MW01701791

Reading Dante

Reading Dante

The Pursuit of Meaning

Jesper Hede

LEXINGTON BOOKS

A division of
ROWMAN & LITTLEFIELD PUBLISHERS, INC.
Lanham • Boulder • New York • Toronto • Plymouth, UK

Published by Lexington Books
A division of Rowman & Littlefield Publishers, Inc.
A wholly owned subsidiary of The Rowman & Littlefield Publishing Group, Inc.
4501 Forbes Boulevard, Suite 200, Lanham, Maryland 20706
http://www.lexingtonbooks.com

Estover Road, Plymouth PL6 7PY, United Kingdom

Copyright © 2007 by Lexington Books
First paperback edition 2010

All rights reserved. No part of this book may be reproduced in any form or by any electronic or mechanical means, including information storage and retrieval systems, without written permission from the publisher, except by a reviewer who may quote passages in a review.

British Library Cataloguing in Publication Information Available

Library of Congress Cataloging-in-Publication Data

Hede, Jesper, 1967–
Reading Dante : the pursuit of meaning / Jesper Hede.
p. cm.
Includes bibliographical references and index.
1. Dante Alighieri, 1265–1321. Divina commedia. I. Title.
PQ4390.H45 2007
851'.1—dc22 2007022932

ISBN: 978-0-7391-2196-2 (cloth : alk. paper)
ISBN: 978-0-7391-2197-9 (pbk : alk. paper)

Printed in the United States of America

™ The paper used in this publication meets the minimum requirements of American National Standard for Information Sciences—Permanence of Paper for Printed Library Materials, ANSI/NISO Z39.48–1992.

Contents

Preface

In 1962, while still a graduate student of philosophy at Yale University, T. K. Seung published a 430-page long book on Dante's *Divina Commedia* under the title of *The Fragile Leaves of the Sibyl: Dante's Master Plan*. Seung's book contains an intriguing theory about the unity of Dante's poem, which is further developed in his two books *Cultural Thematics: The Formation of the Faustian Ethos* (1976) and *Semiotics and Thematics in Hermeneutics* (1982), and has been restated in his long article "The Metaphysics of the *Commedia*" (1988). But for some reason, the theory has never gained any support in Dante studies. In fact, it has largely been ignored by Dante scholars world-wide throughout the last forty-five years.

Seung's theory rests on two fundamental principles of medieval Christian teachings. The first principle is the notion of the three persons of the Holy Trinity: the Father, the Son, and the Holy Spirit. The second principle is the notion of the three parts of the human soul (the vegetative, the sensitive, and the spiritual) and their powers (the concupiscible, the irascible, and the intellectual). The first principle is overtly thematized throughout the poem. As to the second principle, Seung says, its application to the *Commedia* is extratextual. By this he means that it does not lie within the context of discourse. But there are different aspects, both in the text and in the cultural context, that indicate its significance for Dante's construction of the afterworld. For example, Statius's account of the genesis of the soul in *Purgatorio* 25 supports it textually, and the long-standing Judeo-Christian dogma that man is created in the image of God supports it contextually. On this ground, Seung argues that theology and psychology are the two fundamental disciplines for Dante's poetic exposition of God's universal order. They are not two independent disciplines any more than the mirror and its reflections are two separate entities. As Seung argues in "The Metaphysics of the *Commedia*":

> Because the Trinity cannot be an object of direct intuition, it can be known only through its reflections in the soul. Psychology provides the epistemological first principle for theology. On the other hand, the nature and destiny of the soul cannot be fully understood without being traced back to God as its first cause and creator. Theology provides the first ontological principle for psychology.

According to Seung, the systematic correlation of the tripartite soul with its three distinctive powers and the Triune God constitutes the central framework for reading the *Commedia*. The framework provides not only a systematic classification of all the virtues and sins Dante describes in the *Commedia*; it also provides an orderly method for a Trinitarian interpretation of every scene and action in the poem: "The tripartite soul and the Holy Trinity can be said to constitute the joint foundation for the construction of Dante's epic." As far as the structures of Hell, Purgatory, and Paradise are concerned, Seung argues that they are organized in accordance with the medieval table of seven natural virtues (humility, mercy, meekness, fortitude, liberality, temperance, and chastity) and of three supernatural virtues (faith, hope, and love) and their contraries (sins and vices). These ten natural and supernatural virtues and their contraries constitute ten steps on the ladder of grace and are ultimately governed by the two principles of the Trinity and the tripartite soul. These two elements of organization and government are fused into one triadic scheme that gives the different sins of Hell, vices of Purgatory, and virtues of Paradise a theological foundation that is coherent and simple.

However, in spite of its coherence and simple principles of interpretation, Seung's theory remains unexamined and unexplored in Dante studies. Besides a couple of reviews on the publication of *The Fragile Leaves of the Sibyl*, the only reflections on Seung's Dante reading are found in an appendix to Robert Hollander's *Allegory in Dante's Commedia* (1969) and, more obscurely, in the notes to Marc Cogan's *The Design in the Wax: The Structure of the Divine Comedy and Its Meaning* (1999). Since its formulation, there have been very few references to Seung's theory in books and articles on Dante. In fact, the absence of references is striking. For example, in the volume of the American journal *Annali d'Italianistica* (1990) dedicated to modern American Dante studies of the twentieth century, there is no reference to Seung's theory.

But three years after the publication of *The Fragile Leaves of the Sibyl*, Philip McNair wrote an article on "The Poetry of the *Comedy*," whose opening passage seems unthinkable, if it were not for some of Seung's sharpest statements in the beginning of his book:

> For most civilized people, the *Comedy* is the greatest poem ever written. Shakespeare was Dante's peer, but never wrote one work which attempted and achieved so much. The greatness of the *Comedy* is seen in the attempt as well as in the achievement, for whether he succeeds or fails, by any human standard its author has engaged in an enormous enterprise. If he succeeds, his success is Olympian; if he fails, his failure is Titanic. Even if we think that his poem reveals a chaotic mind (and, incredible as it seems, there have been some critics who thought this), at least we should concede that it is the chaos of a great mind.

Though making a different argument, McNair implicitly responded to the question from which Seung starts his inquiry into the *Commedia* in *The Fragile Leaves of the Sibyl*:

> Dante's stage is not only the most wondrous splendor of all poetic creations, but the most baffling enigma. The enigma that has puzzled Dante's readers a little over half a millennium lies in the relation between the form and the content of the *Divina Commedia*. What is the relation between the stage and the action of the poetic drama? This relation of form and matter is one of the oldest problems in philosophy, older than Plato and Aristotle. As a philosophical problem, the relation of form and matter offers only a harmless occasion for theoretical disputations involving no practical consequence. But this harmless philosophical problem has a decisive practical relevance for Dante's epic. For, if there is no relation between its form and content, then Dante's titanic edifice has no unity and should be condemned as the greatest chaos ever created. If there is a definite relation between the stage and the action, Dante's epic can be rightly admired as the greatest single poem ever written since the dawn of human civilization.

McNair's elaboration on Seung's statements shows that *The Fragile Leaves of the Sibyl* was read by some Dante scholars in the years following its publication. Thomas G. Bergin's preface to the book and his references to it now and then in his own writing on Dante might be the major reason for the way in which Seung's reading was assimilated into Dante studies, though only minutely and only in America and only for a short period of time.

Kenelm Foster's review of the book in *Blackfriars* in the year of the publication also indicates that Seung's theory was taken seriously by some Dante scholars. Although Foster criticizes Seung on certain points, he supports his theory that the essential theme of the *Commedia* is the Trinity. Foster emphasized that only few have ever said this of the *Commedia* and no one has ever made "anything like a convincing effort to show that it is true," and that Seung's theory was concerned with "Dante's deepest, also most mysterious claim on our attention—something his great poem seems to say about the very springs of human life and its ultimate significance, the message or meaning that the *Comedy* conveys." Foster was more than half convinced that Seung has seen more deeply and clearly into the structural theological patterns of the *Comedy* than any other author known to him—"more so than Nardi or Gilson or Singleton, with all their learning." To say that Seung's reading was far deeper and clearer than theirs was simply the highest praise Foster could give at the time; Seung's reading was far more convincing than the readings of the greatest authorities in Italy (Nardi), France (Gilson), and America (Singleton). Moreover, about Seung's structural correlation of the three realms of Dante's afterworld, Foster wrote: "The symmetry of this system is exciting and *prima facie* plausible; it makes a grand design." And about Seung's use of the structural correlation for explicating the poem's thematic content: "This triple task of explanation and correlation [Seung] performs with astonishing ingenuity and often too, with superb intuitive insight." This was surely a notable recognition of Seung's effort from a Dante scholar whose works are still cited by contemporary Dante scholars.

According to Foster, it would require extensive space to examine Seung's theory in detail. Therefore he only indicated a couple of points that left him uncertain and unconvinced. But strangely enough, he never went back to Seung's Dante reading. Not even when he argues in *The Two Dantes* that *Paradiso* is particularly Trinitarian in its structure does he refer to it. He says that the Trinitarian feature displays "a typically medieval pattern of ideas," but he associates it only with *Paradiso*. That reveals that Foster's approach to the different parts of the poem is different from Seung's. According to Seung, all three parts of the poem reflect the powers of the Trinity. Whereas Foster identifies Hell, Purgatory, and Paradise as three self-contained schemes of transgression, purgation, and salvation, Seung argues that they constitute one triadic scheme. Every part is a mirror of the other two parts. The three parts are different in that transgression is the subject of Hell, purgation is the subject of Purgatory, and salvation is the subject of Paradise. But the three realms are identical in that they are organized in accordance with seven natural and three supernatural qualities and their organization is governed by the Trinity and the tripartite soul. Despite this fundamental difference in reading Dante's poem, Foster's review shows that he had grasped the substance of Seung's theory. It is not easy to say why Foster never attempted to make an extensive study of it. His commitment to the interpretive practices of Dante studies might be one reason. Another reason might be that he did not find anything faulty in it.

There is no simple explanation for the neglect of Seung's theory in Dante studies. But it is clear that it must be disturbing to the majority of Dante scholars. Many of them might prefer to identify the problem differently. For example, although John A. Scott in his review of Seung's *Cultural Thematics* calls his study of the transformation of the medieval sensibility into the modern sensibility during the twelfth, thirteenth, and fourteenth centuries "courageous and thought-provoking," his sentence on Seung's theory that the Trinity is the ultimate theme of the *Commedia* is severe: "Of course everything is possible in the labyrinth of Dante criticism." In other words, Seung's theory seems to be pure invention, or if not entirely so, a theory imposed on and not deduced from the content of the poem. But neither Scott nor any other Dante scholar has ever taken up the challenge of showing why it is inadequate. Hence Seung's theory has not been dismissed. No examination has shown that it is inconsistent and incoherent.

Only one short observation in *The Fragile Leaves of the Sibyl* is sometimes reproduced in the works of Dante scholars. For example, in *Allegory in Dante's Commedia*, Hollander agrees with Seung that the episode with Francesca reading a book with Paolo (*Inf.* 5) contains a "negative antitype" of Augustine reading a book by St. Paul as described in his *Confessions*. In *Dante: A Life in Works* (2001) Hollander restates Seung's observation, and in *The Metaphysics of Dante's Comedy* (2005) Christian Moevs mentions it in the notes to his study. This type of footnote reference is the only recognition Seung's reading of the *Commedia* has gained in Dante studies. As for his theory about the poem's thematic coherence, it has been suppressed with silence. For that reason, it can be argued that Dante studies do not live up to the scholarly standard of systematic examination of interpretive theories and comparative evaluation of their merit.

In this book on the pursuit of meaning in reading Dante's epic, I try to overcome this problem by critically examining the prevalent methods of reading in Dante studies and comparing the dominant views of the poem's thematic coherence with Seung's theory of the design of the *Commedia*. I depart from two interrelated questions, which any reader of Dante's epic inevitably asks himself: What does the afterworld look like and what is the poem about? In examining the prevalent methods of reading and the dominant theories of thematic coherence, I argue that the two questions are generally unsolved in Dante studies and that the attempts to settle them have generated a large number of interpretive inconsistencies.

In making this argument, the book focuses on two subjects. First, it presents an inquiry into different interpretations of the structure and thematic content of the *Commedia*. Second, it is concerned with principles for literary criticism and historical understanding. The two subjects are due to the focal points of the study. On the one hand, I focus on Seung's interpretation of the *Commedia* as presented in *The Fragile Leaves of the Sibyl*, *Cultural Thematics*, and "The Metaphysics of the *Commedia*." On the other, I take into consideration Seung's interpretive theory as expounded in *Semiotics and Thematics in Hermeneutics* and *Structuralism and Hermeneutics* (1982) and further developed in *Plato Rediscovered: Human Value and Social Order* (1996). My thesis is that these two strongly related sides of Seung's critical work provide a highly resourceful basis for reconsidering the textual meaning (signification) and historical meaningfulness (significance) of Dante's epic and proposing a consistent interpretation of the poem's thematic coherence.

In the first group of work, Seung presents a comprehensive interpretation of the *Commedia* and the cultural texture of Dante's historical context. In the second, he presents an interpretive theory that elucidates the methodology that underlines his interpretation of Dante's text and context. The interpretive theory sheds light on the Dante interpretation, and the Dante interpretation substantiates the interpretive theory. Seung admits that his approach to literary hermeneutics has gone through certain changes from the interpretation to the theory. But the changes have not resulted in a reevaluation of his interpretation of Dante's text. On the contrary, there is continuity from the interpretation to the theory that underlines the significance of the former for the development of the latter. For that reason, the study of Seung's Dante interpretation is also the study of an interpretive theory of principles for literary criticism and historical understanding. The two sides of Seung's critical work are, however, not investigated to the same extent in this book. My primary concern is the signification and significance of Dante's epic. I therefore focus on Seung's Dante interpretation. But due to the affinity between the interpretation and the interpretive theory, the examination investigates some of the principles of Seungs interpretive theory. These principles are those directly related to his Dante interpretation.

My motive for examining Seung's interpretation of Dante's text and context is to try to give consistent and coherent answers to some of the many unsettled questions and inconsistencies in Dante studies, especially on the question of the structure and the thematic content of Dante's epic. As such, the book is an attempt to restate and substantiate Seung's Dante reading. I do not argue that the reading is definitive, nor do I reject the ongoing exploration of the *Commedia* in Dante studies. My objective is to show in what way Seung's Dante reading is a highly resourceful alternative to the main tendencies in Dante studies. In chapter one I outline the essential problems in defining the principles of Dante's vision of God's universal order. On that ground, I consider the different methods of reading applied by Dante scholars in their attempts to define the principles, and I set up certain standards for determining the merit of these attempts. In chapter two I examine the dominant views of the poem's thematic coherence in Dante studies, and I argue that most of these views are incoherent and inconsistent in explicating the poem's thematic coherence. I maintain that, among the great variety of Dante readings, only two studies of the *Commedia* as a whole contain qualified responses to the question of thematic coherence; one is Seung's *The Fragile Leaves of the Sibyl*, and the other is Cogan's *The Design in the Wax*. In chapter three I examine Cogan's theory in detail, because it represents the most qualified response and alternative to Seung's theory. However, I argue that Cogan's theory generates a number of anomalies and ambiguities in Dante's epic, to which it does not find tenable solutions because it is inflicted with inconsistent and incoherent assumptions of Dante studies. For that reason, I maintain that Cogan's theory does not surpass Seung's.

The first three chapters contain my criticism of the prevalent strategies of reading in Dante studies. In the following three chapters, I present a constructive proposal for revitalizing the hermeneutics of Dante studies by considering Seung's theory of the design of Dante's epic. In chapter four I outline some of the most essential points of Seung's Dante reading and hermeneutic theory. The outline takes account of the fact that not all readers of Dante's poem are familiar with Seung's work on Dante. My main purpose is to emphasize why Seung's Dante reading surpasses Cogan's and why it constitutes a highly resourceful alternative to the dominant views in Dante studies. In chapter five I try to substantiate Seung's theory by applying its principles in interpreting a segment of the *Commedia*. The segment consists of canto 8 and 9 of *Paradiso*, which constitutes the heaven of Venus. In chapter six I substantiate the theory further by applying the principles to an episode within a segment of the whole. The episode is Dante's encounter with Brunetto Latini in the seventh circle of *Inferno*. These two examples of how the principles of Seung's theory, on different levels of meaning, can be applied in interpreting Dante's text are chosen in order to elucidate one step on the ladder of grace, according to Seung's parallel reading of the poem's three parts, which identifies the seventh circle of Hell, the third terrace of Purgatory, and the Venus heaven of Paradise as the poem's discourse on wrath and meekness. In the end these three segments turn out to have one unifying theme—they constitute Dante's discourse on political government and bring forth his medieval attitude toward the world of secular affairs.

Abbreviations

CT — *Cultural Thematics: The Formation of the Faustian Ethos* by T. K. Seung. New Haven, Conn.: Yale University Press, 1976.

DDP — *Dante Dartmouth Project.* Online database of commentaries to Dante's *Divina Commedia.* Hosted by www.lib.dartmouth.edu. The reference following the abbreviation refers to the author of the commentary available in the database.

DW — *The Design in the Wax: The Structure of the Divine Comedy and Its Meaning* by Marc Cogan. Notre Dame, Ind.: University of Notre Dame Press, 1999.

ED — *Enciclopedia dantesca.* Edited by Umbero Bosco. Six Volumes. Roma: Istituto della Enciclopedia Italiana, 1970-1976. The reference following the abbreviation refers to the article in the encyclopedia.

FLS — *The Fragile Leaves of the Sibyl: Dante's Master Plan* by T. K. Seung (Swing). Westminster, Md.: The Newman Press, 1962.

IC — *Intuition and Construction: The Formation of Normative Theory* by T. K. Seung. New Haven, Conn.: Yale University Press, 1993.

MC — "The Metaphysics of the *Commedia*" by T. K. Seung in *The Divine Comedy and the Encyclopedia of Arts and Sciences.* Edited by G. C. Scipio and A. Scaglione. Amsterdam, Philadelphia: John Benjamins Publishing Co., 1988.

PR — *Plato Rediscovered: Human Value and Social Order* by T. K. Seung. Lanham, Md.: Rowman & Littlefield Publishers, 1996.

RSV — *Revised Standard Version of the Holy Bible.* New York: Oxford University Press, Inc, 1971

SH — *Structuralism and Hermeneutics* by T. K. Seung. New York: Columbia University Press, 1982.

STH — *Semiotics and Thematics in Hermeneutics* by T. K. Seung. New York: Columbia University Press, 1982.

ST — *Summa Theologiae* by Thomas Aquinas. Translated by Fathers of the English Dominican Province. New York: Benziger Bros. Edition, 1947.

Chapter One

Enigma of Meaning

"The stage of Dante's *Divina Commedia* presents the most wondrous splendor and the most puzzling enigma of all poetic creations" (*FLS* 3). Thus writes T. K. Seung on the first page of *The Fragile Leaves of the Sibyl: Dante's Master Plan*. No doubt, many readers of the poem would approve of the description of Dante's achievement as "the most wondrous splendor." Because of its great variety, T. S. Eliot, for example, argued that as a whole the *Commedia* can be compared only to the entire dramatic work of William Shakespeare, and added: "Dante and Shakespeare divide the modern world between them; there is no third."[1] A similar exaltation of Dante's poetic creation is found in Harold Bloom's defense of a Western canon of literature, at whose centre he places Dante and Shakespeare, "because they excel all other Western writers in cognitive acuity, linguistic energy, and power of invention."[2] Robin Kirkpatrick's suggestion that "it is more accurate to speak of the impact of *The Divine Comedy* upon subsequent generations than of its influence" represents another way of emphasizing the uniqueness of Dante's creation.[3] Because of its monumental character, both in itself and in a historical perspective, it has long been a standard in Dante studies to compare the *Commedia* with a Gothic cathedral.[4] Another standard is to characterize it as an encyclopedic poem or as a sort of *summa* or synthesis of medieval culture and mentality.[5] If the architectonic dimensions of Dante's vision of the universe were visible to others besides enthusiastic Dante readers, it would perhaps even be a common practice to count the *Commedia* among the world's wonders.

But it is one thing to celebrate Dante's achievement; it is another to understand what he articulates with his poetic creation. On this point, there is no consensus among Dante scholars. The elements that are supposed to constitute the monument they claim to see before their inner eyes are insubstantial. In numerous annotated editions and critical studies of the *Commedia*, we are presented with diagrammatic and schematic representations of Dante's universal vision. These representations give us the impression of a well-designed framework for the exposition of the universal order. But what constitutes the nature and essence of the pillars upholding the great edifice of the *Commedia* remains unsettled in these diagrams and schemes. They enumerate thematic and structural elements but do not explain these elements.

Journey and Order

"What is the relation between the stage and the action of the poetic drama" or "between the form and the content of the *Commedia*?" (*FLS* 4). That is the question Seung raises in explaining the reason for characterizing the *Commedia* as "the most puzzling enigma of all poetic creations":

> We know that there are three canticles in the *Divina Commedia*, but do not know how the three canticles constitute one poem. We see three worlds in Dante's creation, but do not see how the three worlds are unified into one cosmos. We hear of many themes and disputations in the course of Dante's pilgrimage, but do not understand how the many topics of discourse and the many scenes of action are woven into the central plot of the epic (*FLS* 21).

The enigma Seung has in mind is the problem of the poem's unity. As he explains in a later examination of this issue, the problem is equivalent to that of one in many and many in one in metaphysics:

> What is the principle of unity that holds together the nine circles of Hell, the seven terraces of Purgatory, and the ten heavens of Paradise? In metaphysics, the principle of unity is convertible to the principle of division and the problem of unity can be restated as the problem of division. What is the principle that divides Hell into nine circles, Purgatory into seven terraces and Paradise into ten heavens? (*MC* 181)

For centuries, this double question has puzzled Dante readers. The reason is that the narrative of the *Commedia*, in various ways, alludes to a well-ordered design. But no statement or passage in the poem or elsewhere in Dante's work makes it certain which principles govern the design. The determination of the poem's unity depends entirely on how we interpret what Dante expresses.

No source elucidates the inspirational background for the design of the three realms. Only in the case of Paradise do we have a formal explanation at the outset. Dante follows the scientific knowledge of his time. He enumerates nine spheres in the superlunar region. To this he adds, in accordance with the theology of the medieval church, a tenth sphere named the Empyreum beyond time and space.[6] But this cosmological standard view sheds no decisive light on Dante's Paradise when it comes to the determination of the qualities he associates with it. It does not provide a basis for understanding the substantive content of the design. Surely, in medieval numerology, the number of ten had great symbolic meaning; it was the perfect number. But by symbolizing perfection, the vision of ten spheres only emphasizes a quality natural to Paradise. Since everything is perfect there, only a perfect number fits the realm of perfection.

That the souls appearing in the superlunar region of spheres actually reside in the Empyreum is a significant example of the complexity of Dante's thought. The standard view does not contain this idea, although it regards the celestial spheres as spiritually animated. But in Dante the distinction between the realm of spheres surrounding the earth and the Empyreum, which he describes as a realm of nine rings of blessed souls and angels surrounding God, attains significant meaning. By creating an essential relation between the geocentric realm of spheres and the theocentric realm of Empyrean rings, Dante rejects the idea that the motions of the spheres are mechanistic phenomena in God's created world. With the appearances of the souls, he argues that the spheres distribute divine providence to the world of the living. But since the souls do not inhabit the spheres but only exemplify their influential capacity, he also rejects the blind belief that the spheres determine the lives of human beings.

When we turn to Hell and Purgatory, the problem of determining the motivation for their design becomes highly complicated. There is no formal explanation. Their design is all Dante's invention. Although there are many medieval visions of Hell as a subterranean realm of punishment, of which some undoubtedly inspired Dante, no source elucidates why he divides it into nine circles. Although the existence of Purgatory was established as a doctrine of the medieval church in 1274, no source reveals why he makes it into a mountain placed in the Southern Hemisphere. Nor is it apparent why the process of purgation is portrayed as a climb of seven terraces associated with the seven capital sins. Dante's originality is striking. He combines a whole range of various sources and develops them creatively. As a result, it is difficult to explain the design of the individual parts of the poem. Since this is a difficult task, it is even more difficult to explain what holds together the three parts of the poem.

In Dante studies there have been many attempts at explaining the poem's unity. One of the most influential examples is Charles S. Singleton's claim that the basic structural principle that holds together the three parts is the account of a journey. According to Singleton, the whole structure of the work will collapse if we take away this element, because "upon the outline of a journey all is threaded." For Singleton, the *Commedia* should be seen as a confessional act comparable to that of Augustine in his *Confessions* (I.i), in which we read at the beginning: "The thought of you [God] stirs him [man] so deeply that he cannot be content unless he praises you, because you made us [mankind] for yourself and our hearts find no peace until they rest in you."[7] Singleton takes the Augustinian notion of the "unquiet heart" and transfers it to the *Commedia*: "The journey of the poem is the journey of the unquiet heart and its presence in the structure constitutes the very heartbeat of the whole."[8]

With this comparison Singleton interprets the *Commedia* as a story about a man who, by traveling through the afterworld, realizes why the human heart finds no rest but in the absolute presence of the "love that moves the sun and the other stars" (*Par.* 33: 145). Since this is true for both the living and the dead, Singleton says that the *Commedia* describes "a journey *there*, through Hell and Purgatory and Paradise, and a journey *here*, an event in this 'our life.'" With this interpretation Singleton ascribes a particular meaning to the poem that finds great support among Dante scholars. The narrative depicts the restlessness of one particular man, but this man represents mankind because his restlessness is common to all men. It describes one particular man's journey to God, but his journey is every man's journey to God. The truth the traveler attains is the same truth for which all men strive.[9]

According to Antonio C. Mastrobuono, this is the allegorical meaning of the poem. On one level, Dante "is still alive and thus, if he should receive an infusion of grace, by the exercise of the freedom of choice, he can still determine his ultimate destiny." On another level, "Dante is symbolic of humanity."[10] Thus Mastrobuono asserts that the ultimate theme of the *Commedia* is man-centered. This is the common assertion in Dante studies. Dante is seen as the hero of his epic, and his experience of the divine order is taken to constitute the poem's thematic content. For similar reasons, A. C. Charity identifies the main theme of the *Commedia* as "conversion": "It is, no doubt, incidentally about much else. But that is its main subject: becoming a Christian." Since this can be understood in several ways, Charity says: "Now it is not a matter of 'becoming a Christian', quite simply. Rather, it is a matter of becoming one truly, of individually appropriating Christianity, of actualizing one's baptism in one's life."[11] In many studies of the *Commedia*, the significance of this theme is emphasized with reference to Dante's characterization of Beatrice's role for the outcome of his journey (*Par.* 31: 85): *"Tu m'hai di servo tratto a libertate"* ("From bondage into freedom you led me").

When unity is understood in these terms, the unity of the *Commedia* is taken to be the account of a journey. It is regarded as the basic structural element that holds together three parts of the poem. At the same time, conversion or the attainment of the universal truth is interpreted as the poem's substantive content. But this understanding of unity is inadequate. The element of journey or the theme of conversion does not explain why the first part consists of nine sections, the second of seven, and the third of ten. It only reveals that the narrator claims once to have traveled through the nine circles of Hell, the seven terraces of Purgatory, and the ten spheres of Paradise. Since the element of journey does not explain these structural characteristics, it cannot be the basic structural element. In fact, it can easily be argued that it is secondary to the conception of order the narrative gradually reveals.

The organizing of the poem with the number of *canti* symbolizing perfection and the poetic rime repetitions (the *terza rima*) that reflect the governing principles of the universe (the Trinity) points beyond the mere description of a travel experience. The form in which the experience is described seems equally important as the description itself. The elements of journey and order are interrelated and interdependent. There is no journey to describe if there is no order through which to travel. There is no order to conceive if there is no account of a journey through which to disclose it. But it is not easy to define the relations between the two elements and settle whether the journey takes place through an already conceived order, or whether the order is constructed as the journey proceeds. To put it simply, what came first in Dante's creative process: the idea of a journey through the afterworld or the vision of the universal order?

The account of the journey is much easier to comprehend than the vision of order. For this reason, Singleton chooses it as the basis for approaching the poem's thematic content, and because of his influence, this approach is paradigmatic for a large number of Dante readings. Singleton does not exclude the vision of order. But due to its complexity, he is fundamentally reserved toward any attempt to describe Dante's conceptual organization of the afterworld behind the suggestive realism of the narrative. In Singleton's view every scene of the *Commedia* displays a variety that defies simple formulation. Dante did not write his poem on the basis of some "preconceived formula mechanically applied." The unique quality of the *Commedia* is that "Each scene arises from its own real center of inspiration." At no point does Dante repeat himself. On the contrary, he creates a great variety of beings and states of being. As a result, it is not only difficult to come to terms with what the poem communicates. In Singleton's view, it becomes impossible. For as he puts it: "It is to the greater glory of the poem that our willful purposes of abstractive analysis are quite defeated in this regard."[12] Hence we will always fail to understand Dante's vision of order in its entirety.

Singleton's reading of the *Commedia* is based on the assumption that every interpretive suggestion proves the limits of all interpretive attempts. Dante's text, as we have it, does not suffer from any serious lacunae. "The lacunae," writes Singleton, "are rather in us, the readers, and reside in that deficient knowledge and lack of awareness which we continue to bring to our reading of the poem."[13] Thus Singleton takes a position similar to that of another influential Dante scholar of the twentieth century, Erich Auerbach. Singleton favors the local perspective on the elements of Dante's account, and this perspective has often been defined as the principle of close reading. In Auerbach the same principle is manifest in his emphasis on focusing on the individual and the concrete in literary texts.[14] In Singleton the individual and the concrete are the complexity of elements that constitutes the variety of Dante's poem. Auerbach claims that that the *Ansatzpunkt* or the point of departure in literary interpretation "should not be a generality imposed on a theme from the outside, but ought rather to be an organic inner part of the theme itself."[15] In Singleton the point of departure is what he calls the real center of inspiration in each scene of the *Commedia.* Auerbach argues that every interpretation is marked by historical relativism. With this claim he puts particular emphasis on the interpreter's act of interpretation and its cultural boundness, while he is less concerned with evaluating the content of interpretation and the interpretive principles as well as setting up standards for determining the merits of interpretive acts.[16] Singleton stresses the inevitable defeat of abstractive analysis in Dante studies. Thus he takes a relativistic stand and avoids formulating principles in determining the merits of interpretations by examining their content and interpretive principles.

In both cases we are dealing with trained scholars of hermeneutics who have made great contributions to Dante studies. No doubt, they would agree that their interpretations reflect the time in which they were made. It is clear that their notion of interpretive indeterminacy is stated in firm opposition to the deterministic tendencies in literary studies at the time. But for some reason, they do not seem to realize that their method of reading is self-defeating. Textual meaning does not arise solely from the particular parts of the text; it depends also on how the parts are perceived from the perspective of the whole. Hence we cannot discover the inner organic part of the theme itself without some general theory about how and where to discover it, and such a theory can have the character of being a generality imposed on the theme from the outside. Nor can we claim that the meaning of the whole will always escape us while at the same time arguing that every scene arises from its own real center of inspiration. The latter view depends on an understanding of the whole as consisting of self-contained scenes with their own real centers of inspiration. But we cannot achieve such an understanding if we are defeated in our willful purposes of abstractive analysis.

The interdependence of the parts to its whole, the text to its context, and the method to its theory has long been common knowledge in hermeneutics. It is known as the hermeneutic circle. This notion has different meanings. For example, textual elements can be understood only in terms of the meaning of their whole, and the whole can be understood only in terms of its elements. Textual meaning depends on contextual understanding, which, in turn, depends on textual meaning. The past can be understood only in the light of the present, and the present can be understood only in the light of the past. A theory is constructed on the basis of data, and data are explained within the framework of a theory. In practical hermeneutics, these distinctions imply that the merit of an interpretation depends on the way in which the interpreter is capable of combining the meaning of the parts with the meaning of the whole, determining the relation of the text to its context, reconstructing the past from present knowledge, and practicing a method of reading in accordance with its theoretical principles.

But in modern literary criticism, practical hermeneutics has often been suppressed by relativistic tendencies in theoretical or philosophical hermeneutics stressing that textual meaning is always indeterminate. Since the hermeneutic circle involves a continuous movement between parts and whole, text and context, past and present, and data and theory, no interpretation can be stable. The circle cannot be transcended. As a result, there can be no generality or universal truth in literary criticism. No doubt, Singleton and Auerbach operated under the spell of this assumption. They saw the notion of interpretive indeterminacy as a way to move further into the complexity of literary meaning without the restraint of predetermined principles of reading and understanding. But there is one problem with the notion of interpretive indeterminacy. It is not indeterminate; it is self-contradictory. To claim that no interpreter can transcend the hermeneutic circle is to make a claim that transcends the circle. To say that every meaning is indeterminate is to establish a determinate meaning. The rejection of universalism involves the acceptance of universalism in one respect. For this reason, though sympathetic and understandable seen in a historical context, the position of Singleton and Auerbach is self-defeating. What we learn from their example is that the problem of unity cannot be resolved only by making close readings of Dante's poem coupled with contextual understandings. The solution to the enigma of the *Commedia* requires consistency and coherence in the formulation and application of interpretive principles.

Skepticism and Indeterminacy

To pose the question of whether the *Commedia* is a well-ordered whole is to engage in a hermeneutic enterprise, and such an engagement requires the establishment of interpretive principles. There are, however, especially two questions that can easily obstruct any attempt to take up the challenge of interpreting the meaning of the *Commedia*. The first question is whether textual interpretation is possible at all; the second is whether incompatible textual interpretations can be equally plausible. Both questions display a fundamental skepticism about the expediency of literary criticism. But their skepticism is of two different kinds. The first question presupposes the enormous difficulty of interpretation; it is so difficult that some say that it is impossible. The second presupposes exactly the opposite; interpretation is so easy that there can be an endless number of interpretations, and nobody can tell which is better than which.

The interpretive problems arising from these two questions have long been pervasive in literary criticism, which the relativistic inclination of Singleton and Auerbach shows. Hence, in order to overcome the problems and engage in the establishment of interpretive principles that can determine whether the *Commedia* is a well-ordered whole, we need to consider the two questions in detail. As for the first question, it is sometimes claimed that all close reading is a matter of rediscovering the impossibility of reading. The claim is a prominent example of the kind of interpretive chaos that pervades modern literary criticism. First of all, the claim is unclear. It involves an implicit distinction between a close reading and an ordinary or superficial reading; they stand for two different levels of reading. Due to this distinction, we may ask whether only a close reading rediscovers the impossibility of reading. Let us assume that a superficial reading of the *Commedia* is capable of recognizing its topic as a journey through the medieval afterworld. If a close reading is a rediscovery of the impossibility of reading, does this mean that such a reading would fail to recognize this topic? If so, a superficial reading is the adequate way for discovering the topic of the *Commedia.* But this is not what the claim intends to demarcate. The intention is to underline that when we make a close reading, the impossibility of reading recognized by a superficial reading becomes more evident. If so, a close reading is a reading that involves a more advanced rediscovery of the impossibility of reading. For that reason, the claim might have stated that all reading is a matter of rediscovering the impossibility of reading.

But how are we to understand that a reading is a rediscovery of the impossibility of reading? A rediscovery implies the recognition of the same thing at least twice. Such recognition can be made if we read the same text twice. If we read two different texts and discover the same impossibility, it is not the texts that generate the problem but the act of reading. Thus it is rejected that any reading can prove the possibility of reading. But the unclearness is not the most important problem with the claim. The problem is that the claim is self-contradictory. If I say that every walking is a matter of rediscovering the impossibility of walking, I would seem to be talking nonsense. A quadriplegic can say that every attempt to walk is a matter of rediscovering the impossibility of walking. But there is a difference between an attempt to walk and walking itself. Some say that reading is impossible because every reading is a misreading. They talk about the impossibility of correct or right reading, not any reading. But if every reading is a misreading, how can we recognize it as a misreading without presupposing the notion of right reading? If we have the notion of right reading, on what ground can we then say that it is impossible to realize? In fact, by the time we say that a reading is a misreading, we are making a right reading. To recognize a misreading as a misreading is the right reading. A misreading takes place only when we make a misreading without recognizing it as such. For these reasons, the doctrine of the impossibility of reading is self-contradictory. Its self-contradiction is of the same type as that of the assertion that there are no truths. If this assertion is true, there is at least one truth, which denies the original assertion. Since the denial of the possibility of reading is stuck in this contradiction, the doctrine is meaningless and serves no purpose in hermeneutics. Its irrelevance is like the irrelevance of total skepticism for scientific enterprise.

As for the second question, we are dealing with a different kind of skepticism. Whereas the denial of the possibility of reading makes reading impossible, the claim of equality of interpretations makes reading chaotic. The chaos arises from the assertion that we have no way of knowing which interpretation is better or worse than which. As a result, all interpretations become equally plausible. This position can be defined as hermeneutic egalitarianism. Some say that it is impossible to tell which interpretation is right. Therefore they conclude that right interpretation is impossible. The impossibility lies not in the act of interpretation, but in the act of determining which one is the right one. It is harder to criticize this position than the previous one. If hermeneutic egalitarianism is true, hermeneutics falls apart. There is no reason why students should study Dante in class. Their readings are as plausible as their teachers'. This is the pragmatic contradiction of the doctrine; it goes against the normal practice in interpretation.

But the doctrine has its own theoretical contradiction. Let us assume that I propose one interpretation of Genesis that is incompatible with Darwinism, and I propose another interpretation that makes Genesis compatible with Darwinism. According to the doctrine of hermeneutic egalitarianism, both interpretations should be equally plausible. But they contradict each other. In logic, once a pair of contradictory statements is accepted, every proposition becomes permissible. For that reason, both the doctrine and its denial are equally permissible. This explanation of the doctrine of hermeneutic egalitarianism assumes that there is only one interpretation of the doctrine. But this is not so. In order to be consistent with the doctrine we would have to say that there are an infinite number of interpretations of the doctrine that are contradictory to one another. We cannot even say that all of them are equally plausible because we should have an infinite number of interpretations of equality and plausibility. As a result, we can never get off the ground. If so, reading becomes truly impossible. But we do not even understand the meaning of its impossibility because there are an infinite number of interpretations for the word "impossibility."

The doctrines of interpretive impossibility and hermeneutic egalitarianism are subversive to hermeneutics. If interpretation is impossible, every hermeneutic enterprise is destined to fail. If incompatible interpretations are equally plausible, no meaning can be established. Meaning becomes a hotchpotch of endless incompatible understandings. But since advocates of interpretive skepticism are well aware that the notion of absolute indeterminacy involves a negative absolutism through an absolute relativism, they are reluctant in defending the two doctrines full-heartedly. Instead, they sometimes claim that every text is an enigma. This is a variant of the doctrine of interpretive impossibility and suffers from the same deficiencies. Just as the notion of misreading depends on the notion of right reading, an enigma is possible only in contrast to its opposite. If every text is enigmatic, something else must be non-enigmatic. But contrary to the full-hearted claim of interpretive impossibility, the notion that every text is an enigma leaves open the possibility that the enigma can be solved. Whether the enigma is solved depends on the substantive content of the suggestion for the solution of the enigma. Most commonly, that requires a comparative study of different suggestions, and their merit is determined on the basis of specific principles that form a method of inquiry.

But advocates of interpretive skepticism often argue that there can be no general method of inquiry because no things have definable meanings. All things are in a constant flux; no object of inquiry is ever stable. As a result, there can be no method of inquiry, because a method requires stable principles in order to function as a method. If an unstable object is subjected to a methodological investigation that provides it with a stable meaning, it is not the object that becomes stable. It is the method that stabilizes it; it provides it with a meaning it does not possess. This critical view is a variant of hermeneutic egalitarianism. The rejection of stable meaning makes it possible that incompatible interpretations of the same object can be equally plausible because the instability can result in different perceptions of the object. But here again, the claim falls victim of self-contradiction. It makes no sense to claim that all objects have instable meanings because the claim implies a stable notion of instability.

Due to this self-contradiction, the view is commonly defended only partially. The reason for arguing that there can be no general foundation for the interpretation of objects is mainly to oppose the criticism that the notion of interpretive indeterminacy is absolutistic. But this reservation is problematic. To say that there can be no general foundation for the interpretation of objects is to oppose generalization. Thus it becomes impossible to pose the questions of whether interpretation is possible at all, or whether incompatible interpretations can be equally plausible, because they arise from a general concern about the status of interpretation. As a result, the impossibility of interpretation or the equality of interpretations cannot be stated as a generality but has to be settled in each single case of interpretation. The impossibility of interpreting one literary text does not prove the impossibility of interpreting every literary text. Nor does the impossibility of interpreting two texts prove the impossibility of interpreting all texts. Due to the countless number of potential interpretations, it becomes impossible to claim that all objects have indefinable meanings, wherefore they cannot be interpreted. If so, it opens up for the possibility that some objects can be interpreted. In fact, the interpretation of an object may not prove the impossibility of interpretation or the equality of interpretations; it may prove the opposite.

Whereas the claim of interpretive impossibility has to prove that all interpretations are failures and the claim of hermeneutic egalitarianism has to prove that all interpretations are equally plausible, the claim that interpretation is possible and some interpretations are more plausible than others needs only to prove that this is true in one single case in order to constitute the claim as a possible truth. This does not mean that the successful interpretation of one object proves that all objects can be successfully interpreted. In fact, many interpretations are not successful in this respect. The possible truth is not a definitive truth. It is essential to distinguish between total and partial indeterminacy. As Seung puts it: "If the meaning of a word is totally indeterminate, it can mean anything and everything. If it is partially indeterminate, its indeterminacy is restricted to only borderline cases." In maintaining the notion of interpretive or semantic indeterminacy, advocates of interpretive impossibility and hermeneutic egalitarianism tend to mean total indeterminacy. But as Seung argues, this assertion is self-defeating: "It does not even allow them to make their case for semantic indeterminacy because the thesis of total indeterminacy eliminates the distinction between determinacy and indeterminacy. For the sake of self-coherence, they must modify their thesis to that of constrained indeterminacy" (*PR* 291-92).

If the meaning of a text is partially indeterminate, some understanding is possible. If some understanding is possible, partial indeterminacy can be restated as partial determinacy. It is the difference between defining a glass of water as either half empty or half full. To say that it is half empty is the negative and skeptical response; to say that it is half full is the positive and constructive response. If the meaning of a text is considered as partially indeterminate, the negative response tends to regard the determination of meaning as pointless because total determinacy is impossible. However, if the meaning of a text is partially determinate, the positive response will be to engage in the determination and construction of meaning because some determinacy is possible. To take the positive stand and accept partial determinacy is to accept the value of constructions of meaning; to move beyond this acceptance is to understand the meaning of constructions. Constructions are understandings, not deceptions. They are not indestructible, but if their elements of meaning are solid, constructions of meaning can have the quality of interpretive completeness without being definitive or conclusive.

The reason for defining understandings as constructions of meaning is due to the nature of these understandings. Their semantic meaning is based on a three-term relation of subject-word-object (*PR* 132-41). In modern linguistics it is common knowledge that no word stands in direct relation to its object. For some practitioners of textual interpretation, this means that the relation between word and object is totally arbitrary. Our understanding of an object is not only divorced from the object itself; our attempt to define it will always be fallacious. Instead of defining objects, our words refer to other words that again refer to other words. In short, we are imprisoned in our language. This is the spell of endless signification. Signifiers create an endless chain of signifiers. We never gain access to the ultimate signified. But if we operate a three-term relation of subject-word-object, instead of the two-term relation of word to object or signifier to signifier, things look different.

The notion of a three-term relation of subject-word-object maintains that the relation between object and word is not direct, and it overcomes the claim of linguistic imprisonment and the spell of endless signification by emphasizing that the relation between object and word is mediated by the subject's conception of the nature of the object. If so, the claim of endless signification is not necessarily due to an inescapable imprisonment in language. It can more likely be due to the subject's sense of linguistic imprisonment in the mediation of the nature of the object. The three-term relation of subject-word-object does not lead to total determinacy. Partial determinacy is the point of case, because one subject's conception of the nature of an object cannot ensure that the conception is the same for all subjects.

Some might argue that this view leads to textual solipsism, the belief that the only interpretation the interpreter can understand is the one produced by the interpreter himself. Textual solipsism is not only a variant of hermeneutic egalitarianism; it is its very foundation. All interpretations are equal, because an interpretation is accessible only to the interpreter himself. But as we have seen, hermeneutic egalitarianism is self-contradictory. Textual solipsism is not only untenable for pragmatic reasons. In general, interpretations are produced either in opposition to interpretations considered as inaccurate or misleading, or in reliance on interpretations regarded as accurate or resourceful. Interpreters normally claim to understand other interpreters; they develop the interpretations of others as well as criticize them for their misinterpretations. But textual solipsism is untenable because it appeals to the very universalism it rejects. Absolute solipsism requires that all interpreters misunderstand each other. But total misunderstanding cannot be verified in the world of absolute solipsism, because absolute solipsism makes such understanding impossible.

To a large extent, the opposition to determinacy can be seen as a reaction to a conflict between two types of logic—the logic of identity and the logic of resemblance. These two types of logic are semantically opposite. In Seung's words, the former is "blessed with semantic determinacy," while the latter is "infected with semantic indeterminacy" (*PR* 177-81 and 291-93). The logic of identity is the classical logic of classes and discontinua, and it is appropriate for natural science. The logic resemblance is the logic of continuum, and it is the logic applied in human sciences. The logic of identity operates with definite and determinate boundaries between classes; things are either included or excluded from the particular class in question. There are no borderline cases. For example, all birds belong to the class of birds; no birds are excluded. In contrast, the logic of resemblance accepts that boundaries between classes are indefinite and indeterminate; there are borderline cases. The question of whether the *Commedia* is a well-ordered whole is a case in point. It shows that textual interpretation is infected with semantic indeterminacy.

At different times in history, it has been believed that semantic determinacy can be attained for textual interpretation. The logic of identity has been forced upon the domain of textual interpretation, although it is not blessed with semantic determinacy. Since the logic of identity permits precision and exactitude, it has been regarded as the only true standard for scientific inquiry. For this reason, the logic of resemblance has been discriminated in different ways. Although textual interpretation is occupied with the most profound questions of human epistemology, it has been considered a pseudo-science, because it does not fulfill the scientific standards of precision and exactitude. The history of literary criticism is full of appeals to such standards that conceal the infection of semantic indeterminacy under the veil of rhetorical eloquence. Some tendencies in literary criticism have been particularly instrumental in encouraging the discrimination and promoting misconceptions about the expediency of literary criticism.

The opposition to total or partial determinacy can be seen as a reaction against the tendency to consecrate the logic of identity as the logic of science and inflict it upon the humanities and social sciences. But instead of accepting the two types of logic and their domains, advocates of total indeterminacy have reacted against the discrimination of semantic indeterminacy by forcing it upon the domain of semantic determinacy. The radical position of total indeterminacy turns out to be as obstinate as the radical position of total determinacy commonly known as scientism.

Segmentalism and Connectionism

The problem of the unity of the *Commedia* is an issue that makes no sense for any reader who has fallen for the doctrines of interpretive impossibility and hermeneutic egalitarianism. If we are to come to terms with the problem, we have to engage in the construction of meaning. Constructive interpretation departs from the assertion that textual meaning is not indeterminate and that its determination depends on the ability of the text to communicate its meaning and the ability of the reader to understand it. These are the two basic premises for a successful interpretation. But it is a complicated matter to establish an adequate relation between a text and its reader. The *Commedia* is a complex text. At the outset, it is not possible say whether the text has been successful in communicating its meaning. The question of the poem's unity makes it evident. In reading the *Commedia*, we have to construct its meaning. Nowhere in the text is the meaning laid out in such a way that we may easily pick it up. Since Dante scholars do not agree on whether the poem displays a coherent conception of the universal order, the question of unity is open for discussion. Maybe Dante did not operate with a set of principles whereby to structure the *Commedia* because the experience it describes did not reveal the principles. Perhaps the narrative implicitly portrays a search for the divine order. Maybe Dante, during the writing process, made minor or major corrections of his initial plan because of new insights into the divine order, which eventually undermined the unity he originally intended. But maybe he did not have a plan at all. Perhaps his intention was to recount an otherworldly experience. Maybe he simply tried to unfold, as best as he possibly could, what he essentially believed was beyond human comprehension. If so, we should not expect to discover a conceptual design beneath the narrative account.

Due to the general uncertainty about the poem's design, some Dante scholars firmly reject the idea of unity. They take any attempt to answer it as an insensitive rationalization of a poetic creation that was not conceived within the limits of discursive speculation and dispute. It arose with astonishing vigor from Dante's genius of imagination and powerful sensibility. For that reason, any such attempt is likely due to the reader's insistence on finding the principles that can save the phenomena in Dante's vision. When Dante scholars are reluctant to conclude that there is no unity, the reason is perhaps that such a conclusion would mean that the *Commedia* is conceptually a gigantic failure, because it does not reflect the order it aims at disclosing and claims to reveal.

The *Commedia* was written in a historical period whose cultural texture we have to reconstruct. This is no easy task. As Wendell V. Harris writes:

> The basic practical principle for finding the intended meaning [of a literary text], then, is obvious: one must know as much as possible of the expectations, beliefs, assumptions, prejudices, knowledge, and current interests the author could have assumed, he/she either shared with or could attribute to the intended reader. Since the interpretation of meaning depends on the reconstruction of presumed background, it can never be certain. All that one can definitely rule out are suggested readings that are dependent on contextual assumptions that the author could not have made.[17]

The difficulty of complying with the principle for finding the intended meaning is further complicated by the different contexts involved in interpretive activities. As Seung explains:

> Just as an interpreter of a literary text cannot situate his act of interpretation in any other context than his own, so an author of a text cannot derive his thematic ideas from any other context than his own. An author may propose certain thematic ideas in a deliberate opposition to the dominant ideas of his own historical context. Even in that case, the emergence of his thematic ideas belongs to the existential dynamics of his existential context. Hence the thematic ideas of a literary text are doubly existential; they are linked to the existential context of the author as well as of the interpreter (*STH* 192).

As a result, every hermeneutic enterprise is always probabilistic and fallible. But as Harris emphasizes, the fact that the possibility of error is never absent should put us on guard against any theorizing that denies the possibility of error on the grounds that there is no alternative to it—"that we are indeed in endless error hurled."[18] To establish an adequate relation between a text and a reader is a methodological problem of great complexity. But what are the criteria for deciding between different attempts at establishing such a relation? This is a crucial problem in Dante studies.

In reading the *Commedia*, one thing stands clear: Dante's synoptic view of the three realms of divine justice presupposes a coherent vision of God's universal order. All that Dante claims in the *Commedia* has to be grounded in a firm vision of the divine justice, which is never accidental but always intentional. His recurring claims of truth are reduced to empty rhetoric if he does not succeed in revealing the truth. While the medieval man wanders around on earth, damnation, purgation, and salvation are issues that pertain exclusively to the science of divine things or theology. Since the *Commedia* explores these three otherworldly conditions, Dante's epic of a mysterious journey is essentially a theological poem, though a highly speculative one. In *De monarchia* (I.ii) Dante argues that man cannot affect the divine things, but he can speculate on them. By this he implies that if such speculations take account of all that is known about the divine things, a comprehensive understanding of God's universal order can be obtained. The *Commedia* presupposes such an understanding if it is to achieve its goal. But the question is whether Dante achieves it. There is no way to settle that question with absolute certainty. But in our reading of the *Commedia* we may render it probable that the poem displays a well-ordered whole. There is good reason for asserting that the *Commedia* reflects more than a search for the divine order. Dante's political ideas and cosmological outlook reveal a firm intention of communicating a vision of the universe as a divinely ordered whole. But in order to render it probable that the *Commedia* has a conceptual design, we need to turn to the topological characteristics of Hell, Purgatory, and Paradise.

To explain these characteristics is perhaps the most difficult problem in Dante studies. If Dante's vision is coherent, the particular elements of the afterworld should create decisive structural and thematic relations, and these relations should constitute the poem as a well-ordered whole. But it is not easy to establish such relations. It is much easier to argue that the *Commedia* is not a well-ordered whole because the relations seem too haphazard and indecisive to constitute such a whole. As a result, Dante studies are full of ambiguous statements about the poem's unity. The question of the relation between the structures of Hell and Purgatory is the classical example of how Dante scholars have pondered about the existence of a conceptual design. At the same time, a treatment of this issue makes clear what is needed for settling the question of the poem's unity. It requires a coherent strategy of reading that takes account of the indications of a conceptual design. The formulation of such a strategy is the major difference between the interpretive method many Dante scholars apply and the method we discover in Seung's work on Dante.

To demarcate the opposition between these two interpretive methods I propose a distinction between two different approaches to the *Commedia*. One is defined as "connectionism." The term is taken from Seung's *Plato Rediscovered* (*PR* xiv-xv), and it defines the analytic approach of *The Fragile Leaves of the Sibyl*. By connectionism or connectionist reading I mean the kind of reading that tries to connect the themes and structural elements of Dante's vision in order to come to terms with the global meaning of the poem. The other approach is defined as "segmentalism." It is a terminological construct intended to demarcate the analytic approach of many studies of Dante's poem. By segmentalism or segmental reading I intend the kind of reading that focuses on the meaning of the different segments or elements of the poem in their local narrative context. Segmental reading is characterized by the neglect of the global perspective essential to connectionist reading. Its interpretive practice often consists in focusing on the divisions Dante states as the basic elements of the structure of the afterworld, such as circles, terraces, or spheres. In some cases, it concentrates on minor issues within these segments of the whole, and sometimes it expands the perspective to major parts of the poem, though without applying a global perspective on its substantive content. In all cases the different segments or elements of the whole are basically treated as self-contained entities.

With this distinction I argue that segmental reading is incapable of providing a comprehensive explication of the poem's thematic coherence. Since its main concern is to explain the meaning of particular elements of the whole, it generally neglects the overall question of how these elements constitute the total meaning of the whole. For that reason, connectionist reading is the adequate reading for determining the poem's thematic coherence; it departs from the assertion that the poem's vision of the afterworld has a conceptual design.

Structural Correspondence

Since the diagrammatic representations of Hell and Purgatory in Daniello of Lucca's edition of the *Commedia* (published in 1568), the question of the poem's unity has been a visible problem.[19] The diagrams visualized the two realms as two inverted versions of the same measure. In 1879 Karl Witte stressed this correspondence in the following manner: "The cone of Purgatory corresponds to the funnel of Hell, so that if we inverted the former we could, as it were, drop into the latter as into a roughly fitting sheath."[20] The two realms seem interrelated. As we descend the diagram of the former, we notice increasingly heavier forms of sin. As we ascend the diagram of the latter, we discern ever lighter forms of sin that undergo purgation. The one depicts a variety of human degeneration, while the other depicts a variety of human regeneration. It is this kind of correspondence, by apparently immediate oppositions, that has incited the pursuit for ordering principles in Dante's vision.

Vergil's explanation of the origins of Hell and Purgatory in canto 34 (121-26) of *Inferno* is an important passage for the representation of the two realms as corresponding constructions. It gives the correspondence a historical foundation. Vergil explains that Hell and Purgatory came into being at the same time in history, when Satan was cast out of heaven.[21] The Mount of Purgatory was created by the giant excavation of the cavern of Hell when Satan hit the earth. The movement that created Hell and introduced the principle of damnation founded Purgatory and subsequently introduced the principle of purgation by repentance in order to avoid damnation. With the revolt and expulsion of Satan, sin became an inescapable existential condition. But in order to prevent the world from falling into eternal misery, God established the principle of purgation by repentance as the way out of sin.[22]

When we turn to the structural divisions of Hell and Purgatory, we detect other indications of a well-ordered design. The infernal sins from the second to the fifth circle (lust, gluttony, avarice or prodigality, and wrath) and the purgatorial sins from the seventh to the third terrace (lust, gluttony, avarice, sloth, and wrath) constitute a partial correspondence in ethical terms with the application of the notion of the seven capital sins (lust, gluttony, avarice, sloth, wrath, envy, and pride). The notion is fully exposed on the Mount of Purgatory. The purpose of ascending the seven terraces consists in the transformation of the seven capital sins to their virtuous opposites. The two parts of the *Commedia* also indicate a correspondence by containing explanations that divide their sections into three major categories.

In canto 11 (79-84) of *Inferno*, Vergil refers to Aristotle's *Ethics* for a distinction between three dispositions that offend heaven: *incontinenza, malizia e la matta bestialitade* (incontinence, malice, and mad bestiality). Traditionally, Dante scholars identify the sins of incontinence as those represented from the second to the fifth circle. The seventh circle is commonly associated with malice, and the eighth and ninth circles with bestiality. As for the sixth circle, Dante scholars normally do not relate it to any of the three categories; it does not seem to belong to any of them. In canto 17 (91-138) of *Purgatorio*, Vergil makes another threefold distinction. In this case, he distinguishes between three forms of love that have led the souls of the penitents astray in the mortal world: (1) perverted love, shown on the first, the second, and the third terrace; (2) defective love, shown on the fourth terrace; and (3) excessive love, shown on the fifth, the sixth, and the seventh terrace. In *Inferno* Vergil makes the distinction in the sixth circle and on the threshold to the seventh circle. If we exclude the first circle from Hell proper, as many Dante scholars do, the distinction is made almost halfway through Hell. This indicates that Hell is divided into an upper part, a middle part, and a lower part. In *Purgatorio* the threefold distinction is made on the fourth terrace—that is, on the middle terrace. This indicates that Purgatory is divided into a lower part, a middle part, and an upper part. But the explanations apply two different sets of principles that do not readily show the correspondence between the two realms.

Yet the two sets are not necessarily incompatible. The distinctive principles of *Inferno* 11 are perhaps chosen for their fundamentally negative meaning. As Vergil explains, they are contrary to the divine will. Although the three dispositions may not be the most offensive according to Aristotle, the *Ethics* emphasizes them in a much more detestable manner than with other repulsive dispositions. When we turn to *Purgatorio* 17, the meaning of the distinctive principles is not negative in a similar sense. The transgressions of the divine will now being purged in Purgatory are classified according to erroneous forms of love. The process of purgation can be accomplished only by the aid of God's loving grace. For this reason, love can easily be seen as the proper means for explaining the categories of sins that are being purged. Hence there seems to be formal consistency between the conception and the description of Purgatory. This also seems to be the case with Hell. Since the sins of Hell are unforgivable and deserve eternal damnation, distasteful expressions of human degeneration are the proper means for explaining the categories.

However, it is one thing to argue that there is consistency between the conception and the description; it is another to explain the meaning of the two categories for the structures of Hell and Purgatory and their correspondence. The correspondence between the two realms seems to dissolve when we look closer at their structural divisions. In *Inferno*, only half of the seven capital sins are exposed as the causes of punishment of sinful souls. The relationship between the two realms is ambiguous. For the rest of the infernal structure, Dante uses other designations for the causes of infernal punishment. He refers to sinful causes that are not represented explicitly in *Purgatorio*. From the sixth circle downward, the correspondence disappears. In that circle the condemned sin is heresy, which is not included among the sins to be purged in Purgatory. Furthermore, the lowest three circles are designated in a way that does not seem to refer to the seven capital sins. Dante also subdivides them into several minor sections. Thus he creates an extensive variety of sinful causes.

Whereas the divisions of sins to be purged in Purgatory give the impression of a conceptual conformity by the use of the seven capital sins, the divisions and subdivisions of condemned sins in Hell create two problems. First, it seems to undermine a potential system of correspondence between the two realms. Second, it complicates the determination of the conceptual principles that govern the structure of Hell. If the seven capital sins are not the structural principles of Hell, there is perhaps no essential correspondence between the two realms. Hell is perhaps structured according to a different notion of the nature of sin. If this is so, we can still ask why Dante apparently associates half of the sinful circles with half of the purgatorial terraces. The correspondence makes us inclined to think that the two realms are interrelated, but since the correspondence is only partial, we are also inclined to dismiss the thought. We are disorientated. Whereas the seven capital sins make the order of Purgatory transparent, the diversity of *Inferno* creates an ambiguous account of the nature of condemnable sins. The partial correspondence puzzles us. It indicates a structural parallelism between Hell and Purgatory; yet the indication is indecisive.

The problem of determining the principles of the poem's design is further complicated by the fact that the question of the relation between Hell and Purgatory concerns only two thirds of the poem's design. The determination of parallel structures between these two realms does not settle the question of whether there is an overall set of governing principles. At best, it provides us only with an analytic framework for interpreting two thirds of Dante's poem. The point of the matter is what the determination of parallel structures would implicate for the understanding of the *Commedia* as a whole. If the structural parallels between Hell and Purgatory are essential, we have to consider whether the understanding of the former is dependent on the understanding of the latter. If so, it might be that the partial application of the seven capital sins in Hell serves the purpose of indicating a conceptual correspondence with Purgatory while at the same time stressing essential differences. If the understanding of the two structures is interdependent, we also have to consider whether the understanding of the interdependence provides us with a basis for understanding the third realm of Paradise. *Paradiso* contains no unequivocal account of the qualities celebrated in the ten heavens similar to Vergil's structural descriptions in *Inferno* and *Purgatorio*.

In comparison with the first two realms, Paradise has a scientific foundation. In contrast to Vergil's descriptions of Hell and Purgatory, the scientific foundation provides only a formal structure to Paradise and does not elucidate its substantive content. The determination of the substantive meaning of Paradise depends on how we interpret the different topics of discourse treated and the different scenes of action shown in the heavens. But this problem need not be overstated. After all, the *Commedia* does not consist of three separate parts; it is a whole divided into three parts. The absence of explicit structural designations for Paradise might indicate that we are to understand it as somehow interacting with the structures of Hell and Purgatory. If so, the understanding of the substantive content of Paradise depends on the understanding of Hell and Purgatory. But this suggestion creates another problem. Since the correspondence between the structures of Hell and Purgatory is only partial, the understanding of these two realms is incomplete. The structural parallels between them do not provide us with any immediate understanding of the governing principles of the poem's design. We seem to have no basis for understanding the structure of Paradise. But this problem need not be overstated either. Since the *Commedia* is a whole divided into three parts, the meaning of each part might lie in the way that it is related to the other two. If so, it is only possible to understand the structure of each part if the structures of the other two are simultaneously taken into consideration.

This is the basic principle in Seung's reading of the *Commedia*. If we are to understand how the three canticles constitute one poem, the reading of the *Commedia* that connects the three parts simultaneously should be the most profitable one. This is the strategy of connectionism or connectionist reading. For Seung it leads to the conclusion that the *Commedia* is "a careful design of the highest order" (*FLS* 130).

Serialism and Parallelism

In Dante studies there have been many attempts at connectionist reading. Themes and structural indications in different sections of the poem have often been compared in order to explain their meanings. One of the most prominent attempts consists in comparing the second circle of Hell, the seventh terrace of Purgatory, and the third heaven of Paradise (Venus).[23] These three sections seem interrelated through a common theme. As for the second circle and the seventh terrace, the theme of lust is explicitly stated as the classificatory principle of the two sections. In the former the sin of lust is condemned, and in the latter it undergoes purgation. As for the third sphere, Dante scholars associate it with the theme of lust due to textual aspects that indicate a lustful behavior of the souls appearing in the Venus heaven while they were still in the mortal world. But this is not the kind of connectionist reading for which Seung argues. It should rather be defined as a comparative reading. Seung's interpretation is not restricted to comparisons of only some segments of the poem. On the contrary, he systematically connects every segment of the whole. Although the comparative reading of the second circle, the seventh terrace, and the third sphere is formally representational of connectionism, the result is segmentalism, because the connectionism consists primarily in combining three separate segmental readings. The objective is only to discuss how Dante treats the theme of lust in three different ways. The difference between the two strategies of reading can be elucidated by applying a distinction from the language of computer science, the distinction between serial and parallel architectures. Whereas Seung's method is a parallel reading of the three parts, the conventional method of Dante studies is a serial reading of the poem.

According to Seung's parallel reading of the poem, the seventh circle, the third terrace, and the third sphere constitute a joint discourse on the capital sin of wrath and its opposite virtue of meekness (or courage). In Hell wrath is condemned, in Purgatory it is purged, and in Paradise its opposite virtue is celebrated (*FLS* 191-217). In the serial reading, such relations are never determined. Its method consists in reading the seventh circle first, then the third terrace, and finally the third sphere. Each section is interpreted as a self-contained entity. However, the parallel relation of Dante's three worlds is vital for the parallel reading. We can go through the seventh circle in its own right, but when we get to the third terrace, we should see it in the light of the seventh circle. When we come to the third sphere, we should understand its significance in the light of the third terrace and the seventh circle. This is the method of parallel contrast, which produces a cumulative effect. In the serial reading, however, what is read is left behind the reader as he or she moves on. In the parallel reading, what is read stays with the reader as he or she moves on. The serial reading is like the flow of a river; the parallel reading is like a dam that collects the flowing water into a lake.

Due to the problems of determining the structural principles, Dante scholars have generated two submethods to the basic method of segmental reading. One is episodic reading. Its analytic focus is set on the different episodes of the text. The objective is not to determine the structural principles but to interpret the narrative action. Robert Hollander defines this method as "microanalysis of particulars of the poem,"[24] and Seung speaks of "episodic exegeses and fragmentary commentaries" (*CT* xvi). For example, the famous passage in *Inferno* 5 with Francesca and Paolo has often been read only with regard to Dante's encounter with the two lovers and the background story for their tragic death. It is not necessarily considered in relation to the overall theme of lust. Nor is the episode related to the theme of lust within the whole of Dante's afterworld. For these reasons, it is questionable whether an episodic reading of the passage contributes to the determination of the total meaning of the poem.

The other submethod is, as already stated, serial reading. This type of reading focuses only on one of the poem's three parts. Its analytic procedure is comparable to the attempt to interpret a whole play on the basis of a single act or the whole work of an author on the basis of a single book. Its interpretive perspective consists of interpreting the poem's segments as constituents of confined series of thematic meaning. Francis Fergusson's reading of *Purgatorio* in *Dante's Drama of the Mind* (1953), in which he focuses on the second canticle in order to explain the poem's composition, is a classical example of this type of reading. A more recent example is John A. Scott's *Dante's Political Purgatory* (1996), in which Dante's political ideas are discussed with explicit focus on *Purgatorio*. Though exploring two different issues, Fergusson and Scott practice a reading strategy that maintains that each of the three parts can be read as a separate entity. However, a complete serial reading would consist of three separate readings. Therefore their readings are only partial or incomplete serial readings.

To be sure, those who practice the method of segmental reading do not exclude connectionist reading. In their analyses they often discuss issues from other sections or parts of the poem and try to determine the meaning of the segment on which they focus by comparing or connecting it to other segments. But they make the comparisons or connections without determining the principles that hold together the different segments of the whole. The connectionist aspects primarily serve the purpose of elucidating the meaning of a particular segment. The characterization of the method of Dante studies as segmental reading might seem to recall Aristotle's contempt for "episodic plots and actions" as expressed in the *Poetics* (1451b). It might seem to imply that Dante scholars prefer segmental reading because it enables them to disguise their incapacity of coming to terms with the total meaning of the text. This is not the argument I pose. The issue is not a matter of disguising the incapacity of understanding, but a matter of neglecting or underestimating the question of unity in the attempt to understand the poem's meaning. Seung's characterization of the *Commedia* as a careful design of the highest order may raise the question of whether Dante exemplifies the ideal poet (according to Aristotle) in that he is a rational maker of artifacts—mimetic structures of action—who sets out the general scheme of his work before elaborating the details.[25] However, any confirmation of this possibility is irrelevant to the present discussion. The purpose of the definition is not to substantiate Eliot's and Bloom's exaltation of Dante's uniqueness or promote a transcultural and transhistorical conception of what makes some authors surpass others. The question is whether Dante achieved what he aimed at. Nowadays we seem well-equipped for answering that question. We have better and more accurate editions of Dante's works than ever before. The material at our disposal is vaster and more instrumental than ever before. Nevertheless, Dante scholars are faced with three difficult problems when they try to answer the question. The first one is the general confusion in modern literary criticism, the second is the complexity of the text, and the third is the tradition of Dante reading.

The *Commedia* is complex and comprehensive, and here lies the difficulty of comprehending its overall structure. This difficulty has fostered the piecemeal reading of the poem. Instead of seeking solid ground for arguing that the *Commedia* is or is not a well-ordered whole, Dante scholars often read the poem as if the question were insignificant. The method of segmental reading is so deeply rooted in Dante studies that its widespread practice constitutes a convincing argument against attempts to find a method to settle the problem of the poem's unity. At best Dante scholars only hint at the problem. Sometimes they seem to regard it as unsolvable because the text is either too complex or too obscure to be understood in its entirety. On other occasions, they seem inclined to reject the idea that Dante has constructed the *Commedia* in accordance with specific principles. In both cases, segmental reading stands out as the adequate way of reading the *Commedia*.

Coherence and Consistency

Segmentalism and connectionism are the two basic strategies of reading in Dante studies. How are we to decide between these two forms of reading? In order to answer that question, it is necessary to consider two essential requirements for literary interpretation—consistency and coherence. We cannot prove that one reading is the correct one. If such a proof were possible, critical disputes about textual meanings would eventually draw to a close. This is the basic difference between a scientific theory and a textual interpretation. It is possible to prove or disprove a scientific theory on the basis of empirical data, but it is not possible to prove or disprove a textual interpretation on the basis of textual evidence. This problem is further emphasized in the case of the *Commedia* because its meaning is not literal but allegorical. A scientific theory is also an interpretation of the available empirical data or phenomena. But it is always empirical and literal. Since literary texts often contain figurative senses, literary meaning is more indeterminate than scientific meaning.

When there is more than one theory proposed to explain the same phenomena, we can have a competition of theories. Sometimes it is hard to decide the outcome of such a competition. In deciding between two competing theories, we should be careful not to say that one is true and the other is false. This distinction is untenable if there can be borderline cases. A borderline case occurs if a theory is defined as true given one set of premises and defined as false given another set of principles. For example, when we consider the two major cosmological theories of the twentieth century, it is incorrect to say that the Big Bang theory is true and the Steady State theory is false. The two theories are based on different sets of premises. The Steady State theory was formulated on the basis of one of set of data, which was later corrected. The correction prepared the way for the Big Bang theory, which was formulated on the basis of another set of data.

Modern cosmology does not postulate definitive truths about the origin, form, and development of the cosmos. It uncovers the structures in the cosmic space that indicate the origin, form, and development. As the modern cosmologist Dennis Sciama puts it: "None of us can understand why there is a Universe at all, why anything should exist; that's the ultimate question. But while we cannot answer that question, we can at least make progress with the next simple one, of what the Universe as a whole is like."[26] On the basis of the available empirical data, the modern cosmologist can prove or disprove a theory about structures in the cosmic space. But he cannot constitute the theory as an ultimate truth. To do that, it would require that he knew the truth about the universe. For these reasons, it is incorrect to say that the Ptolemaic system is false and the Copernican is true. Empirically, both can be true because either the sun or the earth can be regarded as the center for the planetary motions. It all depends on the data applied in substantiating one theory at the expense of another. Since it is problematic to say that the one is true and the other is false, we should rather ask which theory is the better one, or which theory explains the phenomena best. In this respect, the Copernican system is a better theory than the Ptolemaic because it provides a better understanding of the planetary motions. It is for the same reason that the Big Bang theory has replaced the Steady State theory in modern cosmology. It gives a better explanation of the structures discovered in the cosmos.

The distinction of better and worse is different from the distinction of true and false. Since it is impossible to determine which reading of the *Commedia* is true and which is false, we should distinguish between good and bad readings and the better and the worse readings. If I prefer one reading of the *Commedia*, I cannot prove that it is the correct reading. To show that one reading is better than any other reading, I have to make generalizations about the different strategies of reading in Dante studies. I have already argued for such a selective procedure by distinguishing between segmental reading and connectionist reading and between serial or episodic reading and systematic parallel reading. To make such distinctions is necessary for any hermeneutic enterprise; they provide argumentative clarity. But the distinctions also constitute standards for determining the merits of different readings. If we do not set up such standards, we are stuck in hermeneutic egalitarianism.

If we maintain that it is possible to establish an adequate relation between the *Commedia* and its interpreter, the question is what the criteria are for deciding between different readings. The minimum logical requirement for developing a convincing interpretation is that the argumentation is consistent. For example, if I say that the story of Paolo and Francesca in *Inferno* 5 portrays the sin of lust, and say at the same time that it does not portray such a sin, I make a contradictory statement. In this case, I am inconsistent. The criterion of consistency is the weakest criterion because no critic will ever deliberately produce an interpretation that contains a pair of contradictory statements. Since the criterion of consistency is the minimum logical requirement for a theory, it also applies to scientific theories. Inconsistent scientific theories are rare. For example, although the Ptolemaic system turned out to be inadequate for explaining the planetary motions, it was consistent on the basis of the available data. The logical requirement of consistency is a formal criterion because it does not involve any substantive content. By logic alone, it is possible to tell, for example, that "snow is white" and "snow is not white" cannot be jointly true. There is no need to look at the snow. Although each of the two statements has its own substantive content about the nature of snow, their joint assertion cannot have any substantive content because it fails the formal requirement of logical consistency.

The merit of competing scientific theories must be decided by comparing their substantive content, if they are consistent. That requires substantive criteria. What are these criteria? Let us assume that all competing theories take into account the same empirical data. If any of them fails to do so, it should be labeled as inadequate and discarded. If all of them can explain the same empirical data, we should choose the one that organizes those data better than the others. This is the criterion of order or unity. We prefer the Copernican system to the Ptolemaic system because the former gives us a much better and simpler organization of the relevant data than the latter. The criterion of order or unity is also called the criterion of coherence. Coherence is a substantive criterion that applies to textual interpretation. The substantive content of a poem is its thematic content. Every interpretation of a poem tries to secure a unity of its thematic content. In case of competing interpretations, their merit should be decided by the scope and degree of unity the interpretations achieve for the thematic content. Even when a literary text is structured in such a way that its thematic content displays incompatible meanings, the criterion of coherence is operative in textual interpretation. In that case, interpretive coherence consists in explaining how and why incompatible meanings occur. The plurality of meanings can be either intentional or unintentional. If it is unintentional, interpretive coherence consists in elucidating the inconsistency of the thematic content. If the plurality of meanings is intentional, interpretive coherence consists in elucidating how the thematic content undermines or rejects uniform meaning.

Let us assume that our reading of the *Commedia* results in an understanding of the thematic content that complies with the following statement by Natalino Sapegno: "The *Comedy* must be seen as a work that takes shape as it goes along, not an organic preconstituted block of forms and concepts."[27] This view displays a decisive response to the question of unity. It claims that we should not expect to find a conceptual design beneath the narrative account. Since the *Commedia* was gradually shaped, Dante did not operate with a set of principles from the start to the end. As a result, the view dictates a serial reading of the poem. If this is an adequate understanding, the decision between competing serial readings depends on which of those readings explains best the nature of the poem's gradual shaping. The criterion for deciding between these readings is a matter of internal consistency. If I say that "snow is white" and "snow is not white," the inconsistency is internal. It belongs to the statements I make. When readings of the *Commedia* stem from the same assertion but make incompatible conclusions, the inconsistency is internal. But let us suppose that I say that "snow is white" and another person says that "snow is not white." The inconsistency is then external. It does not belong to the statement I make. It appears only when my statement is compared with a statement that does not belong to me. When different readings depart from different assertions, the inconsistency is external.

Since literary meaning is more indeterminate than scientific meaning, the same text is often capable of generating incompatible interpretations. Let us assume that a reading of the *Commedia* results in an understanding of its thematic content that rejects Sapegno's assertion of a gradual shaping. Perhaps the reading complies with Marc Cogan's interpretation in *The Design in the Wax* that "the three structures of the individual cantiche of the Commedia propose variations on a single theme. In those variations the meaning of the theme undergoes change and development, and the content of those changes is the content of the arresting new doctrine Dante expresses in the allegory of the poem" (*DW* 249). If we agree with this assertion, serial reading can no longer be our strategy of reading. If we are to understand Dante's doctrine, we have to engage in connectionist reading. The connectionist reading has to be more than comparative; it has to establish decisive thematic relations between textual elements. If not, we cannot see how the structures of the three canticles propose variations on a single theme. If there are several readings that depart from this assertion, the criterion for deciding between them is internal consistency. It depends on which of these readings best explains the overall theme and its variations.

There are few examples of such readings in Dante studies. The general rule is serial, segmental, or episodic readings. The difference between the rule and the exceptions is a matter of external inconsistency. Sapegno's assertion excludes the possibility of a systematic application of conceptual principles. Cogan, however, asserts that the ultimate meaning of the poem is to be discovered in Dante's application of conceptual principles. These two assertions are incompatible. It is a contradiction to claim that the *Commedia* is a well-ordered whole and yet analyze its thematic content without considering its ordering principles. Let us apply the distinction between the internal and the external consistency to the *Commedia*. By doing so, we can elucidate the problem of deciding between the two assertions on the basis of our reading of the poem.

Because the hierarchy of sins in Hell does not coincide with the hierarchy of sins in Purgatory, we have to say that some sins in Hell cannot find suitable place for purgation in Purgatory. But this assertion produces an external inconsistency, because it is incompatible with the theological teaching of the medieval church, according to which every sin can be purged. But if some infernal sins cannot be purged in Purgatory, we need to ask what the role of purgation is in the *Commedia*. The role of purgation can be understood in two ways—negative or positive. The negative way is to see purgation as a way of getting rid of sin. By the negative process, purgation cleanses the soul of all sins and restores its purity, which makes it into a blank tablet. The positive way is to see purgation as a way of converting sins into virtues. After all, purgation is to make the soul truly Christian, and this goal cannot be accomplished by making the soul into a blank tablet. Virtues and sins involve the powers of the soul and determine its spiritual condition. This condition cannot be neutral for entering the kingdom of heaven. Hence the positive notion of purgation is not only dictated by Christian teaching, it is really operative in Dante's Purgatory, where we observe purgation as a positive process. Given this premise, we have to ask what happens to the virtues gained in Purgatory when the soul ascends to Paradise. There is no way to answer this question since the ten spheres are not named after virtues. There is nothing logically inconsistent between Purgatory and Paradise. One is busily engaged in the regeneration of virtues, but the other does not show any trace of the arduous process. This makes no sense, but it involves no logical contradiction. It would be a logical contradiction if Paradise portrayed one set of virtues incompatible with the set of virtues attained through the arduous process of purgation. But the naming of the spheres in Paradise reveals no set of virtues. The last two canticles appear to have no thematic connection at all. In short, there seems to be no coherence between these two parts of the poem.

Finally, there is one more meaning of inconsistency, which further elucidates the interpretive problems we are dealing with. This inconsistency is not logical but substantive. It is often used for describing the performance of an athlete on the field. For example, a player's performance is said to be inconsistent; that is, he performs well sometimes, but poorly other times. A consistent player is someone who performs well or poorly all the time. We can apply this criterion to Dante studies. The hierarchies of Hell and Purgatory are not totally different, but partially overlap. If they were totally different, they should dictate a purely serial reading of the first canticles. If they were identical, they would dictate a systematic parallel reading. Since they are neither totally different nor totally identical, they seem to dictate a mixed reading—the mixture of serial and parallel readings. This is the problem of inconsistency. The purely serial reading is consistent, and the systematic parallel reading is consistent. But the mixed reading does not have the virtue of consistency; it is inconsistent.

This leaves us with an essential question when we try to solve the problem of the poem's unity. Is Dante inconsistent in his exposition of the universal order, or have Dante scholars been inconsistent in the treatment of the question of coherence? Since it is our interpretation of the poem that determines Dante's consistency, the answer depends on the consistency of our interpretive performance. There are four main options. (1) If we assert that the *Commedia* is a well-ordered whole but do not explain the principles that govern its design, our interpretive performance is inconsistent. (2) If we assert that the poem is not a well-ordered whole but do not explain why the thematic content does not constitute such a whole, our performance is inconsistent. However, (3) if we assert that the poem is not a well-ordered whole and explain why the thematic content does not constitute such a whole, our performance is consistent. (4) If we assert that the poem is a well-ordered whole and explain how the thematic content constitutes such a whole, our performance is consistent.

Interpretive Performance

Choosing between these four options, the interpretive performance in Dante studies has been inconsistent. Although Dante scholars often assert that the *Commedia* is a well-ordered whole, they seldom explain its ordering principles. I detect two major reasons for this inconsistency. First, innumerable studies of Dante's poem display great uncertainty about how to determine the constituents of the poem's structure. Generally speaking, Dante scholars rely too much on the narrative's explicit designations of the structural divisions. By doing so, they overlook how the many scenes of action and the many topics of discourse throughout the narrative contribute to the constitution of the structure. Second, since interpretations of the *Commedia* often contradict the assertion of a well-ordered whole by not explaining the constituting principles, many studies of Dante's poem are caught in a conflict between structuralism and skepticism.

Singleton's approach to the *Commedia* is a case in point that deserves special attention for several reasons. The first reason is due to Robert Hollander's claim that Dante studies world-wide are still "in a Singletonian age."[28] By this he means that the question of the poem's allegorical meaning, which Singleton brought to the fore, is still the predominant issue in many studies of Dante's poem, of which many are indebted to Singleton's work on Dante. The implication of the allegorical perspective is a man-centered reading with exclusive focus on the element of journey in Dante's poem. Due to the analytic characteristic of this view, Hollander's accurate assertion of a continuous Singletonian influence implies that Dante scholars still tend to neglect or underestimate the meaning of the poem's vision of order. Cogan's study of the *Commedia* is therefore a valuable contribution to the revitalization of the question of order in Dante's otherworldly vision.

The second reason is that the conflict between structuralism and skepticism, which still marks most readings of the *Commedia*, was more explicitly stated at an earlier stage of modern Dante studies. Previously, Dante scholars emphasized the poem's complexity as the main hindrance for a comprehensive understanding. The notion of the reader's inescapable subjectivity has now been emphatically added to the sum of hindrances. The third reason for focusing on Singleton's approach is that it helps to clarify on what ground Seung proposed his interpretation of the poem's thematic coherence. The fourth reason is that with this focus it is possible to substantiate historically the distinctions between the different strategies of reading presented in the preceding. I do not claim that Dante studies have seen no progress since Singleton, but I argue that it has not come closer to a comprehensive understanding of the poem's unity. This is due to the man-centered reading Singleton promoted.

Another problem is that most of the innumerable statements in Dante studies about the poem's unity remain on a level of general assumption. They do not show how the unity is materialized into the poem's details. For that reason, their interpretive performance lacks consistency. For example, in *Mimesis* Auerbach claims that the moral system of the *Commedia*, "in its distribution of souls among the three realms and their subdivisions," follows "on the whole . . . Aristotelian-Thomist ethics."[29] Such a claim presupposes an elucidation of how Dante incorporates this ethical position in his poetic exposition of the universal order. But Auerbach never shows how Dante does that. For that reason, his claim is unfounded. Moreover, it is hardly sustainable. As made clear by Seung and Cogan, among others, Dante's use of Aristotle's *Ethics* in canto 11 of *Inferno* is not particularly Aristotelian or Thomistic (*DW* 4-19 and *MC* 186-87). Although Auerbach never refers to this passage, it is quite clear that it underlies his characterization of Dante's moral system. Furthermore, as pointed out by Seung, Aquinas's notion of the seven capital sins cannot be taken as the model for Dante's way of structuring Purgatory proper, since Aquinas is never consistent in his treatment of their hierarchical order (*MC* 212). Consequently, if the reader of the *Commedia* takes Auerbach's statement for a decisive observation, he contributes to the consolidation of an inconsistent view of the poem.

Depending on Etienne Gilson's version of medieval Thomism, Auerbach claims: "That man's existence on earth is provisional and must be complemented in the world beyond, is a concept in keeping with Thomist anthropology."[30] This seems to be a significant insight but is in fact a trite observation. It is the very essence of medieval Christianity to regard earthly existence as only provisional. Why, then, does Auerbach find it necessary to identify it with Thomistic thought? In order to understand this motivation, let us consider another example of performative inconsistency. In an article on Dante and the asceticism of the thirteenth century, Giorgio Petrocchi argues that "the spiritual outlook of the *Commedia* can be identified by the parallel process of mystical-ascetical, and apocalyptic-messianic influences." Petrocchi associates the mystical-ascetical aspects in Dante with the mystical theology of Bernard of Clairvaux, Bonaventure, and the school of Saint-Victor, and he associates the apocalyptic-messianic aspects with Joachim of Fiore and Pietro da Morone (Celestin V), in whose works we find "postures of expectation and invocation of God's emissary, the renewer of mankind and restorer of the Church."[31]

By pointing out these principal aspects, Petrocchi places Dante in the tradition of medieval mysticism. But he emphasizes that Dante is not a mystic *stricto sensu*. He is rather "a man of letter who has claimed for himself, for the convenience of a rhetorical project and through love of a literary form in common use at the time, an experience never truly lavished upon him by God." According to Petrocchi, the *Commedia* is not a report of a supernatural experience. It has the structure of a mystical account, but it is grounded in an earthly experience, which "symbolized, reflected, or hypothesized in the various vicissitudes and encounters in the course of the eschatological pilgrimage."[32] However, Petrocchi's emphasis on the supernatural experience as essential to medieval mysticism involves a narrow definition of the mystical current in medieval Christianity. According to Bernard McGinn, "what we call mysticism today is best seen not as a discrete entity, a special kind of religion, but as a part or element within broader concrete traditions." Its primary themes are "solitude and silence, prayer and contemplation, and the vision of God."[33] These themes can be treated in different ways. What makes a report mystical is not only a matter of whether the reporter truly believes to have experienced a supernatural event. Dante's speculative exposition of God's universal order can also be defined as mystical because Dante fully believes in the vision he constructs.

But Petrocchi excludes this possibility because he conceives mysticism as presupposing a sensation whose cause the mystic identifies as supernatural. Dante's vision is too controlled, constructed, and extraordinary to arise from such a sensation. Petrocchi argues that Dante's inspirational source for the ascetical aspects of the *Commedia* is not to be found in the mystical currents: "The source, as usual, is St. Thomas Aquinas." Petrocchi refers to a specific paragraph in the *Summa Theologiae*.[34] In that paragraph (pt. 2-2, q. 24, a. 9), Aquinas draws up a schema with three ascetic phases of perfection that resemble the growth of the human body and delineate man's possibility of experiencing increasing degrees of divine charity. Petrocchi suggests that Dante might have applied this schema, but he does not show in what way. For that reason, his claim is unfounded. In addition, he is also somewhat reserved toward identifying Aquinas as the source for Dante's threefold ascent to God. He admits that "it would be rash to see a correspondence between the three phases of ascetic perfection and the three parts of the *Commedia*."[35] Therefore, as in Auerbach's case, we may ask why he refers to Aquinas. There are several reasons for the reference that underline Petrocchi's interpretive inconsistency and at the same time elucidate Auerbach's.

By stressing that he was a man of letters, Petrocchi regards Dante, first of all, as a particularly gifted poet but not as an erudite theologian. Whereas his poetic inventiveness was extraordinary, his theological understanding was not. The poetic exploration of the literary form of mystical accounts and eschatological descriptions required comprehensive theological understanding. For this purpose, he relied heavily on the works of the major Christian theologians and especially on Aquinas's two *Summae*, since they are ample summaries of theological doctrines of medieval Christianity. As a result, Aquinas has long endured the fortune of being the preferred source for interpreting the poem's theological content. But the reliance on Thomistic thought in Dante studies is disproportionate with the role of Aquinas in the *Commedia*. Moreover, in theological matters, Dante does not apply distinctively Thomistic terminology. Hence, if Dante scholars maintain a certain affinity between Dante and Aquinas, they have to show how the Thomistic influence is materialized into Dante's poetic construction and detectable in his inventive poetic language. This would require a thoroughgoing comparative study of the poem's theological content and the theological teachings of Aquinas. But such a study has never been made. The reason is that Dante scholars are well aware that Dante was not a Thomist.

The heavy use of Thomistic thought in Dante studies has also a historical explanation. Aquinas was never, in Dante's lifetime, an official or unofficial authority whose teachings were regarded as incontestable. On the contrary, the Parisian bishop Etienne Tempier's condemnations of a number of Aristotelian and Averroistic propositions in 1270 and 1277 had a significant impact on the formation of a posthumous reputation that underlined several controversial elements in Aquinas's works. For example, between 1277 and 1279 the Franciscan William de la Mare composed a correction to 117 passages in his works that restrained his immediate influence.[36] In response to such expressions of suspicion about Aquinas's orthodoxy, the general chapter of the Dominicans found it necessary to express its confidence in his teachings four times during the next twenty-five years. However, with his canonization in 1323 the attacks on Aquinas decreased, and in 1325 the censures were withdrawn. Thomistic teachings were less controversial when Dante wrote the *Commedia* than when he underwent his educational training in Florence. But although Aquinas's influence gradually increased, his modern reputation of the great synthesizer of medieval theological ideas is basically an invention of the Counterreformation.[37] It was consolidated with the rise of Thomistic studies in the nineteenth century. Finally, in 1879, Pope Leo XIII declared Thomistic teachings to be the philosophical foundation of the Catholic Church. This position was largely maintained until the Second Vatican Council in 1962-1965.[38] Auerbach and Petrocchi do not take account of these historical circumstances. Perhaps they were unaware that Thomism is basically a modern invention that reached its peak during the same period in which modern Dante studies took form. Nevertheless, the perception of Dante's inspirational background and historical context, which Thomistic readings of the *Commedia* generate, is not consistent with the historical circumstances.

Performative consistency is a hard but indispensable criterion. To my knowledge, there are only two readings in Dante studies that do not fall down on this criterion. One is Seung's Dante reading and the other is Cogan's. Neither Seung nor Cogan simply presume the existence of a conceptual design, as John Freccero, for instance, does: "We must assume the existence of a coherent pattern and abandon our hypothesis only when our resources or those of the poem are exhausted. Only then may we conclude either that the significance of these details escapes us, or that the poem is unintelligible in this respect."[39] On the contrary, Seung and Cogan propose detailed explanations of what makes up the pattern. In this respect, their readings stand in opposition to the general tendencies in Dante studies. The plurality of these tendencies is here emphasized deliberately. Dante studies are not a homogeneous entity. The vast amount of Dante readings points in many directions. The question of the poem's allegorical meaning displays a great variety of positions and opinions. But the fact that there are few examples of comprehensive explanations of the poem's thematic coherence indicates that the prevalent methods of reading in Dante studies are different than those practiced by Seung and Cogan.

Notes

1. T. S. Eliot, "Dante" in *Selected Essays* (London: Faber and Faber Limited, 1972), 265.
2. Harold Bloom, *The Western Canon: The Books and Schools of the Ages* (New York: Harcourt Brace & Company, 1994), 43.
3. Robin Kirkpatrick, *Dante: The Divine Comedy* (Cambridge: Cambridge University Press, 1996), 107.
4. Benedetto Croce, *La Poesia di Dante* (Bari: Laterza, 1921), 68-69.
5. Giuseppe Petronio, *L'attività letteraria in Italia: storia della letteratura* (Palermo: Palumbo, 1977), 105.
6. For Dante's account of the order of the celestial spheres, see the *Convivio* (II.iii). Dante Alighieri, *Dante's Il Convivio (The Banquet)*, trans. Richard H. Lansing (New York: Garland Publishing, 1990), 44-46. For the development of medieval cosmology, see Edward Grant, "Cosmology," in *Science in the Middle Ages*, ed. David C. Lindberg (Chicago: University of Chicago Press, 1978), 265-302, and David C. Lindberg, *The Beginnings of Western Science* (Chicago: University of Chicago Press, 1992), 245-52. For the emergence of the Empyreum in medieval cosmology, see Edward Grant, *Planets, Stars, & Orbs: The Medieval Cosmos, 1200-1687* (Cambridge: Cambridge University Press, 1997), 371-82.
7. Augustine, *Confessions*, trans. R. S. Pine-Coffin (London: Penguin, 1976), 21.
8. Charles S. Singleton, *Dante Studies II: Journey to Beatrice* (Cambridge, Mass.: Harvard University Press, 1958), 3-4.
9. Singleton, *Dante Studies II*, 5, and John Freccero, *Dante: The Poetics of Conversion*, ed. Rachel Jacoff (Cambridge, Mass.: Harvard University Press, 1986), 70.
10. Antonio C. Mastrobuono, *Dante's Journey of Sanctification* (Washington, D.C.: Regnery Gateway, 1990), 8.
11. A. C. Charity, *Events and their Afterlife: The Dialectics of Christian Typology in the Bible and Dante* (Cambridge: Cambridge University Press, 1987), 167-68.
12. Charles S. Singleton, *Dante Studies I: Elements of Structure* (Cambridge, Mass.: Harvard University Press, 1954), 30.
13. Charles S. Singleton, *Dante Studies II*, v.
14. Erich Auerbach, "Epilegomena to *Mimesis*" in *Mimesis: The Representation of Reality in Western Literature* (Princeton, N.J.: Princeton University Press, 2003), 572.

15. Erich Auerbach, "Philology and *Weltliteratur*," in *Centennial Review* 13: 1 (1969), 16.

16. Erich Auerbach, "Vico's Contribution to Literary Criticism," in *Studia Philologica et Litteraria in Honorem L. Spitzer*, ed. A. G. Hatcher and K. L. Selig (Bern: Franeke Verlag, 1958), 262.

17. Wendell V. Harris, *Literary Meaning: Reclaiming the Study of Literature.* (London: Routledge, 1996), 107.

18. Wendell V. Harris, *Literary Meaning*, 18.

19. Bernardino Daniello, *L'espositione di Bernardino Daniello da Lucca sopra la Comedia di Dante*, ed. R. Hollander and J. Schnapp (Hanover: University Press of New England, 1989).

20. Karl Witte, "The Ethical Systems of the Inferno and the Purgatorio," in *Essays on Dante* (London: Lawrence and Philip H.), 117.

21. Vergil's explanation represents a unique reading of the biblical story of the fall of Satan (Isaiah 14, Ezekiel 28, and Revelation 12). Vergil says to Dante that when Satan was cast out of heaven, he fell toward the Southern Hemisphere. The effect of the fall was two significant movements of the landmasses of the earth. The reason for the movements was fear of Satan. The first movement occurred when he plunged through the spheres and approached the earth like a "lightning from heaven" (Luke 10: 18). Just before the impact, the landmasses of the Southern Hemisphere hid beneath the ocean and fled toward the Northern Hemisphere. This movement raised the level of the Northern Hemisphere, which later in history became the inhabited part of the earth with Jerusalem as its centre. The withdrawal in terror transformed the Southern Hemisphere into a vast ocean. The second movement occurred when Satan hit the earth. In equal fear of him, the landmasses of the interior escaped the impact and rushed up to the surface of the earth. The movement upward created the Mount of Purgatory in the middle of the vast ocean of the Southern Hemisphere and left a huge crevasse in the interior of the Northern Hemisphere, which then became the realm of Hell. See also Jeffrey Burton Russell, *Lucifer: The Devil in the Middle Ages* (Ithaca, N.Y.: Cornell University Press, 1984), 224.

22. Neither in the *Commedia* nor in the biblical sources is it overtly stated when the expulsion of Satan took place. In Isaiah (14: 12-19) we only learn why he was expelled; he tried to place his throne above God's. In Ezekiel (28: 17) the reason is further elucidated; he revolted against God because his heart was full of arrogance. However, in *De civitate Dei* (XI: 14-19), Augustine argues that the introduction of evil must have taken place at an early stage of the creation, since the opposition between good and evil existed as a principle when God created Adam as the first man. According to Augustine, the division between light and darkness and between night and day in Genesis (1: 1-5) also involved the separation between the holy angels and the unclean angels that participated in Satan's revolt.

23. Patrick Boyde, *Perception and Passion in Dante's Comedy* (Cambridge: Cambridge University Press, 1993), 275-301.

24. Robert Hollander, "Dante and his commentators," in *The Cambridge Companion to Dante*, ed. Rachel Jacoff (Cambridge: Cambridge University Press, 1993), 232.

25. Stephen Halliwell, "Aristotle's Poetics," in *The Cambridge History of Literary Criticism, Vol. I: Classical Criticism*, ed. G. A. Kennedy (Cambridge: Cambridge University Press, 1993), 158.

26. Helge Kragh, *Cosmology and Controversy: The Historical Development of Two Theories of the Universe* (Princeton, N.J.: Princeton University Press, 1996), xi.

27. Lettario Cassata, "The Hard Begin," in *Lectura Dantis: Inferno: A Canto-by-Canto Commentary*, ed. Allen Mandelbaum (Los Angeles: University of California Press, 1998), 11.

28. Robert Hollander, "Dante and his commentators," 234; Robert Hollander, *Allegory in Dante's Commedia* (Princeton, N.J.: Princeton University Press, 1969), 49.

29. Erich Auerbach, *Mimesis: The Representation of Reality in Western Literature*, trans. W. R. Trask (Princeton, N.J.: Princeton University Press, 1953), 190.

30. Erich Auerbach, *Mimesis*, 196.

31. Giorgio Petrocchi, "Dante and Thirteenth-Century Asceticism," in *From Time to Eternity: Eassays on Dante's Divine Comedy*, ed. Thomas G. Bergin (New Haven, Conn.: Yale University Press, 1967), 39.

32. Giorgio Petrocchi, "Dante and Thirteenth-Century Asceticism," 44-45.

33. Bernard McGinn, *The Presence of God: A History of Western Christian Mysticism, Vol. I: The Foundations of Mysticism* (New York: Crossroad, 1991), xv-xvi, and *Vol. II: The Growth of Mysticism* (New York: Crossroad, 1994), 119.

34. Giorgio Petrocchi, "Dante and Thirteenth-Century Asceticism," 46.

35. Giorgio Petrocchi, "Dante and Thirteenth-Century Asceticism," 47.

36. Bonnie Kent, *Virtues of the Will: The Transformation of Ethics in the Late Thirteenth Century* (Washington, D.C.: Catholic University of America Press, 1995), 81; Richard C. Dales, "The Origin of the Doctrine of the Double Truth," in *Viator* 15 (1984), 179; Frederick Copleston, *A History of Philosophy, Vol. II: Medieval Philosophy from Augustine to Duns Scotus* (New York: Image Books, 1993), 433.

37. Quentin Skinner, *The Foundations of Modern Political Thought, Vol. II: The Age of Reformation* (Cambridge: Cambridge University Press, 1978), 135-48.

38. Paul E. Sigmund, "Law and politics," in *The Cambridge Companion to Aquinas*, ed. Norman Kretzmann and Eleonore Stump (Cambridge: Cambridge University Press, 1993), 228.

39. John Freccero, "Dante's Pilgrim in a Gyre," in *PMLA* LXXVI (1961), reprinted in John Freccero, *Dante: The Poetics of Conversion*, 71. The citation is taken out of a specific context, but Rachel Jacoff's quotation of the statement in the introduction to *The Poetics of Conversion* points beyond the context in

which it occurs. Among Freccero's articles on Dante, I have not come across one that treats the poem's unity in a systematic way. Freccero often hovers about this question without finding any solution to it. For example, in "The Prologue Scene," Freccero writes: "The coherence of the whole poem may be grasped only with a view to its totality, a view from the ending, just as the coherence of the poet's life could be grasped only in retrospect, from the perspective of totality in death." To put his view of the *Commedia* further into perspective, it is also significant how he distinguishes between the pilgrim's and the poet's view of the world: "The pilgrim's view is very much like our view of history and of ourselves: partial, perhaps confused, still in the making. But the poet's view is far different, for it is global and comprehensive, the total view of a man who looks at the world, his neighborhood, and indeed himself with all the detachment of a cultural anthropologist." John Freccero, "The Proloque Scene," in *Dante Studies* 84 (1966), reprinted in John Freccero, *Dante: The Poetics of Conversion*, 25-26.

Chapter Two

Heraclitean River

In *The King's Two Bodies*, Ernst H. Kantorowicz identifies two difficulties in approaching Dante's *Commedia*. The first difficulty consists in the fact that Dante, "who reproduced the general knowledge of his age on every page, gave every theorem which he reproduced a slant so new and so surprising that the evidence proving his dependency on other writings serves mainly to underscore the novelty of his own approach and his own solutions." For Kantorowicz, the knowledge of various notions and statements of ancient and medieval writers can enable us to get better hold of the essential points of Dante's worldview. At the same time he emphasizes that it would be a grave mistake to see this worldview as representational of a particular branch within medieval thought.

The other great difficulty Kantorowicz detects is that "every Dante interpretation is bound to be fragmentary where Dante himself is complex":

> Dante's hard-riding logic, though perfectly clear and perhaps even consistent within the whole of his work, was yet anything but linear, because every point on the line of his thought was cross-connected with countless other points on countless other lines. Any effort, therefore, to reproduce the thought of Dante the philosopher in a straightforward fashion will hardly escape the danger of falling flat and becoming trite simply because the complexity of the poet's view has been neglected.[1]

For Kantorowicz, Dante is a writer whose achievement defies simple formulation. But his statement contains more than just an acknowledgment of the interpretive act as involving formalization and simplification of its object. It involves an implicit criticism of previous attempts to interpret Dante's line of thought according to specific tendencies in medieval thought. These tendencies are either Aquinas's moderate Aristotelianism or the radical Aristotelianism associated with Siger of Brabant and Boethius of Dacia. Kantorowicz's statement reflects a period in Dante studies in which it was still necessary to underline that Dante's eclecticism was not epigenous.

The same point is emphasized by Etienne Gilson. For Gilson it stands clear that Dante's Thomism

> was neither so complete nor so exclusive as has sometimes been supposed. St. Thomas and his theology clearly occupy a place of honour. Yet he is not the only theologian in the poem, for, to say nothing of St. Bernard, St. Bonaventure is on a par with the Dominican Doctor. Dante, then, has identified Thomistic theology with the *Divine Comedy*, but it cannot be maintained that he has identified the *Divine Comedy* with Thomistic theology.[2]

According to Gilson, whatever inspirational, conceptual, or thematic relationship we might establish between Dante and Aquinas, we should not exaggerate apparent correspondences. The same goes for any other thinker whose writings might have inspired Dante. As Umberto Cosmo puts it: "It is not St. Thomas or St. Bonaventure or Aristotle that is important; it is Dante. St. Thomas, St. Bonaventure and Aristotle can only point to the understanding of the poet."[3]

The reason why we should not exaggerate apparent correspondences is due to what Kantorowicz identifies as cross-connections between countless points on countless lines. The complexity of the poem makes it impossible to give prominence to specific notions or incidents in the narrative. There is no theological key notion to the understanding of Dante's worldview. When Dante elaborates on a notion on one occasion, its importance becomes clear only in relation to similar notions on other occasions. Due to this narrative characteristic, Thomas G. Bergin makes the following comparison, which coincides with Kantorowicz's and Singleton's view of the *Commedia*:

> If one looks at the *Comedy* as a work of art, the image of oriental rug comes very easily to mind. The patterns recur, certain bright threads, creative, rhetorical, or didactic, run through the weaving in ever new combinations, coming together in knots or colorful concentrations at various points, forming designs always sufficiently familiar to be reassuring, never without some element of surprise in their composition.[4]

For Bergin the "crossing and recrossing" of themes and structural elements give the *Commedia* an aesthetic unity that is dynamic: "The whole magnificent artifact, with its separate parts exchanging their splendors even as the stars of heaven, glitters with no static glow, but seems to *spin* before our fascinated eyes."[5] The result is something rare in literature.

Given this appraisal of the *Commedia* as a perhaps coherent whole of cross-connections or a complex pattern of recurring themes, it is not hard to understand why there are so few comprehensive explanations of the poem's thematic coherence. The two major obstacles have been pointed out by Kantorowicz. First, the issues revealed by the content of the narrative are in themselves complex. Second, the form in which they are presented makes them even more complex. Confronted with this complexity, Singleton's claim that abstractive analysis is defeated in front of the poem's totality seems reasonable. As a result, comprehensive explanation becomes impossible. The text is regarded as ultimately impenetrable, because its complexity generates textual ambiguities that obscure the message. If so, we may ask whether Dante never had a plan or lost control over his ambitious enterprise. Singleton suggests neither. To my knowledge, no Dante scholar has ever categorically claimed and systematically shown that Dante did not have a plan or that he failed to complete whatever plan he had. Only the latter has sometimes been suggested but only hypothetically.

The defeat of abstractive analysis, however, can have another reason. It can be due to the method, by which many Dante scholars try to penetrate the text. Maybe it is their way of reading that makes the complexity of the poem's message into a cluster of ambiguous obscurities. It is not necessarily the discipline of abstractive analysis that it is defeated when a comprehensive understanding is not attained. The rareness of comprehensive explanations indicates what constitutes this method. Dante scholars concentrate on minor issues. They often leave the question of the poem's thematic coherence unexplored, as if it does not exist or cannot be determined. This prevalent view in Dante studies, however, is not due to conscious positioning, but by venerating the poem's meaning as indeterminate, many Dante scholars show a specific attitude toward the poem that has the character of a common position.

Foundation of Dante Studies

In the history of Dante reception, there are especially two well-reputed analytic practices that have contributed to the consolidation of the position. One is the commentary tradition that goes back to the first decades after Dante's death. It has been continued throughout the history of Dante reception, though with varying impetus depending on Dante's cultural status at different times. The other is the so-called *lectura Dantis* genre that goes back to Giovanni Boccaccio's lectures on the first half of *Inferno* in 1373. This genre was further developed in the sixteenth and nineteenth centuries into a special kind of narrative interpretive commentary, which in the twentieth century has become a well-established exercise in Dante studies. These two analytic perspectives constitute a historical continuity. The understanding of the *Commedia* has changed radically over a span of seven centuries. But due to the continuous focus on the particular elements, there is a certain affinity between the different stages of Dante studies. In spite of the successful revolt against simplistic Dante readings, which throughout the twentieth century has led to significant reevaluations of Dante's achievement, inquiries into the *Commedia* are still modeled on the same principle as in the earliest times of Dante reading. The problem with these two analytic forms is that they give prevalence to the local perspective on the text.

The commentary practice consists in explaining single, often difficult or ambiguous words, sentences, expressions, and passages of the *Commedia*. Lengthy notes are added to the text informing the reader about biographical and historical facts and potential sources of inspiration. The objective is to reconstruct the overall cultural texture of Dante's medieval context. The problem with this encyclopedic objective is that it does not settle the question of unity. But the commentary explanations are often taken to be the precondition for understanding Dante's text. This is a defensible analytic position, since we cannot interpret what we do not understand. But in Dante studies this principle has a special connotation. Only when the reader has completed an attentive reading of the poem, frequently consulting the commentary explanations, is he or she in the position of engaging in the interpretive act. Singleton exemplifies this with his extensive commentary to his translation of the *Commedia*.[6] The idea has been further advanced by Hollander with the Dartmouth Dante Project, which is a database with a large number of commentaries available for consultation on the Internet (*DDP*). According to Hollander, "the commentary tradition is an extremely useful tool, perhaps less for coming up with 'answers' than for indicating the complexity of the problems which need to be addressed."[7] For the untrained reader, the consultation of the commentary—and, for the professional Dante scholar, the study of the commentary tradition—has the status of a necessary prerequisite for getting hold of the particular elements that constitute the poem's thematic content.

The emphasis on the significance of the commentaries for the reader's understanding of the text has had a decisive impact on the interpretive method in Dante studies. This is exemplified by a *lectura Dantis*, which denotes an interpretive reading of one particular canto out of the poem's one hundred cantos. The procedure corresponds to that of interpreting a passage or a chapter in a novel or a dialogue or a scene in a play as a separate entity. The result is an episodic or purely segmental reading. In most cases, the interpretive perspective is restricted by the extension of the particular canto in question. But the structural design of Dante's afterworld does not coincide with the division into cantos. Therefore the analytic basis for a *lectura Dantis* is only the formal structure of the poem, not its substantive structure. To deal with the substantive structure is to try to determine the meaning of Dante's vision. Like the commentary, the *lectura Dantis* aims at elucidating textual statements in semantically confined contexts. The particular episode, segment, or part attains the status of a self-contained entity. That creates a problem for the determination of the meaning of crossing and recrossing themes. The local perspective is incapable of handling such themes. The themes are seldom investigated systematically but stand out as accidental or arbitrary elements within the whole.

The consequence of the strong focus on textual details is a fundamental ambiguity about how to appropriate the text. The response has resulted in two perceptions of the poem as a whole. These two perceptions are formally related to two different issues in Dante studies and give rise to two different puzzlements. The first perception defines the *Commedia* as a whole greater than the sum of its parts. The second perception identifies it as a work in progress. In the latter case, the work is conceived as concluded in the sense that it has a decisive narrative frame. But it is regarded as incomplete in the sense that the structural and thematic elements we detect within this frame do not add up to a conceptual whole. The two perceptions represent two different responses to the ambiguity. But they have one thing in common—they display a notion of an ungraspable whole. In the one case, it is our perception of the text that identifies the whole as ungraspable. In the other, it is our interpretation of Dante's perception of the universal order that identifies his attempt to grasp the whole as ultimately incomplete. There is, of course, a difference between identifying the notion of an ungraspable whole with the reader's perception of the poem and identifying it with Dante's perception of the universal order. But the two perceptions implicate the same exclusion. It is this exclusion that constitutes the prevalent attitude in Dante studies. Both exclude the possibility of conducting a systematic interpretation of the *Commedia* on the basis of the assertion that the form and the content ultimately unfold a conceptual design. Whether it is our willful purposes of abstractive analysis that are ultimately defeated, or it is Dante's perception of the universe that sets the limits for our interpretive possibilities, it all leads to the same conclusion: the whole is ungraspable. For that reason, the difference between the two perceptions is only formal.

A passage in T. S. Eliot's famous essay on Dante exemplifies the affinity between the two perceptions. In discussing canto 34 of *Inferno*, Eliot argues that "Dante made the best of bad job" in describing Satan's conditions at the bottom of the infernal pit:

> If anyone is repelled by the last canto of the *Inferno*, I can only ask him to wait until he has read and lived for years with the last canto of the *Paradiso*, which is to my thinking the highest point that poetry has ever reached or ever can reach, and in which Dante amply repairs any failure of Canto XXXIV of the *Inferno*; but perhaps it is better, on our first reading of the *Inferno*, to omit the last canto and return to the beginning of Canto III.[8]

Eliot insinuates that Dante failed to present Satan in a poetically suggestive way that convincingly pictures his evilness. For that reason, he recommends the reader to jump certain episodes now and then. The reason is that he basically reads the *Commedia* as a work in progress. For Eliot, the *Commedia* is one of the greatest achievements in world literature. He does not question Dante's genius but eagerly stresses his canonical status. But when he distinguishes between the failure of canto 34 of *Inferno* and the mastery of canto 33 of *Paradiso*, he accepts that there are inconsistencies between the form and the content. These inconsistencies reflect the general development of Dante's poetic creativity and point to certain limits of his ongoing project. As such, Eliot's view of the *Commedia* complies with Sapegno's assertion of a gradual shaping of the *Commedia*.

But Eliot never investigates the implications of his assumption. His aim is to show the greatness of Dante's poetry by pointing out that minor failures in the details are nothing compared to the mastery of the whole. Eliot would not hesitate in confirming the characterization of the *Commedia* as a whole greater than the sum of its parts. He never chooses between the two ways of perceiving the whole, but his acknowledgement of Dante's mastery reveals his position. Since the reader should not make too much of minor failures, he might as well ignore them. The whole is never overshadowed by inconsistent details. The consequence of this view is that we might read the single parts as self-contained entities and interpret them without establishing their significance for the narrative progression and the whole construction. The beauty of the final canto of *Paradiso* is not disrupted by the failure of the final canto of *Inferno*, although the contrast between the ultimate image of the evil and the ultimate image of the good might be significant in terms of the thematic content of the whole.

Structuralism and Skepticism

The reason why Dante scholars do find it problematic to interpret the single parts as self-contained entities becomes clear if we consider Singleton's insistence on each scene as having its own real center of inspiration. The question is what he means by "real center of inspiration." His concern is to reject the idea of a preconceived formula mechanically applied, but he never rejects the idea of a conceptual design. Singleton's discovery of a numerological center of the poem around canto 17 of *Purgatorio* shows that he accepts the possibility of a conceptual design.[9] But the discovery makes him wonder why Dante would construct a numerical symmetry and insert hidden signs in the design, which for many centuries escaped the minds of Dante scholars because of the subtlety.

In order to solve this problem, Singleton argues that the insertion of hidden signs does not necessarily make part of the message Dante wants to communicate to the reader. What the reader perhaps regards as a deliberate textual intricacy on Dante's part is not intended to be so. Singleton emphasizes that with the *Commedia* Dante is not only conversing with himself and the reader about a personal ultramundane experience. The discourse unfolds an existential answer to the question of how God is manifest in the world experienced by human beings both in this life and in the afterlife. Every sign or theme in the *Commedia*, whether it is overtly or covertly stated, has always God as its ultimate point of reference. However hidden a theme might be for the mind of the reader, it is always intelligible for the divine mind. But although Singleton emphasizes that Dante is conversing with God through the insertion of hidden signs, the notion of a hidden symmetry does not make him consider the possibility of a conceptual design.

Singleton does address the question of the poem's unity, but the result is a very broad and undeterminable concept of the inspirational center of the whole. In arguing that the *Commedia* has the character of a "double vision," since it is an account of a real event that contains an allegorical meaning, whereby the narrative has both a literal and a trans-literal meaning, Singleton says:

> The question can and does arise whether Dante could have had some model in mind when he wrote his poem to be read in such a focus of double vision—or the question, say, whether Dante's greatest structure and Dante's art is, in any sense, an "imitation" . . . Dante's structure is an imitation of the two works by God, two books written by God, the created universe with its symbolism as one "book," and Holy Scripture with its allegory as the other.[10]

But this definition of Dante's inspirational background is the broadest possible definition of any inspirational background of a humanly created work. It is the same to say that Dante is inspired by life and subsequently imitates it. The definition only states that Dante imitates the origin of life, which is God, and the manifestation of life, which comes out of God. Dante is inspired by his participation in the universe, whose divine creation has constituted the form of life, and he is inspired by the way in which God has brought his creative wisdom to mankind through the Holy Scriptures, which communicate the essence of life. To say that Dante imitates these two works only underlines that the *Commedia* reflects a medieval concept of life and is inspired by a medieval way of looking at life. To say that Dante imitates life solely underlines that the author's experience of life is his point of departure for the *Commedia*. Hence Singleton's argument only states the fact that the *Commedia* exists because its way of reflecting the conditions of life derives from the experience of life itself.

In order to do justice to Singleton's claim, it should be noticed that his argument is due to the question of whether the *Commedia* is to be read as an "allegory of the poets" or as an "allegory of the theologians." This problem arises from the comparative reading of book 2 of the *Convivio* and the dedicatory *Letter to Can Grande della Scala*, which the majority of Dante scholars regard as authentic.[11] In speaking of Dante's "model" for the *Commedia*, Singleton's objective is not to define the principles that govern the poem's design. His concern is to determine the nature of the poem's "double vision," whereby it differs, for example, from Tolstoy's *War and Peace* due to its way of unfolding another meaning concurrently with the "illusion of reality," which the narrative presents.[12] Nonetheless, Singleton's emphasis on Dante's imitation of God's creative power is characteristic of his way of approaching the question of the whole. By giving the "model" for the *Commedia* the broadest possible definition, the whole remains something that defies simple formulation. Singleton does not claim that the order Dante describes is to be interpreted as perceived only as his project progressed. In this respect, his approach to the *Commedia* differs from that of Eliot and Sapegno. According to Singleton, it does not suit the greatness of the *Commedia* to speak of failures on Dante's part. If there are failures, they are to be found in the reader's appropriation of the text. Whereas Eliot's objective is to underline Dante's mastery, Singleton's objective is to put into perspective the greatness of the mastery by stressing the reader's constant uncertainty of what constitutes the whole. According to Singleton, we can improve our knowledge of Dante's cultural context and intensify our awareness in the reading process. But the whole escapes us, either because it is impossible to grasp, or because it does not exist in principle.

By making the assertion of the ungraspable whole, Singleton undermines his principal claim that every episode has its own real center of inspiration. For how can we determine the inspirational core of each episode without possessing an understanding of the whole? We can only claim that each episode has its own inspirational core, if we have determined that there is no set of ordering principles. Hence Singleton makes a contradiction. He states a conviction but does not consider the premises on which it depends. He is agnostic as far as the understanding of the whole is concerned, but he is not agnostic when it comes to the understanding of the episodes. Singleton's position is a conflict between structuralism and skepticism. His objective is to disclose the elements that constitute the structure of the *Commedia*. In this endeavor he consents to the notion of structure advocated by New Criticism, for which structure is a system of relations between elements and elements have structure if they are related. This assertion is the principle of his structuralism. But the application of the principle results in skepticism. Singleton does not question that the structure of the *Commedia* is a system of relations between particular elements, but his perception of the elements contradicts his notion of a relational system, because he excludes the possibility of defining the relations between particular elements in terms of structuring principles. Singleton's attempt to overcome the contradiction results in his claim that each scene has its own real center of inspiration. Thus he advocates that segmental reading is the adequate reading. In a historical perspective, this position is supported by the traditions of commentary practice and *lectura Dantis*. At the same time Singleton's objective is to advance a global understanding of the poem. He considers his interpretive practice to be characterized by a global focus on the text. But the result is an inconsistent application of the global perspective.

Because Singleton's position is a conflict between structuralism in principle and skepticism in interpretive practice, it is not in his work on Dante that we find the method of segmental reading most clearly defined. The most categorical formulation of its principles that I have come across is one by Fernando Figurelli. Figurelli not only argues that the *Commedia* has a structure that cannot in any way be defined in its entirety, he also claims that it is pointless to say anything general about the structural function of this or that canto or part. The meaning of each canto or part should be specified only in each single case.[13] Figurelli's claim demarcates a prevalent view in Dante studies. It finds support in the comparison of the *Commedia* with a Gothic cathedral. This comparison serves the purpose of illuminating the poem as an extraordinary creation that defies definition due to its overwhelming complexity. At the same time it underlines Dante's craftsmanship as a poet by creating an image of a solid construction that has stood for centuries. But the symbol of the Gothic cathedral reveals nothing of the architectonic characteristics of Dante's edifice. As such, it is a shallow symbol. At best it only emphasizes a certain characteristic of the cultural outlook of Dante's time. According to Jacques Le Goff, the thirteenth century was "the century of organization," where "debate, decision, and implementation, knowledge and its uses, were all systematized."[14]

In addition, the symbol is incompatible with the view of the *Commedia* many Dante scholars promote in applying the method of segmental reading. A Gothic cathedral is composed of arches and segments. Each segment can be appreciated as a self-contained unit, but the segments add up to a grand structure only when they are unified in a grand design. Like the *Commedia*, we can make segmental examinations of a cathedral. But our experience of the cathedral is unsatisfactory if we restrict our view only to a series of fragmentary visions. However fascinating each segment is, our experience of the segment is satisfactory only when it is seen in the context of the grandeur of the cathedral. This comparison spells out the problem of segmental reading in Dante studies. In examining the different segments of the *Commedia*, many Dante scholars do not try to survey the height and depth of the *Commedia*. Instead, they restrict their view to series of fragmentary visions.

Recently Stephen Botterill has proposed a more sophisticated variation on the excuse for not attempting to make a comprehensive interpretation of the poem. Botterill argues that the *Commedia* resembles "a Heraclitean river, into which no reader can ever step twice and find it unaltered."[15] Thus the reading of Dante's poem becomes a neverending journey of discovery or a perpetual reader-response exercise of the erudite kind. More recently, Hollander has used the same symbol for the constant changes in Dante studies: "Like Heraclitus' river, Dante studies are always in motion—one can never step a second time into the same current. One day we may well know more than we do today, but that day, too, shall have to yield—as long as these studies continue."[16] The idea that the understanding of the *Commedia* constantly changes is not new in Dante studies.[17] But the two statements display a far greater skepticism about interpretive determinacy than previously stated in Dante studies. This is manifest in their preference for the Heraclitean symbol. In contrast to the Gothic cathedral, it implies no image of a solid construction. It rather underlines that every reading is ambiguous.

The Heraclitean river might be an accurate symbol of how many people nowadays conceive their experience of being in the world. But the idea that everything passes away and nothing remains would have been heretical to Dante. Heraclitus claimed that the cosmos "was made by no god or man, but always was and is and will always be an ever-living fire, being kindled in measures and quenched in measures."[18] By this Heraclitus does not intend that everything is total chaos. Although the flux perpetually changes, Heraclitus insists, it has its own *logos* or logical form. Although the *logos* is elusive, it does not mean that there is no order. Chaos and perpetual change are not the same. Nevertheless, the ancient naturalist view is diametrically opposed to the medieval notion of an external cause for the creation of the cosmos and to the medieval notion of a spiritual afterlife. If the *Commedia* were to resemble the Heraclitean river, there would be no poem. Like the Gothic cathedral, the Heraclitean river is therefore an inadequate symbol of Dante's achievement. It is inconsistent because it demarcates the opposite of what Dante presents. The inconsistency is further emphasized if we manage to make a comprehensive explication of the principles that constitute the poem's unity. Advocates of the Heraclitean symbol might argue that if no such principles are detectable in the poem, Dante's attempt to disclose God's universal order comes to confirm the universality of the symbol. But even in that case, it is still inconsistent. If Dante's vision of the divine order is incoherent, it is due to inconsistencies in his portrayal of it. The *Commedia* still displays a firm belief in the universe as a divinely ordered whole whose governing principles never change.

Unlike the advocates of interpretive skepticism, Botterill and Hollander do not argue that reading is impossible or that every reading is a misreading. Nor do they maintain that all readings are equally plausible.

Their studies of Dante's poem are concerned with coming up with answers to specific questions. Botterrill tries to determine the relation between Dante and Bernard of Clairvaux, and Hollander tries to delineate Dante's intellectual development. In their interpretive practice, they do not argue for total indeterminacy, but they make use of a symbol that implies it. If every reading is in a constant flow and contributes to the constant flow of other readings, there is no firm ground on which to base an interpretation of the poem's content. It becomes impossible to demarcate interpretive principles. If there are no principles, there is no basis for deciding whether one reading is better than another. The problem of the poem's thematic coherence remains unsolvable. But this conclusion is never drawn in Dante studies. If it were, the result would be interpretive impossibility or hermeneutic egalitarianism.

Source-Dependent Reading

In order to escape the dissolution of interpretive skepticism, Dante scholars have long favored a restrictive perspective on the *Commedia.* They assert that it is impossible to achieve a comprehensive understanding of the poem's meaning. One reason for this assertion is the general view of the *Commedia* as an ungraspable whole. Another reason is the notion of a fundamental historical and cultural detachment from Dante's medieval world that complicates the modern reader's attempt to understand the poem. For example, Singleton says:

> Some day perhaps we shall realize that one of the most important inquiries that might be undertaken in Dante studies would be a searching review of the way in which we lost touch, so to say, with Dante and his time—and with his Poem; for, to go over the record of our *loss* in this respect, and of the way it came about through the centuries, would mean to come into sharper awareness of what we must do to recover his time and his "world," and his Poem that mirrors his time and world.[19]

Singleton stresses the cultural and historical separation between the medieval and the modern world. There is only one way by which the modern reader might recover Dante's medieval world, and that is through complete neutrality in the interpretive act. This is made clear by Singleton's claim that "an out-and-out atheist might achieve an understanding reading of the *Divina Commedia* through a willing suspension of disbelief and an imaginative and sympathetic *surrender* to the experience of the Poem."[20]

The guiding principle for maintaining this neutrality has been expressed most clearly by Michele Barbi, for whom it is not important what does not belong to the poet's conscience or horizon.[21] Thus we are warned against reading into Dante, as Kantorowicz puts it, "things which Dante neither said nor meant to say."[22] But how can we determine what belongs and does not belong to the cultural texture of Dante's time? The acknowledgement of historical detachment and the emphasis on analytic neutrality make it difficult to set up standards for determining the characteristics of Dante's outlook. It easily leads to the assumption that all readings are basically speculative and hypothetical and that Dante studies are in a constant flow of undecidability. This is the impression we get from reading the following statement by William Anderson:

> If there is such a disagreement amongst Dante's commentators on the sources and meaning of so many passages, it is because of the multitude of influences that went into his creative imagination and that were fused there into new amalgams of symbol and expression. This is why there are so many plausible explanations for individual passages and why each explanation can easily be attacked for incompleteness.[23]

Anderson is well aware that the consequence of this view is hermeneutic egalitarianism. As he says, if sustained, Dante studies become "a Dodo's race in which everyone gets a prize for being partly right."[24] But Anderson's claim is inadequate for one particular reason. Since the method of the commentary practice is that of segmental reading, the commentary explanations are not the adequate basis for making claims about the nature of Dante's text. The commentaries do not propose a theory about the poem's order or lack of order. Their function is to explain the individual passages without explicitly engaging the interpretive act and evaluating the sum of explanations.

However, although Dante scholars assert that comprehensive understanding is impossible, they do not argue for total indeterminacy in interpreting the *Commedia*. Instead, they argue for a restrictive procedure. One characteristic of this procedure is the source-dependent method for explaining the content of episodes, segments, or parts. The source-dependent method is one type of extrinsic criticism. The reader sets out from a general understanding of the poem's historical period. On this ground, the reader tries to establish the inspirational sources in order to elucidate the thematic content. As the method is commonly applied, it is based on the assumption that the modern reader can reattach himself to Dante's medieval world only by establishing the precise or proximate sources for Dante's poetic construction. Its practice consists in investigating cognate expressions in Dante's text and other ancient or medieval texts. As such, the method displays a segmental approach to the content of the *Commedia.* A crucial side effect of the neglect of the global perspective is an ambiguous way of coding the structural and thematic constituents of the order of Dante's afterworld. This ambiguity can be elucidated by considering the elements of journey and order.

The *Commedia* is an account of a personal travel experience that embraces a vast range of human reactions to the encounter with the unknown and unforeseen. But besides recounting a personal travel experience, Dante proclaims a specific concept of universal order. The difference between the element of journey and the element of order can be defined in terms of the difference between traveling around in an unknown region without any foreknowledge of its geographic and geopolitical characteristics, and looking at a highly detailed map of that region that shows these characteristics and their variations. It is the difference between observing the earth from its surface and knowing the extent of the region only from what the eye perceives by looking at the horizon, and analyzing and systematizing data received from a satellite system that covers every region of the earth. When we try to settle what constitutes the poem's structural and thematic unity, the question is whether Dante the author only perceives the form and content of his work as he passes through the unknown land he tries to survey, or whether he is illuminated by a vision of the universal order.

In considering this issue, one thing needs to be emphasized. The content of the account unfolds itself only as the traveler perceives and reacts to the experience of the unknown. Although the narrative describes a past event, the narrator does not anticipate the narrative progression. Only occasionally does he reflect on the past event. But on the whole, every theme indicated, explored, or explained has a specific place in the narrative account. This place is defined by the particular incident that introduces the theme. For example, when Dante in the beginning of the poem reveals his initial state of alienation by describing himself as a man lost in the Dark Wood, he only indicates the reason for his desperate situation at this point of his life; he does not reveal the change he subsequently experienced. He refers to the loss of the "straight path" (*Inf.* 1: 3), which in the medieval Christian theological tradition is the one out of two ways of earthly existence. The "strait way," in Gerhart B. Ladner's words, is the one that "leads through a narrow gate to life, that is to say, to steadfastness with God"; the "broad way" is the one "which through a wide gate leads to perdition."[25] But Dante does not explain how he found the "strait way" and what changed his state of alienation into a state of clarification.

Vergil's report in *Inferno* 2 of how three women in Paradise have sent him on a mission of rescue contains no account of the change the traveler is about to experience. It is a report of a past event. Vergil's appearance announces the promise that if Dante puts his trust in him, he might approach the source of rescue and experience an existential transformation by the aid of divine grace. But what the graceful rescue implies is not revealed. It is discovered in the narrative progression. Hence we cannot establish the meaning of the elements of journey and order until we have read the whole account. The meaning of the journey lies in the clarification that characterizes the final vision of order the traveler endures. The difference between the elements of journey and order is comparable to that between time and space. The element of journey displays a temporal experience of the afterworld, while the element of order creates the spatial form through which the experience takes place. Since Dante scholars prefer the method of segmental reading, they are often inconsistent in their treatment of the relation between the temporal and the spatial dimension. The interpretations of the spatial dimension are in most cases sporadic and descriptive. The temporal dimension is normally conceived as a matter of reading the text as an account of a travel experience. The spatial dimension is usually conceived as a matter of producing diagrammatic or schematic representations of the afterworld. As such, the element of journey is understood as intrinsic to the narrative, whereas the element of order is taken to be extrinsic to the narrative. The former is regarded as a fundamental narrative characteristic, whereas the latter is a matter of interpretation and not necessarily as a narrative theme in itself.

The intention with the making of summarizing diagrams and schemes is to produce a static version of the order the narrative gradually reveals. But this enterprise raises a number of problems that are comparable to those involved in geodetic mapping. The problems regard the method applied in coding the matter observed in order to distinguish the different elements that make out the matter as a whole. They also regard the method applied in simplifying and rationalizing the data collected in order to create a comprehensible and usable framework. In Dante studies the fixed points used for determining the structure of the afterworld are normally the explicit statements about what is condemned in Hell, purged in Purgatory, or celebrated in Paradise. But this type of coding is problematic as far as the substantive content of the different segments or sections is concerned. The souls Dante encounters often speak of subjects that are not necessarily related to the explicit statements.

Brunetto Latini's presence in the seventh circle of Hell exemplifies the problem of coding an episode on the basis of explicit statements. Brunetto's damnation is traditionally interpreted as being due to acts of sodomy. The textual basis for this interpretation is a single reference to the biblical city of Sodom (*Inf.* 11: 50). The fix point is one word in *Inferno* 11 used in determining the theme of the episode of *Inferno* 15. But nothing in the episode indicates that the sodomites were sinners of homosexual lust. The result is a puzzling discrepancy between the traditional structural coding of the episode and its substantive content. This case is by no means exceptional. Instead of analyzing the thematic content of the discourses unfolded in the different classificatory sections, Dante scholars focus on singular explicit statements in their attempt to schematize the thematic content of Dante's afterworld. The kind of textual coding that uses explicit statements as fixed points is problematic because it neglects the fact that the narrator does not anticipate the narrative progression. If we are to take it seriously that Dante recounts his travel experience as much as possible in accordance with the encounter with the unknown, we should be cautious in accepting explicit statements as decisive indicators of the structure of the afterworld. If we do not take into account that explicit statements are perhaps only meant as provisional indicators of the spatial form, we might end up simplifying and rationalizing the indicators of order in a way that on the surface constitutes a comprehensible and usable framework but does not correspond with the actual order as it stands out in the final figuration.

The lack of focus on the element of order is characteristic of many studies of Dante's poem. The problem is not only the questionable way in which the text is often coded. The problem is also the general interpretive perspective this type of coding favors. It often results in readings of the *Commedia* that tend to wander off into details, because the single segments or episodes are interpreted as self-contained entities. The outcome is interpretive digressions that do not widen the understanding of what the *Commedia* aims at revealing. This tendency is exemplified by the discussion of Islamic sources for the *Commedia* that arose from Miguel Asìn Palacios's *La Escatologìa Musulmana en la Divina Comedia* (1919). Asìn Palacios argued for a direct influence. The result was a polemical discussion of whether Dante's view of Islam was more sympathetic or less condemnable than normally in medieval Europe. The discussion sharpened the understanding of the fact that, as Norman Daniel puts it, the "differences between the two religions are fewer and smaller than the points they hold in common; in the course of time much greater differences have accrued from the way the cultures understood and practiced the two religions."[26] The *Commedia* might be said to substantiate this argument. As Maria Corti argues, Dante's poem establishes a system of punitive classification and a hierarchical order of the blessed that are absent in the Christian visions of the afterworld predating the poem. The *Commedia* displays certain affinities with Islamic eschatological traditions.[27] In the case of the Islamic *Liber scalae Mahometi* (from the thirteenth century) about the prophet's ascent to the world beyond (published in 1949), some Dante scholars have suggested that we might speak of an inspirational source since the *Commedia* seems to recall precise images of the Islamic text.

But when we try to settle Dante's attitude toward the Muslim world, one thing strikes the reader in considering the extensive literature on the subject.[28] Out of the hundreds of characters in the *Commedia* who speak out, are pointed out, or referred to, explicitly or implicitly, there are only five Muslims mentioned in the text. Less than twenty lines are used to characterize the state of their souls: in the first circle of Hell (Limbo) we encounter the philosophers Avicenna and Averroes and the Egyptian and Syrian sultan Saladin (*Inf.* 4), and in the eighth circle Mohammed and his son-in-law Ali (*Inf.* 28). Apart from these two instances, Dante makes some remarks about the Crusades, the Muslims, and their faith elsewhere in the poem. But the clearest picture of his attitude toward Islam is found in the two episodes. Although statistics cannot account for the themes and their significance in a literary work such as the *Commedia*, this fact does, however, underline the proportions of Dante's relation to Islam and consequently the potentially controversial character of the issue. Nothing indicates that Dante was interested in the Muslim world. In fact, as Richard W. Southern has shown, Dante was greatly ignorant of it.[29] He believed Islam to be a Christian schism and made a gross blunder by placing Mohammed and Ali together, confusing the latter with the Nestorian monk Sergius who in medieval Europe was believed to have been the mind behind Mohammed's envious revolt against the authority of the church.[30]

It is reasonable to argue, as Philip F. Kennedy does, that the *Commedia* "was the product of a Europe engaged, anxiously at times, in the absorption, transformation and reappropriation of literary elements preserved in Arab sources" and that Dante's possible familiarity with the *Liber scalae* provides us with "an understanding of the kind of channels through which these texts were absorbed."[31] The example emphasizes the necessity of applying a broad perspective on the inspirational background for the poem's thematic content. We should not underestimate thematic similarities on a literary and cultural level just because we are incapable of establishing the source of inspiration. But in the case of Islamic influence on Dante and his view on the Muslim world, the similarities do not further our understanding of the *Commedia.* We are dealing with the transfer of literary elements from one cultural context to another but not with the integral meaning of the poem.

This becomes clear if we consider some of the main points of the literary equivalence outlined by Southern:

> In the *Liber de Scala* the role of the angel Gabriel as guide to Mahomet is somewhat similar to the role of Virgil as guide to Dante; the three voices which attempt to deflect Mahomet in his ascent are reminiscent of the three beasts which frighten Dante; the pitiless dry wind of Mahomet's first Hell is not unlike the fierce winds of Dante's second circle; the Great Hell with its walls and seven gates, which Mahomet saw, might be a model for the City of Dis in Dante's sixth circle.[32]

In its general plan of Heaven and Hell, the *Liber scalae* is nearer to the plan of the *Commedia* than any other existing Christian vision. But as Southern makes clear, the correspondence is of no great importance if it does not elucidate the meaning intended by Dante. In order to understand this problem, we need only to recall that the *Commedia* covers more than Hell and Heaven, it depicts also a realm of transition by repentance, Vergil is not the only guide that leads Dante through the world beyond, the three beasts represent evils that are thematically opposed to some of the attributes of the Christian notion of the Trinity, and the City of Dis is described as full of burning *meschite* or "mosques," as if it were populated by Muslims (*Inf.* 8: 70-73). Given these differences, the similarities are by no means substantial. The similarities are only curiosities that perhaps settle formal aspects of the inspirational background, but they do not provide a key to the understanding of the poem.

The treatment of the influence of Islamic sources on Dante exemplifies, and is a remnant of, the kind of literary criticism for which the establishment of precise or proximate sources was regarded as the main objective. But since the validity of such interpretive activities can be questioned when the result is only a handful of recollected images or similar phrasing, the whole controversy represents an interpretive digression when confronted with the question of what Dante aims at and accomplishes with his description of an otherworldly journey. Gabriel's role, the three voices, the pitiless wind, and the form of the infernal city in the *Liber scalae* are analogies that shed no light on that question.

Structural and Thematic Meaning

The significance of the element of journey is one of the major reasons why Dante scholars often fall for interpretive digressions. By favoring that element, every reading of the *Commedia* can be seen as a neverending journey of discovery. The element of journey creates an affinity between the poem's narrative content, the author's creative process, and the reader's understanding of the text. First, the main theme of the narrative is a journey toward divine illumination. Second, the creative process took the author on a spiritual journey through every part of the human soul and the universe, and the process reflects the different stops and changes of direction he made or had to make throughout his life. Third, the reader's appropriation of the text is like a journey because it involves years of studying the text, the historical and cultural setting, the reception history, and the different strategies of reading. Thus the reader gradually attains the knowledge and tools needed for uncovering the different layers of the account. For these reasons, many Dante scholars favor the kind of reading that focuses on the affinity between the text and the author's existential conditions. For example, Sapegno argues:

> The *Comedy* is first and foremost the whole of Dante's life, both emotional and intellectual. But as well as being the expression of its author's personality, the poem crowns and epitomizes a great period in the history of civilization. That period is caught in its final phase, on the very brink of disintegration, and this why it is portrayed in such passionate, emotive and dramatic colors. This, too, is why Dante chose poetry as his vehicle rather than the—theoretically possible—treatise or sermon.[33]

But by focusing on the existential dimension and historical significance of the poem, many studies of Dante's poem pay too little attention to the question of textual and thematic coherence. A side effect is that the structure of the afterworld and the thematic content of the narrative action are treated as two distinct aspects of the same text and not as two sides of the same content.

Structure is a concept that has proved its vitality in many areas of scientific inquiry. In literary criticism it is commonly identified as an analytic concept used in order to describe the compositional characteristics of a literary work. As such, it is a useful concept in textual analysis and a crucial one in many studies of literary texts. However, in speaking of the structure of the *Commedia*, we normally intend the structure of the afterworld. The basic constituents of this structure are the three realms divided into different sections, and what the descriptions of these realms reveal is the poem's thematic content. However, this does not mean that the theme of the *Commedia* is the afterworld. With reference to the *Letter to Can Grande*, Dante scholars sometimes describe the poem's theme as "the state of the souls after death" (viii).[34] But this is an inadequate description of the theme. In the *Commedia* the state of the souls is described with reference to their earthly doings. Formally, the souls are placed in Hell, Purgatory, or Paradise due to their sinful errors or virtuous deeds on earth, but what essentially determines their spiritual state is divine justice. For this reason, it would be more adequate to define the theme of the *Commedia* in terms of what the description of the afterworld reveals about Dante's conception of divine justice. Such a definition would have to include both the order of divine justice, as it is described in the three parts of the poem, and Dante's emphasis on divine justice as ultimately inscrutable. To make a comprehensive interpretation of this conception is to try to explicate the thematic meaning of the poem. But Dante's exposition of the universal order of divine justice is not easily defined.

To say that the *Commedia* consists of three parts is to describe its poetic structure. To say that the *terza rima* is the basic unit of the poem is to make a structural description. These two structural features can be said to constitute a structural unity of the poem. Hence the formal structure is balanced and displays an intentional design. But in literary criticism structure is often given different meanings that make the concept ambiguous. One definition is to say that structure is the sum of the relationships of the elements to each other. But this simple definition can be understood at least in two ways. It can have a quantitative meaning and a qualitative meaning. Structure can be understood as the quantity of relations between textual elements. This is the neutral meaning of structure. Structure only means that textual elements are related. It does not involve an evaluation of the relations. To evaluate the relations is to apply a qualitative concept of structure. This meaning of structure can also be defined as the interpretive meaning. If textual elements are related, the definition of the structure depends on the interpretation of the relations.

To describe the *Commedia* as a whole of three parts, delivered in the poetic form of the *terza rima*, is to make a neutral description of the structure. On the neutral level, we can also say that the poem contains descriptions of the spiritual conditions of the afterworld. However, when we look closer at the different features of these three realms, we immediately discover that it is necessary to engage in interpretation if we are to attain a comprehensive understanding of the structure. Damnation, purgation, and salvation are three related elements in the poem. Damnation and salvation are related because they are diametrically opposed to each other. The latter is the positive outcome of man's existence if he complies with the articles of the Christian faith. The former is the negative outcome as a result of rejecting these articles. Purgation is related to both damnation and salvation by representing the way in which the sinful soul can free itself from damnation and reach salvation. However, when we consider the details of Dante's description, it becomes increasingly difficult to determine the relations between the elements that constitute the structure of the afterworld.

This leaves us with a problem that has to do with the fact that the question of constituting elements can be considered in different ways. On one level, we can speak of the relation between the three parts and how they describe three related aspects of spiritual existence. On another level, we can compare the way in which Dante gives the three parts diverse constructions that complicate the determination of structural relations. In the former case we apply a quantitative concept of structure. In the latter we have to apply a qualitative concept if we are to attain a comprehensive understanding of the relationship between the three parts. The problem is fundamental when we try to determine the meaning of the different topics of discourse or the different scenes of actions. The topics and scenes are often significant for the determination of the essential features of the three diverse constructions, but their meanings are seldom unambiguously stated. They are frequently figurative and contain allegorical and symbolic meanings. For these reasons, the quantitative concept of structure is inadequate for explaining the structure of the afterworld. It can only provide a superficial account of some of the basic constituents. If we are to attain a comprehensive understanding of Dante's afterworld, we have to apply a qualitative concept of structure.

In Dante studies there is great uncertainty about quantitative and qualitative meanings. Qualitative assertions are often taken as quantitative descriptions. No clear distinction is made between textual evidence and textual interpretation. But a significant constituent of the structure can be the content of a particular passage or even the meaning of a specific word. Hence textual evidence is a matter of textual interpretation. The definition of the structure does not only require structural analysis, and the determination of the thematic content does not only require thematic analysis. Structural analysis is often the means for exposing essential aspects of the thematic content, and thematic analysis is often the means for disclosing significant structural elements. To interpret the structure is to determine the thematic content, and to determine the thematic content is to define the structure. For these reasons, the structure and the thematic content are not two distinct sides of Dante's construction. The construction remains obscure if we do not understand its thematic content, and the thematic content remains unsettled as long as we have not defined the principles of the construction of the afterworld. Structural indications contain thematic meanings and thematic discourses are structural constituents. When combined, structure and thematic content constitutes the poem's thematic coherence.

Decisive Reading

Throughout the history of Dante reading, there have been four ways of responding to the question of the poem's thematic coherence. Formally speaking, these four ways can be reduced to three main types: the decisively negative response, the decisively positive response, and the indecisive response. Since the indecisive response can be inclined towards either the decisively positive response or the decisively negative response, we can speak of four types of responses.[35]

According to the decisively negative response, the *Commedia* does not display a coherent vision of God's universal order. Although Dante frequently emphasizes that his vision reflects that order, he never succeeds in describing it in a coherent manner. The characterization of the *Commedia* in the eighteenth century as an obscure, pedantic, disordered, and grotesque poem exemplifies the attitude of this response. For example, Voltaire characterized the poem as mishmash.[36] Also for Coleridge did the impression of performative inconsistency on Dante's part overshadow signs of thematic coherence. He defined the *Commedia* as "a system of moral, political and theological truths with arbitrary exemplification."[37] But at no time in the history of Dante reading has the view of the *Commedia* as an arbitrary, heterogeneous, and chaotic construction been substantiated systematically. The view pervaded the revival of Dante studies in the eighteenth century, but it was primarily prejudicial. Due, for instance, to Karl Witte's studies of the *Commedia*, the prejudicial approach was eventually replaced by a more impartial method of inquiry based on philological principles. Throughout the nineteenth century, Dante studies gradually moved from the evaluation of the poem's validity toward the understanding of its content. Although personal preferences still interfered, interpretations were largely oriented toward the foundation of interpretive standards.

Nowadays, the decisively negative response is basically non-existent. No Dante scholar has ever tried to show that the *Commedia* does not display a coherent vision of God's universal order. Occasionally some Dante scholars challenge the assertion of a conceptual design. But the challenges are made only hypothetically, and their premises are seldom stated explicitly. As a result, it is uncertain whether they reject the assertion of a conceptual design. They rather express a skeptical response to the question of thematic coherence. For example, Lino Pertile speaks of structural adjustments especially in *Paradiso* in comparison with what seems to be the general outline of the poem's content on reading the first cantos of *Inferno*. He argues that the many years of exile matured Dante and made him change his original plans. In Pertile's view, one of these plans was to make St. Lucy appear at the end of the poem instead of Bernard of Clairvaux (*Par.* 31-33). Another plan was to make Beatrice explain the meaning of Dante's exile instead of Cacciaguida (*Par.* 15-18).[38] Whether Pertile thinks that these adjustments undermine the poem's thematic coherence is not clear. He deals with them only as narrative alterations with minor implications for the formal structure and not as thematic transformations of essential importance for the substantive content. In addition, the passages Pertile refers to in support of his arguments are not unequivocal. They can be understood in both specific and general terms. For example, when Vergil in *Inferno* 10 (130-32) says that Beatrice will later on explain to Dante his journey in life, he may refer to what Cacciaguida reveals, whereby Beatrice becomes the intermediary of the revelation, not the revealer herself. But during their flight through the ten heavens, Beatrice says many things to Dante that put his life in perspective, and acts as an intermediary of revelations of others. Hence what Vergil refers to may be Cacciaguida's revelations, but it can also be what the flight through Paradise, with Beatrice as guide, reveals in its entirety and in specific relation to Dante's journey in life.

In contrast, according to the decisively positive response, the *Commedia* displays a conceptual design. Advocates of this view claim to have detected the principles that hold together the poem's three parts. Seung's reading of the *Commedia* represents such a response. Cogan's reading also belongs to this category, but his theory suffers from some serious defects. These defects need to be considered in detail, because Cogan's theory represents the most qualified criticism of Seung's theory. Cogan's reading does not fall down on the criterion of performative consistency. This is true in the sense that he proposes a theory about the poem's unity and substantiates it with textual data. But when we consider his approach to the textual data, his interpretive performance turns out to be inconsistent.

In Seung's reading, the structure and the thematic content merge into a coherent whole. In explicating the poem's unity, he applies no rigid distinction between the form and the content. On the contrary, he stresses the "inseparability of form and content" (*CT* 49). The understanding of the narrative action is not dependent on the understanding of the stage setting. For Seung, the poem's thematic coherence emerges only when the form and the content are combined. The one has no meaning independent of the other. The same is not the case with Cogan's reading. Cogan does not go as far in his interpretive practice as Seung does. Cogan's concern is specifically the question of the poem's structure. He examines the narrative themes or actions only when they shed light on his theory of the constituting elements of the structure. For that reason, his reading involves a rigid distinction between the narrative and the structure. In the beginning of *The Design in the Wax*, Cogan says about the significance of the poem's structure that "there remains no more important subject for our understanding of the poem, or for any inquiries we might wish to make into it. All of our most sophisticated interpretations of the narrative depend on its subtle and erudite structure" (*DW* xix). In short, the understanding of the narrative is dependent on the understanding of the structure.

Whereas Seung combines the content and the form, Cogan subordinates the one to the other. Due to this subordination, Cogan's reading is only a partial examination of the poem's thematic coherence. Though extensive in intent and complex in argumentation, whatever his reading reveals about the structure still has to be substantiated by analyses of the narrative content. What ought to follow from Cogan's disclosure of the meaning of the poem's subtle and erudite structure are sophisticated interpretations of the narrative. But this procedural distinction is untenable. For how can we determine what constitutes the structure if we have not engaged in detailed studies of what the narrative reveals about it? This is possible only if we rely on certain general assertions about the narrative content. We assume that the basic knowledge of what the narrative reveals about the structure has already been established. What remains, and what Cogan claims to accomplish, is to combine the essential features of this knowledge in a way that reveals the structural design of the *Comme-*

dia. But if this is an adequate procedure, Cogan contradicts himself. On the one hand, he gives prevalence to the interpretation of the structure before proceeding to the interpretation of the narrative. On the other, he makes use of interpretations of the narrative in order to disclose the principles of the structural design. This problem can be illustrated by considering the following issue in Cogan's reading.

In arguing that the difference between Hell and Purgatory consists in the difference between act and habit, Cogan uses sodomy or homosexuality as an example. In Hell the act of sodomy is apparently condemned in the seventh circle, which is the third gravest and normally associated with acts of violence. In Purgatory the disposition of homosexuality is purged on the seventh terrace as a species of lust, the lightest of the seven deadly sins. Cogan takes this difference as a clear indication of how Dante distinguishes between Hell as the realm of sinful acts that deserve punishment, and Purgatory as the realm of vicious dispositions that might be purged. But Cogan's exemplification is based on a non-reflective use of a traditional way of coding the substantive content of the seventh circle. He ignores the lengthy debate about the sodomites in that circle. In Dante studies much has been said about who might count as sodomite and who not. One of the most intricate problems has been whether Brunetto Latini is condemned for sodomy or some other sin of violence. The diversity of positions in Dante studies has even led Kirkpatrick to suggest that the question of what Brunetto is condemned for is "a matter of small significance compared with the fact that Brunetto has sinned at all."[39] In other words, since there is no general agreement among Dante scholars about what Brunetto is condemned for, the contribution of the Brunetto episode to our knowledge of the narrative structuring of the afterworld is restricted to the mere knowledge that Brunetto is condemned for being a violent sinner. Hence, if we count Brunetto among the sodomites and use him to exemplify this sin, our argument is vague.

Cogan has taken a precaution against this criticism. He does not mention Brunetto in relation to the sodomites. In fact, he mentions no one. None of the violent sinners are explicitly associated with sodomy. In Cogan's reading sodomy is a structural category that still needs to be substantiated by analyzing the appearances of the sodomites in the seventh circle. Cogan does not consider how the narrative constitutes the association with sodomy. He follows the traditional explanation of the thematic content of the episode and takes it for granted that the seventh circle contains homosexuals. Since Cogan relies on segmental readings, his version of the poem's thematic coherence turns out to be an attempt to systematize segmental examinations. This procedure is not only questionable in methodological terms, the outcome is also an interpretation of the episode that misfits its thematic content. The motive for placing Brunetto in Hell can be interpreted differently if we focus on the thematic content of his speech. The textual basis for associating the episode of the so-called runners of the seventh circle with sodomy is vague. On the one hand, it is due to a single reference to the Biblical city of Sodom, whereby this sinful category was historically coined. On the other hand, it rests on a few (by no means unequivocal) remarks, which can be associated with sodomy, however, only if we accept the biblical reference as implying that sin. For example, Brunetto says that Andrea de' Mozzi had *mal protesi nervi* or "badly stretched nerves" (*Inf.* 15: 114), and Jacopo Rusticucci is said to have been driven to what he is condemned for by his "violent" (*fiera*) wife (16: 45). These statements make sense when related to the theme of violence, but to interpret them as referring to sodomy requires speculative assumptions about medieval psychology that find no support in the episode of the sodomites.

In making the association with sodomy, Dante scholars have failed to take account of two simple facts. First, none of the condemned souls do anywhere refer to the sin. Second, nothing in the biographies of these sinners suggests that they were homosexuals, neither in act nor in disposition. For that reason, the idea that homosexuality is represented in the seventh circle rests upon the mentioning of the city of Sodom along with Cahors and not, as in Purgatory (*Purg* 26: 40), along with Gomorrah. Moreover, when Dante arrives at the third ring of violent sinners, which besides the sodomites includes blasphemers and usurers, he sees "a fall of slowly raining broad flakes of fire showered steadily" on these sinners (*Inf.* 14: 28-30). These flakes of fire refer to the brimstone and fire, whereby God destroyed Sodom and Gomorrah (Genesis 19: 24). Hence the representational meaning of the label comprises more than the sin of sodomy; it covers also blasphemy and usury.

No doubt, Dante's sodomites are violent sinners, but their sin might not have anything to do with lustful acts. By not mentioning Sodom along with Gomorrah, Dante might want to draw our attention to one specific aspect in relation to the destruction of Sodom: the "just revenge of God" (*Inf.* 14: 16) or God's wrath. The sin of wrath (or anger) is the sinful category Seung associates with the seventh circle. He argues that all the sinners of that circle are ultimately sinners of wrath. Wrath is the sinful disposition purged on the third terrace of *Purgatorio*. According to Seung, Purgatory provides the system for categorizing the diversity of infernal sins into some major categories. These categories are the seven capital sins, which are being purged into their opposite virtues on the seven terraces of the mount of Purgatory. Since the end of purgation is the attainment of virtuousness, Purgatory provides also the system for categorizing the unnamed virtues celebrated in *Paradiso* into some major categories. These categories are the virtues opposite to the seven capital sins. On this ground, Seung argues that the opposite of wrath is the virtue celebrated in the Venus sphere of *Paradiso*.

Indecisive Reading

Despite these preliminary objections to Cogan's method of reading, his theory is still representational of the decisively positive response to the question of thematic coherence. This type of response does not belong to the mainstream of Dante studies. The prevalent position is the indecisive response with a positive inclination. This is the third position of the four types of responses. This type of response does not maintain to have detected any constituting principles, but it is still inclined to believe that there might be some. The result is either a sort of intuitive admission to the possibility of a conceptual design or a sketchy proposal for what might be the constituting principles. In the history of Dante reading, there are many examples of such intuitive admissions. Freccero's claim that we must assume the existence of a coherent pattern is one example. Singleton's approach to the *Commedia* is another example, due to his unresolved conflict between structuralism and skepticism.

As far as sketchy proposals are concerned, Francis X. Newman's article "St. Augustine Three Visions and the Structure of the *Commedia*" exemplifies this type of response. According to Newman, Augustine's distinction between *visio corporalis*, *visio spiritualis* or *imaginativa*, and *visio intellectualis* (*De genesi ad litteram*) might be "the ultimate, if not the proximate source" for the pattern whereby Dante structures the three parts of the afterworld, since the *Commedia* has "three points of climax, three centripetal moments of vision, within the larger movement toward finality."[40] But Newman only points to certain general similarities between Augustine's visionary theory and the narrative surface of the *Commedia*. He does not consider any of the complex questions concerning the individual structures of the three realms and their interrelations. Compared with Seung's and Cogan's examinations of the *Commedia*, Newman's theory is superficial and unsatisfactory. He admits that his objective is solely "to show that [the] Augustinian pattern gives us a very direct clue to the structure of the *Commedia* as an act of vision."[41] Hence his interpretation is only a propositional attempt to make a qualified response to the question of the poem's unity. But although his reading displays a positive inclination toward the idea of a conceptual design, his proposal cannot escape the tendency of interpretive mystification. If he is right in his suggestion, the essential question that needs to be addressed is how Dante incorporates Augustine's visionary theory in the structures of the three realms. But since he never attempts to answer this question, his proposal turns out to be mystifying instead of clarifying.

When we turn to the indecisive position with a negative inclination, the tendency of interpretive mystification becomes acute. Advocates of the negative position maintain that since the principles for the poem's design have never been fully established, the idea that such principles can be established should be dismissed. The reason for the dismissal, however, is not necessarily due to a firm opposition to the idea of a conceptual design. The problem is rather that Dante scholars have failed to disclose the design. This is taken to affirm the impossibility of establishing a coherent relation between the form and the content. As a result, the question of the poem's thematic coherence is neglected. Normally Dante scholars do not take this stand explicitly, but their interpretive practice often displays it implicitly. The positions of Harold Bloom and Teodolinda Barolini exemplify this point. The opposition between them also shows that the lack of decisive response increases the puzzlement about what kind of text the *Commedia* is and what it aims at communicating. Neither of the two takes any notice of the question of thematic coherence. They consider only the poem's narrative themes. From a structural point of view, Bloom's and Barolini's interpretations display a fundamental skepticism about the possibility of solving the question of the poem's thematic coherence. Due to their lack of structural understanding, they exemplify how the field of Dante reading can easily be laid wide open for speculative readings.

Criticizing the Dante readings of Auerbach, Singleton, and Freccero, Bloom remarks (in his *Ruin the Sacred Truth*): "Unfortunately, the readers of all three critics sometimes seem to have learned to read Dante precisely as they would read theology. A distorted emphasis upon doctrine is the unhappy result, and soon readers forget the insight of Curtius, which is that Dante's Beatrice is the central figure in a purely personal gnosis."[42] In *The Western Canon*, Bloom develops this idea by defining Beatrice as "the supreme Christian muse," in some sense a parallel to Venus in Vergil's *Aeneid*.[43] In attempting to constitute a basis for a detheologizing reading of the *Commedia*, Barolini argues that Dante scholars basically treat Dante "as he would have us treat him—not as a poet, but as an authority, a 'theologian.'"[44] In a note to this statement, Barolini further remarks: "While Harold Bloom deplores those readers who 'have learned to read Dante precisely as they would read theology,' he does not seem to understand to what extent Dante himself is responsible for this state of affairs."[45] In *The Western Canon* Bloom repeats the position exposed in his previous Dante reading, but adds with implicit reference to Barolini that he thinks "detheologizing Dante would be as irrelevant as theologizing him." For, as he says, "The *Comedy* purports to be the truth":

> Dante was brazen, aggressive, prideful, and audacious beyond all poets, before or since. He imposed his vision on Eternity, and he has very little in common with the flock of his piously learned exegetes. If it is all in Augustine or in Thomas Aquinas, then let us read Augustine or Aquinas. But Dante wanted us to read Dante. He did not compose his poem to illuminate inherited truths.[46]

This dispute between Bloom and Barolini is basically a matter of how we are to handle the apparently doctrinal elements in Dante's poem. Are we entrapped in some sort of a theological frame of understanding due to the suggestive realism of Dante's account and his insistence on recounting a true otherworldly experience? Or have we rather been misled by the theological readings of Dante scholars and have lost sight of his innovative genius and message? The latter question pervades Bloom's opposition to readings that attempt to explain the matter of Dante's textual universe by way of theological conceptions and terminology. The former question constitutes, in Barolini's words, her "attempt to analyze the textual metaphysics that makes the *Commedia*'s truth claims credible and to show how the illusion is constructed, forged, made—by a man who is precisely, after all, 'only' a *fabbro*, a maker . . . a poet."[47] In the one case, Dante is held responsible for the misleading emphasis on theology within Dante studies. In the other, Dante scholars are made responsible for the distortion of the message by the use of theological explanations.

Bloom wants to get rid of theology because it distorts the literary individuality and poetic autonomy Dante incarnates. He claims that we ought to read the *Commedia* as "the third Testament prophesied by Joachim of Fiore."[48] In Bloomian terms, Dante is a "strong poet" driven by "the anxiety of influence" and an arch-individualist who, in fear of non-originality and with artistic pride, persistently tries to avoid that his creation bears any sign of derivation or indebtedness.[49] As a result, Dante, in Bloom's view, moves far beyond theological discourse and materializes through his poetic *tour de force* a profoundly prophetic spirit. Barolini's project seems to have a similar objective. She does not engage in the kind of Bloomian speculation about the nature of the poet's creative force, but, like Bloom, she wants to rehabilitate Dante's visionary and prophetic vocation. In order to do that, she proposes three premises for our reading Dante's poem: (1) we should accept that Dante regards his vision as true; (2) we should acknowledge that Dante fuses poetry and prophecy and avoid distinguishing between them because it diminishes the prophetic character of the vision; and (3) we should realize that Dante differs from all other great prophet-visionaries of the period "in the immensity of his poetic gift," and we should not take this immensity as a reason for doubting the genuineness of his vision. According to Barolini, if we accept these premises, we might get a chance to "look behind the veil" and see how Dante forges "the magic of his compelling realism."[50] That does not mean that she regards Dante as a conscious poetic forger. It only means that she wants to look at the rhetorical and narrative elements that constitute the *Commedia* as a text that captivates the reader by means of sophisticated forms of linguistic and imaginative expressions. Her concern is not what Dante says but how he says it. The issue is not what Dante believes in, but how he persuades us to believe in it.

Although she emphasizes that we ought to believe in Dante and even states the premises for her investigation as a matter of commitment to Dante's truth claims, her interpretation does not bring us close to an elucidation of what he believes in. Whether Dante constructs his exposition of God's universal order in accordance with specific principles, has no significance in Barolini's study. It is never expressed whether it is due to the fact that she believes such principles to be undetectable. But since she interprets the *Commedia* without taking account of the ultimate point of reference for Dante's exposition, her study does not further the understanding of his vision. On the contrary, it draws us away from it. This is made clear by her use of the term *form* in relation to the poem.

Barolini assures us that her project is not anti-theological. In theory, she accepts the existence of some sort of theological frame. This is a reasonable assertion because the premise for detheologizing is that there is a theology to dismantle. But in terms of interpretive practice, she favors the attempt to get out of or behind the theological content by focusing on the devices Dante uses in order to manipulate the narrative "in ways that authenticate his text."[51] In order to release our reading from Dante's grip and find a way out of his hall of mirrors, she privileges form over content. By this she identifies the form as the medium by which

Dante manipulates his readers to believe in his illusion and the content as the medium that constitutes Dante as a theological authority. The form is thus conceived within the context of the thematic content of the narrative. It is defined as a way of speaking. It does not imply the vision of God's universal order. For Barolini the form does not signify the structure of the afterworld. The form is reduced to the medium of rhetorical persuasion. Due to this reduction, the perspective Barolini imposes on the *Commedia* is a non-theistic one. There is nothing left of the belief in Dante she argues for. She defines her interpretive project as a matter of detheologizing the *Commedia*, but this is a misidentification of the characteristics of theological discourse. This misidentification also pervades Bloom's rejection of both the theological perspective and Barolini's project. In theological terms, the ultimate point of reference for Dante's cosmic worldview is normally denoted as God, the divine essence, or the Trinity. But these terms are only technical responses to matters of theistic concern; theology is a conceptualization of theism. Faith is the inner conviction, and theology is the discursive attempt to disclose the essence of faith.

Dante's awareness of this difference is manifest in the fact that there is more to be revealed about the Christian faith after the great theologians Aquinas and Bonaventure have made their appearances in the heaven of the sun. For example, in the heaven of Jupiter we encounter Trajan and Ripheus, who were pagans, but they had faith without any knowledge of theological discourse. With Peter Damian, Benedict, and Bernard of Clairvaux, we are confronted with medieval personalities who were theologically well founded but favored obedience and contemplation as true expressions of faith. Furthermore, it is not a philosophical authority such as Aristotle who acts as guide in Dante's ascent to the Terrestrial Paradise. Nor is it a theological authority who leads him through Paradise. Finally, Dante's failing capacity to describe his vision as he ascends the heavens is another indication of how he regards language, which is the medium of theological conceptions, as insufficient in dealing with the essence of faith. Language can point to the true essence, but it can define it only indirectly by way of signs. It can denote attributes and create meaning through symbols or allegories, but the truth is enigmatic.

When Barolini argues for a detheologizing reading, the consequence should have been a non-theological reading. Such a reading would avoid the sophisticated terminology of theological discourse in explaining the poem's meaning. This is the kind of sophistication Bloom rejects. But since Barolini identifies theism with theology, the result is a non-theistic reading. This is an inconsistent deduction. For what happens if we exclude theological discourse in our treatment of the poem? The narrative does not stop reflecting a man's search for truth. By eliminating theological discourse as a means for explaining the poem's meaning, everything in that world described as just and perfect does not cease to display a fundamentally theistic outlook. The elimination of theology implies only the exclusion of a discursive means for explaining the thematic coherence of the *Commedia*.

One result of the exclusion could be a treatment of the poem on a par with other expressions of religious belief and without any reference to its medieval Christian context. Moreover, if we regard religious expressions as articulations of existential uncertainties, another result could be a psychological perspective on the poem. We could examine Dante's struggle for truth and the good life without making use of medieval philosophical and theological conceptions and terminology. But such an examination easily fails to maintain the theistic outlook and explain its essential characteristics. Imagine, for example, that the walls of the City of Dis or the cleft between the seventh and the eighth circle of *Inferno* were taken to mark a descent into something comparable to the Freudian "unconscious." Maybe the whole *Inferno* is to be understood as a description of man's mental characteristics. But the problem is that Hell is the place of human degeneration and the darkest sides of human activity. It is not simply the realm of conscious, semi-conscious, or unconscious thoughts, feelings, and passions. To make a comparison between Dante's *Inferno* and the conscious and the unconscious in psychology is to propose a negative conception of man's mental activities. If we conceive these activities as also involving distinctly positive dispositions, we need to broaden our psychological perspective on the poem.

This might seem to be an easy task since the *Commedia* depicts more than a descent into the darkest depths of the human mind. In *Purgatorio* we witness the regeneration of the human soul, and in *Paradiso* we see it in its proper form. But in none of these two realms do we find any immediate counterpart to the infernal boundaries that should constitute the affinity between medieval and modern psychology. We might suggest, for example, that the Ante-Purgatory and the common identification of the first three spheres of *Paradiso* (the Moon, Mercury, and Venus) as an Ante-Paradise share certain affinities with the "unconscious." But this suggestion is inconsistent. Even if we achieve a consistent psychological interpretation that identifies structural parallels between the three realms, we will still be missing one essential point. Dante's concern is not simply the proper form of the human soul. Whatever its form is, we still need to take account of the theistic power Dante associates with the creation and individual qualities of the human soul. Hence, if we neglect the theism of

Dante's outlook, we impose a "postmetaphysical" conception of human existence and reality upon a fundamentally metaphysical outlook. For that reason, if we are to get to terms with what Dante believes in and how he tries to persuade us to follow him in his belief, we have to consider the poem's theistic foundation. If our aim by reading the *Commedia* is to understand what Dante expresses, we need to be consistent in our way of explaining the content of his expression. If not, we increase the puzzlement. Though just a minor terminological inaccuracy, Barolini's misidentification of theism with theology has this effect. Although her intention is to set aside the theistic dimension in order to elucidate how Dante textually authenticates his truth claims, it remains unclear on what ground this dimension is put aside. It is never explicitly stated whether she thinks the essence of Dante's theism has already been settled, has never been settled, or cannot be settled. However, a passage in *The Undivine Comedy* reveals that she is most inclined to think that it cannot be settled.

For Barolini, one particular question is more fundamental than any other for all readers of Dante's poem: "How are we to respond to the poet's insistence that he is telling the truth?" To this she further adds: "Logically prior to this query stands another that we cannot answer, but on which we may speculate: Did Dante himself believe in the literal truth of those things for which he claims literal truth?"[52] In considering the implication of such questions in relation to the question of coherence, it should be noticed that the problem of Dante's truth claims is not the same as the question of the poem's thematic coherence. The one concerns the question of whether Dante ultimately believed his own words, whereas the other is a matter of whether he was consistent in his use of the words. According to Barolini, only if we accept Dante's insistence on telling the truth as genuine do we have some sort of certainty about his belief in his own words. If we doubt it, no source will provide a clear answer and not, for example, Boccaccio's legend, as Bloom is inclined to, about some Veronese women who spoke of Dante as Hell's messenger, to which he responded with a smile.[53] But in response to Barolini's insistence on having encapsulated the most essential issue in Dante studies, we might ask what the premise is for the assertion that the question of Dante's truth claims is the most fundamental one to be raised. Imagine that we detect the constituting principles and discover that the *Commedia* displays a coherent vision of God's universal order. Are we to regard such a discovery as insignificant for the determination of whether Dante believed his own words? To this Barolini might answer that although it can never be insignificant, the discovery does not establish the validity of his vision. Dante may still have forged it.

Barolini's intention is to underline Dante's craftsmanship as poet. But to speak of the *Commedia* in these terms implicitly draws upon certain characteristics of modern literary criticism. Modern literary critics are trained to question any claim of truth in literary texts, and modern writers are often persistent on distinguishing their narrative voice from their existential voice. For that reason, it has become a standard to consider the creation and interpretation of literary texts as a matter of posing the right questions and not providing decisive answers. Whatever the meaning of the text is, it is now an issue in which the fusion of horizons in the interpretive act is more likely to result in the delineation of interpretive possibilities than in the establishment of meaning. The result is an inclination toward hermeneutic egalitarianism. Barolini's focus on Dante's truth claims is the misplacement of her concern. She has every right to be concerned with the question of whether Dante's description of the afterworld is true or not. But this was not necessarily Dante's concern. It can be argued that he was solely writing on the religious doctrines of his time, that he regarded them as universally accepted as the foundation of everyday life, and that he was neither questioning their truth nor trying to persuade anyone to accept them. Barolini has every right to talk about the truth values of Dante's assertions and the rhetorical efficacy of his exposition. But that is her problem and concern. We have to distinguish between the question of explicating what Dante says and the question of deciding whether it is true. The former question is the question of interpretation, and the latter is the question of judgment.

The inclination toward hermeneutic egalitarianism makes Barolini's attempt to detheologize the *Commedia* an easy target for Bloom's rejection of whatever is related to theology. But his alternative does not bring us any closer to an understanding of what Dante believes in and how he thinks the essence of his belief is manifest in the universe. For Bloom the *Commedia* is a spiritual testament of Dante's prophetic vocation. But Bloom overlooks the fact that Joachim's eschatological worldview is driven by a profound quest for systematization. The uncertainties and diversities that pervade man's existential experience are in Joachim subjected to a wealth of figures and a complex system of symbolic forms. Joachim might seem to represent yet another arch-individualist driven by the anxiety of influence. But on such a central point, in Joachim's thought, as the division of history into three stages, it is worth noticing that he has forerunners in Rupert of Deutz and Otto of Freising and a fellow in Ralph of Diceto. Joachim does contribute significantly to the expansion of the idea due to his way of relating the three stages to the three persons of the Trinity and provides the course of world history with a meaning that contains more than the demarcation of the world as moving into its final era. The essential result of Joachim's combination of tradition and innovation is a profoundly Trinitarian theology and an attempt at systematic thought; it not an outburst of a prophetic vocation.

In spite of the association with Joachim, Bloom shows no interest in investigating the thematic affinities between Joachim's Trinitarian theology and the constant flow of Trinitarian themes in the *Commedia*. He is satisfied with underlining Dante's individuality and autonomy, and promoting the image of Beatrice as a sort of supreme Christian incarnation of the ancient Venus. Although every triadic element of the *Commedia* displays a Trinitarian meaning and is a sign of the ultimate point of reference for Dante's cosmic vision, Bloom insists on a limited perspective on the poem by turning Dante's divinization of Beatrice into the poetic force of his creation and the central theme of his epic. Anything regarding the constituting principles of Dante's exposition of world order is left unconsidered. By ignoring the issue and focusing on Beatrice's manifestation in the poem's narrative, Bloom avoids formulating a response to the question of thematic coherence. He either favors the rejection of the idea that a decisive response can be made or avoids considering the possibility because the absence of such considerations might ensure that the poem is kept alive.

Bloom's rejection of reading the *Commedia* in the light of theological discourse leads to a serious contextual distortion of the poem's thematic content. If Dante wanted to maintain his poetic autonomy by keeping his work away from the influence of theology, he would indeed be a strong poet driven by the anxiety of influence. But the anxiety of influence is not a medieval ideal. It is a Protestant ideal that can be seen as the poetic version of Martin Luther's sense of revolt against authority. This sense of revolt is contrary to the medieval respect and veneration for authority. For example, Aquinas cannot make an assertion without quoting an authority like Aristotle or Augustine. The same is true of Dante. In the *Commedia*, the dependence on authority is manifest in Dante's reliance on his guides as authoritative figures in the ascent toward divine revelation. This essential feature underlines the fundamental difference between the ethos of the *Commedia* and, for example, that of John Bunyan's *Pilgrim's Progress*, in which the Christian hero fights a lonely battle against sins. The former is medieval, while the latter belongs to the ethos of modernity.

Notes

1. Ernst H. Kantorowicz, *The King's Two Bodies: A Study of Medieval Political Thought* (Princeton, N.J.: Princeton University Press, 1957), 452-53.

2. Etienne Gilson, *Dante the Philosopher*, trans. D. Moore (New York: Harper & Row, 1952), 241.

3. Umberto Cosmo, *A Handbook to Dante Studies*, trans. D. Moore (Oxford: Basil Blackwell, 1973), 154.

4. Thomas G. Bergin, *Perspectives on the Divine Comedy* (Piscataway, N.J.: Rutgers University Press, 1967), 37-38.

5. Thomas G. Bergin, *Perspectives on the Divine Comedy*, 70.

6. Dante Alighieri, *The Divine Comedy*, trans. Charles S. Singleton (Princeton, N.J.: Princeton University Press, 1970-75).

7. Robert Hollander, "Dante and his Commentators," in *The Cambridge Companion to Dante*, ed. Rachel Jacoff (Cambridge: Cambridge University Press, 1993), 235.

8. T. S. Eliot, "Dante," in *Selected Essays* (London: Faber and Faber Limited, 1972), 251.

9. Charles S. Singleton, "The Poet's Number at the Center," in *MLN* 80: 1 (1965), 1-10. The seven cantos constituting the center of the poem in *Purgatorio* have the following lengths of lines: 151, 145, 145, 139, 145, 145, and 151. Canto 17 of *Purgatorio* has 139 (1 + 3 + 9—that is, numbers referring to the Trinity and its unity) and is surrounded by cantos with symmetrical lengths. The symbolism consists in 1 + 5 + 1 = 7, and 1 + 4 + 5 = 10. Both are important quantities in Christian numerology. It is the symmetry around canto 17 that constitutes this canto as the center of the poem. Canto 17 of *Purgatorio* is also taken to be the center of the poem in thematic and not only numerical terms because of Vergil's exposition of the nature of love, which includes an explanation of the design of *Purgatorio* and the reference to three perversions of love as the causes of the sins that undergo purgation in the second realm of the afterworld. For a further development of Singleton's numerical interpretation, see J. L. Logan, "The Poet's Central Numbers," in *MLN* 86: 1 (1971), 95-98.

10. Charles S. Singleton, "The Irreducible Dove," in *Comparative Studies* IX (1957), 131.

11. Robert Hollander, *Dante's Epistle to Cangrande* (Ann Arbor: University of Michigan Press, 1993).

12. Charles S. Singleton, "The Irreducible Dove," 130.

13. Fernando Figurelli, "I canti di Cacciaguida," in *Dante nella critica d'oggi: risultati e prospettive*, ed. Umberto Bosco (Firenze: Le Monnier, 1965), 635.

14. Jacques Le Goff, *The Birth of Purgatory*, trans. A. Goldhammer (Chicago: University of Chicago Press, 1984), 237.

15. Stephen Botterill, *Dante and the Mystical Tradition: Bernard of Clairvaux in the Commedia* (Cambridge: Cambridge University Press, 1994), 2.

16. Robert Hollander, *Dante: A Life in Works* (New Haven, Conn.: Yale University Press, 2001), 3.

17. Francis Fergusson, *Dante's Drama of the Mind: A Modern Reading of the Purgatorio* (Princeton, N.J.: Princeton University Press, 1953), v.

18. Terence Irwin, *Classical Thought* (Oxford: Oxford University Press, 1989), 24.

19. Charles S. Singleton, "The Vistas in Retrospect," in *MLN* 81: 1 (1966), 58.

20. Charles S. Singleton, "The Vistas in Retrospect," 60.

21. Michele Barbi, "Nuovi problemi della critica dantesca," in *Studi danteschi* XXIII (1938), 48.

22. Ernst H. Kantorowicz, *The King's Two Bodies*, 453.

23. William Anderson, *Dante the Maker* (London: Routledge and Kegan Paul, 1980), 332.

24. William Anderson, *Dante the Maker*, 332 and 336.

25. Gerhart B. Ladner, "*Homo Viator*: Medieval Ideas on Alienation and Order," in *Speculum* 42: 2 (1967), 240. Matthew 7: 13-14—"Enter by the narrow gate; for the gate is wide and the way is easy, that leads to destruction, and those who enter it are many. For the gate is narrow and the way is hard, that leads to life, and those who find it are few." Luke 13: 24—"Strive to enter by the narrow door; for many, I tell you, will seek to enter and will not be able" (trans. *RSV*). Thematically applied to the *Commedia*, the notion of the "narrow gate" corresponds with the *cammino ascoso* or "hidden road" (*Inf.* 24: 133) and the *pertugio rotondo* or "round opening" (*Inf.* 24: 138), whereby Dante and Vergil reach Purgatory from the bottom of the infernal pit. In contrast, the Gate of Hell is immense (*Inf.* 3), and the ocean Ulysses tried to cross is wide (*Inf.* 26).

26. Norman Daniel, *The Arabs and Medieval Europe* (London: Longmans, 1975), 10.

27. Maria Corti, "Il binomio intertestualità e fonti: funzioni della storia nel sistema letterario," in *La scrittura e la storia: problemi di storiografia letteraria*, ed. Alberto Asor Rosa (Firenze: La Nuova Italia, 1995), 124-25.

28. Vicente Cantarino, "Dante and Islam: History and Analysis of a Controversy," in *A Dante Symposium in Commemoration of the 700 Anniversary of the Poet's Birth*, ed. William de Sua and Gino Rizzo (Chapel Hill: The University of North Carolina Press, 1965).

29. Richard W. Southern, "Dante and Islam," in *Relations between East and West in the Middle Ages*, ed. Derel Baker (Edinburgh, Scotland: Edinburgh University Press, 1973), 133-45.

30. James Kritzeck, *Peter the Venerable and Islam* (Princeton, N.J.: Princeton University Press, 1964), 129.

31. Philip F. Kennedy, "Muslim Sources of Dante?" in *The Arab Influence in Medieval Europe*, ed. Dionisius A. Agius and Richard Hitchcock (Reading, Penn.: Ithaca Press, 1994), 79.

32. Richard W. Southern, "Dante and Islam," 141.

33. Natalino Sapegno, "Genesis and Structure: Two Approaches to the Poetry of the *Comedy*," in *The Mind of Dante*, ed. U. Limentani (Cambridge: Cambridge University Press, 1965), 15.

34. One of the most influential advocates of this view is Erich Auerbach: "The unity of the poem is convincing. It is due to its all-inclusive subject, which is the *staus animarum post mortem*." Erich Auerbach, "Figura," in *Scenes from the Drama of European Literature: Six Essays*, trans. R. Manheim (New York: Meridian Books, Inc., 1959), 189.

35. T. K. Seung makes a similar argument in *The Fragile Leaves of the Sibyl* (*FLS* 6-8) in speaking of three major schools of opinion in Dante studies: (1) the school of damnation, (2) the school of adulation, and (3) the school of silence.

36. Daniele Mattalia, "Dante Alighieri," in *I classici italiani nella storia della critica, Vol. I: Da Dante al Marino*, ed. Walter Binni (Firenze: La Nuova Italia, 1967), 40-53.

37. The citation is from Coleridge's "Lectura X, 1818." Samuel Taylor Coleridge, *The Portable Coleridge*, ed. I. A. Richards (New York, 1950), 405-6 (cited in *FLS* 6).

38. Lino Pertile, "Does the *Stilnovo* Go to Heaven?" in *Dante for the New Millennium*, ed. Teodolinda Barolini and H. Wayne Storey (New York: Fordham University Press, 2003), 112-13.

39. Robin Kirkpatrick, *Dante: The Divine Comedy* (Cambridge: Cambridge University Press, 1996), 68.

40. Francis X. Newman, "St. Augustine's Three Visions and the Structure of the *Commedia*," in *MLN* 82: 1 (1967), 58.

41. Francis X. Newman, "St. Augustine's Three Visions," 78.

42. Harold Bloom, *Ruin the Sacred Truth: Poetry and Belief from the Bible to the Present* (Cambridge, Mass.: Harvard University Press, 1989), 46.

43. Harold Bloom, *The Western Canon: The Books and Schools of the Ages* (New York: Harcourt Brace & Company, 1994), 95-96.

44. Teodolinda Barolini, *The Undivine Comedy: Detheologizing Dante* (Princeton, N.J.: Princeton University Press, 1992), 17.

45. Teodolinda Barolini, *The Undivine Comedy*, 271.

46. Harold Bloom, *The Western Canon*, 78.

47. Teodolinda Barolini, *The Undivine Comedy*, 20.

48. Harold Bloom, *Ruin the Sacred Truth*, 47, and Harold Bloom, *The Western Canon*, 91.

49. Harold Bloom, *The Anxiety of Influence: A Theory of Poetry* (Oxford: Oxford University Press, 1973).

50. Teodolinda Barolini, "'Why Did Dante Write the Commedia?' or The Vision Thing," in *Dante Studies* CXI (1993), 3-4.

51. Teodolinda Barolini, *The Undivine Comedy*, 19.

52. Teodolinda Barolini, *The Undivine Comedy*, 4.

53. Giovanni Boccaccio, "Trattatello in laude di Dante," in *Opere in versi*, ed. P. G. Ricci (Milano: Riccardo Ricciardi, 1965), 608-9; Harold Bloom, *The Western Canon*, 83.

Chapter Three

Design in the Wax

In *The Design in the Wax*, Cogan presents a decisively positive response to the question of the poem's thematic coherence. His Dante reading is a valuable contribution to the revitalization of comprehensive interpretations of the *Commedia*. But it is questionable whether his reading succeeds in uncovering the poem's structure and its meaning. This is due to his focus on the structure and his reliance on assertions about the narrative content established by segmental examinations. The problem is his mixture of segmentalism and connectionism. The mixture creates more anomalies and ambiguities than Seung's systematic parallel reading. Why this is so is the issue I explore in detail in this chapter.

Mixed Reading

With reference to paragraph 16 of the *Letter to Can Grande della Scala*, Cogan argues that "the field of the *Commedia* is ethics" (*DW* xxii, 232 and 249). By this he means that the principle, which Dante finds in Aristotle's *Ethics* to organize *Inferno* into three major sections, is an ethical one that also applies to the structures of Purgatory and Paradise. The structures of the three realms propose variations on a single theme, whose doctrinal principles are fully revealed only in *Paradiso*. There the diversity, multiplicity, and complexity of the narrative become simple and intelligible. All things in the universe are images of God, who is most simple and most intelligible, but when distanced from their source of origin, they become mixed with dissimilarity from God, making them more diverse and multiple, and less intelligible (*DW* 246). The principles Cogan identifies as the structural constituents are what he calls the three appetitive faculties of the will, the irascible, and the concupiscible. But it remains unclear why he prefers to speak of appetitive faculties. The concupiscible belongs to the category of appetites. But it is not clear why the irascible and the will belong to the same category. The irascible is feeling and emotion, which is different from appetition. Likewise, the will cannot belong to the category of appetites, because the will is in control of appetites. Hence the terminology Cogan uses raises questions his theory does not answer.

Cogan's use of the tripartite soul for explaining the common structure of the three realms seems indebted to Seung's reading. To my knowledge, Seung is the first to propose that the notion of the three parts of the human soul provides a divisional system that underlies the formal structures of the three realms. But Cogan never admits his indebtedness. In a note he only remarks that Seung's use of the terms of the vegetative, the sensitive, and the intellectual for the structural divisions is based on the misidentification of the concupiscible appetite with the vegetative power. With this remark Cogan dissociates his reading from Seung's. He claims that Seung's argument rests on a mistaken interpretation of Aristotle (*DW* 324). But Cogan's claim reveals an inadequate understanding of Seung's theory and method. Seung does not elucidate the underlying structure of the *Commedia* on the basis of a specific interpretation of Aristotle or a special current in medieval thought, because the language of the *Commedia* is poetic, even when it reproduces distinctive notions of medieval scholasticism. Statius's account of the genesis of the soul in Purgatory (*Purg.* 25: 37-108) includes certain technical terms, but it is not possible to associate it fully with a specific current or school of medieval thought. When Seung uses both sets of technical terms interchangeably, they serve the purpose of conceptualizing what Dante visualizes poetically. If we rely strictly on one set of terms, we easily end up imposing a specific system of thought on the *Commedia*, which the poetic language does not display.

Cogan's reading exemplifies this problem. He interprets the ethical content of the *Commedia* in contrast to what he regards as the main stream of medieval interpretations of Aristotle. He identifies Dante's reading of Aristotle as unorthodox and idiosyncratic and divergent from both Aristotle and medieval interpretations of his work. To identify a main stream of Aristotelianism in Dante's time is, however, not easy. Cogan does not take account of this problem and relies almost entirely on Aquinas's work as the main representative of orthodox medieval Aristotelianism. He emphasizes that he uses Aquinas to provide "a sort of background against which Dante's positions are thrown better into relief" (*DW* xxiii-xxiv). He does not argue that when Dante says one thing it is because Aquinas said something like it. Cogan's reading of the *Commedia* is not Thomistic. But because of his heavy use of Aquinas's work, his reading becomes contingent on Thomistic thought. In fact, he finds it likely that "Dante believed himself working in the spirit of Aristotle and Aquinas" and that "the way in which he diverges from them exhibits a characteristically medieval respect for their authority" (*DW* 73). Due to the contingency, Cogan imposes a restrictive view on the poem that distorts its thematic integrity. Instead of letting the poem reveal itself, he is more concerned with placing Dante's positions within or in opposition to a specific current of medieval Aristotelianism.

This problem can be illustrated by considering his criticism of Seung's identification of the vegetative part with the concupiscible faculty. In the *Summa Theologiae* Aquinas follows Aristotle's tripartite theory of the soul that accepts Plato's tripartite theory. Aquinas calls the three parts the vegetative soul, the sensitive soul, and the intellectual soul. The last one is unique for human beings, who share the second one with animals and the third one with plants as well as with animals (*ST* pt. 1, q. 78, a. 1). Aquinas further says that the vegetative soul has three distinct powers: the generative, the nutritive, and the augmentative. Their operations are procreation, the appetites for food and drink, and the desire to mature and expand (*ST* pt. 1, q. 78, a. 2). These operations are reflected in Aquinas's treatment of the concupiscible faculty. For example, Aquinas associates the capital sin of lust with the lower appetite of the concupiscence. At the same time, he emphasizes that the semen is the residue of the action of the nutritive power and needed for the work of the generative power (*ST* pt. 2-2, q. 153, a. 3 and 5).

In explicating the concupiscible appetites, Aquinas recognizes that the powers of the vegetative soul are operative in the human soul. When Seung uses the vegetative part interchangeably with the concupiscible, it does not rest on a misidentification of the one with the other, but it emphasizes an essential affinity between the vegetative soul in plants and the concupiscible faculty in the human soul. This affinity is manifest in Statius's account of the genesis of the soul. But since Cogan reads the *Commedia* on the background of Thomistic Aristotelianism, he insists on following scholastic distinctions, although the poetic language does not reproduce them. This procedure is critical. At first sight, Seung's reading in *The Fragile Leaves of the Sibyl* involves a similar procedure due to his frequent references to Aquinas for doctrinal explanations. But when we consider his original thesis in the light of his later works on Dante, his use of Thomistic-Aristotelian terms mainly serves the purpose of outlining conceptual characteristics and not demonstrating the proximate inspirational sources. In defining Dante's theological outlook, Seung emphasizes that it is has more in common with that of Bonaventure than that of Aquinas. Cogan, however, makes no such conceptual characterization. He never questions whether Aquinas is the most adequate basis for explicating the poem's meaning. He simply regards the two *Summae* as summaries of common medieval positions, although they only attained that position later in history. Hence Cogan's reading represents a continuation of the Thomistic type of reading frequently practiced in Dante studies.

The reliance on Thomistic thought has consequences for Cogan's theory. Although he outlines a common structure for all three parts of the poem, his theory stresses the notion of separation or discontinuity that marks Thomistic thought. Aquinas insisted on distinguishing between the natural and the supernatural order. Like his teacher Albertus Magnus, Aquinas rejected the Neoplatonic conception of scientific inquiry manifest in Grosseteste, Robert Kilwardly, and Roger Bacon, who argued that the different branches of science (the natural, the mathematical, and the metaphysical) represent ascending degrees of illumination. The study of nature can lead to knowledge definable in mathematical terms, and mathematical knowledge can provide the means for understanding metaphysical things. Thus man is ascribed the potentiality of divine illumination through scientific study. But under the influence of Aristotle, this view was rejected by Albertus Magnus, who argued that each science is autonomous in its own sphere of inquiry.[1] By following this view, Aquinas promoted a method of separation or discontinuity which stands in opposition to the notion of relation or continuity manifest in Bonaventure's thought.

The difference between these two notions and their representative thinkers can be illustrated by comparing two different ways of elaborating on the threefold division of the curriculum at the Parisian Faculty of Arts around 1240 into natural, moral, and rational philosophy. The one is found in Aquinas's commentary on Aristotle's *Ethics*, and the other is found in Bonaventure's *Itinerarium mentis in Deum*.[2] In the beginning of his commentary (I.i), Aquinas speaks of the threefold division and treats their relation as naturally given. The object of his analysis is the maturation of the intellect in the natural order. He does not move beyond that order because he rejects the classification of sciences according to ascending degrees of abstraction. With the emphasis on autonomous fields of science, philosophy and theology come to represent two different viewpoints. The subject of the former is the natural order, and the subject of the latter is the supernatural order; they constitute a dyadic structure of thought in Aquinas. In Bonaventure's *Itinerarium* (III.vi), the division between natural, moral, and rational philosophy is given a different interpretation. Its scientific foundation is the Neoplatonic notion of transcendence from the natural to the supernatural order. The three philosophies are interpreted as three phases in the development of the human intellect and represent three steps in the appropriation of the qualities associated with the Holy Trinity. Hence Bonaventure applies a triadic system of thought with Trinitarian content and adds a spiritual dimension to the potentiality of the human intellect. With this dimension he argues for an essential relation or continuity between the immanent and the transcendent features of the universe. In Aquinas this mystical element is not prevalent, while it is a fundamental in Bonaventure.

By following the discontinuous system of thought and yet proposing a common structure for all three parts of the *Commedia*, Cogan's reading turns out to be a mixture of serial and parallel reading. He argues that all three parts have a common structure that thematizes the tripartite soul. This is the principle of his parallel reading. But he also argues that the three parts are diverse in their structure because they thematize the tripartite soul in three different ways: Hell thematizes acts of the tripartite soul, Purgatory thematizes habits of the tripartite soul, and Paradise thematizes powers of the tripartite soul. These three aspects constitute the principles for his serial reading. But the mixed reading does not have the virtue of consistency. Cogan seems to solve this problem by emphasizing that on the surface level there is no symmetry between Hell and Purgatory. The symmetry is found at the level of appetites implicitly thematized in the two parts. But when we consider the substantive content of this separation of acts from habits, the mixture of serial and parallel readings creates problems concerning what Cogan identifies as the essential topic of the *Commedia*.

In arguing that *Inferno* describes only sinful acts and not vicious habits, Cogan emphasizes that virtue and vice depend on habit or disposition, whereas salvation and damnation do not. One can be damned to eternal punishment in Hell because of a single act, just as one can be saved from infernal punishment by a single act (*DW* 10). This means that there need not be any disposition for sin or repentance behind the act of sin or repentance. Sins are not necessarily symptoms of vices. On this ground, Cogan argues, for example, that Ugolino della Gherardesca's betrayal of Pisa, for which he seems condemned (*Inf.* 33: 79-87), was only an exceptional incident in his life and not due to a habit, wherefore his sin was not vicious in Aristotelian terms (*DW* 9). This seems to be a reasonable argument. But it relies entirely on the traditional way of explaining the structural design. Ugolino is traditionally seen as a traitor. There are two principal passages in the text that support this structural designation. First, in canto 11 of *Inferno*, Vergil says that the smallest circle at the center of the earth, "around the throne of Dis," contains traitors (*Inf.* 11: 64-66). Second, Dante remarks that Ugolino was accused of turning traitor (*Inf.* 33: 85-87). But Cogan's interpretation does not take account of the most crucial aspect in Ugolino's appearance. In tears he tells the story how he was locked up with his four sons in a prison and left to starvation (*Inf.* 33: 4-75). While growing weaker and weaker, the sons, in whose faces Ugolino saw himself reflected four times, offered their flesh for the father to eat. First he rejected the offer, but when they died and Ugolino had turned blind, "hunger proved more powerful than grief."

The kind of structural and serial reading Cogan practices does not determine the thematic meaning of this story. It does not take account of how it points toward the vicious disposition of Ugolino's soul that resulted in his terrible act. According to Seung's thematic reading of the episode, Ugolino's story demarcates the nature of Satan's carnal feast as presented in canto 34 of *Inferno*. Seung argues that the Ugolino story should be compared with the scene of the Last Supper, where Christ offered his flesh and blood to his children:

> Ugolino is too powerless to do anything for his sons locked up in the prison, and Christ releases His children from the prison of death with his death and feeds them with His body and blood. Ugolino and his children are the victims on the cross of pride, and Christ and His children are the lambs on the cross of humility . . . The prison in which Count Ugolino was locked is the symbol of the proud will. The proud man locks himself in the prison of his defiant will by alienating himself from the bounty of grace. The proud will has to freeze into itself like the sinners in Cocytus and feed on itself. This is the feast of pride, the feast of sorrow and death. This is the feast of self-destruction; all the three companions [Brutus, Cassius, and Judas] took their own lives in the sin of their pride (*FLS* 163).

If this is so, it is inaccurate to say that "Judas' betrayal of Jesus can only be understood as a singular action, not as a result of depraved habit or habits" (*DW* 9). Cogan's claim does not take account of the cumulative effects the narrative generates.

Traditionally the four zones of the ninth circle are conceived as four separate rings. But Seung argues that they can be seen as three rings with a center. What is thematized in the first three rings finds its cumulative expression in the center. In order to understand the cumulative effect, we have to take account of the names Dante chooses for the first three rings.

In Genesis 4 we read about Cain, who killed his brother; he committed a sin against his own family. In Homer's *Illiade* (III, 146-60 and VII, 345-53) we hear of the Trojan Antenor, who opposed the war against the Greeks. He wanted Helena returned and concluded the peace treaty with the Greeks. According to a medieval tradition that goes back to Servius's fifth-century commentary to Vergil's *Aeneide*, Antenor was the archetype of a traitor against one's own country.[3] In 1 Machabees (16: 11-17) we read about Ptolemeus, who was so greedy for power that he killed his father-in-law and brother-in-law. On this ground, Seung argues that the theme of Caina is related to sinful acts among family members, the theme of Antenora is related to sinful acts against one's own country, and the theme of Tolemea is related to sinful acts against bonds of friendship in the pursuit for power.

In Giudecca these three themes are repeated with cumulative impetus in Satan's imitation of the Trinity. Traditionally the punishments of Brutus, Cassius, and Judas in Satan's mouths have been interpreted as demarcating treachery against the Lord of the Earthly Empire and against the Lord of the Heavenly Empire. Brutus and Cassius betrayed the former by planning and executing the murder of Julius Caesar, and Judas betrayed the latter by pointing out Jesus to the Roman soldiers. But this interpretation is inconsistent with Satan's imitation of the Trinity. With reference to Plutarch, whom Dante knew very well, Seung emphasizes that the two conspirators had different motives for murdering Caesar and played different roles in the conspiracy. According to Plutarch, Cassius was the mind behind the act. His motive was the defense of the country against Caesar's tyranny, and he used his talent to persuade Brutus about the necessity of murdering Caesar. Brutus's motive for participating in the conspiracy was of a different kind. He came out of a family that had long been known as defender of the Roman Republic. When Caesar attained the role of dictator, he did not join the conspiracy because of love for the republican idea. He felt humiliated and found it necessary to defend the honor and proud traditions of his family. According to Seung, Brutus was driven by family pride, whereas Cassius acted in pride for the country. If so, the punishment of Brutus is the cumulative image of the sins portrayed in the ring of Caina, and the punishment of Cassius is the cumulative image of the sins portrayed in the ring of Antenora. Finally, the sins of the ring of Tolemea find their cumulative expression in the image of Judas's punishment. According to Seung, Judas's crime was the sin against the very foundation of Christianity—to love one's neighbor. Judas betrayed his friend Jesus and sinned against the message of Christ's first coming.

Satan imitates the Trinity in sin, and the three sinners Satan is chewing represent the three sins of Satan's pride:

> In rebelling against God, Satan tried to usurp the inheritance of his family. What is the family inheritance he tried to usurp? It is the source of beatitude. It is God, Satan's father, who has this source. Satan attempted to be the source of beatitude like his Creator. Further, Satan was proud of his talent; he was created as the greatest angel. With his talent, Satan masterminded the conspiracy against God and turned one-tenth of the angels against Him. Lastly, Satan wanted to consolidate his power by overthrowing his friend and the original bestower of his power (*FLS* 145).

Hence Judas committed his sinful act against his friend Jesus because he was absorbed in the pride of power. By examining the cumulative effects of the narrative, Seung is capable of bringing forth the dispositions underlying the sinful acts portrayed in *Inferno*. Cogan cannot accomplish such an understanding for two reasons. First, his reliance on segmental examinations involves a discrepancy between his analytic basis and his interpretive objective. The objective is to explicate the principles of the poem's unity, but the explication is made on the basis of restrictive examinations. Second, since Cogan relies on segmental examinations, his method for explicating the structure of every part is basically serial reading. The reliance on segmental examinations makes him focus on the diversity of sinful acts in Hell in contrast to the orderly notion of seven deadly vices in Purgatory. That prevents him from seeing sinful acts as symptomatic expressions of vicious dispositions. This is the basic principle of correspondence between Hell and Purgatory according to Seung's systematic parallel reading. At the same time Cogan's serial reading results in his distinction between a realm of acts (Hell), a realm of habits (Purgatory), and a realm of powers (Paradise). But this distinction is problematic in ethics.

Acts and Habits

Cogan maintains that Judas's betrayal of Jesus can be understood only as a singular act because he insists on separating acts from habits. On the level of appetites, he argues for a symmetrical relation between the acts portrayed in Hell and the habits portrayed in Purgatory. But the symmetry falls apart when we consider the sin of sodomy in the seventh circle as a sinful act of the irascible faculty and the vice of sodomy on the seventh terrace as a vicious habit of the concupiscible faculty. Seung notices this anomaly, but does not explain it. According to Seung's systematic parallel reading, each terrace on the mount of Purgatory reflects the design of the corresponding circle in Hell. On this point, Cogan and Seung clearly disagree. According to Cogan, the locations of corresponding sins and vices in the two realms are often so divergent that they challenge the symmetry of the two realms rather than support it. Seung detects no such divergence as far as these locations are concerned. This means that in a number of cases they propose fundamentally different interpretations of what kind of sin is condemned in which division or subdivision of Hell. This is the case with Ugolino. Only in one case does Seung admit an exception to the rule of correspondence. The exception is the sodomites: "In the *Inferno*, it is not the Circle of lust but the Circle of wrath to which sodomites are condemned" (*FLS* 311). Seung follows here the conventional interpretation of the sodomites in the seventh circle as sinners of lust. Cogan also accepts this interpretation. At no point does he wonder whether the anomaly can be due to an inadequate interpretation of the episode in Hell.

According to Seung, the sins portrayed in Hell are acts arising from the seven capital sins portrayed in Purgatory. Due to this correspondence, Seung's connectionist reading stresses the intimate relation between acts and habits in accordance with medieval ethics. For example, with reference to Aristotle, Aquinas says that "habits of virtue and vice are caused by acts," and that "a habit of virtue, and for the same reason, other habits [i.e., vices], is not caused by one act," but only by many acts. Once attained, a virtue is not destroyed by a single act of vice. Virtues are decreased or destroyed by the lack of exercise (*ST* pt. 1-2, q. 53, a. 2 and 3). In short, the standard position is that habits are formed by acts and acts display habits. Aquinas stresses this intimate relation between act and habit by saying that for an act to be human it must proceed from a deliberate will act (*ST* pt. 1-2, q. 1, a. 1 and q. 6, a. 1). This emphasis on the significance of the will led William of Ockham to maintain that all acts are morally neutral in themselves. An act is neither good nor bad in itself. The same act can be good when combined with one intention and evil when combined with another. Whether an act is morally permissible or impermissible can be established only by considering the agent's intention.[4] This intimate relation between act and habit and act and will is not maintained in Cogan's reading, since he emphasizes divergence as far as the locations of corresponding sins and vices are concerned. This is manifest in his interpretation of the locations of the sodomites in the

Commedia. Cogan repeatedly stresses Dante's idiosyncratic position and its paradoxical outcome. But since the separation of acts from habits is problematic, the idiosyncrasy and the paradoxes can also be due to Cogan's way of coding the thematic content. Either Dante is making a gross blunder or Cogan is imposing one on Dante.

Cogan is right in asserting that Hell punishes acts and that Purgatory corrects habits. But the assertion that the subject of discourse is sinful acts in Hell and vicious habits in Purgatory is problematic. That presupposes the distinction between sins and vices; that is, sins are only acts, whereas vices are not acts but only habits. In order to understand the problem of this distinction, let us first consider the distinction of virtues and vices. These are only dispositions and should be distinguished from acts of virtue or acts of vice. If a person has the virtue of courage, he has the disposition to perform acts of courage. Such a disposition constitutes the character. But having a character does not mean that the person also performs a certain act. The relation between a virtue and an act of that virtue is the relation between potency and act. By the time the person performs an act of courage his virtue of courage is translated from potentiality to actuality.

Performing a certain act, however, does not always mean that it is the actualization of a disposition. A person can perform an act of courage, but he may not have the disposition for the act in his character. In that case, the act is out of his character. It is an accident, and as such, it has no moral merit. The connection between the character and the act is essential for virtue. The same relation holds between a vice and an act of vice. The vice of gluttony is only a disposition that becomes real when translated into an act. Whether the translation takes place or not is determined by the will. It would be incorrect to punish a person for having a disposition for an act of vice he does not make. It would also be incorrect to punish a person for an accidental act for which he has no disposition. Aquinas is explicit about the incorrectness of such a punishment: "A man is justly punished for a vicious act; but not for a vicious habit, so long as no act ensues. Therefore a vicious action is worse than a vicious habit" (*ST* pt. 1-2, q. 71, a. 3). But it is correct to maintain that the target for punishment is the act and not the disposition for it. From this it follows that Hell is for the punishment of acts and not of dispositions.

Given these distinctions, let us add some final remarks to the question of Judas's betrayal of Jesus. The betrayal can indeed be a singular act, if Judas never betrayed anyone before. But that does not make his act an accidental event, which is out of his character. He may not even have the disposition to betray anyone if he has not betrayed anyone before, because a disposition is formed by the repetition of the same act. Likewise, anyone who commits a murder for the first time cannot act out of the disposition to murder. The murder cannot be an act of sin if the basis of sin is the disposition for that sin. The reason for this absurd consequence is that there are two ways of understanding dispositions. One is to regard dispositions as the results of repeated acts. This is the narrow understanding of dispositions. The other involves a broad understanding of the nature of dispositions. For example, although a person may not have the disposition for murder, he may be said to have a disposition to harm others. Likewise, although Judas may not have had the disposition to betray because he never betrayed anyone before, he may have had the disposition to disloyalty because of selfishness. For these reasons, it is incorrect to explain Judas's act by his disposition to betray. It is much better to explain it by his pride, which is a broader disposition than the disposition to betray.

It is the narrow understanding of dispositions Cogan intends when he rejects the idea that Judas's betrayal of Jesus as due to a disposition. It is the broad understanding of dispositions Seung applies in identifying Judas's sin as the satanic sin of pride. The difference between these two understandings of the nature of dispositions is not just a matter of two different conceptual approaches to the poem's substantive content. Since Cogan does not take account of the broad understanding, his theory can be criticized for imposing a limited perspective on the poem's substantive content. Since Seung applies the broad understanding, his theory gives the substantive content a more profound meaning than Cogan's.

As said, the function of Hell is to punish acts and not dispositions. But the function of purgation is different. The object of purgation is not an act but a disposition. There is no way to purge an act once it is done because it belongs to the past. But the disposition is still there even after the act. In Purgatory there can be penance (or punishment), but no purgation for acts of vice. The only thing that can be purged is what is in the heart or soul: the character of dispositions. Therefore it is correct to say that the moral character is the target of purgation. But it is incorrect to say that sins are not the target of purgation. The *Commedia* clearly says that the seven deadly sins are purged on the seven terraces of the Mount of Purgatory.

The word "sin" has two meanings—narrow and broad. In its narrow sense, sin means sinful acts. In its broad sense, it means not only sinful acts but also sinful dispositions. In the *Summa Theologiae* Aquinas says: "Sin is compared to virtue, as evil act to good habit" (*ST* pt. 1-2, q. 71, a. 4). Hence Aquinas identifies sin as an act. But he also says that sin can take place on different levels, for example, on the three successive levels of thought, word, and deed (*ST* pt. 1-2, q. 72, a. 7). To illustrate this point, he takes the sin of anger: it can begin with angry thought, turn into angry words, and finally become angry deeds. Of these three, the last level clearly belongs to the level of acts, while the first belongs to the level of dispositions. The second level can be consigned to either of the two levels. The angry words can be regarded as verbal acts or only as signs of a disposition for angry deeds.

This ambiguity is not restricted to the word "sin." It is also operative in the meaning of "virtue" and "vice." Although we sometimes distinguish virtue as disposition from the corresponding act, we also use the word "virtue" to cover not only the disposition but also its acts. For example, if we say that Abraham Lincoln had the virtue of honesty, we do not mean only that he had the disposition. What we mean is that Lincoln had not only the disposition of honesty, he also performed honest acts. It is difficult to determine that a person has a disposition of honesty if he does not perform honest acts. For that reason, acts are essential for determining whether a person has a certain disposition. The same thing goes for vice. A person can be called gluttonous if he not only has the disposition for gluttony, but also performs gluttonous acts. In the *Commedia* this ambiguity is manifest in Dante's use of the same words (*colpa della gola*) for describing the acts of gluttony in the third circle of Hell (*Inf.* 6: 53) and the disposition for gluttony on the sixth terrace of Purgatory (*Purg.* 24: 128). When we compare the narrow and the broad meaning of virtue and vice, the broad is the standard meaning. The narrow one is usually reserved for technical usage. When we speak of courage, the usual meaning covers both the disposition and the corresponding act. The broad meaning is the standard meaning, because there is an intimate connection between a virtue or a vice and the corresponding act. If acts are separated from habits, they are out of character and belong neither to virtue nor to vice.

The distinction between act and habit is a basic distinction in ethics, ancient, medieval, and modern. However, it is inadequate when we try to solve the problem of sodomy in the *Commedia*. The classification of sodomy makes no sense in ethics. Although a sin can have two aspects (act and disposition), they belong to the same sin. It is impossible to assign the act to one sin and the disposition to another sin. Nevertheless, that is what Cogan does. Sins of sodomy are not only related to two different types of sin, they are also said to be prompted by two different types of passions. But there is no independent definition of sinful dispositions, independent of sinful acts. For this reason, it makes no sense to separate the act and the disposition of a sin and assign them to different regions.

Philosophy and Theology

In arguing that Hell is structured in accordance with sins and Purgatory in accordance with vices, Cogan relies on two assertions. First, Dante believed that it was possible to separate acts from habits. Second, by separating acts from habits he wanted to give Hell a philosophical structure, so that the pagan sinners would understand why they are punished, and Purgatory a theological structure that the Christian penitents understand. Cogan claims that Hell is organized by principles that have their origin in nature and not in Christian faith, and that its structure is articulated by philosophy and intelligible for anyone.

This seems to be a reasonable argument, since there are many pagans in Hell. But if Hell is organized by pagan principles and Purgatory by Christian principles, Dante makes a serious mistake as far as the historical origins of the concepts of vice, virtue, and sin are concerned. The concept of virtue and vice is a legacy from Greco-Roman antiquity, whereas the concept of sin is a Judeo-Christian legacy. The latter did not have the concept of virtue, wherefore Christians adopted the Greco-Roman notion of virtue. Since Christians had their own notion of sin that resembled the pagan notion of vice, they used the two concepts interchangeably. Cogan admits that medieval thinkers used the terms *peccatum* and *vitium* interchangeably, but he emphasizes that they always denoted vices. For that reason, Cogan argues, the seven deadly sins should be called the seven capital vices; they are vices because they denote sinful dispositions, and they are capital because they are the head or origin of other vices and sins (*DW* 85). Nevertheless, if the function of Hell is the punishment for sins, its organization should be based on Christian principles, and if the function of Purgatory is the purgation of vices, its organization should be governed by pagan principles. The Greco-Roman doctrine of vice had its origin in nature and was intelligible to natural reason, but the doctrine of sin was not. Its origin was not in nature but in revelation. As Søren Kierkegaard says, the concept of sin becomes possible only in the face of God; it is the rebellion against God. The concept of virtue and vice, however, is possible in the world of nature.

Dante might have disregarded the historical origins of the concept of virtue and vice and that of sin. But the view that the organization of Hell is based on natural reason or pagan principles goes against Dante's text. Hell contains many sins, such as suicide, heresy, and simony, that are uniquely Christian. For example, suicide was never condemned as a sin in the pagan tradition. In fact, it was considered to be a noble act in defense of honor, as in the case of Cato of Utica, whose soul is the first Dante meets in the Ante-Purgatory. Cato killed himself because he did not want to fall in the hands of his adversary Julius Caesar when the defeat in the Roman Civil War, in which he had fought on the side of Pompey, was certain. In the *Commedia* Cato is described as one who died for the sake of liberty (*Purg.* 1: 70-75).

Cogan tries to solve the problem of suicide by focusing on how the act stems from the irascible faculty. For example, he argues that the suicide of Pier della Vigna was not an act of desperation but an attempt to exact a certain revenge on his enemies, which is the natural goal of anger. But his anger turned out to be unnatural because it was directed toward himself instead of his enemies (*DW* 56-57). Thus Cogan proposes a philosophical explanation to the sin of suicide. This explanation implies that when confronted with God's justice, which in Cogan's view is implicit in the philosophical structure of Hell, pagans will recognize the noble act in defense of honor as an erroneous act of the irascible faculty. But there are no pagan suicides in the seventh circle to support Cogan's reading. The pagans that could have supported it are placed elsewhere. This indicates that Dante regards suicide as a uniquely Christian sin and that he is aware of the difference between the Christian and the pagan attitude toward suicide. For example, Cato is not condemned for his suicidal act, but stands on the shore on the Mount of Purgatory. Although Dido committed a ritual suicide because of forsaken love, she is not condemned for the act, but for her lustful behavior.

These two cases make it clear that it is not always the gravest act of sin that determines the destiny of the soul in the afterworld. Hence, when Cogan says that a person can be damned because of a single act of sin, it should be emphasized that damnation can be cancelled if something in the person's character speaks for another destination in the afterworld. This is exemplified with the presence of Rahab of Jericho in the Venus heaven. Although she was a prostitute, she was the first to rise to Heaven when Christ harrowed Hell before his return to the Father. The reason is that she made Joshua's first glory in the Holy Land possible, whereby the Coming of Christ was prefigured (*Par.* 9: 118-26). In the case of Cato, his sense of liberty prevails over his suicide, wherefore damnation is cancelled. In the case of Dido, her lustful behavior is stressed at the expense of her suicide and makes her representational of a lighter sin than the one that put an end to her life. This does not make sense if a person can be damned for a single act that does not arise from a habit. As an act, suicide should still be a graver sin than lust.

Cogan argues that in order to understand why Dido is placed in the second and not in the seventh circle, we have to take account of the appetite that prompted her act. He claims that her suicide had its source in the concupiscence, and that Dante explicitly states that "she committed suicide for love, that is under the influence of concupiscible passion." For that reason, her suicide lacks the irascible passion or intent of Pier's (*DW* 57). This means that in principle, suicides can be placed in different sections of Hell depending on the passion that prompts the acts. But the placement of Dido in Hell can be given a different explanation. The reason why she and other pagan suicides are not condemned for their suicidal act might be that they did not know that suicide was a sin. Since they did not know that it meant a rebellion against God, their suicides could not be influenced by the same passion that prompted Pier's act. As a Christian, Pier knew that suicide was a sin, but he fell victim of a perverted passion of the irascible faculty. By disregarding the sacredness of human life, he rebelled against God.

Dido and the other pagan suicides were not disposed to the suicidal act. If it had been a vice in the pagan tradition, they could have been condemned for the act. But since it was not, to condemn them for the act would have been to punish them for an accidental act that has no moral merit. Hence, when Dante refers to the fact that Dido committed suicide for love, he may be implying something else than what Cogan proposes. Instead of underlining that the same act can be influenced by different passions, Dante may implicitly be emphasizing that the precondition for a sinner's placement in a specific section of Hell is that there is an intimate relation between the act he commits and the disposition that incites the act.

According to Cogan, the second circle thematizes lustful acts. But Dante explicitly says that Semiramis was corrupted by the *vizio di lussuria*, the "vice of lust." Because of the vice, she licensed laws that would cleanse the stain of scandal she spread (*Inf.* 5: 55-57). In reading Paulus Orosius's *Historium adversum Paganos*, from which Dante borrowed several phrases, it becomes clear that her sin of lust involved more than a single act. Orosius says (I, iv, 4, 7-8):

> Burning with lust and thirsty for blood, Semiramis in the course of continuous adulteries and homicides caused the death of all those who she had delighted to hold in her adulterous embrace and whom she had

> summoned to her by royal command for that purpose. She finally most shamelessly conceived a son, godlessly abandoned the child, later had incestuous relations with him, and then covered her private disgrace by public crime. For she prescribed that between parents and children no reverence for nature in the conjugal act was to be observed, but that each should be free to do as he pleased.[5]

On this ground, it is misleading to maintain that the second circle only thematizes lustful acts. Due to the intimate relation between act and habit, its ultimate theme can be the disposition as well as acts of lust. If so, the famous story of Francesca and Paolo implies more than a single act that ended tragically when the love affair was discovered by the husband Gianciotto, Paolo's older brother. The story implies that the two lovers responded to a lustful impulse because they both had the disposition to the act of lust. Because of the intimate relation between act and habit, the lustful act reveals that the two lovers had the lustful disposition. Cogan observes that it is unlikely that Francesca and Paolo "would have been considered vicious in an Aristotelian sense" (*DW* 28). But due to the intimate relation between act and habit, they can be considered sinners of both the vice and the act of lust in a Christian sense. They developed the disposition to lust through thoughts and words and finally realized it in the fatal act.

In dealing with the episode of Francesca and Paolo, Dante scholars have generally been misled by Dante's apparent empathy for the two lovers. The empathy tends to overshadow the fact that they are sinners of lust. As Giovanni Boccaccio recounts the background story, there are good reasons for the empathy. The marriage between the high-spirited Francesca and the physically deformed Gianciotto was due to political scheming. Francesca fell in love with Paolo at first sight but was deceived. When Francesca and Paolo became intimate, their love ended in brutal death between family members.[6] But although Dante's empathy is clear and the course of events was tragic, we should not neglect the fact that Dante's conception of divine justice identifies the two lovers as sinners of lust.

As Dante employs the Aristotelian distinction between incontinence, malice, and bestiality, the souls of the second circle are sinners of incontinence. Incontinence denotes the inordinate appetite that escapes the control of the will and is the vice of soft and weak people (*Ethics*, 1148a12). According to Aquinas, "the incontinent man goes astray from that which is in accord with reason" and "plunges into shameful pleasures" (*ST* pt. 2-2, q. 156, a. 2). The sinners of the second circle are all condemned for such a behavior. To paraphrase Aquinas, the lower parts of their soul (the concupiscible appetites) were strongly moved toward the object for their lust. As a result, the higher parts of their soul (reason and will) were hindered and disordered in their acts (*ST* pt. 2-2, q. 153, a. 5). For this reason, Cogan is right in asserting that the second circle implicitly thematizes lust as a sin influenced by the concupiscible passion. But his argument that the lustful acts in Hell cannot be seen as different species of the capital vice of lust is inconsistent.

Dante says that the lustful sinners have one thing in common: they made reason slave to appetite (*Inf.* 5: 37-39). Moreover, they are whirled about together in a dark and stormy wind. Since the sinners form a communal entity, we may wonder why Cogan is reluctant to take his argument one step further. He does not relate their acts to the vice of lust, which is an erroneous disposition of the concupiscible faculty. The concupiscible faculty (as well as the other faculties) generates dispositions, and dispositions can be developed correctly or incorrectly. If developed correctly, the dispositions become virtues, and if developed incorrectly, they become vices. If they become vices, they can result in vicious acts. However, to fully substantiate this argument, we need to make a systematic parallel reading of *Inferno* and *Purgatorio* and thematically connect the second circle of Hell to the seventh terrace of Purgatory. We cannot identify the sinful acts in Hell as the results of vicious dispositions if we only consider the description of sinful acts in Hell. Since Hell is for the punishment of acts, the vicious dispositions that incited the acts can be thematized only implicitly. Likewise, since the moral character of a sinner is the target for purgation, the sinful acts that are now forgiven in Purgatory can be established only when connected to the sinful acts portrayed in Hell, whose sources, in turn, become clear when connected to the description of vicious dispositions in Purgatory.

In addition, Cogan's focus on the diversity of sins in *Inferno* in contrast to the uniformity of vices in *Purgatorio* creates another anomaly concerning medieval theological teaching. As Cogan interprets the punishment for sins in Hell, there is no room for the doctrine that every sin can be purged. If we agree with Cogan, a large number of sins cannot be purged. This is the case with heresy, vandalism, murder, suicide, blasphemy, usury, seduction, flattery, simony, soothsaying, bribery, hypocrisy, theft, false counsel, schismatic conduct, forgery, and treachery. According to Cogan, no penitent in Purgatory does anywhere show that these sinful acts can be forgiven and the dispositions that incited them can be purged. And yet he claims that "the actions committed by the souls in Purgatory have already been forgiven. Were that not so, the souls would be in Hell rather than in Purgatory. But though the actions are now behind them, the dispositions, that is, vices, that led to those actions are not themselves necessarily removed by that forgiveness" (*DW* 90). At the same time Cogan emphasizes that in Hell the souls are fixed in the image of the worst evil they have committed (*DW* 93).

But if there are no thematic connections between the actions forgiven in Purgatory and those portrayed in the fifth, seventh, eighth, and ninth circles of Hell, and if the evil actions condemned in Hell cannot be seen as perverted reflections of the dispositions that are now being purged in Purgatory, we have to conclude that not all sins can be purged. Cogan's assertion that as a disposition sodomy is a vice of the concupiscible faculty, which becomes a sin of the irascible faculty when turned into an act, puts this anomaly into perspective. However, if the acts in Hell and the dispositions in Purgatory are thematically related, we can deduce two essential doctrines from their interrelation. First, the acts in Hell show what happens if a person develops the dispositions portrayed in Purgatory incorrectly. The consequence is evil and the degeneration of the soul. Second, the correction of vicious dispositions in Purgatory shows how the dispositions of the tripartite soul ought to be developed in order to prevent evil and regenerate the soul for the attainment of virtues.

Cogan's reading does not result in such simple doctrines. He cannot claim that the sinful acts of Hell show what happens if the dispositions of Purgatory are developed incorrectly, because there is no direct relation between the acts of the former and the dispositions of the latter. Since the relation between Hell and Purgatory exists only at the level of appetites, he can only claim that the sinful acts show the consequences of inordinate appetites and the purgation of sinful dispositions portrays the regeneration of these appetites. As a result, in Cogan's reading the *Commedia* comes to display a complicated doctrine about how to avoid acts of sin. The condemnation of sodomy cannot be taken to show the immediate consequence of an act arising from the homosexual disposition. Likewise, the purgation of the homosexual disposition cannot be taken to show directly how to avoid acts of sodomy. Moreover, when we consider his interpretation of *Paradiso*, the doctrinal meaning Cogan imposes on the *Commedia* generates more anomalies. By interpreting Hell as the realm of acts, Purgatory as the realm of habits, and Paradise as the realm of powers, his theory dissolves the intimate relation between act, habit, and power in ethics.

Cultural Contextualism

There are two major problems with Cogan's interpretation of *Paradiso*. One is the fact that he separates power from act and habit. The other is his account of what the properties of the powers of Paradise are. The first problem concerns his interpretation of the relation between the three parts of the poem, and the second concerns his interpretation of *Paradiso*. I will start with the first question, because it naturally follows from what I have discussed until now. At the same time, an examination of that question makes it easier to see why his interpretation of *Paradiso* is problematic.

In the sphere of the Prime Mover (*Par.* 29: 31-36), Beatrice explains to Dante that the order of the created world displays, from the lowest point to the highest, an order of potency and act. The lower one gets, the more one exists in potency than in act; the higher one gets, the more one exists in act than in potency. For example, Beatrice says that the angels of Paradise are "pure act" because of their closeness to the absolute act, which is God. On this ground, Cogan says that Dante's journey is "a journey from the realm of potency toward that of act" (*DW* 271). But how are we to understand this order of potency and act, when he says that Hell is the realm of acts, Purgatory is the realm of habits, and Paradise is the realm of powers? Cogan admits that this is a paradox. In order to solve it, he turns to the question of appetitive faculties: "Hell not only shows us the appetites in their most corporeal form, it also shows them to us in their most contingent form" (*DW* 272). By this he means that Hell implicitly describes what happens when acts of sin degenerate the appetitive faculties and prevent the soul from actualizing its potentialities in the proper way. The proper way is to actualize the potentialities so that the soul can reach Paradise, whose entrance prescribes a specific order of the soul. According to Cogan, *Purgatorio* describes how this order can be attained, and *Paradiso* describes what the right order is when fully actualized.

But this interpretation does not make his insistence on the act-habit-power distinction less problematic. On the contrary, especially in considering Aquinas's explanation of the relation between act and power, Cogan's theory becomes ambiguous. In the *Summa Theologiae* (*ST* pt. 1, q. 77, aa. 1-8), Aquinas stresses that powers are known by their actions and that the essence of the soul is not its powers. The reason is that power is potency. If it is actualized, it becomes act and habit. If it is not actualized, it is nothing. It cannot be identified because it has not been actualized through an act. When Cogan speaks of act and potency in distinguishing between the highest and the lowest point of Dante's afterworld, it cannot be the Thomistic distinction he intends. If it were, he would contradict Dante as well as his own interpretation.

Since Dante insists that Paradise is the realm of actuality, it cannot be the realm of powers in the Thomistic sense, because Aquinas stresses that powers are only potentialities, and Paradise permits no potentiality, only actuality. If Cogan relied on the Thomistic distinction, he would have to admit that the acts in Hell and the dispositions in Purgatory are organized in accordance with the principle of actuality. Moreover, the sinful acts and the vicious dispositions would not be on the same level of actuality. On the contrary, the former would be on a higher level of actuality, because act is actuality and disposition lies somewhere between actuality and potentiality. Finally, Paradise would be organized in accordance with the principle of potentiality, which is a lower principle than the principle of actuality. This would be the consequence if Cogan followed medieval Aristotelianism.

But Cogan mentions no alternative to the Aristotelian tradition. He seems to suggest that Dante organized the three realms of the afterworld on the inspiration of the medieval Aristotelianism but gave the concepts of act-actuality and power-potentiality ambiguous meanings as concepts. For example, although Cogan says that Hell is organized according to acts, it cannot properly be called the realm of acts, because it is distanced from the realm of true actuality, which is Paradise. Likewise, although he says that Paradise is organized according to powers, it cannot properly be called the realm of powers, because powers are only potentialities and Paradise is full actuality. However, the reason for this ambiguity is that whereas the power-act distinction made by Aquinas and the act-potency distinction used by Dante are common medieval distinctions, Cogan's act-habit-power distinction is his own invention. He invents the distinction because he detects no direct parallels between the three realms, as far as sins, vices, and virtues are concerned.

According to Cogan, no description of a sinful act in Hell describes a vicious habit. If just one act of Hell could be related to a habit, Hell would no longer be organized strictly according to acts. Cogan's theory would collapse. If Hell occasionally thematized habits, it would no longer be the realm of acts but also of habits. Moreover, if the description of habits were not restricted to Purgatory, there would be no basis for saying that it is organized strictly according to habits, because Hell would also thematize habits. But the second circle of Hell can been seen as thematizing the intimate relation between act and disposition. This suggests that Cogan's act-habit-power distinction is a rigid distinction imposed on and not deduced from Dante's text. But why does he maintain such a rigid perspective on the poem?

I have already pointed out that Cogan's reading is problematic because his attempt to explain the ordering principles of the afterworld relies on segmental examinations, and I will further elucidate this problem in considering his account of what the properties of the powers of Paradise are. To give his reading a consistent foundation, he would have to reexamine the narrative in order to determine whether the structural constituents established by segmental readings are ultimately adequate. On this point, Seung's reading surpasses Cogan's, because Seung does not interpret the meaning of pre-established structural constituents; he also examines the thematic content of the narrative. Cogan's reliance on Aquinas displays the same interpretive inconsistency. Nowhere does he discuss whether Thomistic Aristotelianism is the proper way to substantiate or explicate Dante's philosophical and theological outlook. This problem becomes acute when Cogan argues for divergence from medieval Aristotelianism; it makes his references to it ambiguous. Cogan's reading lacks cultural contextualism. On this point, Seung's reading also surpasses Cogan's. Seung makes an extensive examination of the thematic texture of Dante's cultural context, which emphasizes that the thematic content of the *Commedia* has more in common with Bonaventure's Trinitarian theology than with Thomistic Aristotelianism. Seung also develops a theory about the principles for cultural contextualism. The former is presented in *Cultural Thematics* and the latter in *Semiotics and Thematics in Hermeneutics*.

Cogan's reliance on Thomistic Aristotelianism involves also a cultural contextualist perspective on the poem's content. Although he underlines that Dante's reading of Aristotle is often unorthodox and idiosyncratic and Dante's conception of Purgatory and Paradise is paradoxical, he regards the doctrinal content of the *Commedia* as firmly linked to the Thomistic current of medieval thought. But there is a major difference between Cogan's and Seung's identification of Dante's philosophical and theological leaning. Seung's cultural contextualist interpretation of the *Commedia* involves the theory of cultural thematics that favors the global perspective on cultural themes in historical contexts. His association of the *Commedia* with Bonaventurian theology does not emphasize proximate inspirational sources but conceptual affinities. By outlining the conceptual landscape of medieval thought in Dante's time and pointing out how he incorporates elements from different currents, Seung's account of Dante's cultural outlook also underlines the unique character of his leaning.

In defining this unique character, Seung outlines two streams of medieval Platonism. One is the Augustinian Platonism defined as the dualistic wing and characterized by the logic of discontinuity, because it maintains that the transcendent God is impossible to comprehend. The other is the Dionysian Platonism defined as the monistic wing and characterized by the logic of continuity, because it maintains that it is possible to comprehend the essence of the transcendent God through contemplation: "The development of the Latin West after the ninth century may be viewed as a dialectical interplay between the Augustinian upper current and the Dionysian undercurrent" (*CT* 59). To this Seung adds:

> The Gothic culture of the thirteenth century may be regarded as a systematic attempt to tame the rampant Dionysian ethos beneath the Augustinian yoke. Of course, in the vanguard of this battle were the followers of St. Francis and St. Dominic. In theology, the taming of the Dionysian ethos assumes two forms, that is, to reinforce the sagging authority of the Augustinian yoke, and to impose the old yoke on the new bull. St. Thomas takes the latter course, while St. Bonaventure takes the former (*CT* 69).

Cogan's study of the *Commedia* contains no such cultural contextualist specifications. His cultural contextualist perspective reflects the type of extrinsic criticism previously defined as the source-dependent method that primarily focuses on inspirational sources for local expressions. Cogan's insistence on reading the *Commedia* in the light of Thomistic Aristotelianism leads to a rigid cultural contextualist perspective that emphasizes only two options: Dante is either an orthodox or an unorthodox Aristotelian. Since this perspective is not contextually substantiated, the anomalies Cogan's reading generates may not be the outcome of an idiosyncratic use of Thomistic Aristotelianism on Dante's part; they may simply be due to Cogan's choice of interpretive perspective.

The act-habit-power distinction is a symptom of his insistence on reading the *Commedia* in the light of the logic of discontinuity. The notion that act is the proper target for infernal punishment and habit is the proper target for the purgatorial process is taken to mean that Hell is the realm of acts and Purgatory is the realm of habits. On this ground, he assumes that Paradise must be the realm of powers, because acts and habits reflect the powers of the soul. Since the distinction he imposes on the *Commedia* is not in accordance with the Thomistic act-power distinction, he concludes that Dante on this point apparently diverges from medieval Aristotelianism, although he still follows the logic of discontinuity characteristic of this current of thought.

Deficiencies and Attributes

The second problem of Cogan's interpretation of Paradise concerns the properties of the powers of Paradise. This interpretation creates more ambiguities than his invention of the act-habit-power distinction. In dealing with the virtues of Paradise, Dante scholars take often two assertions for granted. The first assertion is that the first three spheres (the Moon, Mercury, and Venus) display some sort of deficiency, because they all lie within the shadow of the earth (*Par.* 9: 118-19). This is taken to mean that the souls Dante encounters there are still marked by earthly limitations. The second assertion is that the following four spheres in some sense thematize the four cardinal virtues of prudence, fortitude, justice, and temperance. In Cogan's reading, the first assertion is fully accepted, whereas the second one is only partially accepted.

The two assertions are problematic. Later in this book I will argue extensively that both of them should be dismissed. At this point, I will only draw the attention to a particular issue that has been totally neglected by the advocates of the first assertion. The issue regards the relation between the statement about the shadow of the earth and a passage near the end of *De monarchia*. The relation in itself does not determine whether the assertion should be dismissed or not, since Dante never claims that the understanding of the former depends on the understanding of the latter. But the relation indicates the complexity of thought characteristic of Dante and underlines the superficiality of reading that marks the assertion. To claim, on the basis of the statement, that the first three spheres of the *Commedia* display some deficiency because of a certain attachment to the conditions of earthly existence is to ascribe a specific symbolic meaning to the statement. But Dante never says that it should be understood in this manner. To ascribe such meaning to the statement is therefore a matter of interpretation. That raises one simple question: Is it probable that Dante would ascribe such meaning to the first three spheres? To answer that question, it is necessary to examine the context in which the statement is made. In chapter five of this book, I will argue—on the basis of an examination of the discourse and Dante's references to Venus in the *Commedia*—that the assertion is unfounded. Instead of being the result of an attentive reading that takes account of the poem's thematic integrity, the assertion is grounded in an interpretive tradition that has never been questioned.

The passage in *De monarchia* supports the rejection of the assertion. In the treatise Dante shows that he is well aware that the question of the influence and meaning of the planetary spheres, to which the Moon, Mercury, and Venus belong, is not easily answered. In speaking of the emperor in relation to the Moon and the pope in relation to the Sun and the division of powers in temporal government, Dante emphasizes the complex qualities of the planetary spheres (III.iv): "Although the moon does not have light in abundance except in so far as it receives it from the sun, it does not follow from this that the moon derives from the sun. For it must be grasped that the moon's existence is one thing, its power another, and its function another again."[7] This is a crucial argument in the treatise. It makes part of his rejection of the assertion that the temporal power should receive its authority from the spiritual power. If it did, the pope could claim to stand above the emperor in all matters. For this reason, it is essential for Dante to distinguish between existence, power, and function.

If we take account of this distinction in considering the reference to the earth's shadow, it clearly says something about the existence of the first three spheres, but nothing about their power and function. It can be argued that in the case of the Moon, the idea of earthly attachment makes the planet the proper symbol of temporal power, because the empire is grounded in the mortal world. But Dante emphasizes that its power and function transcend the mortal world and that the authority of the emperor flows down into him without any intermediary from the fountainhead of universal authority. This notion is incompatible with the assertion that the Moon of the *Commedia* thematizes some deficiency. It makes no sense to associate an authority that stems directly from the fountainhead of universal authority with a symbol of deficiency. If we still maintain that the Moon is the proper symbol of temporal power, we have two options when we try to explain the power and function of the Moon: either Dante is inconsistent or he believes that God is inconsistent.

If the spehere of the Moon displays some deficiency in the *Commedia*, Dante's identification of the proper meaning of the symbol in *De monarchia* is inconsistent, because it ascribes deficiency to a divinely willed and guided institution. But this cannot be, because the work and power of the divine will cannot be deficient. If Dante believes that a planet whose power and function are somehow deficient is the proper symbol of the work and power of the divine will, he ascribes deficiency to the work and power of the divine will. If this is so, there is no need to expect that the *Commedia* ultimately displays a coherent vision of God's universal order because Dante no longer maintains that the universe is an ordered whole. In both cases Dante's vision of the divine order is ultimately incoherent. That is one of the consequences of asserting that the first three spheres display some deficiency. Let us point out another consequence before considering Cogan's reason for supporting the assertion.

In the *Commedia* (*Par.* 33: 104-5), Dante says that all in the Empyreum is perfect, whereas everything outside is imperfect. How are we to understand this statement when we consider the relation between the first three spheres of the geocentric realm and the three angelic orders of Angels, Archangels, and Principalities in the theocentric realm? If the spheres display deficiency, are the angelic orders also associated with deficiency? All the spheres of the superlunar region are incorruptible. The deficiency of the first three spheres cannot be due to some external influence; it has to do with the properties they represent. The souls Dante encounters in the spheres actually reside in the Empyreum, where all is perfect. But if the souls of the first three spheres display deficiency when they appear before Dante in the geocentric realm, does it mean that they are still marked by the deficiency when they move around in the theocentric realm? If so, we may ask whether the Empyreum can properly be called the realm of perfection, since deficiency is associated with the most distant triad of angels in the theocentric realm, which corresponds with the lowest triad of spheres in the geocentric realm. Cogan does not solve the problem. He only says that the relation between appearance and actual residence is paradoxical (*DW* 149-53). Thus he avoids saying that Dante's vision is ultimately incoherent, because the assignment of deficiency to the first three spheres contradicts the notion of perfection as the essential property of the Empyreum.

Given these consequences, why does Cogan still support the assertion? The reason why he incorporates it in his theory is that he wants to divide the nine spheres of the geocentric realm into three triads. These triads correspond with his association of the Moon, Mercury, and Venus with the will, the Sun, Mars, and Jupiter with the irascible, and Saturn, the Fixed Stars, and the Prime Mover with the concupiscible. Cogan uses the assertion to divide the three lowest spheres from the three middle spheres. But this insistence on triadic divisions becomes problematic when he divides the three middle spheres from the three highest spheres. He claims that the highest spheres are distinguished from the middle spheres "by being traversed by the golden ladder Jacob had seen" (*Par.* 21: 28-30) (*DW* 191). Jacob's ladder appears to Dante only when he has reached the seventh sphere, but the ladder does not divide the sixth sphere from the seventh. On the contrary, it leads up to the eighth sphere; it is the means by which Dante reaches the sphere of the Fixed Stars. For that reason, the ladder rather constitutes a divisional line between the seventh planetary heaven and the three highest heavens (*FLS* 313-32). Hence Cogan does not take account of what the text actually describes, but twists its meaning in order to promote his triadic divisions.

The reason why Cogan insists on these divisions is that he formally bases his treatment of *Paradiso* on Pseudo-Dionysius the Areopagite's exposition of the angelic hierarchies. In the *Celestial Hierarchy*, Pseudo-Dionysius divides the angels into three triads. Cogan relates these three triads to the three persons of the Trinity and their attributes in two ways. He relates them to the triads in terms of primary and secondary attributes. In support of his association of the angelic hierarchies with the Trinity, he turns to the *Convivio*, where Dante associates the hierarchies with the Trinity (II.5). Although Dante makes no explicit mention of the association, "there is no reason not to believe that he continued to be convinced of the appropriateness of the interpretation" proposed in the *Convivio* (*DW* 183). But this argument is problematic. In the *Convivio* Dante enumerates the angelic orders according to the tradition of Gregory the Great, as presented, for example, in Brunetto Latini's encyclopedia *Li livres dou Tresor* (I.12). But in canto 28 of *Paradiso*, Dante explicitly corrects this concept and says that it was Pseudo-Dionysius who contemplated the right order of angels. He further says that when Gregory died and ascended to the heavens, he realized that the Areopagite had revealed the truth and then laughed at his own mistake. The reason why Dante believes that Pseudo-Dionysius and not Gregory had contemplated the right order of angels is due to the belief that the former had been the disciple of St. Paul, who after his visit to the third heaven (*II Cor.* 12: 2-4) had revealed "this truth and many other truths" to his disciple (*Par.* 28: 98-139). Due to this conceptual change, we cannot conclude that Dante incorporates one aspect of the rejected concept of the *Convivio* in the concept of the *Commedia.*

The replacement of the Gregorian concept with the Dionysian does not necessarily imply an association of the angelic triads with the Trinity, because Pseudo-Dionysius never makes the association. Cogan admits that. But it is clear that the triadic elements of the *Celestial Hierarchy* encourage the association, and many medieval readers of Pseudo-Dionysius took it as naturally implied. At times, the two concepts were even mixed or mentioned as two alternative models. In his commentary on the *Celestial Hierarchy*, Hugh of St. Victor comments on the Dionysian model and gives it a Trinitarian interpretation. But as an alternative, Hugh mentions the Gregorian model and divides it into the three triads of the Dionysian model, although Gregory does not make such divisions. In his *Sententiae* (2 *Sententiae* 9.1), Peter Lombard applies the Gregorian model and he gives it a Trinitarian interpretation, although Gregory does not propose the association. In most commentaries on the *Sententiae* of the thirteenth century, the Dionysian model is the preferred one. This is the case in the commentaries of Bonaventure and Aquinas. But as David Keck points out, whereas the former frequently explored the Trinitarian intimations of the Dionysian hierarchies, the latter argued against a direct association on the basis of the assumption that the Trinity does not exist in a hierarchy.[8] Hence there is no uniformity in the way medieval theologians dealt with the angelic hierarchies.

To associate the angelic orders with the three persons of the Trinity on the basis of the Dionysian triads was, however, in Dante's time a common practice in angelological theology. But the absence of any direct association in the manner outlined in the *Convivio* does not mean that Dante would naturally follow the common practice of his time. To take that for granted is to regard Dante's conceptual inventiveness as limited. It is excluded that Dante could propose a concept that draws on the Dionysian tradition but results in a concept different from the tradition.

Orders and Attributes

There are two parts to the question of the celestial order of *Paradiso*. The first part is the hierarchy of the nine angelic orders, and the second part is their association with the Trinity. As we have seen, there is some difference on the first part between Gregory and Pseudo-Dionysius. As for the second part, it is inspired by Pseudo-Dionysius, who according to M.-D. Cheny provided medieval thinkers with a "total hypothesis," or a framework for understanding everything comparable to the evolution theory today, as Keck puts it.[9] Dante can have adopted the celestial hierarchy of the latter in the *Commedia* and still retained the Trinitarian association of the nine angelic orders proposed in the *Convivio*. But nowhere in the poem is it made manifest that Dante applies the Dionysian divisions. According to Cogan, Dante changes the first part but maintains the second. In contrast, Seung argues that Dante changes both the first and the second part. The result is a new theory of the relation between the angelic orders and the three persons of the Trinity. Seung suggests a radical difference between the *Convivio* and the *Commedia*, whereas Cogan argues for an affinity between the two works. But Cogan's argument is built on the assumption that the Dionysian divisions are implied in the *Commedia* and that Dante associate them with Trinity as shown in the *Convivio*. Seung's argument is not based on any particular extratextual source, but deduced from Dante's text. Hence Seung's reading respects the thematic integrity of the poem, whereas Cogan's tends to neglect it.

Cogan's argument is problematic because he does not substantiate why there should be a clear affinity between the two works. In support of his argument, he refers to a passage in Boyde's *Dante Philomythes and Philosopher*, where Boyde argues in favor of an affinity between the *Convivio* and the *Commedia*.[10] However, as it turns out, Boyde relies on Kenelm Foster. This is an example of how Dante scholars often defend assertions on the authority of other scholars with whom they share the assertions. According to Foster, *Paradiso* is in a sense "a discourse about God," who is viewed under various aspects, and underlying the variations he finds "a typical pattern of ideas," whose Trinitarian elements he points out by using Dante's description in the *Convivio*.[11] Foster emphasizes the significance of the angelic orders and their relation to the Trinity for our understanding of the structural design of Paradise. But in contrast to Boyde, he assigns no attributes to the three persons of the Trinity. He only states that the nine angelic orders contemplate the three persons. He does not consider Dante's distribution of their attributes of power, wisdom, and love in the *Convivio*. In this respect, Boyde's reading is an improvement of Foster's, because he takes account of the attributes Foster ignores. But both readings suffer from the same limited interpretive perspective on the poem in dealing with the Trinitarian elements of the *Commedia*. The Trinitarian concept stated in the *Convivio* is considered only in relation to *Paradiso*. Hence both treatments reflect the method of serial reading. Foster and Boyde basically interpret *Paradiso* as a self-contained entity. Since Cogan relies on Boyde who refers to Foster, and the method applied by both Foster and Boyde is that of serial reading, Cogan's theory of the structure of Paradise turns out to be an attempt to systematize assertions established by segmental readings.

Nevertheless, with his scheme of appetites, angelic qualities, and Trinitarian attributes, Cogan tries to determine the nature of Paradise. In order to determine which virtues are celebrated in *Paradiso*, he combines the qualities associated with the angelic creatures and their influences with the attributes associated with the three persons of the Trinity. But the result diverges considerably from the traditional scheme of Trinitarian attributes as stated in the *Convivio* and restated by Boyde. In speaking of divine attributes, Cogan does not follow the medieval tradition of the triadic scheme of the Father-power, Son-wisdom, and Spirit-love association, which, in Dante's time, was a well-established legacy that went back to Augustine. He uses the notion of Trinitarian attributes of the former in his treatment of the latter, but he does not apply the traditional attributes of power, wisdom, and love consistently to the nine heavens and angelic orders of *Paradiso*. To complicate the matter further, he adds other attributes to the three persons of the Trinity.

Cogan also diverges from the tradition by not defining the attributes unequivocally. For example, as far as the middle triad of angels is concerned, Cogan says that it is primarily associated with the Son and his attributes: "On the one hand, as the Word, he is associated with wisdom, science, and reason. On the other hand, the central event in the human life of the Son was his passion and the fortitude, even daring or courage, that it implies" (*DW* 192). Cogan argues that the souls present in the middle triad of spheres exhibit these attributes of the Son in one way or another. But since Mars, as its middle sphere, is associated with the attributes of the Son both primarily and secondarily, its souls exhibit the attributes in the most direct way. Cogan further says that "in Dante's linkage of sphere to angelic order, these souls would have their characters formed by the order of angels called virtues, and with regard to this order the quality to which Dionysius calls special attention, most appropriately, is their fortitude" (*DW* 193). Hence, in Cogan's interpretation, the Son is given more than one attribute. In the first citation he mentions the traditional attribute of wisdom stated in the *Convivio*, and in both citations he stresses fortitude. Let us consider these two attributes in order to show how arbitrary his assignment of attributes is.

In the first citation, Cogan does not make it clear whether wisdom is an attribute of the Son or only a virtue associated with or determined by the attributes of the Son. If wisdom is the attribute of the Son, it belongs to the category of primary attributes. But if it is a virtue only associated with the attributes of the Son, to what category does it then belong? This is just one of the many uncertainties Cogan's interpretation generates. The same is the case with the question of fortitude in the second citation. If it is only a virtue, Cogan should also operate with a category of virtues only associated with and not identical to the Trinitarian attributes. But he does not operate with such a category. Perhaps we are meant to infer that the categories of primary and secondary attributes are categories containing virtues that are only associated with the Trinitarian attributes. But if wisdom and fortitude are associated only with the attributes of the Son, it is unclear what the attributes of the Son are. If this is so, the attributes of the Son as well as those of the Father and the Holy Spirit are either blank checks or indeterminable. If they are blank checks, they contain no meaning, wherefore they can be given any meaning and associated with any virtue. If they are indeterminable, it means that we cannot say what they stand for and that no virtue can be associated with them. These are the consequences if the account of divine attributes is not unequivocal.

In addition, Cogan's treatment of the question of fortitude creates another problem. The problem is that he does not explicate on what ground he justifies the association of fortitude with the Son. He says that fortitude was a central aspect of the passion of the Son. By this he seems to intend that fortitude is a virtue of the Son that his passion displays. In that case, fortitude is an attribute of the Son. But why does Cogan restrict the passion of the Son only to the virtue of fortitude? The passion of the Son displays many virtues. It displays the virtue of humility even more frequently than fortitude. It displays his love of human beings because he was crucified for his love of human beings. It displays his virtue of mercy because he forgave his persecutors while on the cross. It displays his virtue of liberality because he gave his life liberally. It displays his virtue of justice because his passion was meant to be the restitution for the sin of Adam. Why are these virtues not associated with the passion of the Son in Cogan's account? The fact that he leaves them out and only takes fortitude shows how arbitrary his assignment of attributes is. It would be odd not to accept humility, love, mercy, liberality, and justice as virtues of the Son. But why are they dormant when wisdom and fortitude pop up? Cogan does not answer that question. He is not concerned with that kind of inconsistency.

Cogan emphasizes fortitude in relation to the passion of the Son because he supports the widespread assertion that the cardinal virtue of fortitude is somehow thematized in the sphere of Mars. He singles out fortitude because it fits with the interpretive tradition. The same is the case with the sphere of Jupiter. There he draws on the assertion that the sphere is somehow associated with the cardinal virtue of justice. This association, Cogan argues, is possible to establish by combining Trinitarian attributes with angelic qualities. His treatment of Mars and Jupiter displays his partial acceptance of the assertion that the cardinal virtues are somehow thematized in *Paradiso*. But since he accepts it only partially, his interpretation becomes arbitrary. In the case of the Sun and Saturn, which have often been associated with prudence and temperance, he proposes different interpretations. As for the Sun, Cogan says, its primary attribute is the wisdom of the Son, and its secondary attribute is the power of the Father. He also says that in Pseudo-Dionysius the angelic order of Powers is specifically associated with the intellect. This interpretation is an expanded version of another common assertion in Dante studies. According to this assertion, the Sun contains teachers or theologians. Cogan combines two different ways of coding the structural constituents that share the method of segmental reading. One is the use of the cardinal virtues for the fourth, fifth, sixth, and seventh spheres. The other is the demarcation of some basic characteristic that does not disclose the virtue the souls in each sphere incarnate but points to something they have in common, especially when we take account of their earthly existence. Whenever one of them is inadequate for explicating the structural constituents, he turns to the other for support.

In the case of Saturn, Cogan argues that it makes part of the highest triad, whose primary attributes are those of the Father. He does not reproduce the assertion that it somehow thematizes temperance. Instead, he identifies it as the sphere of the contemplatives. This is also a standard view in Dante studies. Cogan says that all the souls in the spheres of Saturn and the Fixed Stars (the Prime Mover contains only angels) can be said to have known God directly, without mediation. The apostles of the eighth sphere knew the Incarnate Son directly, and the contemplatives of the seventh sphere, such as Peter Damian and Benedict, came to know God directly through contemplation. According to Cogan, the notion of direct knowledge of God is what distinguishes the sphere of the theologians from that of the contemplatives. For the latter, the knowledge of God was not discursive or mediated, while it was acquired by the former. Cogan argues that the reason for this difference is that the Sun has the attributes of the Father only secondarily, whereas Saturn has them primarily as well as secondarily.

But how can the notion of direct or acquired knowledge of God be an attribute of the Father? If this is an attribute of the Father, we can also say that the Son has the attribute of being born in Bethlehem and the attribute of being crucified in Jerusalem. Anything associated with the one of the three persons of the Trinity can be turned into an attribute. The direct knowledge of God is not a divine attribute. On the contrary, it concerns man's contemplation of God. Instead of speaking of divine attributes, Cogan should be talking about human attributes. He connects the direct knowledge to the Father by saying that the Father alone can give it. By doing that, he converts the human contemplation to the divine gift. But as soon as he makes this conversion, he has to say that everything that the Father does becomes an attribute. For example, if a person reads Genesis and attains knowledge of the creation, he attains knowledge of God. According to Cogan, only the Father can provide such knowledge.

Hence the creation and the human knowledge of the creation are attributes of the Father. If this is the true meaning of attributes, it should also be true of the attributes of the Son and the Spirit. The knowledge of the passion of the Son is an attribute of the Son. In fact, every single detail of that passion can be converted into an attribute.

The whole business of attributes becomes more arbitrary when we consider Cogan's basis for associating the sphere of the contemplatives with the Father. In support of the association, he cites Pseudo-Dionysius's *Celestial Hierarchy* (VI.ii and VII.i-ii). But as noticed, Pseudo-Dionysius does not make the Trinitarian association. He speaks of God, Jesus, and spiritual aspects of the celestial hierarchy, but he does not speak of the Father, the Son, and the Holy Spirit. Hence the motive for singling out the Father as the source for direct knowledge of God is weak. Moreover, Cogan's interpretation of the distribution of divine knowledge goes also against his own theory. In his reading, the members of the church in the eighth heaven are said to have their direct knowledge of God through the Son. But the Son is not the Father, strictly speaking. Does this mean that the knowledge of the Son is only an attribute of the Father? If the members of the church have their knowledge of God through the Son, the proper object for their contemplation of God should be the Son, not the Father.

Finally, what about the ninth heaven, which contains the angelic order of the Seraphs? They are said to be associated with the attributes of the Holy Spirit. Does that mean that they have their knowledge of God through the Holy Spirit, just as the members of the church have their knowledge of God through the Son? If the divine knowledge of the former comes through the Spirit and the divine knowledge of the latter comes through the Son, why is it then necessary to stress that in both cases, the divine knowledge comes from the Father? Are the three persons of the Trinity no longer equal? Of course, Cogan does not claim that the Son and the Spirit are simply attributes of the Father. But by not solving the problems, which his assertion about the distribution of divine knowledge generates, his explication of the structure of Paradise increases our puzzlement about what Dante is trying to reveal.

Contemplation and Redemption

Given these objections, we can now see how arbitrary Cogan's application of the celestial concept of the *Convivio* to the *Commedia* is. In presenting the concept in the treatise (II.5), Dante does mainly three things: (1) he names the hierarchy of the nine angelic orders and talks about their function, (2) he speaks of the contemplation of the nine angelic orders on the Trinity, and (3) he speaks of the attributes of Trinity. (2) and (3) are given together. For example, Dante says: "For it is possible to contemplate the supreme power of the Father, upon which the first [highest] hierarchy gazes, that is, the one which is first in nobility and we count as last."[12] Then he compounds this primary assignment with a secondary assignment. He says: "Since each person of the divine Trinity can be considered in a threefold manner, there are in each hierarchy three orders that contemplate in different ways."[13] For example, the Father can be contemplated all by himself or in respect with the Son or in respect with the Holy Spirit. This secondary assignment is necessary because without it the three angelic orders of each triad would have the same contemplation of the same person. There are nine angelic orders, and Dante wants to assign a unique way of contemplating the Trinity to each one of them.

This is the original framework, from which Foster, Boyde, and Cogan derive their theories. Foster takes (2), and Boyde takes (3). However, (2) and (3) are inseparably joined together in Dante's theory. But Foster and Boyde separate them. Foster takes one side, and Boyde takes the other. Both of them disregard the secondary assignment. Cogan follows in the footsteps of Foster and Boyde, while at the same time trying to restore the secondary assignment. In his hand, the primary and secondary assignments become the primary and secondary attributes. As shown, he does one more thing. He adds more attributes to the original three attributes of power, wisdom, and love. All these moves are limited to (3). Occasionally, Cogan tries to retain something of (2) in speaking of (3). For example, as we have seen, Cogan says that the highest triad is given the direct knowledge of God. This belongs to (2) and not (3), because direct knowledge of God is not a divine attribute. By retaining something of (2) in the treatment of the highest triad, Cogan's talk about this triad becomes different from his talk about the lowest and the middle triads, which is limited to (3). Hence, in his treatment of Paradise, Cogan mixes up (2) and (3). This mixture is different from the performance of Foster and Boyde. As said, Foster takes (2), and Boyde takes (3). They do not take both at the same time. Moreover, when they occasionally try to move from (2) to (3) and the other way round, the moves are never conducted systematically. As a result, their theories are incomplete. Since Cogan wants to have both (2) and (3), his theory should be more consistent than Foster's and Boyde's. But the result is interpretive inconsistency. When Cogan takes account of (2) while focusing on (3), it is not because he maintains that (2) and (3) are inseparable. Cogan's theory could have been consistent if he had applied (2) and (3) to all the nine angelic orders. But he does not do that. He applies (2) only to the highest three orders and (3) to the lowest six orders, while now and then flavoring them with some of (2).

Finally, Cogan uses (1). He argues that the function of the angelic orders is to determine the virtues displayed in each heaven. But it is never made clear why this function should be needed if the virtues have already been determined by the divine attributes. We can only wonder why Cogan at no point takes account of the fact that in the *Convivio* (II.13), Dante also associates the seven planetary heavens with the *Trivium* and the *Quadrivium*, the eighth heaven with physics and metaphysics, the ninth heaven with moral science, and the tenth heaven with theology. The reason might be that this association cuts across the association of the first nine spheres with the nine angelic orders. It does not fit with Cogan's theory. In his eagerness to find some ground on which to interpret *Paradiso*, Cogan seems to forget that the nine angelic orders of the *Convivio* have nothing to do with Paradise. As Dante describes them in the *Convivio*, they are nine angelic orders who move the nine spheres. Dante's afterworld of Hell, Purgatory, and Paradise is an invention presented for the first time in the *Commedia*. None of these three realms of the afterworld can be found in the *Convivio*. Even in the *Commedia*, Dante says that the blessed souls actually live in the Empyreum. Paradise is not located in the nine spheres. Dante uses them to display the virtues of the blessed souls. For this reason, there is no basis for associating the nine spheres of the *Convivio* with the virtues of the blessed souls in the *Commedia*. On the basis of the *Commedia*, which displays a different concept of the celestial world than that of the *Convivio*, Cogan assumes that Dante intends something in the treatise, which he does not say.

The *Convivio* and the *Commedia* represent two different stages of Dante's intellectual development. To emphasize the major difference between the two works, as far as the role of the Trinity is concerned, I propose two technical expressions: the contemplation scheme and the redemption scheme. When Dante discusses the nine angelic orders in the *Convivio*, he describes the contemplation scheme—that is, how the nine angelic orders contemplate the three persons of the Trinity. The three attributes of power, wisdom, and love are presented as the objects of angelic contemplation. In the *Commedia*, however, Dante describes how the three persons are engaged in the redemption of human beings. The redemption scheme is fully elaborated in Seung's interpretation of the role of the Trinity in the *Commedia*. Seung argues that the virtues of the blessed souls are ultimately derived from the Trinity. The virtues of the blessed souls are the consequences of the divine redemption project. The redemption scheme, however, is not necessary for the *Convivio*, because Dante is concerned only with the relation of the angelic orders to the Trinity, and angels do not need redemption. But the redemption scheme is paramount for the *Commedia*, because it is devoted to the problem of redemption.

Let us return to the theories of Foster, Boyde, and Cogan and see how they take account of these two schemes. Foster takes over the contemplation scheme from the *Convivio* and does not notice its inadequacy for the problem of redemption in the *Commedia*. Boyde's theory looks different because he mentions the divine attributes of the three persons. It can be taken to refer to the contemplation scheme or to the redemption scheme. For example, Boyde asserts that the three lowest spheres are primarily dedicated to love and the Holy Spirit. This can be taken either in the contemplation or in the redemption scheme. It can be taken to mean that the three lowest spheres are dedicated to the contemplation of the Holy Spirit, or that they are dedicated to the works of the Holy Spirit and love in the redemption of sinful souls. But since Boyde does not clarify this difference, it is likely that he follows the contemplation scheme. He advocates the retention of the *Convivio* doctrine for the reading of the *Commedia*. Finally, in Cogan's reading, the contemplation and the redemption scheme get mixed up. He uses the redemption scheme for the first two triads and the contemplation scheme for the highest triad.

Seung uses the redemption scheme in his interpretation of the *Commedia*. In this regard, Seung's reading is fundamentally different from Foster's and Boyde's. Before Cogan, Seung was the only one to advocate the redemption scheme of the Trinity in interpreting the *Commedia*. Hence, when Cogan applies it, his reading seems inspired by Seung's. But since Cogan's application is inconsistent, he has not got the redemption scheme right. The problem of determining the relation of virtues to divine attributes arises only in the redemption scheme. In the contemplation scheme, the question concerns only the possibility of contemplating the divine attributes or virtues. In the redemption scheme, however, this question turns into the problem of determining how the divine attributes or virtues are related to the virtues of the blessed souls.

Let us consider this problem in relation to the question of primary and secondary attributes. If we only contemplate the attribute of the Father (power) as the primary attribute and the attribute of the Son (wisdom) as the secondary attribute, we do not run into any conflict of attributes. But if we try to figure out the relation between these attributes in determining the virtues of the blessed souls in the different spheres, we face the problem of deciding which attribute overrules which attribute. This problem becomes complicated when we have more than one attribute for the primary and secondary attributes. For example, if the Son has three or four attributes, we can contemplate them all without any problem. But if these attributes determine the virtues of the blessed souls on the Sun, we have to decide which of them should overrule the others.

Virtues and Soul

In speaking of Cogan's demarcation of the virtues thematized in the three triads, another thing should be noticed because it complicates further the doctrine he imposes on the *Commedia*. His association of fortitude and justice with Mars and Jupiter does not imply that these virtues are strictly speaking those normally identified as the cardinal virtues. With his combination of angelic qualities and Trinitarian attributes in determining the virtues displayed in the other spheres, he emphasizes that all virtues of Paradise are supernatural. As we have seen, Cogan argues that Hell punishes sinful acts and Purgatory purges vicious habits. As far as the purgation is concerned, he further adds that Purgatory does not merely transform "mundane vices" into their conventional counterparts, "the mundane virtues," but into "ultramundane virtues" (*DW* 125). By this he means that the virtues Dante describes in *Paradiso* transcend all human understanding of virtues. They constitute a different set of virtues than the one we might have expected to find, because the preparation of the soul for the heavenly bliss is described as implying the purgation of the seven capital sins into their counterparts. For this reason, we might have expected to find the seven capital virtues celebrated in *Paradiso*. But in Cogan's view, this is not the case. For example, the purgation of the vice of pride into the virtue of humility on the first terrace does not mean that humility is thematized as a supernatural virtue in one of the spheres of *Paradiso*.

In support of the idea that *Paradiso* thematizes a different set of virtues than the one found in *Purgatorio*, Cogan draws the attention to the fact that the seven Beatitudes Dante uses in demarcating the seven capital virtues on the seven terraces are in fact six. On the fifth and the sixth terrace, Dante uses the Beatitude that begins "Blessed are they who hunger and thirst." The angel of the fifth terrace sings "Blessed are they who thirst" (*Purg*. 22: 1-6), and the angel of the sixth terrace sings "Blessed are they who hunger" (*Purg*. 24: 151-54). Cogan argues that through sharing Beatitude, Dante wants to signal that avarice shares with gluttony an underlying, authentically concupiscent nature (*DW* 114). This is in accordance with what he has previously said about the sinful acts of gluttony and avarice in Hell. But he also takes the sharing of the Beatitude as indicating a significant change that gradually takes place in Purgatory. According to Cogan, this change implies that *Purgatorio* should be interpreted in two ways—in the light of sin and in the light of Heaven. The use of the same Beatitude indicates that "while Dante sees the purgatorial process as one of replacing vices with virtues, he is at the same time deliberately substituting a new set of virtues for an older one" (*DW* 124).

Cogan outlines this new set of virtues by combining angelic qualities and Trinitarian attributes. But it is by no means clear what this new set of virtues consists of. The combination of angelic qualities and Trinitarian attributes leads to a far-reaching reinterpretation of the presence of the three appetites in Paradise. This reinterpretation is due to his insistence on seeing Purgatory from two different perspectives. On the one hand, he says that it is manifestly relevant to pious action in this world that the source of vices and sins is designated as disorders of the appetitive faculties: "Medieval interpretations of Aristotelian ethics stressed the goal of bringing the appetitive powers into properly orderly operation." On the other hand, Cogan argues that the same cannot be said of the souls of Purgatory:

> They are not returning to the world of action. The narrative insists that their rehabilitation is for the sake of their entry into Heaven . . . Rectification of the appetites by which action is initiated in this world scarcely seems relevant to that new life. These appetitive faculties would seem to have to disappear, and even their virtues with them, for want of any function to perform in Heaven (*DW* 121).

In support of this view, Cogan cites a passage from Aquinas (*ST* pt. 1-2, q. 67, a. 1), and stresses that the medieval Aristotelianism Dante follows denies that the sensitive appetites endure after death:

> All that could be eternal in human soul, according to this tradition, were its intellectual faculties, reason and will foremost among them. The sensitive faculties (whether of apprehension, as the five senses, or of appetition, the concupiscible and irascible appetites) would, because of their dependence on the body, have to disappear almost entirely with the body's death. And, as they perished, so did their virtues (*DW* 121).

In support of this view, Cogan once again cites Aquinas (pt. 1, q. 77, a. 8) who argues that when the human body is destroyed, the powers of the sensitive and nutritive parts of the soul do not remain actually but only virtually in the soul.

For Cogan's reading of *Paradiso*, this Thomistic notion implies that the order of the third realm appears to be the same as the order of the human appetites, but its ultimate order "must be understood in a way appropriate to the wholly intellectual nature of both angels and souls whom we encounter in Heaven" (*DW* 223). This means that the presence of the three appetites in the structure of Paradise is not real or actual but rather virtual or potential. But since this goes against the notion of Paradise as the realm of actuality, we are stuck in a contradiction. For that reason, the properties of the powers cannot be the appetites. But Cogan says that Hell and Purgatory share a common structure on the level of appetites. He also says that the appearance of this structure is different in the two realms, because in Hell it is manifest in the order of sinful acts, whereas in Purgatory it is manifest in the order of vicious habits under purgation. But what about Paradise?

Cogan argues that the angelic characters are described in a way relative to the operations of the human appetites. The appetites should become detectable in the structure of Paradise through the qualities associated with the angelic orders. For example, the irascibility associated with the middle triad is, in Cogan's view, echoed in the descriptions of the Dominions, the angels of the sphere of Jupiter. At the same time he uses other arbitrary associations of the triads with the Trinity in order to bring forth other appetitive aspects in the structure of Paradise. For example, he argues that since the Dominions, on the secondary level of Trinitarian attributes, are associated with the Holy Sprit, and the Holy Spirit is associated with the will, the Dominions are also associated with the will, though only secondarily. With this double association, Cogan finds a way to explain why Dominions in the Dionysian tradition are said to exercise their dominion humbly. Since the virtue of humility in Purgatory is, according to Cogan, apparently associated with the will, and the will is apparently associated with the Holy Spirit, the reason why the exercise is humble is that the secondary attributes of the Dominions are those of the Holy Spirit.

Hence Cogan turns to Purgatory in order to explain why the sixth sphere thematizes humility. But is that thc proper way to explain why the Dominions apparently exercise their dominion humbly? Has he forgotten his own claim that the purgation of the "mundane vice" of pride does not lead to the "mundane virtue" of humility but to some sort of "ultramundane virtue"? Is the virtue of humility achieved in Purgatory different from the one displayed in Paradise? If it is different, what should it then be called? Is it an attribute of the Holy Spirit or an ultramundane virtue only associated with attributes of the Holy Spirit? Perhaps Cogan only intends to say that humility is a virtue of the will when realized in the mortal world. But if this is so, we would expect to find it explicated in his treatment of how the lowest triad of the celestial hierarchy is still somehow related to the world of earthly existence. But the explication does not mention humility. Since humility makes part of the influence of the Dominions, which are associated with the Holy Spirit, though only secondarily, we can only wonder why it is apparently dormant or perhaps even absent in the lowest triad, which is associated with the will, and whose primary attributes are those of the Holy Spirit.

It is clear that when Cogan says that Paradise is organized according to powers, it is not the appetitive faculties of the tripartite soul he has in mind. The powers influence the human faculties, but their properties are not concupiscence, irascibility, and volition. The properties of the powers are the attributes of the Trinity. The angelic orders transmit these properties to the world of the living through the celestial motions. These transmissions are the workings of divine providence, which, along with nature, determine the character of each human being. When the soul of a human being is influenced by the powers, certain qualities of their properties are imprinted in the soul. The imprint is unique for every soul, wherefore every soul is unique. To be sure, all souls have the same end, but the routes they take or the choices they make in order to reach that end are never the same, because the human will is free.

Cogan argues that when the human soul is imprinted with a certain quality, the quality is imprinted in a certain part of the soul, because the property of the power from which the quality originates is associated with a certain faculty, when it is imprinted in the human soul. For example, Cogan argues that the primary properties of the power associated with the Dominions are those identified with the attributes of the Son—namely, fortitude and perseverance (*DW* 196). He further argues that these properties are associated with the irascible faculty, when imprinted as qualities in the human soul. But according to Cogan, the power associated with the Dominions does not only influence the irascible faculty of the human soul. The influence of the Dominions is also associated with the Holy Spirit by way of secondary attributes—namely, charity and justice—and these attributes are associated with the faculty of the will when imprinted in the human soul. Therefore, the power that the Dominions transmit to the world of the living is also imprinted as a quality in the faculty of the will.

According to Cogan, this explains why the souls Dante encounters in the sphere of Jupiter are different from those in the other two spheres of the middle triad of angelic orders, whose primary attributes are also those of the Son, but whose secondary attributes are those of the Father (the Sun) and those of the Son (Mars), associated with the concupiscible and the irascible faculty, respectively. The difference is due to the combination of primary and secondary attributes and their association with the human faculties. This combination provides a doctrinal explanation to the theme of just rule displayed in the sphere of Jupiter. In Cogan's view, just rule implies a combination of the virtues of fortitude and perseverance and the virtues of charity and justice, and at the same time it implies a balance between the irascible faculty and the faculty of the will in the manner prescribed by the power transmitted by the Dominions. Hence, according to Cogan, Dante conceives just rule as requiring especially fortitude and perseverance of the irascible faculty sustained by charity and justice of the faculty of the will.

The same principle, Cogan argues, applies also to the qualities that the other properties of the powers imprint in the human soul. The combination of primary and secondary attributes and their association with the faculties of the soul makes each power different from all the others. But since the attributes of the three persons of the Trinity are somehow present in each triad, there are also cross-relations between the three triads. For example, Cogan argues, due to the charity of the Holy Spirit associated with Venus, Jupiter, and the Prime Mover as their secondary attribute, these three spheres all share an association with love:

> What in the shadow of the earth first appears in the third sphere as terrestrial love, naturally contingent and particular, finds echoes and comparisons in the sixth sphere in the ultramundane love of justice that directs communities, and ultimately, in the ninth sphere, in a simple and immediate love of God, that is, in fact, beyond human capacity, and of which only angels are truly capable of (*DW* 217).

If this is so, similar cross-relations should be detectable in the relations between the Moon, the Sun, and Saturn, and between Mercury, Mars, and the Fixed Stars. But Cogan does not systematically explain the other cross-relations. For this reason, it remains uncertain whether the cross-relations always occur or whether they are not always significant. As a result, the whole business of attributes becomes extremely complicated and arbitrary. There is nothing left of the medieval assumption that the order of the divine things are ultimately simply, although they appear complex to human beings.[14]

As mentioned, Cogan associates especially the two virtues of charity and justice with the Holy Spirit. The association of charity or love with the Spirit is traditional, but justice is Cogan's addition. As we have seen, he also associates the virtue of humility with the Spirit, because the Spirit is associated with the will. That is also an addition to the traditional view of attributes. In speaking of the lowest triad of angels, he also says that the nature of these angels is particularly adapted to the role of communication. If this is so, communication seems to be a virtue associated with the attributes of the Spirit, which the triad has primarily. This is yet another addition on Cogan's part. But at no point does he explain systematically the presence of these different attributes or virtues in the different sections associated with the Holy Spirit. For example, the virtue of communication is not mentioned in his treatment of the sphere of Jupiter. Is it because the primary attributes of the Son have eliminated or overpowered the virtue of communication? Cogan makes no effort to explain the exact relation between primary and secondary attributes. In his treatment of the lowest triad, he only speaks of love and communication, not of humility and justice. Finally, in his treatment of the angelic order of Seraphs in the Prime Mover, he speaks of love, not justice, humility, or communication. Similar problems occur in his treatment of the other virtues associated with the Father and the Son, both primarily and secondarily. For that reason, in the end, Cogan's association of virtues with the Trinity turns out to be a will-o'-the-wisp. It is totally arbitrary as soon as it diverges from the medieval tradition of the triadic scheme of the Father-power, Son-wisdom, and Spirit-love association, and when Cogan begins to make his own additions.

On the basis of the Thomistic notion of the disappearance of the sensitive and nutritive powers of the soul at the death of the body, Cogan argues that liberality and temperance have no place in Paradise. They are only mundane virtues opposed to the mundane vices of avarice and gluttony purged in Purgatory. To be sure, in the celestial world the blessed souls are not going to worry about food and clothing. Therefore their virtues cannot be employed in handling such earthly matters. But that does not mean that their virtues of liberality and temperance have no place for their celestial life. They can still be applicable to celestial matters. The fact that Aquinas stresses that the sensitive and nutritive powers remain virtually in the soul after the body is destroyed indicates that any quality or virtue that can be associated with those parts can still be important for the celestial life. Consider, for example, the virtue of justice. In Paradise this virtue cannot be used for distributing material goods or for punishing criminals, but it can still be needed for maintaining the justice of the celestial world. The same can also be the case with liberality and temperance as well as the other virtues achieved by the penitents in Purgatory.

Particular and Universal Judgment

In dealing with the nature of Paradise, Cogan confuses two questions. On the one hand, there is the question of which virtues are needed for the celestial life. What is the spiritual condition of the soul once it has entered Paradise? But that is not the same as to ask which virtues are needed for entering Paradise. The description of the purgation of the seven capital sins into their counterparts makes it clear what is needed for salvation, but it does not reveal how the celestial life is in all its actuality. In addition, there is the question what kind of virtues Dante describes when he ascends the celestial spheres. In the *Commedia* Dante never raises or discusses the question of which virtues are needed for the celestial life. It is therefore irrelevant. The only important question is which virtues are displayed in *Paradiso* and which virtues Cogan recognizes in his reading of *Paradiso*.

That Dante does not discuss the virtues needed for the celestial life makes perfect sense, given the fact that what he describes is the world of particular judgment, not the world of universal judgment. He cannot know the life of the latter, because it has not occurred. It is inconceivable to man, because the ways of the Lord are inscrutable. Hence, if Dante wants to say something sensible about the order of divine justice, he can deal with it only as it appears to man when he considers the doctrines concerning particular judgment. In *Purgatorio* Dante shows that the purgation of the seven capital sins is necessary for entering Paradise. He shows what is needed for the salvation of particular judgment. To say more than that is to deal with the salvation of universal judgment. But that is impossible for man. What happens at universal judgment is inconceivable to man.

With his notion of primary and secondary attributes, Cogan argues that what Dante describes in *Paradiso* is the virtuous state of the celestial life, somehow consistent with life at universal judgment. But since the conditions of that life cannot be fully determined, Cogan argues that

Paradiso only describes glimpses of what makes up the celestial life. Due to this idea that the attributes only occur as glimpses in the different sections of Paradise, Cogan finds it justified to assign different virtues or attributes to each section and vary their number for each section, both on the primary and on the secondary level. But what Cogan regards as glimpses of the divine attributes are in fact reflections of the ambiguities and anomalies that characterize segmental interpretations of the structural constituents of the afterworld, which he tries to systematize with his assignment of virtues or attributes. For this reason, Cogan's reading of the *Commedia* can hardly be said to show its readers, as the back cover of the book claims, "how to discover the single consistent principle which organizes each part and the poem overall." Cogan presents a theory about how the poem is organized, but the principle he detects is not consistent. Due to the ambiguities and anomalies arising from his way of coding the structure of the afterworld, there is no consistent principle that holds together three parts and constitutes them as a coherent vision of God's universal order. Therefore, if Cogan is right, his reading fully justifies Petrocchi's verdict on Dante that, as a poet, he was particularly gifted, but as a theologian, he was not.

Notes

1. J. A. Weisheipl, "Classification of the Sciences in Medieval Thought," in *Medieval Studies* 27 (1965), 82-87.
2. Bonaventura, "The Journey of the Mind to God," in *The Works of Bonaventure, Vol. I: Mystical Opuscula*, trans. J. de Vinck (Patterson, N.J.: St. Anthong Guild Press, 1960); Thomas Aquinas, *Aristotelian Commentary Series, Vol. I: Commentary on Aristotle's Nicomachean Ethics*, trans I. C. Litzinger (Notre Dame, Ind.: Dumb Ox Books, 1993).
3. *DDP* Singleton on *Inf.* 32: 88.
4. Peter King, "Ockham's Ethical Theory," in *The Cambridge Companion to Ockham*, ed. Paul Vincent Spade (Cambridge: Cambridge University Press, 1999), 229-31.
5. *DDP* Singleton on *Inf.* 5: 52-60.
6. *DDP* Singleton on *Inf.* 5: 96.
7. Dante Alighieri, *Monarchy*, trans. Prue Shaw (Cambridge: Cambridge University Press, 1996), 72.
8. David Keck, *Angels & Angelology in the Middle Ages* (Oxford: University of Oxford Press, 1998), 54.
9. Marie-Dominique Cheny, *Nature, Man, and Society in the Twelfth Century: Essays on New Theological Perspectives in the Latin West*, trans. J. Taylor

and L. K. Little (Chicago: University of Chicago Press, 1968), 82, and David Keck, *Angels & Angelology*, 53.

10. Patrick Boyde, *Dante: Philomythes and Philosopher: Man in the Cosmos* (Cambridge: Cambridge University Press, 1981), 187.

11. Kenelm Foster, *The Two Dantes and Other Studies* (Berkeley: University of California Press, 1977), 121-22 and 140.

12. Dante Alighieri, *Dante's Il Convivio (The Banquet)*, trans. Richard H. Lansing (New York: Garland Publishing, 1990), 51.

13. Dante Alighieri, *Dante's Il Convivio*, 52.

14. For more on this issue, see Jesper Hede, "Unity and Difference in Dante's Universal Vision," in *Classica et Mediaevalia* 57 (2006), 239-81.

Chapter Four

Fragile Leaves of the Sibyl

Cogan's interpretation of the *Commedia* is the most qualified response to Seung's theory, but it is mainly displayed in the notes to his study. Nowhere does Cogan explicitly discuss his opposition to Seung's theory. The two theories are different both in terms of substance and in terms of method of inquiry. Cogan's method is the source-dependent reading of episodes, segments, or series, while Seung's method is the method of cultural thematics, which implicates a strong emphasis on the global perspective on the cultural texture of the poem's historical context (*STH* ix-xi). In determining the poem's thematic meaning, Seung's method of cultural thematics emphasizes the significance of conceptual affinities between the thematic content and the cultural texture. There are two premises for the determination of such affinities. First, it requires a comprehensive understanding of the poem's thematic content. Second, it requires a comprehensive understanding of the cultural texture of the poem's historical context. The former is accomplished in *The Fragile Leaves of the Sibyl* and the latter in *Cultural Thematics*. In *Semiotics and Thematics in Hermeneutics* Seung explicates the principles of his method of reading and historical understanding. He argues for decisive coherence between his textual interpretation and historical understanding. Such coherence is the basic criterion for evaluating the formal merit of any interpretation. Its substantive merit, however, depends on the adequacy of both the textual interpretation and the historical understanding.

The focus on conceptual affinities does not involve the neglect of inspirational sources. These are considered to be significant indications of how the text is constructed and elucidate the author's creative process and contribute to the explication of the thematic content of the text. But since the investigation of inspirational sources is primarily confined to particular textual units, it seldom moves beyond the local perspective. On the local level, if such an investigation is productive, the result can be defined as concordant with the formal criterion for interpretive adequacy, because it establishes coherence between a textual passage and an inspirational source. But the investigation deals only with a local entity. It is not possible to verify whether the result is concordant with the substantive criterion. In order to verify that criterion, it is necessary to consider the result within the global context of meaning. Such a context involves a comprehensive understanding of both the poem's thematic meaning and its cultural context. Local inquiries are therefore subsidiary to global considerations. Global meaning presupposes inquiries into local entities, but the meaning of these entities can be established only on the basis of the global understanding.

The predominance of the restrictive and source-dependent method of reading is one of the main reasons why Seung's theory has not gained support in Dante studies. With the source-dependent reading it seems excluded that the reader can achieve a resourceful understanding of the *Commedia* if he attempts the kind of interpretive experiment I. A. Richards explored in the 1920s when he made students analyze poems without extratextual foreknowledge.[1] In *Semiotics and Thematics in Hermeneutics* Seung says that *The Fragile Leaves of the Sibyl* was inspired by two Richardian principles: (1) the principle of textual fidelity, and (2) the principle of interpretive coherence. The former prescribes that the reader should be faithful to what is in the text and let it reveal itself. The latter implies the assertion that the entire range of thematic references (implicit and explicit) can be articulated only by appealing to the principle of textual and thematic coherence (*STH* 170). In *Cultural Thematics* Seung says that the application of these two principles was inspired by "the Brooks-Winsatt stronghold of New Criticism in New Haven" (*CT* xiv).

But in spite of the influence of New Criticism, Seung's Dante reading is not an example of intrinsic literary criticism. He interprets Dante's text without depending on the problems Dante scholars regard as those that need to be addressed. In this respect, Seung's reading can be defined as "experimental" in the Richardian sense. By appealing to the principle of textual and thematic coherence, he stresses the significance of the poem's thematic integrity for the interpretive act. The result is not a reading that disregards contextual understanding. Seung emphasizes that the merit of phenomenological reading depends on how it accords with the understanding of the historical and cultural context. Although *The Fragile Leaves of the Sibyl* was inspired by intrinsic criticism and *Cultural Thematics* was inspired by extrinsic criticism, the contextual understanding of the latter represents in all a continuation of the textual analysis of the former. In *Structuralism and Hermeneutics* Seung examines the tension between intrinsic and extrinsic criticism, and in *Semiotics and Thematics in Hermeneutics* he presents a theory of how the two positions can be combined and the tension resolved. As a result, Seung's Dante reading is not only a literary analysis of the text of the *Commedia*; it also involves an interpretation of its cultural context and a commitment to a specific theory for literary criticism and historical understanding. Seung's interpretive theory is not only a theory; it has been practiced on the text and context of Dante's *Commedia.*

For these reasons, Seung's reading of the *Commedia* occupies a unique position in Dante studies. In many studies of Dante's poem interpretive suggestions are made on the basis of principles that are only implied and seldom explicated theoretically. Due to the development of his interpretive activity and theory from *The Fragile Leaves of the Sibyl* to *Semiotics and Thematics in Hermeneutics*, the study of Seung's Dante reading cannot be reduced to a discussion of his textual analysis in *The Fragile Leaves of the Sibyl.*

Structure and Thematic Content

A decade before Seung published his Dante reading, Morton W. Bloomfield made the following statement in *The Seven Deadly Sins*:

> The most important section of the *"Purgatorio"* (Cantos X-XXVI) is built around our concept [i.e., the seven deadly sins], and some investigators have attempted to find the cardinal sins in the scheme of punishments in the *"Inferno."* This last attempt seems to me, as well as to more competent Dante scholars, to be forcing material into a preconceived mold.

Bloomfield admits that several of the chief sins can be found in *Inferno*, but he sees no reason to assume that the sins make part of a consciously applied system of classification in the first part of the poem.[2] Bloomfield's statement can be read as a warning against what Seung proposes in *The Fragile Leaves of the Sibyl.* But Bloomfield's treatment of the seven capital sins is so committed to the source-dependent method of reading that he is incapable of handling issues that are only implied and not overtly stated. Due to his commitment, he claims that the general merging of the capital and deadly sins did not take place until the fifteenth and sixteenth centuries, although the identification of the two labels were made by Aquinas in his two *Summae.*[3] Dante never says that the notion of capital sins is the system of classification of sins in *Inferno*, but from that it does not follow that the system cannot be implied. Seung argues that Dante is saying all that is essential and necessary except the things that are obvious; he leaves the meaning of the poem to our intuitive understanding; he does not overtly reveal the right order of things but incarnates it in the poem (*FLS* 327). In short, the poem's ultimate theme may not be overtly stated (*STH* 142).

According to Seung's theory, Hell, Purgatory, and Paradise are not three separate entities. They are three diverse but interrelated manifestations of the powers of God's universal order. The state of sin in Hell and the state of virtue in Paradise are directly opposed consequences of human behavior. As such, the two realms are fundamentally diverse: "Damnation is the actualization of the soul in the material and natural order, and salvation is the actualization of the soul in the spiritual and supernatural order. The soul achieves its natural end in the former, and its supernatural end in the latter" (*FLS* 77). At the same time Hell and Paradise are uniform in that they both show the state of the souls as fixed and stationary. In the former the souls have received their reward in punishment; in the latter they await for God's final kingdom, but their finality is settled. The finality constitutes the affinity between the two realms by way of opposition. The evilness depicted in *Inferno* is contrasted to the goodness portrayed in *Paradiso*.

Purgatory, however, is diverse from Hell and Paradise insofar as the purgation of sin to virtue involves transition. But the notion of transition constitutes an affinity between the three realms. Purgatory is related to Hell and Paradise because it elaborates on the notion of opposition between sin and virtue. In Hell and Paradise, this notion is revealed in terms of unchanging conditions. In Purgatory it is revealed in terms of transitory conditions. The latter stands out as the link between the lower world of infernal darkness and the higher world of heavenly light. Purgatory is partly related to Hell, because the transition from sin to virtue takes place in a world that is still attached to the lower world of darkness. Yet it is partly opposed to Hell, because it is directed toward the higher world of light. In like manner, Purgatory is partly related to Paradise, because the transition from sin to virtue involves a movement away from the world of darkness toward the world of light. Yet it is opposed to Paradise, because the movement from darkness to light has not been concluded.

The basic principle for this pattern of thought can be defined as oppositional thinking: sins are opposed to virtues, just as darkness is the opposite of light and death is the opposite of life. Aquinas's *Summa The-*

ologiae demonstrates this pattern of thought. In the second part of the second book, he explores it under the heading of the three theological virtues of faith, hope, and charity and the four cardinal virtues of prudence, justice, fortitude, and temperance. In the *Summa* the method of oppositional thinking plays an important part in the determination and definition of sins and virtues. The oppositions constitute a pattern by which to investigate and discuss significant elements of the divine order. But the *Summa* is not unique in this respect. Oppositional thinking was a basic feature of medieval thought. It is manifest in the invention of the literary genre of the treatise on vices and virtues.

The genre is characteristic of medieval Christendom. It finds only few counterparts in the Jewish and Islamic cultures.[4] The inspirational background was the rabbinical literature of the first century BC. But it was not until the fourth century AD that the genre was invented by the Egyptian Christian mystic Evagrius Ponticus, who stressed the existence of a specific number of basic evil forms of behavior.[5] Evagrius was the first to formulate the concept of primary sins within the context of Eastern monasticism. John Cassian played an important role in the transmission of the Evagrian corpus into Western monasticism, where the *tractatus de vitiis et virtutibus* early gained lasting popularity. The existence of around seven hundred manuscripts of Martin of Braga's *Formula vitae honestae* from the second part of the sixth century shows the popularity of the genre.[6]

Evagrius originally enumerated eight major sins. But from Gregory the Great, who was the first to make the concept accessible to a larger non-monastic audience, and to the end of the medieval period, the number of capital or deadly sins was basically identified as seven. The order was never stable nor the terminology fixed. But the general pattern was that they consisted in lust, gluttony, avarice, sadness (or sloth), wrath, envy, and vainglory.[7] The seven sins were regarded as stemming from the same source. Pride or *superbia* was the root of all sins; it caused Satan's fall from the Heaven and the expulsion of Adam and Eve from the Earthly Paradise (*ST* pt. 2-2, q. 162, aa. 7-8; pt. 2-2, q. 163, a. 1). Among the contributors to the development of the genre, we find Alcuin, Fulbert of Chartres, Bernard of Clairvaux, Hugo of Saint-Victor, Grosseteste, William of Auvergne, and Jean Gerson. Treatises were ascribed to Alexander of Hales, Albertus Magnus, and Bonaventura. Besides Greek and Latin, many of the treatises were written in vernaculars. William Peraldus's *Summa de vitiis et virtutibus* written around the middle of the thirteenth century has even been seen as a possible source for Dante's system of classification.[8]

Nevertheless, despite the affinity between oppositional thinking, which was intrinsic in the cultural texture of Dante's times, and the basic features of Dante's afterworld, Seung is the only one who has ever systematically tried to apply this type of thinking to the structure of Dante's afterworld and its thematic content. It is the basic principle for his systematic parallel reading. But it is only a formal aspect of his explication of the poem's thematic coherence. According to Seung, the basic structural element of the *Commedia* is not the account of a journey; it is the coherent vision of universal order. The hero of the epic drama is not Dante the traveler, but the Holy Trinity. The primary subject is not the state of the souls after death, but the manifestation of the Trinity in all things. The ultimate theme is not the traveler's progressive realization of the divine truth, but the actions of the Trinity in the all-encompassing whole. As a result of his Trinitarian reading, Seung argues that Dante's use of the fourfold allegory (literal, allegorical, moral, and anagogical), which he defines as "poetic figuralism," has three interrelated dimensions:

> [the] three spiritual senses revolve around the Three Persons of the Holy Trinity: the allegorical sense is the figural representation of their works in this world (the macrocosmic dimension); the moral sense is the figural representation of their works in the individual soul (the microcosmic dimension); and the anagogical sense is the figural representation of their works in the Kingdom of Heaven (the supracosmic dimension) (*CT* 48).

Hence oppositional thinking is only a formal aspect of the poem's structural thematics; the substantive aspect is the Trinitarian principles that govern the oppositional thinking.

Seung argues that Hell, Purgatory, and Paradise are organized in accordance with the medieval table of seven natural virtues (humility, mercy, meekness, fortitude, liberality, temperance, and chastity) and three supernatural virtues (faith, hope, and charity) and their contraries. These ten natural and supernatural virtues and their contraries constitute ten steps on the ladder of grace divided into two sections—the natural and the supernatural. The seven natural virtues and their contraries constitute the seven steps of the natural section, and the three supernatural virtues and their contraries constitute the three steps of the supernatural section (*CT* 43-44). Seung combines these ten virtues and their contraries with the notions of the tripartite soul (and its powers) and the triune God.

Humility and mercy and their contraries (pride and envy) are related to the spiritual part of the soul (and the power of the intellect) and associated with the Son. These natural qualities are thematized in the ninth and eight circles, on the first and second terraces, and in the spheres of the Moon and Mercury. Meekness and fortitude and their contraries (wrath and sloth) are related to the sensitive part (and the irascible power) and associated with the Holy Spirit. These natural qualities are thematized in the seventh, sixth, and fifth circles, on the third and fourth terraces, and in the heavens of Venus and the Sun. Liberality, temperance, and chastity and their contraries (avarice, gluttony, and lust) are related to the vegetative part (and the concupiscible power) and associated with the Father. These natural qualities are thematized in the fourth, third, and second circles, on the fifth, sixth, and seventh terraces, and in the heavens of Mars, Jupiter, and Saturn. Faith is related to the spiritual part (and the power of the intellect) and associated with the Son. This supernatural quality is thematized on four occasions: as absent in Limbo and as present in the upper section of the Ante-Purgatory; it is celebrated with the procession in the Terrestrial Paradise and shown in purity in the heaven of the Fixed Stars. Hope is related to the sensitive part (and the irascible power) and associated with the Holy Spirit. This supernatural quality is thematized on four occasions: as absent in the Vestibule of Hell and as present in the middle section of the Ante-Purgatory; it is celebrated with the tribulations of the chariot in the Terrestrial Paradise and shown in purity in the heaven of the Prime Mover. Finally, charity is related to the vegetative part (and the concupiscible power) and associated with the Father. This supernatural quality is thematized on four occasions: as absent at the entrance of Hell and as present in the lower section of the Ante-Purgatory; it is celebrated with the fountainhead of Lethe and Eunoe in the Terrestrial Paradise and shown in purity in the heaven of the Empyreum.

In the natural section of the ladder of grace, each of the three parts of the soul is associated with more than one virtue or sin. In order to understand how each part of the soul is associated with more than one virtue or sin, Seung makes two distinctions. First, he distinguishes between active and passive expressions of the powers of the souls. Second, he distinguishes between virtues and sins that are private or individual, and virtues and sins that are public or communal. These two distinctions represent two ways of demarcating the qualities of the different virtues and sins described in the *Commedia*. The virtues and sins of the active power of the soul can be called private or individual virtues and sins because their chief domain and concern are the individuals in privacy. The virtues and sins of the passive power can be called public or communal because their chief domain and concern are the communities in public (*FLS* 34-59).

Seung explains the distinction between active and passive expressions of the powers of the souls with reference to the difference between subject and object in Thomistic thought. The three powers of the soul (the intellectual, the irascible, and the concupiscible) are the subjects of act. The soul acts through these three powers, but it requires objects for its act: "The relation between the subject and the object can be either active or passive. The active act is called action, and the passive act, passion. In action, the subject acts as an agent on the object. In passion, the subject is acted upon as a patient by the object" (*FLS* 34). For example, the passion of Christ is a passion because Christ is acted upon by his crucifiers and suffers as a patient. God's creation of the world, however, is an action. Satan's revolt against God elucidates the relation between action and passion. He was originally the most beautiful of all the angels but became envious of God. While still only envious, his revolt was a secret passion. But when he tried to place his throne above God, it became an action. Envy spurred him on, but his act was one of pride. The distinction between action and passion delineates that humility and pride are qualities of the active intellect, and mercy and envy are qualities of the passive intellect. Meekness and wrath are qualities of the active irascible, and fortitude and sloth are qualities of the passive irascible. Liberality and avarice are qualities of the active concupiscible, and temperance and gluttony are qualities the passive concupiscible. Chastity and lust are qualities of the concupiscible and have at the same time both an active and a passive quality: "Love is neither active nor passive; rather it is both active and passive. In a perfect love, one loves and is loved, is an agent and a patient" (*FLS* 36).

Operational and Orientational Virtues

Seung further explains the relation between the natural and the supernatural set of virtues and sins on the basis of a distinction between operational and orientational virtues and sins: "The orientational virtues orient the soul to its end, but do not give it the power to achieve the end. The operational virtues are the powers of operation for achieving the end. The theological virtues only orient the soul to the supernatural end" (*MC* 205). Only Christians can achieve the supernatural end. By baptism the

Christian is oriented to the supernatural end, but he can lose this orientation if he forsakes his Christian faith. If lost, he cannot develop the powers of operation necessary for achieving the supernatural end. He can still act virtuously due to virtuous dispositions, but his virtuousness only reflects an orientation to the natural end, not the supernatural end. As a result, he cannot be saved. Though perhaps virtuous in character, he will end up in Hell, because he has deliberately forsaken his Christian faith. The importance of baptism for the orientation to the supernatural end is emphasized by Vergil, who calls it "the gateway to Christian faith" (*Inf.* 4: 36), which Dante identifies as "the first step on the road to salvation" (*Inf.* 2: 29-30). This also explains why pagans cannot be saved. Since they were unbaptized, they did not have orientation to the supernatural end. They could still act virtuously, but their virtuousness was not oriented to the supernatural end.

This means that there are two kinds of operational and orientational virtues—the natural and the supernatural. In the medieval period the operational virtues for achieving the natural end were most commonly identified as the moral and intellectual virtues. These are the virtues Dante mentions in *De monarchia* (III.xvi) in emphasizing the goal for the emperor's guidance of mankind. In the treatise Dante also says that the orientation is temporal happiness. This distinction elucidates Dante's identification of the powers of operation and their orientation in achieving the natural end. But the treatise's subject is the division of power in the temporal world; it is therefore not directly concerned with the operational and orientational virtues neccesary for achieving the supernatural end. In speaking of the goal of the pope's guidance of mankind, Dante mentions the three theological virtues and says that their orientation is eternal happiness. But he does not say which powers of operation are needed for achieving the supernatural end. The three theological virtues are not such powers; they are only virtues that orient the soul to the supernatural end.

According to Seung, the operational virtues for the theological virtues are not the moral and intellectual virtues, "because they are natural virtues useful for the fulfillment of the natural end. The operational virtues required for the fulfillment of the supernatural end can be given only by God. St. Thomas calls them the infused virtues (*ST* pt. 1-2, q. 63, a. 3)." The infused virtues resemble the natural virtues in certain respects, but as Aquinas points out, they are different:

> Whereas the principle of natural virtues is the ideal of the golden mean, the principle of infused virtues is the standard of excessive rigor and

> abstinence (*ST* pt. 1-2, q. 63, a. 4). St. Thomas says little about the nature and number of the infused virtues beyond this general account. Dante has given a systematic tabulation of infused virtues by naming the virtues contrary to the seven deadly sins and then relating them to the powers of the soul. Those seven virtues are not natural but infused virtues. They are operational in fulfilling not the natural but the supernatural end (*MC* 206).

The natural virtues, both orientational and operational, are humanly possible, because they can be developed on the basis of what man has been given by nature. But the supernatural virtues are humanly impossible, because these virtues, both orientational and operational, become possible only by the aid of grace—that is, by divine infusion.

The function of infused virtues, Seung argues, is the substantiation of the theological virtues. By this he means that the former gives substance to the latter. Through the operational virtues the orientational virtues are fully actualized:

> The infused virtue of liberality provides the principal power for the substantiation of the theological virtue of faith, while the infused virtue of humility and mercy provide the ancillary powers. The infused virtue of temperance provides the principal power for the substantiation of the theological virtue of hope, while the infused virtues of meekness and fortitude (zeal) provide the ancillary powers. The infused virtue of chastity provides the principal power for the substantiation of the theological virtue of love, while the infused virtues that have been used in the substantiation of faith and hope provide the ancillary powers (*MC* 206).

The substantiation relation is not only detectable in the context of Paradise. The same principle is also detectable in Purgatory and Hell, though in two different ways:

> The substantiation relation between the infused and the theological virtues endows the ascent of Purgatory and Paradise with cumulative effect. The virtues developed on the lower terraces or heavens are not left behind, but sent upwards to be fused and perfected for progressively higher purposes. On the other hand, the descent of Hell produces the opposite effect; it is weighted down with the feeling of dispersion rather than of accumulation (*MC* 207).

With this explanation of the two sets of virtues and their relation, Seung presents a fully elaborate interpretation of the redemption scheme. The

Commedia does not simply describe how human or angelic beings can contemplate the powers of the Trinity. It thematizes how the powers of the Trinity work in the human soul in order to direct it toward its redemption. Let us draw up the grand picture of Dante's redemption scheme according to Seung's reading. Satan's expulsion from Heaven introduced evil into the created world. When God created the first man, he made him capable of experiencing the true joy of human existence in the natural world. At the same time God gave him the free will to choose between good and evil. But the first man fell victim of Satan's evil temptation. He chose to disobey God's warning against the eating of the Tree of Knowledge. But with the Coming of Christ, the order was restored in the world, and man was shown the way to overcome original sin. With the three theological virtues revealed by the Word, man has been given the orientation necessary for his attempt to redeem his sinful soul. With the notion of virtues contrary to the seven capital sins, man knows which powers of operation he has to develop in order to redeem his sinful soul.

Seung's theory for a Trinitarian interpretation of every scene and action of the *Commedia* does not result in the kind of ambiguities and anomalies that pervade Cogan's reading. On the contrary, it shows that the ambiguities and anomalies we detect in the narrative are only apparent. In the end, they turn out to be elements of a coherent vision of God's universal order. Hence the *Commedia* can be said to describe implicitly the human experience of differences in the mortal world, while at the same time confirming the Christian faith in the unity of the eternal world. Seung accepts that act is the proper target for infernal punishment, and disposition the proper target for purgation. But he rejects the idea that no dispositions can be linked to the acts portrayed in Hell.

The purgation of vicious dispositions portrayed in Purgatory displays a doctrine on what is needed for preventing sinful acts. Purgatory also shows how the soul should be properly ordered if it is to obtain salvation. But in Dante studies this doctrine becomes ambiguous for two reasons. First, there does not seem to be any correspondence between the acts of Hell and the dispositions of Purgatory. Second, it is never overtly stated which virtues are celebrated in Paradise. But with the use of the table of seven capital sins for interpreting circles two to nine of Hell, Seung provides a systematic explanation of what has incited the acts for which the sinners of Hell are condemned. Thus he underlines the intimate relation between act and disposition normally maintained in ethics. Moreover, with his use of the table of seven capital virtues for interpreting the seven planetary spheres, Seung provides a systematic explanation of how the virtues that the soul gradually attains in Purgatory are celebrated in full actuality in Paradise.

Seung's basis for interpreting the circles of Hell and the planetary spheres of Paradise is not some extratextual source but the textual content of the poem itself. For example, Seung does not turn to Aristotle's *Ethics*, as Cogan does, in order to explain the structure of Hell, insinuating that it can be understood only on the basis of some idiosyncratic reading of Aristotle. Seung turns to *Purgatorio* in order to find the principles for explaining the structural design of Hell. The same is the case with his interpretation of *Paradiso*. Seung does not turn to the *Convivio*, as Cogan does, in order to explain the structure of Paradise, suspecting that some element of the celestial concept of the *Convivio* might be implied in the *Commedia*.

There are especially two reasons for not imposing the Dionysian triads on the structure of Paradise. First, their presence is never overtly stated. Therefore the triads have to be transferred to the structure by way of some extratextual source. Cogan tries to do that by assuming that there is a thematic relation between the *Convivio* and the *Commedia*. At the same time, he limits the relation. He takes only the angelic triads of the celestial concept of the treatise, which he then links to Pseudo-Dionysius, although the treatise is ambivalent on that point. Finally, he uses other extratextual sources in order to explain what function and meaning the triads can have within the structure of Paradise. The principles for disclosing the structure of Paradise could hardly be more complicated and arbitrary. Second, no extratextual source is needed for associating the seven planetary spheres with the seven capital virtues. The association combines two thematic elements within the textual universe of the *Commedia*. Such a combination requires only an attentive reading that respects the thematic integrity of the poem.

In explicating the content of *Paradiso*, Seung does not speculate on what the celestial life might be according to Dante. He concentrates on disclosing the virtues displayed in the nine spheres. These virtues belong to the redemption scheme, not the contemplation scheme. They are not the virtues to be used in the celestial life of the blessed souls; they are the virtues these souls developed for their redemption on earth. The souls have learned them by learning from the three persons of the Trinity, who display them in their redemption of the sinful human souls. The description of the ultimate vision of the Empyreum Dante experiences at the end of his journey can be taken to be his attempt to visualize poetically what life will be at universal judgment. But Dante does not say that the vision reveals that life. That makes perfect sense. If he made such a statement, he would claim to know what life would be at universal judgment. But that cannot be, because it is beyond human comprehension.

According to Cogan, the virtues celebrated in Paradise are ultramundane and not merely the counterparts to the mundane virtues attained by the penitents of Purgatory. But the notion of ultramundane virtues does not show which virtues are displayed in *Paradiso*. Cogan only links the virtues to an arbitrary number of ambiguously defined attributes of the Trinity. He claims that Paradise implicitly thematizes the conditions of the celestial life, although Dante never makes that claim. In Cogan's hand, the message Dante tries to deliver becomes jumbled and blurred. As a doctrine, it becomes useless for the medieval man, because it does not show him unequivocally what is needed for his compliance with the will of God. In contrast, by locating the seven capital virtues and the three theological virtues in the structure of Paradise, Seung gives an unequivocal account of what is needed for salvation.

The only extratextual element Seung uses in his interpretation is the notion of the tripartite soul. To use this notion for the *Commedia* is both textually and contextually supported; it was a legacy from Augustine that all Christians shared. In Seung's reading, the notion constitutes the essential link between the three persons of the Trinity and the table of seven natural and three supernatural virtues and their opposites. As such, it is fundamental for understanding the overall structure of Dante's afterworld. But as soon as we recognize its presence in the design, it gives the ethical and psychological aspects of the *Commedia* a coherent theological foundation. With his use of the tripartite soul, Cogan can only show what power of the soul its state of sin, purgation, or blessing might be linked to. Seung, however, is capable of pointing out what it is in the character of a person as a whole that can lead to the depravation of the soul, give it a second chance to regenerate itself by the aid of divine grace, or make it experience the joy of eternal bliss. To do that, Seung applies a broad definition of the potential dispositions of the soul. Disposition does not simply mean a state of the soul due to repeated acts or recurring thoughts. Disposition implies something in the soul we might define as a fundamental inclination. In the general sense of the word, fundamental inclination can mean that a person is inclined to do good or inclined to do evil. Both types of fundamental inclination do not only concern whether the person does good or evil to himself and others. In the medieval Christian context, the true value of fundamental inclinations is ultimately a matter of whether the person does good or evil to God by doing good or evil to himself and others. The notion of capital sins encapsulates this meaning. They are capital because they are the head of other sins. By being that, they represent the seven basic ways to do evil to God by doing evil to oneself and others.

In examining the acts of evil portrayed in Hell, Seung explains the dispositions underlying the acts, not as arising from seven habits acquired through repeated acts, but as arising from seven fundamental evil inclinations. To give an example, the broad definition of envy also provides an explanation of Dante's condemnation of Mohammed as a sower of discord. As Francesco Gabrieli argues, in the medieval period Mohammed was sometimes believed to have been a monk or perhaps even a cardinal who split the church in envy of not being elected pope.[9] That does not mean that Dante might have taken it for granted that Mohammed committed similar acts before splitting up the church. It only means that this particular act reveals his fundamental inclination to evil acts of envy. In addition, the fact that Mohammed is condemned along with Ali adds further aspects to Dante's thematization of the capital sin of envy. Dante probably believed Ali to have been the teacher that led Mohammed astray; the former was the brain behind the latter's revolt. According to Southern, this explains why Ali precedes Mohammed in the ninth *bolgia*, because thought precedes act.[10] With this relation between act and thought, Dante emphasizes two horrific aspects of the capital sin of envy. Mohammed represents the brutal rage in envious acts, whereas Ali stands for the secrecy of envious planning.

However, when we read *Inferno*, the seven fundamental evil inclinations can be detected in the structure of Hell only if we recognize that they can manifest themselves in different ways. This is particularly the case with circles seven, eight, and nine of Hell because of their subdivisions. Because of the subdivisions, it is difficult to come to terms with the structural principles that govern the design of Hell. But conceptually it makes perfect sense that the inclinations can manifest themselves in different ways. Evil does not only mean the opposite of goodness; it means also disorder, just as goodness implies order. Since evil means disorder, the evil soul can be disordered in different ways and its evil inclinations can manifest themselves in different ways. That does not mean, however, that Hell should be without order. Just because the same evil inclination can result in different acts, it does not mean that Hell is by necessity arbitrary and chaotic.

Order and Disorder

Seung's explanation of the function of the operational and the orientational virtues makes it clear why the structure of Hell is formally different from that of Purgatory. Since every Christian through baptism is oriented to the supernatural end, his soul is, at the outset, an orderly soul in potency. But in order to redeem itself, the soul has to be developed in the proper manner and become an orderly soul in actuality. It has to avoid the seven capital sins and develop their opposite virtues. If not, the soul degenerates and can be lost for good. But the degeneration of the soul does not imply chaos. The degenerated soul is a disorderly image of the orderly soul. For that reason, the order of Hell is not immediately comparable with the order of Purgatory. Hell displays a number of ways in which the proper order of the soul can be corrupted. Purgatory shows that the corrupted soul can be reordered only in one way. Since the attainment of the seven operational virtues, along with the restoration of the three orientational virtues, implies an orderly process, it is reasonable to suggest that the same scheme provides an orderly basis for detecting the virtues of Paradise.

With his interpretation of the parallel structures of Hell and Purgatory, Seung shows that the Christian notion that every sin can be forgiven is fully integrated in the structure of Dante's afterworld. The sinners of Hell cannot be forgiven their sinful acts. As they appear in Dante's Hell, they are totally absorbed in their sinful inclinations they now fully enact and therefore incapable of repenting their sins. If they were capable of repentance, they would be in Purgatory. In Purgatory, however, it is not the sinful act that is being purged, but its disposition. The premise is repentance. As soon as the soul repents, it engages in the process of purgation, and through the engagement, the sinful act is forgiven. Hence, in the parallel reading, every sin can be forgiven because every sinful disposition can be purged. Seung provides a much better explanation of the punishment of pagans in Hell than Cogan. If Hell were organized according to philosophical principles, none of the souls in Hell would be able to understand why they have been sentenced to eternal damnation by divine justice. It would be a mystery to the pagan sinner, because with his philosophical or natural orientation, he would know only what is needed for achieving the natural end and what impedes the achievement. But the subject of discourse in the *Commedia* is the achievement of the supernatural end and what impedes it. Since no philosophical or natural orientation can penetrate what is needed for achieving that end, the pagan sinner would not know why he is eternally damned if Hell were organized according to philosophical principles. He would not know that his damnation is due to the fact that he lacked the orientation to the supernatural end and did not develop the powers of operation necessary for achieving that end.

At the same time, if Hell were organized according to philosophical principles, the sentence to eternal damnation would also be a mystery to the Christian sinner. Every Christian has been given by baptism the orientation to the supernatural end. If he practices his Christian faith, he will know that any act related to the seven capital sins hinders him in developing the powers of operation necessary for achieving that end. If he violates his faith, he destroys the orientation. As a result, it becomes impossible to develop the powers of operation for achieving the supernatural end. But that does not make the Christian sinner equal to the pagan sinner. The Christian sinner still has to account for his violation of the belief in the supernatural end. But if Hell were organized according to philosophical principles, he would not be able to understand that his punishment has to do with his violation of the belief in the supernatural end. Due to the limits of philosophy, a philosophical organization of Hell would conceal the supernatural meaning of divine justice.

The pagan sinners may not have believed in divine justice while they lived in the mortal world. But when they enter the afterworld, they immediately experience it and cannot avoid submitting to it. Their experience of divine justice erases their unbelief. The unbeliever comes to know that God exists and that his unbelief was erroneous. The pagan sinners in Hell account for their lack of belief in the supernatural end. If Hell were organized according to philosophical principles, the unbeliever would remain an unbeliever. He would not know that he is being punished because he did not pursue the supernatural end. He would believe that his punishment is due to an erroneous pursuit of the natural end. But with the knowledge of God's existence, the pagan sinner is not given a second chance to take on the belief he once renounced. He comes to know that he should have believed in what he is now for ever prevented from ever making a commitment to. With the sentence of divine justice, the pagan sinner knows the cause of his punishment according to divine justice. He knows that he is a deliberate sinner. There are no accidental sinners in Hell, because it is incorrect to condemn a person for a sin he had no intention of committing or he perhaps does not even know he committed. Every sentence of divine justice spells out the difference between good and evil. The evil soul understands and experiences its own evilness through punishment. But the knowledge does not provide it with any means to amend its evil disposition. Since the soul's knowledge of its own evilness comprises the knowledge of its opposite, the knowledge only increases the soul's experience of its own evilness.

These are the basic principles of the medieval Christian Hell, which the ancients did not share. Since every sinner of Hell is aware of the principles of divine justice and the difference between good and evil, it would be strange if Dante maintained that Hell should be organized according to philosophical principles. It would be inconsistent to apply uniquely Christian principles in describing the principles of divine justice and, at the same time, follow philosophical principles in outlining the design of Hell. The problem of determining how Hell is organized is not a question of whether Dante believes that all souls have basic virtuous potentialities at birth. This is a standard assertion in medieval theology—the human soul is a divine creation. But what are these basic virtuous potentialities according to Dante?

Let us recall the distinction between act and power. The latter is only potency, but when actualized, it becomes act and habit. If it is not actualized, it is nothing. The same is the case with the basic virtuous potentialities. According to Seung's reading, virtuous potentialities can become virtuous actualities in two different ways, depending on what end is pursued. They can become natural virtues if their orientation is the natural end, and they can become supernatural virtues if their orientation is the supernatural end. A Christian has the orientation to the supernatural end and can develop the powers of operation necessary for achieving that end. A pagan has only the orientation to the natural end and can therefore develop only the powers of operation necessary for achieving that end. But Dante maintains that the Christian conception of divine justice is the true one. It is reasonable to suggest, as Seung does, that the powers of operation needed for achieving the supernatural end are the seven capital virtues described in *Purgatorio* because Dante mentions no alternative to this set of virtues.

The distinction between natural and supernatural orientation and between natural and supernatural powers of operation also resolves the problem of Limbo. The problem consists in the fact that Limbo is placed in Hell but at the same time different from the other infernal circles. As Seung argues, it is even protected from the seven capital sins that constitute Hell proper. The souls of Limbo are generally recognized as sages and include a large number of pagans but also three distinguished Muslims. The sages of Limbo are placed in the first circle of Hell, not because they were born before Christ, but because they had no knowledge of the truth revealed by Christ. The sages of Limbo are placed in Hell because they lacked the orientation needed for the redemption of their souls. They are properly called sages because they actualized their basic virtuous potentialities to natural perfection as mortal beings. But they could not develop them beyond that because they lacked the orientation to the supernatural end. This explains why Limbo thematizes the absence of the supernatural virtue of faith. Only with the supernatural orientation can the basic virtuous potentialities be truly actualized.

Since the sages of Limbo lack the supernatural orientation, they cannot enter Purgatory. But since they had achieved a natural perfection, they do not belong to Hell proper. With this explanation we can now understand the principles underlying the placement of Christian and non-Christian sinners in Hell proper. The pagan sinners are placed in the different sections of Hell proper for two reasons. First, they are in Hell proper because they lack the supernatural orientation. Second, they are in Hell proper because they have degenerated their basic potentialities through erroneous acts. To degenerate these potentialities is the same as to sin, because it involves disrespect for what God has installed in the soul through its creation. If a pagan degenerates the basic potentiality Christians identify as the capital virtue of humility, he becomes a sinner of its counterpart, which is the capital sin of pride. The sin of Brutus and Cassius can properly be associated with the capital sin of pride. The former acted out of family pride, and the latter in pride for the country.

In the case of the Christian sinners, the reason for their placement in Hell proper should be explained in a different way. Christians have the supernatural operation by baptism and should be able to develop the powers of operation needed for achieving the supernatural end. Like the pagan sinners, they degenerate the proper powers of operation, but unlike the pagan sinners, they degenerate the supernatural orientation; they degenerate the means they have been given for regenerating the powers of operation in case of sinful transgression. This means is repentance. This is possible only for those who have the supernatural orientation. That the Christian sinners degenerate the orientation and impede the proper development of operational powers does not mean that their sins are much graver than those committed by the pagan sinners. It only means that the pagan and the Christian way of sinning can produce different types of sin.

As far as the pagan sinning is concerned, Limbo exemplifies the difference. Although the sages are not, technically speaking, sinners, because they attained a natural perfection, they still count among the irredeemable souls because they did not pursue the supernatural end. What Limbo reveals is a particularly pagan type of sin. There can be no Christians in Limbo because Christians have the supernatural orientation. Suicide, however, is a Christian type of sin. As Pier della Vigna reveals the cause of his suicide, it involves the attempt to revenge injustice. But instead of turning the anger, essential for vengeful acts, against the enemy and the cause of injustice, Pier turned it against himself. As a result, his sin has two essential features, whose combination makes his sin uniquely Christian. First, he acted contrary to the operational virtue of meekness; he committed an act associated with the capital sin of wrath. Second, as a Christian, Pier should have known that suicide involves the sin against the sacredness of life, according to Christian teachings. With the supernatural orientation, this sacredness is imprinted in the soul. In contrast, in the ancient world, suicide was regarded as an act in defense of honor. To take one's life was not be an act of wrath and the perversion of meekness as operational virtue.

Guidance and Missions

Seung's theory is ultimately simple. The seemingly complicated and confusing construction of the three worlds is governed by two simple principles of organization: the three persons of the Trinity and the three parts of the soul. These two elements are fused into one triadic scheme that gives the different sins of Hell, vices of Purgatory, and virtues of Paradise a coherent theological foundation. Seung's theory of the master plan underlines a basic principle for all types of communication. The attempt to communicate a message is likely to turn out successfully more often if the communicator has a plan for communicating the message than if he does not. It is easier to write a complex poem such as the *Commedia* if one operates with a set of principles for its design at the outset instead of creating them on the way. The incarnation of the ordering principles in the poem is complex and the poetic representation tends to obscure them and make them enigmatic. That disturbs and puzzles the reader in his attempt to understand the structures of the three realms and their thematic content. Seung says that the figural presence of the Trinity in the *Commedia* is not easily discovered:

> Although man is an image of God and as such reflects his glory, Augustine says, this divine reflection in the human mirror is indeed obscure (*enigma*; *De trinitate*, bk. 15, chaps. 8 and 9). He goes on to explain that an enigma is one of the species of allegory, that is, the obscure allegory. Dante's allegorical mirror is as obscure as Augustine's.

> Both of them are so obscure, indeed, that the figural reflection of Trinity is supposedly visible only to the eyes of the faithful. Even a fleeting glimpse of it is meant to be an act of faith and a gift of grace (*CT* 42).

Seung argues that Dante is keenly conscious of the obscurity of his poetic mirror. This is manifest in the way he ceaselessly draws our attention to the "veiled" (*ombra*) or "figural" (*figura*) character of his visionary world: "Throughout the *Commedia*, in fact, he is almost obsessed with the fear that the vivid realism of his poetic creation may mislead his readers to mistake it for an ultimate reality and fail to perceive its obscure, figural function" (*CT* 42).

However, once the reader accepts Seung's theory, Dante's achievement becomes extraordinary. It becomes inaccurate to identify the *Commedia* as "the book of the dead," which has often been the case in Dante studies. Since everything in Dante's vision can be traced back to the universal source of origin, the *Commedia* turns out to be a book of all the existential conditions in the all-encompassing whole; it encompasses both the corporeal and mortal conditions and the spiritual and eternal conditions. But the fact that the narrative action is situated in the world beyond makes some Dante scholars inclined to dismiss the universality of the *Commedia*. This is the case in Harold Bloom's reading of Dante's epic. In demarcating the essential quality of Dante's achievement in contrast to Shakespeare's, Bloom claims that "Dante surpasses all other writers, before or since, in emphasizing an ultimate changelessness in each of us, a fixed position that we must occupy in eternity." Shakespeare, however, "surpasses all others in evidencing a psychology of mutability."[11] In Platonic terms, Bloom seems to intend that the former depicts things at rest, while the latter depicts things in motion; their poetic creations incarnate two super-ideas from which all other writers draw, but never comprehend to the same degree. But Bloom's claim is problematic. If the *Commedia* is taken as a description of the other world, we can say that Dante and Shakespeare divide the entire world between them—this world for Shakespeare, and the other world for Dante. But in the Western canon of literature, to which Bloom appeals, Dante faces no competition as long as the *Commedia* is taken as a description of the other world. Not even Milton's *Paradise Lost* qualifies for the competition Bloom suggests, because Adam's fall takes place in the Garden of Eden, situated in this world, not in the world beyond.

To make Dante the undisputed master of the eternal world of the dead is to make him irrelevant for the mutable world of the living. The *Commedia* becomes the book of the dead, not the living. If so, he is the master over the dead, while Shakespeare is the master over the living. Dante may rule over one half of the universe, but he is ruling over nothing. Bloom's ranking of Dante and Shakespeare as the two greatest writers of the Western canon is not a tribute but an insult to the greatness of Dante's poem. Instead of admiring it as a great book of the living, he is burying it as a great book of the dead. Bloom's distinction between immutability and mutability is misleading. A more adequate way to demarcate Dante's domain from Shakespeare's is the demarcation between the natural and the supernatural. Shakespeare's domain is the natural world. Even the world of his romances is natural; its spiritual beings are essential components of the natural world. Dante's world, however, is supernatural because his entire universe is governed by the supernatural entity. But God is not confined to the eternal, timeless world; his powers permeate the mutable and temporal world. Because his omnipotence and omnipresence is the central theme of the poem, the *Commedia* is a book of the living, not the dead.

According to Seung's theory, the permeation of divine powers is manifest in the meaning of Dante's guides. With his Trinitarian reading, Seung rejects the traditional view that Dante is led through the three otherworldly realms only by two guides—Vergil and Beatrice. Instead, the journey involves three guides that represent the three persons of the Trinity: Vergil stands for the Son, Beatrice for the Holy Spirit, and Bernard of Clairvaux for the Father. To many Dante readers, this is perhaps the most radical implication of Seung's theory, because they are more concerned with the element of journey or the narrative content than with the element of order or the thematic content. But Seung's rejection of the twofold leadership is a consistent extension of his Trinitarian reading. It emphasizes the inseparability of form and content, structure and theme, order and journey, or as Cogan prefers it, structure and narrative. Seung rejects the traditional interpretation of Vergil as Reason and Beatrice as Faith. This is the allegorical interpretation Dante scholars have maintained most often in the history of Dante studies.[12] This type of allegory is the one normally identified as the personification allegory. Seung also rejects the reading that identifies Vergil and Beatrice as figures of John the Baptist and Christ. This is the allegorical interpretation developed out of the Auerbach-Singleton tradition in Dante studies (*CT* 11-13). This type of allegory is the one normally defined as the figural allegory.

The emphasis on figural meaning is one of the great achievements of Auerbach and Singleton. The identification of Beatrice as a Christ-figure is a significant advance beyond the traditional identification of her as Faith. The significance consists in the fact that the interpretation brings

Beatrice closer to God. Her role is not only to represent Faith as the assurance of things hoped for and the conviction of things not seen (Hebrews 11: 1). By identifying her as a Christ-figure, she becomes associated with the divine essence. But Singleton's audacious move creates an anomaly. Why is only the Son singled out for this identification? Why are the Holy Spirit and the Father left out? Singleton never explains the anomaly. He takes his interpretation to be consistent with the medieval theology, but it is inflicted with Protestant theology. Whereas medieval theology is always Trinitarian, Protestant theology is Christological. Martin Luther said that the only God who had any meaning for him was the God who suffered on the cross. Singleton's interpretation reflects this unique feature of Protestant theology. With his identification of Beatrice as a Christ-figure, Singleton imposes the Christological perspective of Protestant theology on the *Commedia*.

The personification allegory and the figural allegory have generated two different interpretations of Vergil and Beatrice in the history of Dante studies. But as Dante scholars have applied the two allegorical approaches to the *Commedia*, they have never resulted in a reevaluation of the assumption that Vergil and Beatrice constitute a twofold leadership. In this respect, the two allegorical interpretations reflect the same pattern of thought. The pattern is dyadic in accordance with the Thomistic distinction between the natural and the supernatural domain. For example, Singleton reaches his conclusion that Beatrice is a Christ-figure by identifying her role as that of the light of grace and Vergil's as that of natural light.[13] That is the same as to say that Vergil's role as guide belongs to the natural domain and Beatrice's belongs to the supernatural domain. Drawing on Singleton's interpretation of Vergil's role as a preparation, within natural bonds, for a higher reality that comes with Beatrice's appearance, Hollander suggests that while Beatrice is a Christ-figure, Vergil is related to John the Baptist, "whose desert voice leads to Christ, and who performs the first baptism."[14] The dyadic pattern of thought is thus given a figural meaning.

In doing so, Singleton and Hollander create an anomaly between the basic elements of the *Commedia* and the pattern of thought they use in order to establish the figural meanings of Vergil and Beatrice. The pattern of thought is incompatible with the basic elements, because the pattern is dyadic, while the elements are triadic and Trinitarian. To apply the dyadic pattern to the *Commedia* is to imply that Dante described the afterworld in triadic terms but conceived its meaning in dyadic terms. If so, we have to conclude that the *Commedia* is incoherent. But the incoherence can have another explanation. Since the Auerbach-Singleton school is still grounded in the tradition of Thomistic reading, it continues to produce disputable readings. Cogan's interpretation of the *Commedia* is an example of how Dante scholars find it difficult to look beyond Aquinas. Another example is Botterill's *Dante and the Mystical Tradition*. In examining the relation between Dante and Bernard of Clairvaux, Botterill says that "Aquinas definitely belongs to—more, is a central figure in—the mainstream of the Western Church's thinking about mystical experience." For that reason, he claims that Dante need not have looked beyond Aquinas for theological grounding of his mystical ideas.[15]

Seung's denunciation of Vergil as associated with the natural domain is theologically well-founded. In accordance with medieval Christian teachings, Seung stresses that Purgatory does not belong to the natural order. On the contrary, it is the realm of grace and beyond the natural order. Hence, if we claim that Vergil's role as guide belongs to the natural domain, we create an anomaly between his capacity as guide and the perspective of his guidance. Seung has been the first to notice this theological anomaly:

> Natural reason ceases to be natural as soon as it is aided by the supernatural power of grace. To inject grace into the workings of natural reason is the essence of the theological doctrine called the infusion of grace, which transforms man's natural powers into supernatural ones. Hence Vergil the guide cannot stand for natural reason if he is aided by the power of grace. As an allegorical representation of natural reason, Vergil is theologically too anomalous to be accommodated within the teachings of medieval Christianity. He concludes this anomalous role by crowning and mitering Dante the pilgrim on the top of Purgatory (*Purgatorio* 27.142). That is, he confers the awesome power of temporal and spiritual autonomy on the sanctified Christian soul, which is an incredible role for natural reason (*STH* 156).

Nevertheless, Dante scholars still maintain the twofold leadership, despite the fact that the interpretation of Vergil's role is incompatible with Christian teachings.

Doctrinal orthodoxy is not in itself a criterion for determining the theological content of the *Commedia*. But if we maintain that Dante identifies Vergil's role with the natural domain, we have to explain why he is not in accordance with the basic doctrines of the medieval church. No Dante scholar has ever convincingly explained Dante's motivation for this apparent discordance. To say that Dante was unaware that Vergil's guidance through Hell and Purgatory involved doctrinal violation is not a convincing argument. If this is the case, the description of Vergil's guidance becomes ridiculous. It comes to reflect an ambitious author's incapability of contemplating the object of his poetic discourse. If so, it is reasonable to assume that the *Commedia* is constructed as a work in progress that ultimately fails to accomplish what it aims at. The *Commedia* is reduced to mere rhetoric, since its claim of truth does not arise from a vision of order.

To say that Dante objected to the basic doctrines of the church concerning the natural and the supernatural domain and the infusion of grace, because he maintained a different view of the preconditions for the salvation of the soul, is not a better argument. In that case, we have to explain why he apparently eliminates the supernatural dimension of Purgatory by making it intelligible to natural reason. If so, there is no reason to speak of Purgatory as the realm of grace; it should rather be defined as the realm of reason. Moreover, if Purgatory is accessible to natural reason, purgation becomes a natural process. If so, nothing hinders us in concluding that Dante regards salvation as attainable by reason alone and even in the mortal world.

Some medieval thinkers argued about whether man could raise himself from the state of sin by his own will without the aid of divine grace. Those who maintained such a view or displayed an inclination toward it were, in the medieval period, condemned as sinners of the Pelagian heresy. This was a serious charge. It was one of the reasons why some parts of Aquinas's work were censured following Tempier's condemnations of 1277, because Aquinas's *Sententiae* were believed to maintain a position similar to the Pelagian view. But the question of whether man possesses the power to raise himself from the state of sin by his own will is irrelevant when we try to determine the essential quality of Vergil's guidance. In the medieval period, the question was raised only in relation to the human conditions of the mortal world; it was never discussed in relation to the other world of perdition or purgation. In the *Commedia* Dante makes it clear that there is only one will that can raise a sinner from the state of sin, and that is the will of God who acts through grace. The irrelevance of the question of the autonomy of the human will is made clear by the fact that Dante's journey through Hell and Purgatory is not due to an autonomous act of his will. On the contrary, he is guided by Vergil. Moreover, Vergil is not acting as Dante's guide due to an autonomous act of his will. On the contrary, he has been sent on a mission by Beatrice, whose descent into Limbo is directed by St. Lucy, who acts at the behest of St. Mary.

Seung argues that Dante's dependence on his guides during his otherworldly journey is one of the strongest evidences of why his epic is fundamentally different from the epics of the ancient tradition:

> Dante the traveler, unfortunately, makes a shabby epic hero, because his chief function is to see and report, the function of a traveling reporter. There are a few things he does on his own during his journey, but all of them are no more than the normal actions and reactions one can expect from any alert and attentive observer. Dante discharges even this function of a traveling reporter under the tutelage of his divinely appointed guides (*STH* 136).

In comparison with the relation Odysseus and Athena in Homer's *Odyssey* and Aeneas and Venus in Vergil's *Aeneid*, Dante the traveler is too powerless and helpless a creature to assume a heroic stature comparable to that of the ancient heroes. At the same time Dante's dependence on his guides is a strong evidence of why the cultural outlook of the *Commedia* is fundamentally different from that of modern times: "Dante the traveler is destined to play the humble role of a powerless and helpless agent. But this is what constitutes the virtue of humility, the foundation of medieval Christian ethos" (*STH* 141-42).

The meaning of the workings of grace is an essential question for any reading of the *Commedia*. Singleton interprets the development of the narrative action as "a movement towards justice and advent," in which Vergil's guidance through Hell and Purgatory represents a preparation, under the natural light of reason, for "sanctifying grace." According to Singleton, Dante receives the sanctifying grace only when Beatrice appears in the Terrestrial Paradise.[16] But the theological basis for Singleton's thesis has been repudiated by Antonio C. Mastrobuono, who rightly observes that "Singleton's thesis is based on an erroneous interpretation of St. Thomas." Instead, Mastrobuono argues, Dante's journey "takes place as an effect of—not a preparation for—sanctifying grace." Dante has already received grace when he enters the afterworld. According to Mastrobuono, Dante's experience of grace involves "justification," which is the effect of operating grace, and "merit," which is the effect of cooperating grace: "Once the soul is justified, the moral process begins whereby Dante, in the exercise of the freedom of his choice, will cooperate with God in the process of his self-sanctification by performing works of charity in order to earn merit of his future glory."[17] For Mastrobuono, the difference between his and Singleton's position could hardly be more divergent.

The question of whether grace is operative for Dante right from the start is important for our understanding of Dante's epic. If Dante cannot descend Hell and ascend Purgatory with the aid of grace, it is untenable to assume that Vergil can guide Dante through these realms without the aid of grace. Since his guidance must be the work of grace, Vergil cannot stand for natural reason, because grace is imperceptible to natural reason. Singleton's association of grace with only the part of the journey under Beatrice's guidance should therefore be dismissed. But Mastrobuono's counterargument does not solve the problem of grace either. This becomes clear when we compare his argument with Seung's. Mastrobuono argues that the special miracle that has been granted Dante with the appearance of Vergil implies a sort of re-experience of the effects of original sin: "Before [Dante] ascends the mountain of Purgatory in order to be regenerated, he will have to undergo an actual tribulation and anguish of Hell as punishment for the sins he has committed. The descent into Hell is such a punishment that will renew Dante in humility . . . The ascent of Purgatory is also punitive but more obviously regenerative."[18] Hence, according to Mastrobuono, for Dante the workings of grace involve a punitive and a regenerative element before Dante's transformation by grace is accomplished.

In *The Fragile Leaves of the Sibyl*, Seung argues that in the *Commedia*, sin is conceived as the precondition for grace: "Grace comes through sin; it would not have come without sin . . . Sin is the indispensable progentrix for virtue." Dante's descent to Hell is his life in sin, and his ascent of Purgatory is his death in sin: "The latter is impossible without the former. No one can climb the *Purgatorio* without the power of sin any more than without the power of grace. Grace does not come and work in the soul which has not been fermented in sin. Grace works its miracle where sin has prepared a fertile soul" (*FLS* 114-15). Seung and Mastrobuono agree that Dante regards grace as a miraculous gift to the sinful soul and as a precondition for its transformation. But there is a major difference in the way they characterize the descent into Hell and ascent of Purgatory. Mastrobuono speaks of the former as "punishment" and of the latter as "regeneration," while Seung speaks of "degeneration" and "regeneration."

Mastrobuono criticizes Singleton's misreading of Aquinas, but he never questions the premise for Singleton's interpretation of Dante's notion of grace. Like Singleton, Mastrobuono reads the *Commedia* primarily as a narrative that recounts a journey of a traveler from one place to another. By doing so, he tends to neglect the vision of order. The transformation of the traveler becomes the key to the allegorical meaning of the poem as a whole. The traveler is interpreted as more than an ordinary sinner; he is a symbol of humanity. Singleton and Mastrobuono share this idea, because they follow the same analytic procedure. The fact that Mastrobuono's interpretation is rooted in the same tradition as Singleton's explains why he characterizes Dante's descent to Hell as punishment. Since Dante is a sinner when he enters Hell, the descent depicts, according to Mastrobuono, the punishment of his sins. The descent into Hell and the ascent of Purgatory are the punishment or satisfaction Dante has to pay.

To identify Dante's descent of Hell with punishment is misleading. In support of his characterization of the descent, Mastrobuono relies on a passage from the *Summa Theologiae*, where Aquinas deals with the triple loss by sinning (*ST* pt. 1-2, q. 109, a. 7). Aquinas distinguishes between the stain on soul, the corruption of the good of nature, and the debt of punishment. Mastrobuono relates this notion to the effects of sin in the soul of Dante the traveler. Its ultimate consequence would have been eternal perdition if the infusion of grace had not been initiated by the mercy of St. Mary. But Mastrobuono's use of the Thomistic doctrine is inaccurate. According to Aquinas, when man sins it involves the withdrawal of divine grace, which is a punishment in itself. When man is deprived of the aid of grace, he is overcome by his passions, and passions and devilish temptations are the causes of sin (*ST* pt. 1-2, q. 87, a. 2). But if punishment were the essential meaning of Dante the traveler's experience of Hell, it would implicate the withdrawal of grace. In that case, the traveler would become subject to his passions. But if he became subject to his passions, he would not be able to get out of Hell. For that reason, punishment is not the proper meaning of the traveler's experience of neither Hell nor Purgatory.

It is the power of grace that empowers Dante to travel through the afterworld. It is also the power of grace that helps the sinners in Purgatory and gives the saints in Paradise their bliss. This does not mean that Dante experiences the essence of punishment in Hell, purgation in Purgatory, and bliss in Paradise. The function of grace for Dante is not identical with the function of grace for the souls of the afterworld. Since Mastrobuono treats them as identical, his interpretation of Dante's notion of grace is inaccurate. Dante can descend into Hell only with the power of grace, but the sinners do not need such a power for their descent into Hell. The sinners are precisely in Hell because they do not enjoy the benefit of grace. This is why Dante is in no position to go through the same experience as that of the condemned. He can only observe and report. The same thing applies to his experience of purgation and salvation.

The grace that empowers Dante to travel through Purgatory and Paradise is the same grace that enables him to go through Hell. This grace is different from the grace that brings regeneration and salvation to virtuous Christians. It is inaccurate to speak of grace for Dante the traveler as though it were the same as the one essential for the process of purgation and sanctification in Christian theology. Mastrobuono is incapable of making this distinction because his interpretive focus is set on the element of journey. He assumes that the account of the journey is the unifying principle of the poem's thematic content.

It is the same assumption that makes Dante scholars maintain that Dante is led through the afterworld only by two guides. By focusing the narrative action, they assume that the guidance of Dante toward the ultimate vision can be assigned only to those characters that bring Dante from one place to another; Vergil brings Dante through Hell and Purgatory, and Beatrice brings him through the celestial spheres to the ultimate heaven. But this view has led to what Seung regards as one of the greatest embarrassments in Dante studies: the neglect of Dante's third guide, Bernard of Clairvaux (*CT* 31 and *STH* 157). According to Seung, Vergil's mission for Dante represents the visible mission of the second person for every human soul. By this he means that it consists in showing the soul how to die in the world of sin and how to be born again in the world of grace. Beatrice's mission, however, represents the invisible mission of the third person. By this Seung intends that it consists in sanctifying the reborn soul and guiding it to the heavenly mansion of the Father (*STH* 158). In support of his reading, Seung argues that Dante highlights this allegorical significance of Vergil's and Beatrice's missions of salvation by using two words, *mia salute* (my salvation), in his final description of the two guides (*Purg*. 30: 15 and *Par*. 31: 79-81). Since Dante uses this expression only in these two instances, Seung argues: "By this unmistakably stringent poetic device, Dante is trying to tell us that Vergil and Beatrice allegorically stand for the Son and the Spirit, the only two agents of salvation known in Christianity. To hand over the missions of salvation to either natural reason or revealed theology would be an act of heresy or lunacy in any part of Christendom" (*STH* 159).

On the basis of this consistent theological understanding of the principles of salvation in medieval Christianity, Seung explicates the allegorical significance of Bernard's appearance in the ultimate heaven:

> It is the Father who sends his Son on his visible mission and his Spirit on his invisible mission. He does not himself go out on any mission of salvation, but remains in his heavenly mansions. His function is not to

> redeem fallen souls from the sinful world, but to receive, with the beatific vision, the souls redeemed by the Son's visible mission and the Spirit's invisible mission (*STH* 159).

According to Seung, this is the allegorical meaning of Bernard's role in the *Commedia*. Like the heavenly father, Bernard "awaits for Dante in the Empyreum and concludes the work of Vergil and Beatrice by elevating his soul to the ecstatic vision of the Holy Trinity" (*STH* 159).

The seven natural and three supernatural virtues and their contraries can formally be defined as the structural display of the poem's ultimate theme. The association of the roles of Vergil, Beatrice, and Bernard for Dante's journey with the three persons of the Trinity is formally the most tangible evidence for Seung's theory that the Trinity is the ultimate theme. But since the framework of Trinitarian theology pervades the entire work, it is misleading to distinguish the structure of the afterworld from the narrative action when we consider the substantive content of the *Commedia*. In Dante studies each of the three realms of Dante's afterworld is often interpreted as having its own moral order. Although the moral order of *Paradiso* is never overtly revealed, the standard reading argues that the *Commedia* displays three individual moral orders and therefore dictates the method of serial reading. Seung, however, proposes one universal moral order for Dante's three realms. In order to reveal the global moral order, he stresses the inseparability of structure and theme: the structure of the afterworld cannot be separated from its thematic content. The structure of the afterworld is the moral order, and the moral order is the thematic order, and the thematic order is the substantive content.

Secular and Sacred Reading

The problem of discovering the covert dimension or the enigmatic meaning of Dante's epic is not only a matter of methodological differences in interpreting the *Commedia*. It also involves a difference between two cultural approaches to the poem's content. These two approaches produce two different types of reading. One can be called the secular reading, and the other can be called the sacred reading. This distinction is as important as the distinction between the systematic reading and the segmental reading with its different submethods.

In Dante studies, one of the most prominent spokesmen for the secular reading has been Benedetto Croce. His work on Dante may not any longer be influential, but the interpretive perspective he encouraged is still widespread. Croce recommends that the readers "should read Dante just as all ingenious readers do and are right in doing, paying little heed to the other world, very little to the moral divisions, none at all to the allegories, and greatly enjoying the poetic representations, in which all the poet's multiform passion is condensed, purified, and expressed" (*FLS* 20). In reading the *Commedia,* Croce gives prevalence to its poetic dimension and dismisses entirely its conception of order; he regards it as irrelevant for the enjoyment of the poem's aesthetic qualities. Seung's response to this perspective is severe:

> Croce may be showing us the right way to enjoy Dante's epic, but he certainly shows us the sure way to lose it. A significant poem is like life itself, because it is a reflection of life. Once you begin merely to enjoy it, you begin to lose it or you have already lost it. You have already lost its significance in frivolity and triviality and the only thing you can do is to sport with it (*FLS* 20).

The distinction between the secular and the sacred reading is not used in Dante studies to demarcate opposing approaches to the *Commedia.* Instead, Dante scholars prefer to distinguish between two other types of reading. These two types can be associated with the secular and the sacred reading, but they are not identical with them. One is the poetic or literary reading, and the other is the theological or philosophical reading. The often debated question of whether Dante's motivation for writing the *Commedia* is primarily that of a poet or that of a theologian indicates the interpretive problems these two types of reading generate. At the same time, it illustrates the kind of whirlwind into which the reader of the *Commedia* is thrown at once when he tries to understand the thematic complexity of Dante's text by consulting scholarly investigations of his conceptual characteristics.

For example, Hollander suggests that Dante is not a *poeta-theologus* but a *theologus-poeta.* With this distinction he argues that "while the former freely admits that his fictions are fictions, Dante creates a fiction which pretends to consider not to be literally fictitious, while at the same time contriving to share the knowledge with us that is precisely fictional."[19] By this Hollander intends that the theological poet (*poeta-theologus*) does not insist that his fiction is anything else but a fiction. His poetic creation is not to be understood as an account of a real event. However, the creation of the poetic theologian (*theologus-poeta*) is not to be understood as something entirely fictional, but as something real, since it claims to be real although it is fictional. In Hollander's view, the relation between theology and poetry in Dante's poem is not easily defined; it implies a tension whose resolution requires a subtle distinction. The nature of the tension becomes clear when we consider the distinction between the poetic and the theological reading.

The theological reading gives prevalence to the doctrinal content of the poem. As such, it focuses on the order of the afterworld. This type of reading is characteristic of the early readings of the poem, since their main concern was often to explain the doctrinal content of the poetic account. But none of these readings ever managed to give the doctrinal content a systematic explanation. In contrast, the poetic reading concentrates on the poem's narrative characteristics, such as its linguistic, rhetorical, metaphorical, allegorical, or symbolic elements. This type of reading represents primarily a modern approach to the poem. There are especially three reasons for its consolidation in Dante studies. The first reason is the development of modern literary criticism with its extensive terminological and conceptual apparatus; the theoretical means for scrutinizing Dante's poetic construction has never been more instrumental. The second reason is the preference for aesthetics, and the third is the modern detachment from the sensibility of medieval Christianity.

In the case of Croce, the combination of a literary aesthetic approach and a modern cultural outlook has serious consequences. His preference for the poetic dimension implies that since the poem's doctrinal content has no significance for the modern sensibility, the reader is free to focus on any aspect of Dante's poetic construction that stimulates his interest. According to Croce, Dante's focus on the theological order restrains the unfolding of his poetic genius. This idea, however, is not a new one. In the sixteenth century, Pietro Bembo expressed a similar objection to Dante's poetry. In his admiration for Petrarch, Bembo criticized Dante's poetic language as too harsh and for lacking elegance and harmony, and he criticized the *Commedia* for containing too much philosophy.[20] The distinction between the theological and the poetic reading does not only demarcate the difference between two historical periods of Dante studies; it demarcates also two different modes of reading detectable in different historical periods.

In *Dante Philomythes and Philosopher*, Patrick Boyde observes that Croce managed "to persuade a whole generation of critics in Italy that the ideological framework and content of the *Comedy* has proved an obstacle to the free expression of Dante's poetic genius." Boyde remarks that "in the longer term, Croce's attempt to banish content, structure and context from any discussion of the poem as poetry has only served to convince subsequent generations of their importance and indispensability."[21] This may be so for the majority of Dante scholars, but the Crocean reading has not vanished. It is manifest in Bloom's assault on theological readings in Dante studies. The assault explicitly aims at restating the Crocean preference for the poetic force of Dante's creativity. But Bloom's approach differs from Croce's and Bembo's in one respect. For Bloom, the problem of the theological reading in Dante studies is that it imposes too much conventionally theological or Augustinian-Thomistic order on the poem's content. The extensive study of what Boyde defines as the ideological content and regards as indispensable for any reading of the poem has blocked the access to the poetic dimension. Bloom opposes the view that Dante, as Boyde claims, "is first and foremost a poet of the intellectual life" and "that most of the distinguishing features of his mature poetry derive from his study of philosophy."[22] For Boyde, Dante's creative writing was simply "nourished by philosophy."[23]

The distinction between the theological and the poetic reading does not encapsulate the distinction between the secular and the sacred reading. As in the case of the poetic and the theological reading, the difference between the secular and the sacred reading can be viewed in two different ways. It can be viewed as the result of a historical process. But it can also be viewed as involving two different modes of experiencing the world. Sapegno's observation that Dante's poem epitomizes a period in history that is caught in its final phase, on the very brink of disintegration, helps to clarify the former view. If the period is seen as the beginning of the disintegration of the sacred or theocentric ethos of the Middle Ages and as the preparation for the emergence of the modern secular ethos, it becomes clear why the reception of Dante's poem has generated more secular readings than sacred readings. The disintegration theory helps to explain why the early readings of the *Commedia*, which formally belong to the medieval period, did not manage to disclose the substantive content of the *Commedia*. The historical process of intellectual secularization, which can be traced back to Dante's time, meant that the early readers imposed a cultural view on the poem that reflects the emergence of the secular ethos. Their readings are not secular readings, but the move towards the secular ethos can be detected. The secular inclination is manifest in the interpretation of Vergil as Reason and Beatrice as Faith. It reflects the Thomistic distinction between the natural and supernatural order. It gives prevalence to the dyadic pattern of thought in interpreting the *Commedia*. In order to understand how the move toward the secular ethos is reflected in the preference for the dyadic pattern of thought, let us again consider the difference between Bonaventure and Aquinas.

In *Semiotics and Thematics in Hermeneutics*, Seung argues that throughout a great part of the medieval period, the concern for this world was totally suppressed for the sake of the other world. But by the twelfth century, secular concern was no longer totally suppressed but became subordinated to religious concern. This change from suppression to subordination was not problematic as long as medieval Christians took no strong interest in the natural order, but once they started showing positive attitudes toward nature, the result was the tension between secular and religious concerns. One way to resolve the tension was the allegorical sensibility that flourished in the twelfth and thirteenth century. The beauty of nature was not appreciated for its own sake; it was taken as the allegorical medium for the reflection of the beauty of the supernatural order:

> The subordination of secular interest to religious concern through allegory reached its fullest bloom in St. Bonaventure's theology, and Dante's figural allegory in the *Commedia*. Bonaventure's theology was to see the allegorical reflections of the Holy Trinity in every natural object and historical event; Dante's figural allegory was to portray the workings of the Trinity through the allegorical medium of the entire universe and its history (*STH* 205).

Seung points out that Aquinas tried to solve the same conflict with his doctrine of the natural and supernatural orders by subordinating the former to the latter.

> But there is a delicate point of difference between his way and Bonaventure's. Although both recognized positive values for the natural order, these positive values were quite different. Bonaventure saw the positive values of nature mainly in her function as allegorical medium. It was essentially an instrumental value. However, Aquinas took the bold step of recognizing the intrinsic value of nature in addition to her instrumental value. This was the main reason why he was considered a radical theologian by his contemporaries. Although Aquinas insisted on the subordination of the intrinsic value of the natural order to that of the supernatural order, the very recognition of the former was a scandal and blasphemy to the conservative Christians who could recognize no intrinsic values outside the supernatural order (*STH* 205-6).

With Aquinas's recognition of the intrinsic values of nature we are still far from the secular ethos of modern times. But the recognition advanced the secular orientation. By demarcating the natural from the supernatural order, Aquinas secured the domain of human autonomy in the natural order: "Human beings have the power to fulfill their natural end, Thomas Aquinas holds, although they do not have the power to fulfill their supernatural end. This is a far clearer recognition of human power and dignity, albeit limited, than the traditional Christian teaching, which had systematically stressed human impotence without a clear discrimination of the natural from the supernatural order" (*STH* 161). To point out how Aquinas's view of human power differs from Dante's, Seung stresses the difference between how Dante tries to scale the mountain in canto 1 of *Inferno* and how the Thomistic man would climb it. In accordance with the general view of Dante studies, Seung says that the mountain represents the kingdom of natural end and bliss. Since human beings, according to Aquinas, have the power to enter that kingdom, the Thomistic man would have the power to climb the mountain on his own. This is not possible for the Dantesque man we encounter in the beginning of the poem:

> His attempt to climb the Delectable Mountain only turns him into a helpless victim of three beasts. Hence the *Commedia* embodies the medieval notion of human impotence and dependence far more emphatically than the Thomistic conception of humanity. With its recognition of partial autonomy, the Thomistic conception constituted the transition from the medieval notion of total impotence and dependence to the Renaissance notion of total human autonomy or sovereignty (*STH* 161-62).

The recognition of the partial human autonomy is the result of Aquinas's adoption of the Aristotelian dyadic outlook against the traditional triadic one displayed most significantly in Bonaventure's works.

In addition, Seung emphasizes another aspect of Thomistic theology that makes it differ from Bonaventurian theology. This difference is the difference between theology of analogy and theology of allegory. Thomistic theology is representational of the former, and Bonaventurian theology is representational of the latter (*CT* 77-89 and 243-55; *STH* 142-53 and 162). These two medieval theologies are two indirect ways of speaking of God. Their basis is the assumption that human language cannot make direct statements about the infinite God, because it belongs to the realm of finite beings or things. Human language can speak of God only indirectly by way of analogies and allegories. But analogies and allegories are two different ways of speaking of God indirectly. The difference between them can be explained by using the distinction between the overt and the covert system of reference. The allegory has two systems of reference—overt and covert. To exemplify this, let us take the allegory of an ant and a grasshopper. The two animals belong to the overt system of reference. If we take this story as the allegory of a hardworking person and a lazy one, these two belong to the covert system of reference. The two persons are not mentioned at all in the story. By recognizing the two systems of reference, we have a complex system that combines the overt and the covert systems. This is the case with the personification allegory. Its literal sense is the overt system and the allegorical sense is the covert system. In the figural allegory, the system of reference becomes more complex. The literal sense is also the overt system, but the covert system has at least three senses—the allegorical, the moral, and the anagogical.

By contrast, there is no covert system of reference for analogy. Suppose that I say that "God is wise" and that the statement is not literal but anagogical. As far as the system of reference is concerned, there is no difference between the literal and the anagogical discourse. Both of them employ only the overt system of reference. Their difference lies in the function of predicate or attribute. The predicate functions literally in one and analogically in the other. For example, "man is wise" and "God is wise" are two sentences that refer to the concept of wisdom. But medieval theologians argued that the two sentences should not be understood univocally. The concept of wisdom is a human concept. If it is applied to God in the same sense as to man, it says something false about God, because God cannot be wise in the same sense as man. The concept of wisdom applied to man is literal, whereas it is analogical when applied to God. Due to the difference between the simple and the complex system of reference, Seung says, "literal theology is a more direct way to talk about God than analogical theology, which is in turn a more direct way than allegorical theology" (*STH* 162).

The allegorical mode emphasizes the radical difference between God and human beings. God can be known primarily by way of covert signs or allegorical language. The medium of understanding is the complex system of reference. In contrast, the literal mode stresses that God is not radically different from human beings. God can be known, more or less, in the same way as human beings. Hence the medium of understanding is the simple system of reference. The analogical mode is the in-between mode of understanding. It is based on the simple system of reference. It insinuates that human beings can know God by way of human language, but it stresses, at the same time, that the human knowledge of God is incomplete, precisely because it is human and therefore limited. These three types of theological conceptions (literal, anagogical, and allegorical), however, are not just three different modes of speaking of God; they also demarcate a historical development. In Seung's words: "Thomistic theology [of analogy] constituted the historical transition from the medieval allegorical tradition to the univocalism and literalism of the Renaissance" (*STH* 162).

Given these distinctions, we can now see why Singleton's interpretation of Beatrice as a Christ-figure and Hollander's interpretation of Vergil as a figure of John the Baptist are problematic. In both cases, the allegorical and triadic outlook is mixed up with the analogical and dyadic outlook that marks the transition from the Gothic to the Renaissance ethos. This mixture can be the reason why Singleton stresses that the modern reader of the *Commedia* is fundamentally detached from Dante's cultural outlook. When the two theological conceptions get mixed up, it is no longer possible to disclose the thematic coherence of the poem's substantive content. On the inspiration of Auerbach's argument that the *Commedia* displays figuralism, Singleton and Hollander maintain that in the *Commedia* Dante makes use of the allegory of the theologians as outlined in the *Convivio* and the *Letter to Can Grande della Scala* and combines it with the allegory of the poets. The former is the figural allegory and the latter is the personification allegory. Although they object to the traditional interpretation of Vergil as Reason and Beatrice as Faith, they do not completely discard it. They keep the twofold leadership intact. Reason prepares the way for Faith, just as John the Baptist prepares the way for Christ. As such, their interpretations are more in accordance with the dyadic outlook of Thomistic theology than with the triadic outlook of Bonaventurian theology. This is the first move away from Dante's cultural outlook.

In arguing in favor of the figural interpretation of the *Commedia*, Singleton and Hollander make a second move away from Dante's cultural outlook. The move concerns Dante's use of the notion of promise and fulfillment in medieval Christian exegesis, which is the essential characteristic of the figural allegory. Also in this case, Singleton and Hollander are indebted to Auerbach. In speaking of Beatrice as a Christ-figure in his *Journey to Beatrice*, Singleton does not refer to Auerbach, but it seems clear that he must have got the idea from Auerbach's essay "Figura," which appeared in 1938 in an Italian version. In that essay Auerbach speaks of Beatrice as a "*figura* or *idolo Christi*."[24] Singleton elaborates on this idea while at the same time taking Auerbach's distinction of promise and fulfillment for granted. In his *Allegory in Dante's Commedia*, Hollander admits his indebtedness to Auerbach and takes

Singleton's elaboration on Auerbach one step further by adding a figural meaning to Vergil. Since the interpretations of Singleton and Hollander are clearly elaborations on Auerbach's original thesis, they should be seen in the light of the latter.

In medieval Christian exegesis, the New Testament was seen as the fulfillment of the promise given in the Old Testament. Both testaments were regarded as historical documents. Their account of events was read literally. But the relation between the promise and the fulfillment was a matter of interpretation. For example, Joshua was seen as a figure of Christ. The former's conquest of Jericho prefigured the latter's entry in Jerusalem. One was the promise, and the other was the fulfillment. Both events were historical. But their ultimate meaning could be disclosed only on the basis of the Christian revelation of the ultimate end. According to Auerbach, Dante makes use of the notion of promise and fulfillment in his figural allegory. He argues that the relation between the historical Vergil of ancient times and the Vergil of the *Commedia* corresponds to the relation between promise and fulfillment. The same is the case with the relation with the historical Beatrice of Florence and the Beatrice of the *Commedia*: "Their appearance in the other world is a fulfillment of their appearance on earth, their earthly appearance a figure of their appearance in the other world."[25] Auerbach identifies these figural relations as the figural realism of the *Commedia.* But as Seung points out: "In order to maintain his figural realism, [Auerbach] advances the absurd view that Dante's Vergil is as real as the historical Vergil. It is one thing to grant the concreteness of Dante's Vergil, but quite another to claim his reality" (*CT* 11).

Singleton and Hollander do not follow Auerbach completely on this point. According to the former, "the fiction of the *Divine Comedy* is that it is not a fiction." According to the latter, the *Commedia* is a poem "in which the events may not have happened but are to be understood and treated *as though* they had actually happened." In short, "Dante *feigns* that his fiction is literally true."[26] Singleton and Hollander adopt Auerbach's figural program, but they are reluctant to accept his realist program. Yet their approach is still infected with the realist program. Their concern for the fictitious character reflects their problem in coming to terms with the literal sense of the *Commedia.* The literal sense is the basis for Auerbach's realist program. As Seung points out: "Auerbach's thesis concerning Dante's figuralism has two features: (1) the literal sense of the *Commedia* belongs to history and not to fiction (his literal fundamentalism); and (2) its spiritual senses are figural and not personification allegory (figural allegorism)" (*CT* 27-28). Singleton and Hollander accept (2), but have problems in accepting (1). They elaborate on (2), but find no solution to (1). They try to solve (1) by speaking of the fictitious character. But as Seung points out:

> Unfortunately, this admission of the "as-if" tone, or fictional pretense, gives the whole show away. It is precisely the as-if tone of reality or fictional pretense that gives a fiction its fictitious character. I know of neither a fiction that is not written as it were a true story, nor a fiction that is written as if it were a false story. To say that the *Commedia* has the as-if tone it to admit that it is a fictitious work (*CT* 12).

Hence what Singleton and Hollander say is something trivial about fictional works. But since they elaborate on Auerbach's thesis and try to adopt the allegory of the theologians to the *Commedia*, they find it necessary to address the question of the literal sense.

In medieval Christian exegesis, the literal sense is always historical. Does Dante's adoption of the exegetical scheme mean that the literal sense of the *Commedia* is historical, too? This question has haunted modern Dante studies. It has led to speculations on whether Dante saw himself as a prophet or whether he believed to have seen the afterworld in some extraordinary vision. There are differences between mystical speculations and the concern for the poem's fictitious character. But as Dante scholars have practiced the mystical and the literary approach to the *Commedia*, the two approaches hold one thing in common: they display an obsession with the literal sense of the *Commedia*. The mystical reading is guided by Dante's claim of revelatory insight in the order of the afterworld. It is taken as an evidence of how the medieval Christian did not make a clear distinction between the physical and the spiritual world. Spiritual experiences were sometimes regarded as actual revelations of the spiritual world in physical things. As a result, the accounts of such experiences could be taken to contain actual or literal meaning. In the literary reading, the obsession with literal meaning follows a different path. Whereas the mystical reading makes the medieval sensibility highly mysterious, the literary reading results in a contextual error. About Auerbach's figural program, Seung says:

> [Auerbach's] blinding obsession with literal sense inevitably leads to the contextual error of interpreting the *Commedia* in the context of modern, Protestant literal sensibility rather than in that of medieval allegorical sensibility. In order to avoid this context error, we must separate figural allegorism from literal fundamentalism and shift all the emphasis from the latter to the former (*CT* 29).

Since Singleton and Hollander interpret the figural meaning of the *Commedia* on the inspiration of Auerbach, they are still puzzled by his literal fundamentalism. As a result, they cannot make the shift from literal fundamentalism to figural allegorism. They cannot make a figural reading of the *Commedia* without unnecessary concern for its literal truth. In *The Fragile Leaves of the Sibyl*, Seung makes such a figural reading. In *Cultural* Thematics, he shows how the figuralism of the *Commedia* matches the Bonaventurian theology of allegory rather than the Thomistic theology of analogy.

The interpretations of Singleton and Hollander display a conflict between literal fundamentalism and figural allegorism. They improve Auerbach's original thesis by emphasizing the inadequacy of taking the literal sense of the *Commedia* at face value. They emphasize the figural meaning and try to release the *Commedia* from the traditional yoke of personification allegory. But they do not seem to be aware that Auerbach's obsession with literal meaning is influenced by the modern Protestant literal sensibility. If they were, they would not have proposed their interpretations of Beatrice as a Christ-figure and Vergil as a figure of John the Baptist. The latter presupposes the former; Hollander's interpretation is an extension of Singleton's. But Singleton's interpretation elaborates on Auerbach's figural thesis, influenced by the Protestant literal sensibility. Therefore the problem with Singleton's interpretation of Beatrice (and consequently also Hollander's interpretation of Vergil) is the strict reliance on Auerbach's figural thesis. Singleton's interpretation is theological. It is influenced by Christology, but Christology is still Christian and religious. Hence his Christological approach to the *Commedia* is not a secular reading. But since it involves a reading that accepts God only in the form of man, it imposes a conception on the *Commedia* that belongs to the Protestant literal sensibility and not the medieval allegorical sensibility. To impose this perspective on Dante's poem is to make a move away from its cultural context. Its thematic content comes to display an inclination toward the secular ethos.

A clear indication of the prevalence of the secular reading in Dante studies is that the twentieth century has produced a far greater number of English translations of *Inferno* than those of the other two parts. The reason is that *Purgatorio* and *Paradiso* are irrelevant to our irreligious or secular age. In contrast, *Inferno* can still make sense for us because it is a record of sins and evils. We can read it without believing in the existence of the afterworld, because Dante's Hell resembles our own secular world. Although we no longer believe in the possibility of salvation, we do not doubt the actuality of perdition and degradation. No one is willing to believe in the workings of the Holy Spirit, but everyone, even the non-Christian secularist, can have empathy with the suffering Christ in the evil world. Our secular age is willing to read the *Commedia* only if it is read as a book of the natural world. *Inferno* can still make a convincing case as a book of this world, because the sins and crimes it narrates appear to be right out of our own world. But *Purgatorio* and *Paradiso* are altogether different. It is impossible to take a single step in those two realms without sensing the brooding omnipresence of the Trinity, which assures us the possibility of repentance and salvation. In our secular age, it is difficult to read *Purgatorio* and *Paradiso* as stories of the living God. As Nietzsche says, "God is dead," at least for our age.

Due to our secular ethos, we have difficulties in identifying ourselves with the medieval worldview and gaining a synoptic view of Dante's vision. To comprehend the *sovrasenso* or covert meaning of the *Commedia* is to have the synoptic vision of all its parts. To read the three parts without a synoptic framework is to have a segmental reading. The problem of attaining a synoptic view can be further elucidated by considering a passage in Foster's review of *The Fragile Leaves of the Sibyl.* Foster refers to Dante scholars who have tried to gain a synoptic vision, and he describes their efforts as follows:

> Those who have tried hardest to see the poem as a whole have tended, in recent years, to concentrate precisely on that part of the *Comedy* where the personal and public elements of Dante's vision, the subjective and the objective, the poetic and the theological are most tightly and puzzlingly interwoven; I mean *Purgatorio* 30-33, the encounter with Beatrice. Now there is a great deal to be said for focusing on this famous episode—"the very heart of the *Comedy*," "the pattern at the center," as Mr. Hardie and Professor Singleton respectively call it.[27]

Colin Hardie and Singleton used two imposing expressions—the heart of the *Commedia* and the pattern at the center—because they believed to have located the ultimate meaning of the *Commedia.* But what takes place on the top of Purgatory is only the preparation for Dante's flight up to the ten heavens of Paradise. Using the language of space travel, we can say that the top of Purgatory is the launching station for Dante's flight to the Empyreum. How can this preparatory ground be the heart or center of the *Commedia*?

In support of their views, Hardie and Singleton argue that Dante's union with Beatrice on the top of Purgatory represents his "return to Beatrice." In the *Vita Nuova* Dante fell in love with her, but in the *Convivio*, he deserted her for the Lady Philosophy. In the *Commedia* he returns to her for their final reunion in the last four cantos of *Purgatorio*. If Dante's reunion with Beatrice is the heart of the *Commedia* or its ultimate message, his love should be consummated on the top of Purgatory. Instead, she replaces Vergil as Dante's guide and leads him to the highest heaven, where she hands over her charge to Bernard for the fulfillment of Dante's love of God in his beatific vision. The love relation between Dante and Beatrice is far from the normal relation between a man and a woman. In the *Commedia* Dante approaches her not simply as his beloved. He approaches her as if she were his lord and master. In return, she rebukes and admonishes him like a school kid. His reverence for her is as evident as his reverence for his first guide, the aged Vergil. When Beatrice finally takes Dante to the Empyreum, she does not stay with him. For some time, he does not even know that she has left him because she did not even say good-bye to mark her departure. Their reunion could not end in such an unceremonious way if it were the heart of the *Commedia*.

About the theory of Dante's return to Beatrice, Foster says that "it remains by no means clear what precisely Dante was returning *from*—what sins or errors or both he was renouncing—nor precisely what he was now returning *to*." According to Hardie, these questions concern the purely private affair between Dante and Beatrice. If so, the entire *Commedia* degenerates to the celebration of Dante's private relation with Beatrice. According to Singleton, Dante's return to Beatrice is his return to Christ because she is a likeness to Christ. In that case, Dante's love of her is his love of Christ. But his poems about her in the *Vita Nuova* depict the love between a boy and a girl. If he now sees her as a Christ-figure in the *Commedia*, his heterosexual relation with her has turned into a homoerotic relation. These are the consequences of Hardie's and Singleton's attempts to locate a synoptic view of the *Commedia* in the reunion of Dante and Beatrice. The prevalence of the secular reading in Dante studies is also the reason why it is a common practice to emphasize that Dante never got his beloved Beatrice in the mortal world. But that is to miss the point. As it turns out in the *Commedia*, Dante's love for Beatrice is not a secular love. What Dante implicitly describes is the manifestation of a sacred or divine love in the mortal world. Beatrice is not the ultimate object for Dante's love. The object is the divine love. In the *Commedia* Beatrice represents the divine love by being the allegorical representation of the Holy Spirit, whose attribute is Love. It is manifest in the beauty of her spiritual appearance, as it was once manifest in the beauty of her physical appearance.

In the review, Foster tries to explain why Seung's reading never gets entangled in the kind of problems that trouble the learned readings of contemporary Dante scholars. He says that Seung's *felix culpa* is that he is not well-versed in contemporary Dante studies. For this reason, he is never swept into the whirlpool of *Purgatorio* 30-33. Instead of getting lost in this whirlpool, Foster says, Seung is "free to leap straight to the 'ladder of joy.'" By this he means to say that if Seung had known more about Dante commentaries and their established traditions and conventions, he might have been entangled in the ticket of the Terrestrial Paradise and would never have got out of it. But this is uncharitable account. It is almost the same as to say that if Seung had received the normal training in Dante studies, he might have been awed by the immense prestige of learned Dante scholars. His understanding of the *Commedia* might have been more concerned with what the learned scholars had said about the poem than with its thematic integrity.

Human and Divine Meaning

In understanding Seung's theory, it is important to distinguish two features: (1) the method of reading, and (2) the content of reading. His parallel reading concerns (1) and his Trinitarian reading concerns (2). Since the method of reading reveals the content of reading, (1) leads to (2). Seung's method of reading is the parallel reading in distinction from the serial reading, which can take different forms such as the segmental and the episodic readings. The parallel reading reveals the ladder of virtues, which in turn reveals the triadic structure of the soul. Since Seung takes the triadic structure of the soul as the image reflecting the nature of the Trinity, the former reveals the latter. This is the sequence of Seung's phenomenological revelation or disclosure. It begins with the parallel reading and leads to his Trinitarian reading, which involves two trinities: (1) the trinity of God, and (2) the trinity of man. Because man is created in the image of God, the trinity of the human psyche reflects the trinity of divine nature.

The Trinitarian relation of man to God was a common heritage for the medieval Christians. Given this heritage, the man-centered reading inevitably leads to the God-centered reading. There are two ways of conducting the man-centered reading. One is the standard way. It is to take the *Commedia* as a description of human affairs. This turns Dante's epic into a *Commedia Umana*. The other way is to take one step further and read the *Commedia* as the reflection of God. This elevates the *Commedia Umana* into the *Commedia Divina*. The ultimate question is whether in Dante's epic humanity should be understood as a self-contained entity or as the reflection of God. To say that humanity is self-contained is to say that humanity is independent. It can be known and described without reference to anything else. However, to take humanity as a reflection of God is to say that humanity is not an independent entity. If so, its description can never be given without pointing to what it reflects. If we assume, as medieval Christians did, that human beings reflect the Trinity, any description of humanity automatically turns into a description of the Trinity.

Seung's God-centered reading opposes the man-centered reading of Dante studies. He regards the man-centered reading as an inaccurate projection of the man-centered ethos of the Renaissance on Dante's poem:

> In justification of this reading, many [Dante scholars] have hailed Dante as the supreme poet of his vernacular tongue in celebration of the Renaissance secular ethos, and his *Commedia* as an immortal monument to the vitality of that ethos. For the same reason, Erich Auerbach has labeled him a poet of the secular world. As a great poet of the secular and the profane, he is often teamed up with Petrarch and Boccaccio to make the celebrated trio of Italian Renaissance literature (*STH* 169).

The man-centered reading is the preferred one by Dante scholars. It is perhaps the greatest hindrance for accepting Seung's theory. In addition, the man-centered reading generates problematic readings of the *Commedia*. To give a radical example, Lee Siegel argues that the *Commedia* is a portrayal of the "subversive ego."[28] Siegel uses the postmodern notion of "subversive" in characterizing the nature of Dante's poem. But is he only flaunting a fashionable word, or does he mean something important? Dante the traveler by himself cannot be a subversive ego, but if Dante presents himself as the epic hero of his otherworldly journey, he becomes an agent of subversion because he supplants God as the epic hero. To pose a human being as the hero of the *Commedia* subverts the medieval theocentric ethos. Siegel's notion of the subversive ego comes down to the question of whether the *Commedia* is anthropocentric or theocentric. Should we read it as a man-centered or a God-centered epic?

In order to bring forth the subversive ego of the *Commedia*, Siegel first emphasizes that our modern culture is one of "almost occult self-centeredness." In this culture, he argues, many people "turn inward to find that part of themselves that is connected to a larger life, that exists beyond their self-interest and their banal desires." But these people often lack the proper means for making "good self-examinations" that does not result in "bad narcissisms." In Siegel's view, the *Commedia* displays "a style of self-description . . . to which we might aspire." He regards it as "the most effective epic of the self," driven by a "torsion of self-conflict." But Siegel's argument for a man-centered reading of the *Commedia* rests on the fact that it is the first epic in world literature in which the author is the main character. This is why he finds it subversive, because the author poses himself as the epic hero. This suggestion has never previously been made by Dante scholars who take the *Commedia* as a first-person epic. But its implication brings nothing new to Dante studies. It only reflects the tendency to see Dante as a modern writer instead of a medieval one. But this view is tenable only if we restrict our focus to the poetic form. It is untenable as soon as we focus on the thematic content. The polysemantic dimension of Dante's poetic language may resemble the polyfonic dimension Mikhail Bakhtin identifies as the essential characteristic of the discourse of the novel.[29] But if Dante's modern strain is identified on that ground, modernity is reduced to a question of how one speaks; what one speaks about becomes irrelevant.

The first-person account was a new invention for the epic but not for other poetic forms in Dante's time. The *Dolce stil novo* persistently explored the first-person account. Dante's choice of poetic form is in accordance with the poetic style of writing in his time. If he had chosen the third-person, he would have broken with the poetic tradition of the *Dolce stil novo*. He would have gone back to a poetic form that was not in accordance with the poetic tradition of the period. The reason why Siegel bases his argument on Dante's choice of poetic form is due to the emphasis on the individual perspective. In contrast to the collective, the emergence of the individual has often been taken to be an essential characteristic of modernity. Since the rise of modernity is often associated with the Renaissance, many readers of the *Commedia* have found it reasonable to suggest that modernity is detectable in Dante's poem and that Dante's first-person account reflects the first step towards the Renaissance individual. If so, it leads to the anthropocentric view of the world. The *Commedia* then belongs to the Renaissance ethos and is subversive of the medieval theocentric ethos. But Dante's choice of poetic form can be given a different explanation. It can be seen as an expression of piety. By this I mean that it underlines the way in which Dante wholeheartedly believes in his vision. This does not mean that he sees himself somehow as a prophet to whom God has spoken directly. It rather means that he considers his vision of order to be as accurate as possible.

Notes

1. I. A. Richards, *Practical Criticism: A Study of Literary Judgment* (London: Routledge and Kegan Paul, 1929).

2. Morton W. Bloomfield, *The Seven Deadly Sins: An Introduction to the History of a Religious Concept with Special Reference to Medieval English Literature* (East Lansing: Michigan State University Press, 1967), 157. The book was originally published in 1952.

3. Morton W. Bloomfield, *The Seven Deadly Sins*, 43-44 and 157.

4. Richard Newhauser, *The Treatise on Vices and Virtues in Latin and the Vernacular* (Turnhout, Belgium: Brepols, 1993), 14-15.

5. Richard Newhauser, *The Treatise on Vices and Virtues*, 99.

6. Richard Newhauser, *The Treatise on Vices and Virtues*, 108-13.

7. Richard Newhauser, *The Treatise on Vices and Virtues*, 60-64.

8. Mancini, Franco. "Un' 'auctoritas' di Dante," in *Studi danteschi* 45 (1968), 95-119.

9. See *ED* on the article *Maometto.*

10. Richard W. Southern, "Dante and Islam," in *Relations between East and West in the Middle Ages*, ed. Derel Baker (Edinburgh, Scotland: Edinburgh University Press, 1973), 138.

11. Harold Bloom, *The Western Canon: The Books and Schools of the Ages* (New York: Harcourt Brace & Company, 1994), 46.

12. In the history of Dante studies, Vergil and Beatrice have been attributed different allegorical meanings, but the prevailing tendency has been and still is to distinguish between a natural domain (reason or philosophy) and a supernatural domain (faith or theology). For more on this issue, see *ED* under the articles *Virgilio* and *Beatrice.* For a recent example of this tendency, see J. A. Scott, *Dante's Political Purgatory* (Philadelphia: University of Pennsylvania Press, 1996), x. Scott uses the distinction of *De monarchia* (III. xvi) between man's two goals and the two guides (the emperor and the pope) for mankind's attainment of these goals. The different concepts Dante scholars apply for demarcating the difference between Vergil's and Beatrice's guidance is not of great importance. What is important is the implicit application of the theological distinction between nature and supernature, which supports the assertion of a conceptual affinity between the *Commedia* and Thomistic theology.

13. The idea of Beatrice as a Christ-figure has been repeated time and again in a great number of Dante readings, but the most influential is Singleton's Dante readings. As for his allegorical identification of Beatrice and Vergil, see Charles S. Singleton, *Dante Studies II: Journey to Beatrice* (Cambridge, Mass.: Harvard University Press, 1958), 30, 33, and 89.

14. Robert Hollander, *Allegory in Dante's Commedia* (Princeton, N.J.: Princeton University Press, 1969), 261; Charles S. Singleton, *Dante Studies II*, 53-54.

15. Stephen Botterill, *Dante and the Mystical Tradition: Bernard of Clairvaux in the Commedia* (Cambridge: Cambridge University Press, 1994), 221.

16. Charles S. Singleton, *Dante Studies II*, 93-94.

17. Antonio C. Mastrobuono, *Dante's Journey of Sanctification* (Washington, D.C.: Regnery Gateway, 1990), v and 124.

18. Antonio C. Mastrobuono, *Dante's Journey of Sanctification*, 6-7.

19. Robert Hollander, "Dante *Theologus-Poeta*," in *Studies in Dante* (Ravenna: Longo, 1980), 86.

20. Marga Cottino-Jones, "Literary-critical Developments in Sixteenth- and Seventeenth Century Italy," in *The Cambridge History of Literary Criticism, Vol. III: The Renaissance*, ed. G. P. Norton (Cambridge: Cambridge University Press, 1999), 570; Fernand Hallyn, "Cosmography and Poetics," in *The Cambridge History of Literary Criticism*, 446.

21. Patrick Boyde, *Dante: Philomythes and Philosopher: Man in the Cosmos* (Cambridge: Cambridge University Press, 1981), 1.

22. Patrick Boyde, *Dante: Philomythes and Philosopher*, 1.

23. Patrick Boyde, *Perception and Passion in Dante's Comedy* (Cambridge: Cambridge University Press, 1993), xii.

24. Erich Auerbach, "Figura," in *Scenes from the Drama of European Literature: Six Essays*, trans. R. Manheim (New York: Meridian Books, Inc., 1959), 75.

25. Erich Auerbach, *Mimesis: The Representation of Reality in Western Literature*, trans. W. R. Trask (Princeton, N.J.: Princeton University Press, 1953), 195.

26. Robert Hollander, *Allegory in Dante's Commedia*, 78 and 258; Robert Hollander, "Dante *Theologus-Poeta*," 63-64; Charles S. Singleton, *Dante Studies I: Elements of Structure* (Cambridge, Mass.: Harvard University Press, 1954), 129.

27. Kenelm Foster, "A Propos of a New Book on Dante," in *Blackfriars* 43 (1962), 481-82.

28. Lee Siegel, "Out of the Dark Wood: Dante and the Subversive Ego," in *Harper's Magazine* (May, 2002), 79-83.

29. Mikhail Bakhtin, "Discourse in the Novel," in *The Dialogic Imagination: Four Essays*, trans. C. Emerson and M. Holquist (Austin: University ofTexas Press, 1981).

Chapter Five

Courage of Venus

Seung's reading of the *Commedia* is highly resourceful because it proposes a consistent and coherent theory about the principles that hold together the poem's three parts and shows how the principles are displayed in the narrative content. But what can be attained if Seung's theory about the poem's thematic coherence is applied in the act of textual analysis? This is the question explored in this and the following chapter. Seung's Dante reading is not conclusive or definitive, and although it has the quality of completeness, there are still many things to be examined and explored before Seung's theory might be accepted as better than the prevalent theories in Dante studies. I will exemplify the kind of work that still needs to be done in two ways. First, I will examine the two cantos of *Paradiso* that constitute the heaven of Venus. Second, I will investigate the episode with Brunetto Latini in the seventh circle of *Inferno*. As far as the methods of reading traditionally applied by Dante scholars are concerned, the former concerns the problem of segmental reading and the latter the problem of episodic reading.

The Venus heaven and the Brunetto episode are not just two elements of the whole. With the third terrace of Purgatory, the third heaven and the seventh circle constitute what Seung calls the rung of meekness and wrath. By focusing on the problem of the Venus discourse and the problem of sodomy, my method of inquiry follows the method of segmental reading. By formally applying the segmental approach while taking account of Seung's systematic parallel reading, my intention is to underline the inadequacy of segmental reading The following investigation, however, is not exhaustive for two reasons. First, it is concerned with only one step on Dante's ladder of divine love, which has ten steps. Second, the investigation is mainly concerned with two questions: What is the thematic content of the Venus discourse? And why has Dante placed Brunetto in Hell? Due to the limited perspective, I define my method of reading as thematic reading. The reading relies on Seung's method of reading, but it does not accomplish such a reading. The reading is defined as thematic because it regards the structure of the afterworld and the themes of the narrative as two sides of the same issue. But the reading is not a systematic thematic reading. Such a reading can be accomplished only if we investigate each step on the ladder of divine love. This is what Seung does in *The Fragile Leaves of the Sibyl*. However, although Seung examines each step of the ladder of divine love in detail, the examinations are not exhaustive due to the complexity of Dante's text and the ambiguities that innumerable studies of the text have generated.

Finally, since I regard the three parts of the poem as thematically connected, my reading opposes one of the standard assertions in Dante studies. For example, Lino Pertile argues that *Paradiso* is the least dramatic *cantica* of the *Commedia*, "if by drama we understand strong contrasts between characters, excited action, abrupt movement, sudden shifts of mood and poetic register and so."[1] A similar view is advocated by Cogan, for whom "the *Paradiso* is the most fundamentally—one might say, organically—allegorical" (*DW* 149). These views are tenable only if we regard each of the poem's three parts as a self-contained entity. But as soon as we recognize that *Paradiso* interacts with *Inferno* and *Purgatorio*, it is untenable to regard it as less dramatic or more allegorical than the other two parts. If *Paradiso* interacts with the other two parts, it makes part of the drama the three parts constitute as a whole. Since the theme of meekness in the third heaven is thematically related to theme of wrath in the seventh circle, the dramatic action of the latter is fully reflected in the seemingly undramatic content of the former. The same goes for the allegorical dimension. *Inferno* is no less allegorical than *Purgatorio* and *Paradiso*, just because the souls in Hell are more heavily marked by the conditions of the temporal world than the penitents of Purgatory and the blessed souls of Paradise. Studies of Dante's poem are often incapable of recognizing the dramatic character and the allegorical dimension of the whole poem because they conduct their inquiries into the narrative without having determined what holds together the three parts and their particular elements.

Myth of Venus

In Dante studies it has long been a standard reading to associate the Venus heaven with lust, although it belongs to the virtuous realm of Paradise.[2] This standard reading makes part of a widely accepted assertion that the state of the blessed souls in the first three spheres in Paradise (the Moon, Mercury, and Venus) is relatively imperfect, since according to medieval cosmology the earth cast its shadow on the three planets.[3] The assertion seems to be textually supported by the fact that Dante mentions this cosmological aspect near the end of the last of the two cantos (8 and 9 of *Paradiso*), which constitute the sphere of Venus (*Par.* 9: 118-19). For these reasons, some Dante scholars argue that three spheres represent a sort of Ante-Paradise analogous to the Ante-Hell (Entrance, Vestibule, and Limbo) and the Ante-Purgatory of the other two parts. This Ante-Paradise is said to display the three theological virtues of faith, hope, and charity in a defective or marred version.[4] Robert Hollander claims that Frank Ordiway has shown that this is the proper meaning of the first three spheres.[5] Hence there should be no reason to question the assertion.

The idea of Ante-Paradise reflects the natural instinct for parallel reading. Because there are an Ante-Hell and an Ante-Purgatory, the readers expect to find an Ante-Paradise by their sense of symmetry. But this expectation is too mechanical. If the function of Ante-Paradise is to prepare the soul for the entrance to Paradise proper, it is served by Purgatory. The notion of Ante-Paradise assumes that Hell, Purgatory, and Paradise stand as three independent domains, each of which has its own beginning and its own end. This is true of Hell. The end of Hell does not lead anywhere. It ends in the frozen lake of Cocytos. But the structure and function of Purgatory is different. It does not end on the top of the Mount of Purgatory, which serves only as the launching station for the flight to Paradise. In one respect, Purgatory is like Hell. Each of them makes a new beginning. That explains the existence of Ante-Hell and Ante-Purgatory. But Paradise does not make a new beginning, but continues the process that has been initiated and completed in Purgatory. Hence Purgatory serves the function of Ante-Paradise for Paradise proper.

The continuity of Purgatory to Paradise is established by the descent of Beatrice to the top of Purgatory to take Dante to the ten heavens. Although Vergil guides Dante through both Hell and Purgatory, he does not establish the continuity of those two domains. He serves the function of contrast between the sins punished and the sins purged. The symmetry between the Ante-Hell and the Ante-Purgatory is only on the surface. The Ante-Hell does not serve the function of initiating the souls to Hell proper. It is for those souls who are not fit to be allowed into Hell proper. It serves the function of exclusion. In fact, every circle of Hell serves the same function of exclusion. No circle allows any intrusion from the other circles. Purgatory, however, is the domain of movement from one terrace to another. This movement begins in Ante-Purgatory and ends in the Terrestrial Paradise, and it continues to the ten heavens. For these reasons, there is no need for an Ante-Paradise. The suggestion that the first three spheres of *Paradiso* constitute an Ante-Paradise seems to be due to a misunderstanding of the function of Purgatory and a mechanical notion of correspondence.

Nevertheless, many Dante scholars maintain some sort of Ante-Paradise for the first three heavens, although they do not always explicitly identify them as constituting an Ante-Paradise. The association of Venus with lust is essential for the interpretation of the first three heavens as displaying a marred version of the three theological virtues. The association is normally established through a combination of textual analysis of the *Commedia*, interpretations of intertextual relations between Dante's works, and the use of extratextual references especially in the commentary tradition, sometimes linked up with Thomistic distinctions as in Ordiway's case. This analytic practice is due to the fact that Dante nowhere says that Venus is associated with lust. The association can be established only if we assume that the *Commedia* repeats the notion of the planet's potential influence on man's behavior in this world as stated in book 2 of the *Convivio*. There Dante cites Vergil and Ovid, and remarks, "because the ancients recognized that this heaven was the cause of love here below, they said that Love was the son of Venus."[6] However, when ascended to the third heaven in the *Commedia*, Dante immediately says two things about Venus that do not coincide with the association with lust. First, he says that the belief in the ancient world that Venus was the cause of carnal love was a dangerous one. Second, he says that the fact that she, her mother Dione, and her son Cupid were worshiped and honored in accordance with this belief was an ancient error (*Par.* 8: 1-6):

> *Solea creder lo mondo in suo periclo*
> *che la bella Ciprigna il folle amore*
> *raggiasse, volta nel terzo epiciclo;*
> *per che non pur a lei faceano onore*
> *di sacrificio e di votivo grido*

le genti antiche ne l'antico errore.

The world once dangerously believed the lovely
Cyprian, whirling in third epicycle,
rayed down her frenzied beams of love on man,
so that the ancients in their ancient error
offered their sacrifice and votive cries
to honor her and not just her alone.
(Trans. Mark Musa)

According to Ordiway, Dante warns his reader to be on the guard against the wrong type of love.[7] But this is a superficial interpretation of the warning. Dante speaks of the error of believing in Venus as the initiator of "mad love." By claiming that the ancient myth of Venus was erroneous, Dante warns his reader against simplified assertions about the celestial influences on man. The implication of this warning is even emphasized long before Dante's ascent to the sphere of Venus.

On the third terrace of Purgatory, Marco Lombardi says that the world is blind because human beings tend to believe that everything is predestined by the motions of the stars (*Purg.* 16: 64-84). But if this were true, Marco says, no free will would exist: "It would not be just to render bliss for good and pain for evil." According to Marco, the stars can only initiate tendencies in man; man is a free subject of a greater power, over which the stars have no control. Since man is a free creature, he alone can make the present world go astray, due to his free will. Hence, when Dante in the third heaven warns us against the ancient belief in Venus, he has already through Marco's speech given us good reasons for not applying the astrological stereotypes of ancient mythology to the function of the heavens in the *Commedia*. Nevertheless, many Dante scholars maintain that the ancient myth constitutes the connection between the theme of lust and the planet's representational function in the *Commedia*. This leads to one simple question: Why does Dante characterize the myth of Venus as erroneous? This problem has largely been ignored in Dante studies. As a result, we are left with a puzzle: How can an idea (the ancient myth), which is characterized as dangerous and erroneous, still be the foundation for the function of an entity (the Venus heaven), whose property is explicitly said to be controlled by a different and more powerful idea (God)?

In order to resolve the discrepancy between the traditional interpretation of Venus and Dante's explicit warning, it is necessary to look at the arguments that make out the traditional view of the third heaven. Normally it involves an attempt to synthesize Dante's treatment of the Venus heaven in the *Convivio* and a handful of textual passages in the *Commedia*, where the name of Venus or her pseudonyms occur and the theme of lust in the sphere seems indicated by way of extratextual references. But the argumentation neglects a fundamental aspect of the Venus discourse. If we focus on what is said in the sphere, the notion of lust misfits the discourse of canto 8 and 9 of *Paradiso*. The discourse has a different thematic content. This not only indicates that Dante's warning is likely to be understood as a refusal of the association of Venus with lust, it also suggests that the state of the souls present in the sphere is not relatively imperfect or decreased because of sexual experiences, which three of the four souls Dante encounters have had.

To many Dante scholars, the suggestion that the representational function or symbolic meaning of Venus is not associated with lust might seem to raise more questions than our available sources can answer. It is admittedly problematic in two ways. First, it implicates an extensive criticism of an interpretive tradition that goes back as long as to the earliest commentaries and is still maintained. The criticism has to show why the treatment of the two Venus cantos has long been inconsistent. Second, the rejection of the association with lust raises one essential question: What does Venus represent? If it is not associated with lust, what is then its representational function? Seung's theory of thematic parallelism resolves the question. It cannot be determined through a segmental reading of the two Venus cantos.

In many studies of the Venus cantos, the *Convivio* plays a prominent part. In the treatise Dante examines the question of the representational function of the planet of Venus. This examination is due to the question of what celestial concept is implied with the initial line of the canzone: *Voi che 'ntendendo il terzo ciel movete*. In chapter 1 of book 2 the question results in the formal explication of the different levels of meaning according to the poets and the theologians. From chapter 2 Dante explores what he calls the literal meaning of the different parts of the canzone. This includes a description of the celestial hierarchy of which the third heaven is Venus. In chapter 3 he outlines the historical development of the concept of the celestial hierarchy. He corrects Aristotle for having followed the ignorance of the astrologers who believed that there were only eight heavens of which the last one (the Fixed Stars) contained the whole. According to Dante, Ptolemy got closer to the truth when he pointed out the necessity of a Prime Mover as the ninth heaven. In accordance with the Ptolemaic system, Dante enumerates nine moving heavens, and in accordance with the Christian teachings, he places outside these heavens the Empyrean heaven. The final heaven is God's domicile, which is motionless, because "stillness and peace are the qualities of the place of that Supreme Deity which alone completely beholds itself."[8]

In chapter 5 Dante assigns the different intelligences or angels to the nine celestial spheres. He explains how these nine spheres are divided into three principal hierarchies. On this ground, he presents a Trinitarian concept where the three principal divisions are related respectively to the power of the Father, the wisdom of the Son, and the love of the Holy Spirit. The spiritual creatures of the Venus heaven are named Thrones, and, like the Angels in the sphere of the Moon and the Archangels in the sphere of Mercury, these intelligences have received their nature from the love of the Holy Spirit. They perform "their operation, which is innate in them, namely the movement of that heaven, filled with love, from which the form of the said heaven derives a potent ardor by which the souls here below are kindled to love, according to their disposition."[9] Then Dante gives the above mentioned remark about the ancient belief in Venus, and cites Vergil and Ovid. In accordance with the distinction between the literal and the allegorical meaning, Dante's explanation of the placement of the third planet and its angels is to be understood as factual.

In the beginning of chapter 12 Dante says that he will now proceed to the second level of meaning. In chapter 13 he connects the heavens to the different disciplines of sciences in the medieval world. The seven planetary heavens are linked to the *Trivium* and the *Quadrivium*, the eighth heaven to natural science (physics and metaphysics), the ninth to moral science, and the tenth to divine science (theology). Venus is associated with the discipline of rhetoric in the *Trivium*. He gives two reasons for this association. First, Venus is associated with rhetoric because of "the brightness of its aspect, which is sweeter to look upon than that of any other star," and second, because of "its appearance now in the morning, now in the evening."[10] In chapter 15 Dante makes his concluding remarks on what he has already said about the literal and the allegorical meaning of the canzone. He believes that the resemblances between the heavens and the sciences make it clear whom he is addressing when he refers to those who are the movers of the Venus heaven in his canzone. Finally, he names Boethius and Cicero as those who with the sweetness of their discourse guided him along the path of love and into the pursuit of the most gentle Lady Philosophy.

From this summary of Dante's treatment of Venus in the *Convivio*, it is clear that Dante does not say that the ancient belief in Venus was dangerous and erroneous. In his explication of the planet's celestial characteristics, Dante simply points out a certain resemblance between the ancient myth and his Christian account. In the ancient world, Venus was regarded as the star of love. Now, in Dante's Christian world, it is associated with the love of the Holy Spirit. The idea of love as the planet's property gives the two concepts a certain affinity. The pagans had no idea of the Christian God but their idea of the goddess of love resembles that of the Holy Spirit, whose attribute is Love. For that reason, Dante's attitude toward the ancient myth of Venus in the *Convivio* does not state the same unconditional refusal as in the *Commedia*. He rather sees the myth as a partial or defective truth; it exemplifies the pagan way of groping for the ultimate truth without revelation.

The *Convivio* and the *Commedia* display two different concepts. In the treatise Dante follows the Gregorian model, which he divides into three triads implicitly following the Dionysian model. Besides that, he assigns Trinitarian attributes to the three triads implicitly following the medieval tradition of interpreting the Dionysian model. He combines two models and gives the result a Trinitarian interpretation. This is the contemplation scheme of the *Convivio*. Dante speaks of how the angelic intelligences contemplate the Trinity. He does not speak of how the Trinity works for the redemption of the human soul. In the poem, however, Dante applies the Dionysian order of angels and emphasizes its accuracy in comparison with the Gregorian model. In *Paradiso* he never divides the order of angels into three triads, nor does he say that the angelic order should be divided into other units and associated with the attributes of the three persons of the Trinity.

Because of the conceptual change, there are at least three important questions Dante readers should consider before making any conclusive remarks about how the *Convivio* supports the interpretation of the Venus heaven as associated with lust. (1) Since Dante with his statement in *Paradiso* about the true contemplation of Pseudo-Dionysius explicitly enters into the Dionysian tradition, the readers should consider whether his change of position influences the thematic content of the celestial hierarchy as a whole. (2) Since the thematic basis for the celestial hierarchy in the *Convivio* is a Trinitarian concept, the readers should consider whether the same theme is present in the *Commedia*. (3) Since Dante in the *Commedia* follows a different concept of the angelic order and corrects his former concept, the readers should consider what the change implicates as far as the representational function of Venus is concerned. The reason for raising these questions is that in the *Convivio* it is the Trinitarian concept that constitutes the relation between the ancient view of Venus as the goddess of love and the Christian notion of love as the attribute of the Holy Spirit. If a similar concept cannot be found in the heavens of the *Commedia*, and the angels of the third heaven cannot be related to the love of the Holy Spirit, there is no principal basis for ascribing lust to the sphere of Venus.

Cogan tries to answer the three questions by using certain aspects of the concept of the *Convivio* in his interpretation of *Paradiso*. But his answers are unsatisfactory. As far as (1) is concerned, Cogan connects *Paradiso* to the Dionysian model of three angelic triads by turning to the *Convivio*. But neither the *Convivio* nor the triads are ever mentioned in the *Commedia*. His motive for turning to the *Convivio* is therefore suspect. As far as (2) is concerned, Cogan gives the triads a Trinitarian interpretation, but he is inconsistent in his use of Trinitarian attributes in interpreting the properties of the angelic hierarchies. He mixes up the contemplation and the redemption schemes and his interpretation becomes arbitrary. Finally, as far as (3) is concerned, he follows the traditional way of coding the thematic content of the Venus discourse. Since the traditional coding implies that the first three spheres display some deficiency, he assumes that the Venus heaven thematizes an earthly limitation, which he associates with terrestrial love. As a result, he neglects Dante's warning against any simplified interpretation of the property of the Venus heaven.

Cogan's interpretation of the representational function of Venus basically reproduces the traditional view of Dante studies. In order to understand why Dante scholars maintain this view, let us consider how the argument is sometimes presented. For that purpose, I will turn to Foster's interpretation of the Venus heaven, because it exemplifies the method of segmental reading. Foster does not investigate (2) and (3), but he takes account of the divine attributes in his attempt to come up with a solution to (1). But the result is unsatisfactory. He interprets the function of the Venus heaven in the *Commedia* in terms of a love-influence due to the planet's relation to the love of the Holy Spirit as stated in the *Convivio*. He thinks that "it is with this [relation] in mind that we should understand those otherwise strangely 'erotic' declarations, in *Paradiso* 9, of Cunizza and Folco,"[11] and that some statements of the *Commedia* should be understood in the light of the *Convivio*. Hence he argues for the same interpretive procedure as Cogan does.

Foster is well aware that Dante's claim in *Paradiso* 8 that the belief of the ancients was erroneous requires some explanation. Since he maintains that the representational function of Venus is related to sexual behavior, the problem is to determine in what sense the ancient belief was an error. In order to answer that question, he proposes the following interpretation of Dante's apparent refusal of the ancient myth:

> To think that a love-influence came from the third heaven was not false, but it was a mistake to derive "*folle amore*," insane irrational love, from the heavens . . . as the two Venus cantos continue we can see Dante quite evidently correcting this error with allusions to the angelic hierarchies; and so, implicitly, to the Providence that governs the star-influences generally. It is in effect a Christian demythologizing: the veil of the fable is removed, the goddess dethroned, and her planet revealed now in its true relation to the angels, and through them to their Creator.[12]

Although Foster regards Dante's warning against the ancient myth as an act of demythologizing, the representational function of the heaven is by no means revealed to the reader. Its relation to the angels and their creator remains unsettled. The problem is that the use of the concept of the *Convivio* in interpreting *Paradiso* can only indicate why the virtuous state of the souls in the sphere is apparently deficient or decreased. It cannot determine what virtue is associated with their presence in Paradise.

Whether the theme displayed in the Venus cantos is interpreted as a defective display of the theological virtue of charity or as a defective display of the virtue of temperance due to carnal love, the interpretation has to rely on a preconceived idea that the sphere through the motions of its angels exerts an influence on man that can lead to a corrupted disposition of the soul. The Venus cantos do not state this idea by themselves. According to Foster, the association of Venus with lust explains why Cunizza and Folco say that on earth they were overcome by the light of the love-star. He maintains that if this notion is not applied, these declarations, which he claims to be erotic, would otherwise be strange. But Cunizza's and Folco's referent (*stella* and *cielo*) is nowhere identified as a love-star associated with lust. It is either extratextual references or statements in the *Commedia* made outside the sphere that determine the association with lust. The declarations are not erotic in themselves. They might seem strange since the thematic meaning of the referent is not explained. But they become erotic only as a result of ascribing lust to the star by way of references extrinsic to the discourse of the third heaven. Foster is right in saying that Dante's refusal of the ancient myth should be understood as if Dante now reveals the planet's true relation to the angels and God. But to point out such a change of position is far from sufficient for understanding what the change implies. The intertextual relations between the *Convivio* and the *Commedia* do not reveal the implication.

In the *Commedia* references to Venus made outside its sphere fall in two groups. The referent is either the mythological goddess or the planet in the celestial hierarchy. If we look at the first group, there are three instances. First, in relation to the theme of chastity on the seventh terrace of Purgatory, Dante makes use of the ancient myth of the goddess Diana, who disguised herself as a huntress in the woods in the attempt to preserve her virginity. Dante tells us that Diana chased out the nymph Helice, who was seduced by Jupiter and felt the poison of Venus (*Purg.* 25: 130-31). Second, in Purgatory Dante refers again to the ancient goddess when he describes the light in Matelda's eyes as more radiant than Venus's eyes when she, as a result of kissing her son Cupid, unintentionally fell madly in love with Adonis (*Purg.* 28: 64-65). Third, in *Paradiso*, when ascended to the Fixed Stars, Beatrice invites Dante to look down on the seven planetary heavens below, and subsequently the third planet is named by reference to the ancient myth of Venus as being the child of Dione (*Par.* 22: 143-44).

In each of these cases, Dante uses the ancient myth as an allegory within the narrative to describe something factual. The purgation of lust, the light of Matelda's eyes, and the position of Venus among the planets are all events that should be understood as factual within the textual universe of the *Commedia.* The mythological references, however, are used as descriptive elements within the factual discourse. When Dante in the *Convivio* explains the four levels of meaning, the issue is the potential polysemy of the factual or literal discourse and not the operative function of mythological allegories within the literal discourse. The semantic value of their function is primarily symbolic or metaphorical and not "a hidden truth beneath a beautiful fiction," as assigned to the second level of meaning in the *Convivio.* This is particularly the case with the first two instances, which have certain descriptive qualities, whereas in the third case the allegory is weakened to only a pseudonymous way of naming the planet. Hence it would be incorrect to appeal to this type of reference in support of the association of Venus with lust. Dante uses this type of reference descriptively only in a very limited context. In addition, the references to the lustful influence of Venus are made before the real character of the third heaven is revealed to Dante—before his ascent in *Paradiso* 8. The allusion to Venus's mythological origin in *Paradiso* 22 has not a similar meaning as the other two. It is allegorically neutral. It only displays an alternative naming of the planet. This is due to the fact that in the first Venus canto the name of the planet is reduced to a linguistic shell. In Dante's celestial hierarchy, Venus has a different meaning than in the ancient world. The name still refers to the ancient myth, but it does not represent the myth. The planet bears the name of the goddess, because the ancients took it and gave it to the planet, but the basis for the assignment was erroneous. Thus both the signifying and the signified have changed, but the signifying still reflects the ancient myth.

When we look at the other group of reference concerning the planet of Venus, it should be noticed that they occur before the ascent to the Venus heaven. There are two instances in Purgatory where the association of Venus with lust seems textually supported. First, in the beginning of *Purgatorio*, Dante refers to the planet, which at this point, before the ascent of the Mount of Purgatory has begun, is described as making the Eastern sky smile in her light veiling the constellation of the Fish. The issue is here medieval astrology, whereby the day and the hour of the day before the ascent are determined. But when Dante scholars cite this passage in support of their interpretation, it is due to the predicate Dante gives the planet. Venus is here called "the beautiful planet that kindles love in man" (*Purg.* 1: 19-21). For further support, Dante scholars sometimes explain the meaning of the verb *confortare* with reference to Dante's poem *Io son venuto al punto de la rota*. In the poem Saturn is said to "strengthen the frost," and Venus is described as "the star of love." Second, on the seventh terrace of Purgatory Dante uses medieval astrology in a similar way. The purpose is to determine the hour of his third dream in Purgatory. Here again it is the predicate that seems to support the notion of lust as the planet's representational function. Venus is described as one "whose flames of love always seem burning" (*Purg.* 27: 96).

Since it is the planet and not the goddess that constitutes the symbolic representation of Venus in the *Commedia*, the association with lust, based on references made outside the sphere, is supported only by the two predicates. It might be argued that Dante's references to the ancient myth of the goddess contribute to the consolidation of the association. But references to either the goddess or the planet need to be kept apart. If the separation is not upheld, the references to Diana and Venus's falling in love with Adonis would naturally support the association, since they state an influence of lust. But if we juxtapose the two types of reference and treat them as representing the same idea, we not only give Dante's two allusions to Ovid's *Metamophorses* (II, 401-530; X, 525-32) a significant representational and allegorical function within the literal discourse, we also neglect the fact that Dante warns us against believing in the ancient myth on which Ovid's stories are based. What remains in support of the association are only the two predicates stating Venus as a planet that may comfort man's relation to love and whose flames of love are always burning.

Both statements occur before Dante ascends to the third heaven and puts forward his warning. In order to understand what kind of love the statements implicate, the two references have to be interpreted retrospectively in the light of the thematic content of the Venus cantos. However, there is no need to do that. Such an interpretation would only give meaning to the references made before the ascent to the Venus heaven and therefore not determine the meaning of the Venus heaven. In addition, the two instances can hardly be said to confirm the association with lust. This is only the case with the allusions to Ovid, but as pointed out, they refer to the goddess whose attribute no longer denotes the planet's meaning. The references to the planet are more likely striking a love-theme comparable to the one explicated in the *Convivio*, where the relation between the ancient and the Christian notion is love, once represented by the mythological Venus and now by the Holy Spirit.

The question is not whether the sphere of the *Commedia* is related to love—that is, the attribute of the Holy Spirit. The question is whether the relation implicates an association with lust. But such an association would have to rely on the assumption that the potential lustful influence of the mythological Venus is to some extent maintained in Dante's concept of the planet's representational function. The references to Venus made outside the third heaven do not elucidate whether this is the case. For that reason, we have to turn the Venus cantos in order to determine the theme of its discourse.

Nature and Providence

In the Venus heaven Dante encounters four souls: Carlo Martello, Cunizza da Romano, Folco of Marseilles, and Rahab of Jericho. The first three are identified through their speeches, while the last one is pointed out by Folco. In Dante studies the association with lust is normally established on the basis of the three aspects. First, there are the two already mentioned textual references to the influence of the star made by Cunizza and Folco. Second, certain extratextual aspects concerning their lives indicate a lustful disposition and lustful acts. For example, Cunizza was married several times and was more than once involved in love affairs outside marriage. Folco lived an amorous life while still a troubadour and poet. But later on, he entered the Cistercian order, and, due to his monastic service, he was appointed first abbot and then bishop. Finally, there is Folco's reference to Rahab, whose status as the harlot of Jericho (Joshua 2: 1) is often stressed by Dante scholars at the expense of her deed as the one who hid Joshua's men in her house, wherefore only she and those in her house were left alive when Joshua ordered the destruction of the city (Joshua 6: 17). Many Dante scholars maintain that these aspects give sufficient support to the association. But when we examine them more closely and place them within the discourse of the two Venus cantos, the argumentation is poorly founded.

Dante's first interlocutor is Carlo Martello, who, after having explained that the souls in the sphere move about in a circular dance, greets the poet by citing the first line of Dante's canzone: *Voi che 'ntendendo il terzo ciel movete*. It might be argued that this reference shows the complexity of intertextual references in Dante's works, since the canzone is the analytic subject of book 2 of the *Convivio*. For that reason, Carlo's greeting has sometimes been interpreted as referring not only to the canzone but also to the *Convivio*. The reference has been taken to support the practice of applying the celestial concept of the *Convivio* in the interpretation of the structure of *Paradiso*. But this practice overlooks two essential things. First of all, it is important to keep in mind that the *Convivio* is never mentioned in the *Commedia*. Nothing in Dante's biography indicates that the four existing chapters of the unfinished treatise were known to anyone but Dante before his death. In our treatment of the relations between the two works, this problem should not be neglected. Since there is no evidence of any circulation of manuscripts of the *Convivio* in Dante's time, we cannot conclude that the implicit corrections of his former statements in the *Commedia* reflect more than a personal response to his former misconceptions. For the same reason, it cannot be determined whether Dante wants his reader to have knowledge of the celestial hierarchy as explained in the *Convivio* in order to understand the structure of Paradise. To paraphrase Singleton, the discrepancy between the *Convivio* and the *Commedia* on certain issues may simply reflect Dante's personal conversation with God about his past errors.

The second point is that we do harm to the temporal integrity of the *Commedia* if we assume that Dante expected his reader to know the content of a work which besides being incomplete was written after the Jubilee of 1300, where his otherworldly journey takes place. All allusions in the *Commedia* to events that take place after that year have formally the shape of prophecies. We only have to think of the condemnation of Pope Boniface VIII (*Inf.* 19: 52-57; *Par.* 30: 148) and the celebration of Emperor Henry VII of Luxemburg (*Par.* 30: 133-38), who both died after that year, in order to understand the significance of the temporal integrity. The two souls have not yet arrived at their destination, but their future destination in the afterworld is stated as a fact. No similar connection is traceable in the case of the *Convivio*. If we focus on whether Dante corrects, rejects, or projects former assertions in the *Commedia*, our understanding of the text can easily be distorted by our effort to read it as if the complexity of intertextual references were the key to its thematic content.

If we leave aside the speculation on Dante's use of implicit references to his own works and consider what is overtly stated, Carlo's citation of the canzone is significant at least in two ways. On the one hand, it helps to date the composition of the canzone, and on the other hand, it suggests a personal relationship between Dante and Carlo. As often mentioned in the commentaries on the episode, Dante might have met the Angevin heir to the thrones of Naples, Provence, and Hungary during his successful visit to Florence the year before he died (1295) at the age of twenty-four. The canzone was probably written around that time, and Dante might personally have made the prince familiar with his new poetic composition.[13] These historical and biographical aspects emphasize the significance of Carlo's presence in the Venus heaven. But what is more important for our present discussion is that the episode with Carlo nearly occupies one half of the entire discourse in the third heaven. This not only suggests that the meeting with Carlo was significant for Dante, it also emphasizes the significance of Carlo's words for the understanding of the Venus discourse. It is therefore puzzling that the advocates of the association of Venus with lust ignore the fact that the theme of lust is absent in Carlo's speech. No extratextual aspects concerning his life elucidate why he is supposedly a representative of the category of religiously affectionate but sensual characters in the virtuous realm of Paradise.

Some kind of eroticism can be imputed into his speech if the citation of the canzone is understood as referring implicitly to the *Convivio*. But such a proposition disregards two facts: (1) the treatise does not state that the influence of the Venus star arouses sexual behavior, and (2) Dante warns us against such a simplified notion. Since nearly one half of the entire discourse in the third heaven does not confirm the association with lust, the content of Carlo's speech is important for both the repudiation of the traditional interpretation and the formulation of a thematically consistent interpretation. In theological terms, Carlo's speech deals with the relations between the inherent nature of man and the workings of divine providence. The central issue is formulated by Dante's question of how "a sweet seed can produce a bitter fruit" (*Par.* 8: 93). The question causes a change of perspective in Carlo's speech. Carlo first says that if he had lived longer, much evil would have been prevented. He could have fulfilled his obligations as the heir to the titles and possessions of the Angevin family. Besides the already mentioned territories, Carlo also names Sicily, which could still have been reigned by Angevin descendants if the tyranny of his grandfather had not alienated the people. The consequence was the rebellion known as the Sicilian Vespers (1282), whereby the Sicilian crown was lost to the house of Aragon. Thus the theme of *mala segnoria* or "evil rule" (*Par.* 8: 73) is introduced for the first time in Carlo's speech. He continues his exemplification of its serious consequences by referring to his brother Robert. Although Robert descended from a generous nature, his character was niggardly. The contrast in character within the same family leads to Dante's question about heredity addressed to Carlo. In the following explanation Carlo unfolds a universal truth concerning nature and providence.

Carlo says that the good moves the heavens and they are filled with all the power of providence (*Par.* 8: 98). The power originates in the perfect "mind" (*Par.* 8: 101). Every type of human nature and its end are foreseen in the divine mind. Every arrow (providential inspiration) shot from the bow (transmitted from the heavens) has a predetermined end (a particular human being). If the heavenly transmissions were not governed by predetermination, the heavens would cause ruins. No work of art would exist, since the inspiration that gives life to it would not reach its end. But according to Carlo, this arbitrariness is impossible, because the intelligences that move the heavens are agents of the divine will. If they do not perform this will, they are defective in their performance, and if they are subdued to imperfection, their creator is also imperfect because his creation is defective.

After his explanation of the transmission and significance of providence, Carlo turns to the question of nature's part in the generation of the human character. He first asks whether man's conditions on earth would be worse if there were no social order. Dante's reply is positive. He then asks whether any social order would exist if men did not have different natures and were not created to serve different ends. His own reply is negative. Hence the Aristotelian notion of man being a social creature must be true. Since all human beings serve different purposes, their "roots" (*Par.* 8: 123) are always diverse. The nature of a legislator (Solon) is created differently from a general (Xerxes), a priest (Melchizedek), or a mechanic (Daedalus). Carlo says that in the generation of each man, nature never fails. Nor is she ever concerned with man's lineage.

This explains why the good father could have two sons (Jacob and Esau), of which the latter had a character that came to express the opposite of the father's, and why the father of the great Quirinus (Romulus) could be a base man. These differences are due to the workings of divine providence. What causes the problems in the social order is neither nature nor providence. The problems arise when human beings do not respect what they have been given by nature and providence, as when a man disposed to being a priest is made a warrior, or a man disposed to preach is made a king. Human disrespect for nature and providence produces "a bitter fruit" that disrupts the social order. In Carlo's speech, this consequence is exemplified by his references to the evil rule within his own family.

Carlo's speech gives a more profound understanding of the significance of nature and providence than previously stated in the *Commedia.* But he does not explain the ontological principle that can lead man to disregard his given nature. There is a good reason for this. Some of its essential aspects have already been explained by Marco Lombardi on the third terrace of Purgatory. Carlo's speech presupposes some of the notions stated in Marco's. This does not mean, however, that Marco's speech is more crucial than Carlo's. On the contrary, a comparison of some of the essential themes displayed in the two episodes makes it clear that Carlo completes the discourse initiated by Marco. For example, Marco says that the human soul is brought into being by a creative act of God (*Purg.* 16: 85-90). By emphasizing that the differences between human beings are due to the workings of divine providence, Carlo makes it evident that the soul is not transmitted by generation. Marco stresses the importance of the free will in man's life on earth (*Purg.* 16: 70-72). Carlo shows the consequences if man draws it to the extremes and disregards his nature. Marco says that the stars can only initiate some tendencies in man, but not all (*Purg.* 16: 73-74). Carlo explains the providential aspects of these tendencies but emphasizes that a harmonious being on earth depends on the balance of nature and providence. Marco says that the evil of social disruption does not come from corrupt nature, but corrupt leadership (*Purg.* 16: 103-5). Carlo says that nature never fails in her generation; social disruption is due to human disrespect for providential dispositions, as when a man through his free will neglects nature and providence. Marco emphasizes the necessity of both secular and ecclesiastical power on earth, and he points out how the latter has extinguished the former (*Purg.* 16: 106-9); the church has fused two powers into one (*Purg.* 16: 127-29). Carlo shows the failure of secular power and explains what has led to "evil rule" and exemplifies its consequences. The reason for the extinction of secular power, once represented by the empire, falls back on its own representatives as in the case of the Angevin family.

These thematic correspondences between Carlo's and Marco's speech emphasize the necessity of connectionist reading for understanding the poem's thematic content. But this type of reading is never systematically applied in Dante studies. Although Patrick Boyde stresses the importance of connectionist reading, when it comes to the Venus discourse he takes the traditional stand and only compares it with the discourses on lust in the second circle of *Inferno* and on the seventh terrace of *Purgatorio*. Since he does not go any further, his comparison is problematic; it reflects the traditional way of coding the thematic content of the Venus discourse. To give another example, in his interpretation of the seventh circle, Richard Kay suggests that the bishop Andrea de' Mozzi, who is condemned as a sodomite together with Brunetto Latini, can be seen as an "antitype" or "antithesis" to Folco because different aspects of their lives make the former stand for improper episcopacy and the latter for proper episcopacy.[14] Hence Kay's interpretation implicitly supports Seung's theory since it argues for a thematic correspondence between the Venus heaven and the seventh circle. But Kay only suggests the correspondence. He does not investigate its meaning on the grand scale. Since he does not place the thematic correspondence within the context of the poem as a whole, we are left with the impression that he regards it as intentional and yet considers its meaning to be somewhat arbitrary, because no principles motivate the correspondence apart from the mere notion of Hell as the realm of erroneous behavior and Paradise as the realm of righteous behavior.

To the best of my knowledge, Seung has been the first to suggest a thematic correspondence between Carlo's and Marco's speeches. The affinities between them support Seung's theory and emphasize that the former concludes issues raised in the latter and presupposes notions applied in the latter. As a result, neither of the two episodes can be analyzed independently; the mutual dependence of the two speeches makes each speech incomplete analyzed independently. Dante scholars do not normally engage in such far-reaching thematic readings. For example, following Singleton and Hollander, John A. Scott argues that the cantos 16-18 of *Purgatorio*, in which Marco makes his appearance, are "numerically and doctrinally," not only at the center of the second canticle, but of the entire *Commedia*.[15] But if this structural aspect is essential for our understanding of the poem's thematic content, our reading becomes problematic. The thematic content is subdued to a numerical structure; medieval mathematics becomes the ruling principle for medieval epistemology. But the thematic relation between Marco's and Carlo's speeches suggests that no singular message or doctrine is fully intelligible before the last word is uttered. Hence, if we speak of the center of the poem, it is rather to be found in our understanding of the whole text, when the whole message is concluded.

Since Marco's speech takes place only when one half of the whole message has been presented, the doctrinal content of the issues he deals with is incomplete. For example, when Marco says that the church has absorbed the secular power, originally installed for the empire by divine providence, it may seem that Dante blames the church for leading Christ's flock astray.[16] But Carlo makes it clear that the fusion of the two powers into one body is also due to the failure among those who have been given the means to secure the separation of the secular power from the ecclesiastical. If we do not see Marco's speech in the light of Carlo's, the political aspects of the former results in a disturbance of the theological message, not only of the latter, but of the whole work. Whereas Marco stresses the ontological principle that characterizes man's condition as a free creature, Carlo places it in a theological context. By pointing out the necessity of taking account of both natural and providential dispositions, Carlo makes it clear that the free will is the means by which man can comply with both types of disposition. This is the epistemological principle for realizing what causes social disorder. The significance of divine providence is further emphasized in the beginning of canto 9 with the concluding remarks of the encounter with Carlo's soul. Dante says that Carlo also informed him about the plots that the progeny of Carlo and his wife Clemence of Habsburg would suffer in the future. But Carlo stresses that Dante should not reveal these future facts to anyone, for those who do wrong will pay with tears.

Then Carlo disappears. No reason for his presence in the sphere of Venus is explicitly stated. But it is implicit in his speech. First of all, he has said that he died before he was able to accomplish his task as the future heir to the Angevin possessions. Hence he is not placed in the realm of virtues because of an earthly accomplishment. But his speech reveals that he was a man who by his own effort realized the evil the disrespect for nature and providence can lead to. It can lead to the disruption of the social order. He has not realized this because he has entered into Paradise. On the contrary, it is the reason for the virtuous state of his soul. His speech shows that he is well aware of the reasons why his own potential governance and that of his progeny have been violated by the tyranny of his family. Thus the cause of evil rule becomes a crucial theme in the sphere of Venus. This is manifest also in the speech of the next soul Dante encounters.

Evil Rule and Social Disorder

When Carlo has disappeared, another radiant light draws near to Dante who eagerly invites the soul to speak. It turns out to be Cunizza da Romano. In her initial utterance, the depraved state of Dante's contemporary Italy (*Par.* 9: 25-6) is emphasized. Whereas Carlo's speech about the evil rule of the Angevin family exemplifies the failure of secular governance in the territories that surround the center of the empire, Cunizza's speech stresses the evil at its center. The empire stands out as an amputated body, both in the way it has been chopped up into various pieces and how its power has degenerated from within. The first example of the degeneration is stated through the outlining of a territory in Northern Italy, where once a firebrand laid waste the countryside around. Cunizza is referring to her atrocious and bloodthirsty brother Ezzelino III da Romano, whom Dante has placed among the tyrants in the river of boiling blood in the seventh circle of Hell (*Inf.* 12: 110). In accordance with Carlo's explanation of how a father can have two children with completely different characters, Cunizza says that they had the same "root" (*Par.* 9: 31). Thus she stresses the difference between her and the brother. The one has ended up in boiling blood, while the other participates in a heavenly dance. This contrast has not drawn any attention in Dante studies, although it is a textual evidence in favor of Seung's connectionist reading, since the brother and the sister are placed in two sections of the rung of meekness and wrath.

However, it is the following remark by Cunizza Dante scholars have been most interested in. It has been taken as a clear evidence for identifying the representational function of Venus with the theme of lust. Cunizza says (*Par.* 9: 32-33):

> *"e qui refulgo*
> *perché mi vinse il lume d'esta stella."*
>
> "I shine here
> for I was overcome by this star's light."
> (Trans. Mark Musa)

According to Ordiway, from this remark the reader learns that Venus holds the souls who on earth were guilty of the wrong type of love.[17] Following that remark, Cunizza also underlines an aspect she shares with Folco and Rahab (*Par.* 9: 34-36):

> *"ma lietamente a me medesma indulgo*
> *la cagion di mia sorte, e non mi noia;*
> *che parrìa forse forte al vostro vulgo."*
>
> "but gladly I myself forgive in me
> what caused my fate, it grieves me not at all—
> which might seem strange, indeed, to earthly minds."
> (Trans. Mark Musa)

Later on, in Folco's speech, the state of eternal peace is also emphasized twice. He says that in Venus the souls do not repent but smile (*Par.* 9: 103). In addition, he describes Rahab as being at peace with herself (*Par.* 9: 115-16). Hence none of the three souls are any longer tormented by the memory of their past.

There is especially one reason why it is highly suspect to associate Venus with lust on the basis of Cunizza's remarks; it involves an insertion of a theme into her speech that completely misfits its content. The problem is rather obvious, but it has never been considered in Dante studies: Why is the idea of Venus as exerting lustful influence on man almost abruptly struck and then forgotten for the rest of her speech? The answer I propose is simple. The idea is never stated. Dante scholars have inserted it into Cunizza's speech in their attempt to understand the never explicitly stated order of virtues in Paradise. By doing that, they neglect the fact that Cunizza does not refer to the *folle amore*. On the contrary, she speaks of the *lume d'esta stella*. That light can be associated with mad love only if we have determined that the star's influence can lead to it. The problem of interpreting Cunizza's presence in the Venus heaven can be pointed out by raising the following questions: How are we to understand her statement about self-forgiveness? What does she mean by *la cagion di mia sorte*? What has been her fate, and what has been its cause? In the commentary tradition, her fate is frequently described with reference to her love affairs and especially the one with the Provençal troubadour Sordello, whose soul is found in the Ante-Purgatory (*Purg.* 6). Subsequently, it has been a common practice to explain the cause by seeing Cunizza as a former subject to lustful influence from the love-star of Venus. But if we interpret this aspect of her life as the essence of her fate, we once again neglect the significance of Dante's warning in *Paradiso* 8. There we have clearly been taught that what is left of Venus as the influence of carnal love is only the name of the goddess.

The traditional reading raises a number of questions that have never been answered. Why did the light of the star in her case result in sexual behavior? How can she forgive herself for having lived an amorous life? How come she does not grieve her past? Why does she not repent her misbehavior like the penitents on the seventh terrace of Purgatory? Why is she not placed in Purgatory? Has she been forgiven? And if so, why and how? But there is no reason for trying to answer these questions. There is a better solution. The solution is to reject any association of the Venus heaven with lust. The few things we know about Cunizza's life show that besides her love affairs she was repeatedly subjected to acts of violence. She was refused any freedom of choice and more than once forced to marry for political scheming. She was widowed and abducted as a result of violent intrigues, but later in her life, we are told, when the fortunes of her family had declined and the cause of her personal suffering had vanished, she became religiously devout.[18]

One of the persons who determined her misfortune was the ruthless brother Ezzelino. In the same sentence, where she mentions the influence of the light of the Venus star, she stresses her communal root with the brother. Hence, when she says that she forgives in herself what caused her fate, she elaborates on Carlo's notion of how two different persons can stem from the same nature. Although she cannot be blamed for Ezzelino's brutal character, she still, however, bears the imprint of its source. On earth, she suffered from its effects, but in the Venus heaven she does not grieve; she now accepts every aspect of her destiny. The acceptance is twofold. On the one hand, it involves the acceptance that her life was haunted by violence. She cannot change the past but she can accept it. On the other hand, it involves the acceptance of what nature has given her. Since the brother and the sister were generated from the same source, the acceptance also regards that part of herself she shares with the brother and which for various reasons produced a tyrant.

If we apply this perspective in our interpretation of her presence in the Venus heaven, she is no longer associated with lustful transgression that has now been forgiven. On the contrary, she stands out as a victim of the brutal evil that rages in the depraved peninsula of Italy. As Seung interprets the capital sin of wrath in the *Commedia*, it is an active sin of the irascible that overpowers reason and makes a person act ferociously and selfishly upon his fellow beings. The result is violence. However, though a victim of violent political scheming, Cunizza managed to avoid the depravation of her soul. That her life ended in the service of God makes manifest that her faith was much stronger than the violence inflicted upon her. As Seung interprets the theme of meekness in the *Commedia*, it is an active virtue of courage that is in accordance with reason. Meekness is a private virtue that controls the animal passions and makes a person act faithfully in the service of God. *Beati pacifici* sounds the Beatitude of the third terrace of Purgatory; that is, blessed are the meek or the peacemakers, for they shall inherit the earth. The virtue of meekness in Cunizza's soul was suppressed by the violence inflicted upon her. But in the end, she actively chose the course of her life and the nature of her acts by making the commitment to the service of God. Although she was engaged in love affairs and perhaps acted out of lust, she came in control of her animal passions and reconciled herself with her fate. Hence Seung stresses the virtue she now incarnates and not the sinful transgression she overcame by actualizing the virtue.

That Cunizza's virtuousness should be seen in the light of the violence inflicted upon her is supported by her speech, which continues the theme of evil rule introduced by Carlo. Besides her own sad story of fierce suppression, she points out three other cases of violent crimes. The first and the third one explicitly involve the conflict between the Guelph and the Ghibelline parties, while the second one accentuates once more the potential difference in character within the same family. In the first case, the subject is the hostility between Padua and Vicenza. Before Folco appears, Cunizza refers to the everlasting fame of his deeds (*Par.* 9: 39). She contrasts it to the violent corruption and tyranny in the March of Treviso, bound by the rivers of Tagliamento to the East and of Adige to the West. Such deeds mean nothing there. The mutual rancor of its rulers is so profound that not even the scourge of war can make them repent. But it will not last, she says. Soon the Paduan Guelphs (who since 1265 ruled in Vicenza) will color the waters around the city with their blood. The reason is that they have stubbornly neglected their duty to the imperial authority. By this remark, she states the future conquest of the city by the Ghibellines (1314), in which Dante's protector Can Grande della Scala took part, and whereby he obtained the position of the city's imperial vicar.

With this example Cunizza elaborates on that part of Marco's speech where he points out how the region of Po and Adige once flowered with worth and courtesy (*Purg.* 16: 115-29). But Marco says that the campaign of Emperor Frederick II of Hohenstaufen made an end to this. The reason is that it enhanced the hostility between the different cities and of the church against the emperor and his supporters. In this confrontation, the da Romano family was openly involved. With the help of the emperor and the Ghibellines, Ezzelino became the ruler of Padua in 1237. But in 1256 the pope proclaimed a crusade against him, and subsequently, the Paduan Guelphs and the Venetians expelled Ezzelino from the city.[19] This is the historical background for the conquest of Vicenza in 1265 by the Paduans, who, according to Cunizza, soon will suffer defeat. Marco has prepared the contextual premises for Cunizza's condemnation of the Paduan Guelphs. Whereas Marco's ironic statement about how a man who feels ashamed in the company of honest people can now travel safely in the March of Treviso strikes the theme of the misery of the region (*Purg.* 16: 118-20), Cunizza discloses it by exemplifying the historical implications. If we take these historical connotations into further consideration, the implicit reference to the recapture of Padua by the Guelphs can be said to resound two things: (1) Marco's notion of the church's fusion of two powers into one, since it was a papal proclamation that united the forces against Ezzelino, and (2) Carlo's notion about the disruption of the social order when a priest is made a warrior. Papal interference in political affairs is exactly what Dante condemns time and again. The misery is even greater the more local the affairs are. This interpretation accentuates the complexity and significance of Cunizza's exemplification. The same is the case with the second example.

Cunizza refers to the lordship of Treviso, where in 1306 the "arrogant" Rizzardo da Cammino—*con la testa alta* (*Par.* 9: 50)—replaced the "good" father Gherardo, which is the word Marco uses on the third terrace to describe the "old man" still living in the year of Dante's journey (*Purg.* 16: 124 and 138). But Cunizza says, "the nets have already been spread for him" (*Par.* 9: 51). In 1312 Rizzardo was murdered while playing chess in his palace. The assassination was planned by his chess partner, who wanted to revenge Rizzardo's seduction of his wife. If we connect these two passages, the key notion is the opposition between the character of the son and that of the father. The argument for such a connectionist reading is that the reference to Rizzardo is made in a textual context where differences in characters are explicitly discussed and settled in theological terms. That Dante would think in this manner is made evident by a similar discussion in the *Convivio.*

In his speech about lack of honesty in the March of Treviso, Marco mentions, along with the good Gherardo, two other "old men" who still represent the former virtue: Currado da Palazzo and Guido da Castel (*Purg.* 16: 121-26). When Dante in the *Convivio* discusses the nature of nobility, he mentions, among others, Gherardo and Guido as persons of great nobility, and in the *Ottimo Commento* it is made clear that Currado had the same reputation in Dante's time.[20] What is significant for the present argument is that in the case of Gherardo, Dante makes use of the same distinction between "baseness" and "nobleness" as Carlo about Romulus and his father, whereby the noble character of Gherardo becomes indisputable (*Convivio*, 4.12).[21] Further on, Dante elaborates on the implication of this distinction by mentioning Guido in a discussion about the absurdity of associating nobility with the sense of being "known by many." Dante ironically says that if this were the true meaning, a certain cobbler of Parma could claim to be nobler than all his fellow citizens (*Convivio*, 4.16). Hence, on this point, the reasoning of the *Commedia* and that of the *Convivio* are analogous. But it is Carlo's speech about nature and providence that grounds the reasoning theologically.

On the third terrace Marco points out three exceptions from the rule in the March of Treviso. In the third heaven Cunizza elaborates on this rule by establishing a thematic connection to these exceptions. As such, Cunizza continues Carlo's speech. It might be argued that the basis for this correlation is vague or insubstantial, since Dante does not make more than one connection. But one example is enough to elucidate the problem involved. There is no need for repetition. This is one of the essential characteristics of Dante's way of presenting his ideas. He economizes and condenses his message. He avoids digressions that impede the progress and objective of his discourse. This accentuates Dante's political and theological commitment in the *Commedia*. In *De monarchia* we experience the same commitment formally presented within the confined pattern of a treatise. But in his *Letter to the Italian Cardinals* (XI) we find it expressed in the most direct manner. His argumentation for a change of conduct within the church is sometimes almost furious and his entreating appeals are almost uncontrolled.[22] The difference in expression indicates a significant element of the nature of his commitment. It might be that Dante often exposes the themes of the *Commedia* in a condensed form, but the seriousness of the matter in question is always present, even in the smallest details.

Cunizza's third example also continues Carlo's speech. The subject is a bloody contraposition between the Ghibellines of Ferrara and the bishop of Feltre, Alessandro Novello of Treviso, who belonged to the Guelph party. Cunizza says that Feltre will come to mourn the treachery of the bishop. The historical incident implicit in her statement is the flight of a group of Ferrase Ghibellines to Feltre (1314) after a failed conspiracy against the Guelph ruler of Ferrara, Pino della Tosa, who was the vicar of King Robert of Anjou. The fleeing Ghibellines thought that they were under the protection of the bishop. But Pino demanded their return, and the bishop complied with the demand. Subsequently, they and several others were executed publicly. This act of violence led to great hatred against the bishop, and he was forced to leave Feltre and retired to a monastery.[23] The reason Dante gives for the violence is that the bishop wanted to show himself faithful to the Guelph party (*Par.* 9: 59). The condemnation is absolute. The act of violence is the gift the bishop has given to the way of life in that area.

Then Cunizza ends her speech. She becomes silent and absorbed in distant thoughts when she reenters the dancing wheel. In short, she becomes peaceful. This is the proper expression of the virtue of meekness. But before her silence, she refers to the angels (Thrones) of the seventh heaven of Saturn. She says they are mirrors (*Par.* 9: 61) through which God shines his judgments down on the souls in Venus. Here Dante makes use of Gregory the Great, who says that through the Thrones God accomplishes his judgments.[24] The discourse of the souls in Venus about the misdeeds of others is therefore justified.[25] Then another soul full of sincere joy appears to Dante. He describes its light as a "fine ruby" (*Par.* 9: 69) struck by the sun, and he stresses the contrast between the heavenly joy and the sadness "below" (in Hell or on earth).

Violence of Despair

Dante addresses himself to the appearing soul because his longing is still unfulfilled. The soul is Folco of Marseilles. His presence in the Venus heaven is the most difficult to interpret. On the one hand, he accomplished some deeds on earth that gave him great fame. He therefore now shines in the heaven. On the other hand, the only thing we learn about these deeds is their fame, which is contrasted by the vicious indifference in the March of Treviso. Folco's accomplishments are undeniably virtuous according to Dante, but their factual significance is extratextual. The problem of interpreting his presence is that since his name intrinsically signals greatness, he speaks of things extrinsic to his virtuous fame. The notion of greatness is implicitly present in his explicit speech. It is a great man who reveals truths. The words of a man of lesser fame would not have the same weight. Whatever Folco says, his saying it emphasizes its importance.

Folco's speech starts with a geographic description of the Mediterranean and the great ocean Dante thought surrounded the inhabited world.

Folco says that he lived by the shores of this basin between the rivers of Ebro in Spain and of Macra in Northern Italy. He establishes the name of his native city by referring to the naval battle in 49 BC between Caesar and Pompey's local supporters in the harbor of Marseilles, which Lucan describes in his *Bellum civile* known as the *Pharsalia* (III). After naming himself, he reveals his relation to the heaven of Venus (*Par*. 9: 95-96):

> *"e questo cielo*
> *di me s'imprenta, com'io fe di lui."*
>
> "this sphere bears my imprint now
> as from my day of birth I bore its own."
> (Trans. Mark Musa)

The statement has been taken as yet another evidence for the association of Venus with lust; the heaven is now imprinted by Folco as he once was imprinted by it while still a mortal. In the following line Folco compares his former emotional state to the one exemplified by three ancient tales, which according to the traditional interpretation support the association with lust.

Folco mentions first Dido (*Par*. 9: 97), whom Dante has placed among the lustful in the second circle of Hell. Despite this thematic relation to lust, it should be remembered that Dido committed not one but two sins: (1) she lived a lustful life, and (2) when Aeneas left her, she took her life by stabbing herself on a funeral pyre; she committed the sin of violence against one's life, which is condemned in the seventh circle of Hell. But the fact that Dante does not condemn her for her suicide indicates that he makes a distinction between accidental and intentional acts of sin. The former are out of character, and the latter are due to a disposition. For that reason, since Dido did not know that suicide was a sin, she cannot be condemned for her suicide. The same is not the case with her lustful acts. They were due to a fully actualized disposition of lust. As already stated, the sin of lust involves the corruption of the operational virtue of chastity. If she had been a Christian and had been given by baptism the orientation to the supernatural end, her suicide would have been a sin against nature. Due to the supernatural orientation, her soul would have been imprinted with the sacredness of life, which every suicide violates. But in the Venus heaven Dante wants to draw the reader's attention to a particular aspect of her life: her love was a violent one.[26] The violence is even emphasized in *Inferno* 5, where she is identified, not by name, but by the effect of her love—that is, her suicide (*Inf.* 5: 61-62).

There are two ways of interpreting Folco's comparison of his inner burning with Dido's. First, we can take it, as many Dante scholars do, as a reference to his life of pleasure before he entered the Cistercian order. In that case, the imprint of the Venus heaven only suggests that in a certain period of his life Folco was overcome by a love-influence transmitted from the Venus star. But as already emphasized, this does not coincide with Dante's warning in the beginning of *Paradiso* 8. Second, we can interpret his statement as not only implying an amorous life but also the violence that characterized Dido's love. But this leaves us with a question the sources only answer partly: Why did he abandon his former way of life? In the commentaries on the passage, we read that while still a troubadour, he frequented several important courts. At a certain time, he became attached to the wife of Barral de Baux (the viscount and lord of Marseilles). Folco wrote songs to her, but it seems as if she rejected him. When she and other distinguished friends had died, he became a monk and persuaded his wife to enter a convent with their two sons. Later he became first an abbot and then a bishop, and subsequently, he was seriously involved in the crusade against the Albigensian heretics.[27]

If we follow the line of thought of the first interpretation, the notion of a lustful past does not elucidate the aspects of Folco's character that first resulted in a life of pleasure and later excelled in severe persecution of heretics; it does not elucidate his presence in Paradise, which is, after all, the realm of virtues. But if we ensue the second line of thought, we may suggest—on the basis of the historical circumstances of his life—that the rejection of his love by the viscountess led to great despair, since he compares his situation with Dido's. But instead of turning against himself the violent despair that caused Dido's death, he underwent a transformation. The transformation became an active force in defending the tenet of the church by persecuting its adversaries. That this might be the right perspective in which to read Folco's reference to the imprint of the Venus heaven finds support in the other two ancient tales.

In these two cases, the primary source for the references is most likely Ovid's *Heroides*, which contains both a speech of Phyllis to Demophoon (II), in which the betrayal of the latter is described (*Par.* 9: 100-101), and one of Deianira to Hercules (IX), in which the consequences of the latter's love of Iole are disclosed (*Par.* 9: 101-2).[28] But before we look at these two speeches, it should be noticed that the Ovidian collection of *Epistulae Heroidum* also elucidates on what ground Dante might be moralizing Dido's death. In her regard, Dante most likely based his judgment on Vergil's *Aeneid*. But her speech in the *Heroides* (VII) spells out the despairing violence of her love. In the epistle she is about to kill herself because her heart has been torn by her love of Aeneas. In its final lines her tragic despair is even made physically manifest. She says that it should be written in the marble of her tomb that the knife and the cause of her death came from Aeneas, while the blow that killed her came from herself. No doubt, Dido is primarily associated with lust in the *Commedia*. This is made clear in *Inferno* 5. But in the Venus heaven the connotation is different. The Ovidian text about Dido supports this impression but not entirely on its own. It is by comparing it with the other two tales in the *Heroides* that we find out what Dante is intending by thematically combining these three ancient tales.

The second one Folco mentions is the princess of Thrace, Phyllis (*Par.* 9: 100). The question is: What is the central theme of her story? If we assume that Dido only represents lust in the *Commedia*, we create a discrepancy between Dido and Phyllis. The problem is that the Ovidian text about Phyllis does not justify the association with lust. Since they are mentioned within the same periodic sentence, it would be strange if one represented lust and the other not. The central aspect in the case of Phyllis is that she hanged herself because she believed to have been abandoned by her lover Demophoon. In the Ovidian text we hear the voice of the abandoned bride who thinks that she has been tricked by her lover's ensuring words of faithfulness and early return from his journey. Phyllis, an innocent and faithful woman full of chaste love, grows weak day by day in her waiting and praying for his safe return. In the end she chooses death. But, as in the Dido tale, she does not want future generations to believe that she was the cause of her death. She says that her tomb shall bear the inscription that Demophoon, a guest in the Thracian land who stole her love, killed her, although death came from her own hand. This is an example of violent despair caused by unrequited love, in which the emotion is turned against its own subject; the Phyllis tale displays the sin of violence against one's life. It is this sin she shares with Dido, not the one of lust. The Phyllis tale substantiates the allusion to violence as in the case of Dido. This interpretation is supported by Folco's next comparison with his inner burning.

The third example refers to the consequences when Hercules (*Par.* 9: 101), who was the son of Jupiter and Alcmene, enclosed the Thessalian princess Iole in his heart. The source of the reference is likely Ovid's *Heroides* (IX), once again. But it is only the illicit love affair between Hercules and Iole that is noted in traditional Dante readings because it seems to confirm the traditional coding of the theme of the Venus cantos:

Hercules was married to Deianira but fell in love with Iole. But this is an inadequate reading of both Dante's reference and the tale about Hercules. For what were the consequences of Hercules's and Iole's love? In order to understand them and the content of Deianira's speech in the *Epistulae Heroidum*, we need first to know some of the story's background. It might be that not all of it was known to Dante, but before making any hasty conclusion, we should bear in mind that in the twelfth century Ovid entered into the educational curriculum for young students in medieval Europe. He was never read or studied as intensely as Vergil and other ancient writers, but some of his works were commentated for educational purposes. The medieval commentaries give us a picture of how he was presented to medieval readers still in the formative years of their education.[29]

As an illegitimate child of Jupiter, Hercules was constantly haunted by the anger of the chief god's wife Juno, the guardian of the marriage bed, as said in Phyllis's speech to Demophoon. While still a child, Juno tried to kill him by placing two snakes in his cradle, but the already strong Hercules strangled them. When grown up, he first married the Theban princess Megara with whom he had three children, but under the influence of Juno's hatred, he killed his wife and children in madness. In order to purge this tragedy, he was given a penance of twelve difficult tasks, which he completed. Afterward, he married Deianira. When the centaur Nessus tried to violate her, Hercules shot the half-man with a poisoned arrow. But the wounded Nessus told Deianira that his blood had the power over love. When Hercules later fell in love with Iole, she dipped a robe with the centaur's blood and sent it to Hercules in order to win back his love. But the centaur had tricked her. Hercules was poisoned and died, and in despair Deianira committed suicide.

In Ovid's *Heroides* we hear the voice of the forsaken wife, near the end mixed with the repeated question: "Deianira, why do you wait to die?" She has heard of the dying Hercules and is now about to take her life. She delivers a speech on her faithfulness and chaste love and bids farewell to the world, since madness now rules her love. She admits that it seems as if she had planned the death of Hercules, but she asks for forgiveness for defending the sacred bonds of marriage. No inscription in marble is to be made, but the message is clear. Once more we are confronted with an example of violent love. Hercules's enclosing of Iole in his heart cannot be seen as only representing an illicit love affair. The Ovidian text makes it clear that there is more at stake. The consequences of Hercules's love of Iole did not only bring about his own death, it also resulted in the suicide of his faithful wife.

What we see here, when the three ancient tales are compared, is a thematic relation between love and violence. In *Inferno* 5 we learn that love can result in lust when two persons follow the same impulse. But it can also turn into violence in despair, when one person's love for another is unrequited. The three tales, as presented by Ovid, display the fatal response when love is unbalanced. That is their common feature. In the Venus heaven it is this notion that is applied when Folco's inner burning is described with reference to the three tales. Folco's three examples constitute a thematic relation to the sin of violence against one's life, condemned in the seventh circle of Hell. In that circle Dante even meets the centaur whose blood was directly the cause of Hercules's death and indirectly of Deianira's suicide (*Inf.* 12: 67-69):

> *"Quelli è Nesso*
> *che morì per la bella Deianira*
> *e fé di sé la vendetta elli stesso."*
>
> "That one there is Nessus
> who died from loving lovely Dejanira,
> and made of himself, of his blood, his own revenge."
> (Trans. Mark Musa)

Furthermore, Nessus is given the task of bringing Dante and Vergil over to the other side of the boiling river of Phlegethon in which Ezzelino, among others, is stuck forever. Thus they reach the ring of suicides. In that rung the theme is not violent love, but one related to the cause of its despair: faithfulness.

In that place Dante meets Pier della Vigna, Frederick II's most intimate adviser. Pier says (*Inf.* 13: 62-63):

> *"vi giuro che già mai non ruppi fede*
> *al mio segnor, che fu d'onor sì degno."*
>
> "I was so faithful to my glorius office,
> I lost not only sleep but life itself."
> (Trans. Mark Musa)

Faithfulness is thus emphasized twice. But Pier fell victim of the special vice of courts: calumny. Since he believed that only death could free him from all disdain (*Inf.* 13: 71), he took his own life. But the result was a sin of violence. That is the knowledge he now possesses. But like Dido and Phyllis in Ovid's *Heroides*, he wants future generations to know the real cause of his death. Dido and Phyllis demand an inscription on their tomb. Pier says to Vergil and Dante (*Inf.* 13: 76-78):

> *"E se di voi alcun nel mondo riede,*
> *conforti la memoria mia, che giace*
> *ancor del colpo che 'nvidia le diede"*
>
> "If one of you should go back to the world,
> restore the memory of me, who here
> remain cut down by the blow of that Envy gave."
> (Trans. Mark Musa)

No doubt, the sin of self-violence is most clearly illustrated by Pier della Vigna and the unknown Florentine in the rung of suicides. But the thematic parallel reading brings forth the complexity of Dante's judgment. In principle, the sin of suicide is equal to murder. But Dante is well aware that self-murder can have different reasons than the one illustrated in the seventh circle. Since there is no need to repeat what has already been revealed in Hell, he makes a variation on its theme by comparing Folco's former situation with the one exemplified by the three tales. The complexity of his thought is further confirmed by the fact that on a few occasions, which refer to pagan suicides, he makes some subtle distinctions as to how they should be punished.

As already mentioned, Dido's sin of lust prevails over her sin of violence. We only have to think of Phyllis in order to see that the disposition to self-murder can easily be more acute than in Dido's case. In Limbo we meet Lucretia and Seneca (*Inf.* 4: 128 and 141). The former killed herself after being raped, while the latter, when charged with conspiracy, took his life by command of Emperor Nero. In the one case, self-violence was caused by innocent despair. In the other, achievements in philosophy prevail. In one single case in the *Commedia*, self-violence might even in the long run be purged due to a struggle for a noble cause. The case is Cato of Utica whose soul is the first one Dante meets in the Ante-Purgatory. Cato killed himself because he did not want to fall in the hands of his adversary, Julius Caesar. But in the *Commedia* he stands out as one who died for the sake of liberty (*Purg.* 1: 70-75).[30]

These exceptions from the rule show that on the matter of self-violence, Dante's view is complex. As we have seen, Seung's notion of natural and supernatural orientation and natural and supernatural powers of operation provides a consistent explanation of why the ancient figures cannot be condemned for their sin against nature. But the tales about suicidal acts in despair of love can still display the sin against nature to a Christian in whom the sacredness of life is imprinted by baptism. As a result, Folco's references not only continue the theme of self-violence, they extend the understanding of what leads to suicide by drawing the attention to the consequences of violent love. Once Folco found himself in a situation comparable to the one that drove the three forsaken lovers to suicide. Now the notion of his fame proves that he overcame the despair and conquered the passion that caused it. Due to this conquest, he was transformed; he became an "excellent man" (*Par.* 9: 41) who fought for a just cause. The virtue he now represents prevails over his former sins. For that reason, the state of his soul cannot be relatively imperfect. If it were, he could not say that he does not repent. He would still feel some remains of his former sins. But Folco's soul does not belong to the purgatorial realm of repentance. It is his virtuous conduct that has given him a life in Paradise. It has made him shine like a "bright and dear joy" (*Par.* 9: 42). Folco smiles because nothing troubles him anymore; nothing disturbs his state of bliss. He is at peace with himself. That is the proper expression of the virtue of meekness.

Core of Venus

What we have learned by now is that nothing is imperfect in the third heaven. If that is so with the Venus heaven, it should also be the case with the Moon and Mercury. If the Venus discourse does not support the notion of an Ante-Paradise, the standard reading of the first three spheres falls apart. To be sure, what Dante sees outside the Empyreum is imperfect when compared with the perfection of the Empyrean realm, which is outside the creation. But that does not mean that the first three spheres display some deficiency. First of all, the imperfection to which Dante refers concerns the imperfection of the entire creation, not only the first three spheres of the celestial realm; it concerns also the spheres above Venus, which Dante scholars do not associate with any deficiency (*Par.* 33: 104-5).[31] Medieval philosophers and theologians maintained that the superlunar region was incorruptible. If so, it is a mistake to assert that any of the spheres of the superlunar region can be taken to display some deficiency. There can be no deficiency in the world of incorruptibility. The notion of incorruptibility in God's created world is so prominent in Dante's worldview that he maintains that nature never fails in her generation. This makes perfectly sense, because natural law is the manifestation of eternal law in the natural order. For these reasons, it is untenable to associate any deficiency with the state of the souls in their circular dance, the intelligences in their ability to move the sphere, and the heaven in its transmission of divine providence. It cannot be otherwise. Carlo has explained the reason. A perfect mind distributes the power that moves all the heavens. Since neither the power nor the distribution is anyway imperfect, neither the motion of the intelligences nor that of the souls can be imperfect. If the motion were imperfect, the distribution of the power would also be imperfect. If so, its originator would be imperfect, too. Since the presence of imperfect souls in a perfect motion would resolve in an imperfect motion, the state of the souls cannot be imperfect.

The imposition of imperfection on the souls of the Venus heaven is to a large extent due to a misinterpretation of the cause of Cunizza's refulgence. As already mentioned, she says that she shines in the Venus heaven because she was overcome by the light of the star. The question is whether she shines because of virtue or whether something else is at stake. The traditional interpretation follows the latter proposition. Cunizza's statement is taken to mean that on earth she was dominated by the star-influence and the domination generated a lustful behavior that now in the realm of Paradise makes her virtuous state imperfect. The star-influence is interpreted as being so strong that it can give rise to lustful behavior. With reference to Dante's warning in *Paradiso* 8, it is, however, generally admitted that the star is no longer directly related to *folle amore* as believed in the ancient world. But its influence can be absorbed in a wrong (lustful) manner by an unbalanced mind.

The consequences of this line of thought are serious. First, it means that it cannot be a virtue that rays down from the Venus sphere. If we still maintain it to be so, we have a problem in explaining why the heavenly transmission of the power of the divine mind can be so excessive that it dominates the behavior of a human being. Carlo's speech on nature and providence makes it clear that no such domination can take place. Although he speaks of the disruption of the social order, the argument is the same. Nature never fails, nor does providential influence ever lead to excesses. Second, if Venus exerted an influence on man that could result in lustful behavior, it would mean that the divine mind had a purpose in creating excesses, since everything is foreseen in that mind, and that since the excesses serve a purpose, the origin of lust can be traced back to the divine mind. Lust would then stem from providence, which is transmitted from the Venus heaven, which is moved by the angels of Principalities, whose impetus comes from the distribution of the power of the divine mind. But this idea is absurd. Since excesses of any kind bear no resemblance to the essence of the divine mind, the idea of excessive influences has to assign some uncontrolled component to the heavenly transmissions. If the transmissions are uncontrolled, they are not in complete accordance with the divine will. If they do not carry out this will in the intended manner, they are wrong, defective, and imperfect in their operation. If so, the same goes for the originator in the creation. Hence the argument for Venus as a love-influence with excessive potentialities is untenable. Cunizza must be intending something else when she refers to her refulgence.

When a soul in the realm of perfection has no reason for regretting a sinful behavior of the past, it is because it is absorbed in virtue. When a soul in the Venus heaven is absorbed in virtue, it enters the circular dance. The dance is directed by the motion of the heaven, and the heaven is set in motion by the power of the divine mind. Hence it is a virtue that moves the souls around. In *Paradiso* 8 Dante says that the souls in this motion stand out as lights (*Par.* 8: 19-21). Their radiance is holy (*Par.* 8: 25) and expresses their happiness (*Par.* 8: 47); it outshines any resemblance to their former appearance on earth. Since we nowhere in the Venus cantos find any hint at an imperfect element in their spiritual appearance, it must be a virtue that makes Cunizza and the other souls shine. When Cunizza says that she was overcome by the Venus light, she does not allude to a love-influence that resulted in lust. The reason for the misinterpretation of the presence of Cunizza, Folco, and, as we shall see, Rahab is that their former sinful behavior is not seen in the light of the essential force of their life.

In the case of Cunizza, her amorous life should be seen in the light of the violence that determined her fate. When she now shines, it is because the providential transmission from the Venus heaven turned out to be much stronger than the violence she suffered and the sins of lust she committed. She survived the fate ruthlessly forced upon her. With her survival and final religious devotion by her free will, she now stands out as a virtuous *exemplum*. Folco's story states a similar transformation. Violence was not forced upon him, but he experienced its force. Dante does not say how, and our sources to Folco's life do not reveal it. But it might be that it was due to unrequited love. Folco's references to the three forsaken women suggest it. In any case, the difference between Cunizza's and Folco's experiences of violence is clear. In the former case, violence came from outside; in the latter, it came from within. Although the circumstances were different, the outcome was identical. They devoted themselves to the service of God and were ultimately granted access to the heavenly bliss. The importance of the outcome of their lives is stressed in two different ways: (1) Dante establishes Cunizza's virtuous state by contrasting it to her damned brother, and (2) by referring to Folco's everlasting fame, he makes it clear that the virtuous deeds have annulled the former sins of lust.

The attainment of virtuousness among the souls of the Venus heaven is not just a minor detail of the discourse displayed in the two cantos. On the contrary, it elucidates why Dante puts forward the warning against the ancient belief in the goddess. It also elucidates why he incorporates in the discourse examples that connote lustful behavior and seem to constitute a relation to the ancient idea. When Dante ascends to the third heaven, he does not just reach a new sphere. He enters the sphere of the heavenly hierarchy whose meaning has been perhaps most grossly misunderstood in the past. This is made clear right from the start by the warning. But the rejection of the ancient belief is not to be seen only as a statement in favor of the Christian account. Dante is aware that the statement needs to be supported by exemplification. In this respect, the rejection constitutes the premises for approaching the true core of the heaven.

Dante's exposition of the Venus heaven has two interrelated ends. On the one hand, he intends to reveal the true meaning of the heaven on the basis of his Christian notion of virtues and sins. On the other hand, he wants to illustrate how the dangerous misunderstanding was framed. The first end is accomplished through the words of the interlocutors and the description of the state of their souls. The other is disclosed through Dante's encounters with souls whose lives seem to display a certain relation to the *folle amore* of the ancient myth. But the relation is only apparent. In the ancient world their behavior would have been explained with reference to the frenzied beams raying down from the Venus star. But Dante excludes this possibility. Therefore the presence of Cunizza and Folco in the Venus heaven should rather be taken as a thematic elaboration on the ancient failure to understand the true meaning of Venus's providential influence. Just as the Venus heaven by its name still bears a formal relation to the ancient myth, so do the stories of Cunizza and Folco display a formal resemblance to the ancient notion of lustful influence. But Venus is no longer associated with lust; it is associated with the Love of the Holy Spirit. In like manner, the essential meaning of the lives of Cunizza and Folco is by no means related to a lustful influence of the star. Dante's exemplification in the Venus heaven elaborates on the formal difference between the signifying and the signified of the planet's representation, between the ancient error and the Christian truth. By doing that, Dante emphasizes twice the incompatibility of the two notions.

On the one hand, it is emphasized explicitly by the initial warning. On the other, it is emphasized implicitly by the exemplification.

When we consider Cunizza's and Folco's lives as a whole, their amorous affairs should not be seen as mere acts of hedonistic pleasure. Their final conversion to the service of God sheds a tragic light on their previous life. The tragedy consists in the circumstances that delayed their conversion. For different reasons, they were led astray from the right path—Cunizza by violent suppression and Folco by violent love. Their situation was thus similar to that of the pilgrim in the *selva oscura* at the beginning of the *Commedia*. For him as well, at a certain time of his life, the path of truth (*Inf.* 1: 12) was out of sight. But by the work of divine grace, he was brought back to life. Dante says nothing of how the same change came about in Cunizza's and Folco's case. There is no reason to explain it. The premises for their conversion have been revealed; it implies grace.

In Dante's case, it is the mercy of the Holy Mother that initiates the distribution of divine grace. She makes St. Lucy report Dante's despairing aberration to Beatrice, who then descends to Limbo and instructs Vergil in how to initiate the aid and perform the first operation. What we learn from this distribution of divine grace is that man's experience of grace is first of all related to Virgin Mary. In the final canto of the poem, Bernard of Clairvaux teaches us, with his prayer to "Virgin Mother, daughter of your son," that the wish of man, who seeks grace and does not turn to her, would fly upwards without wings (*Par.* 33: 13-15). In the distribution of grace, saints play a prominent part. For the living they stand as the link between the mortal and the immortal world. St. Lucy's participation in Dante's rescue exemplifies this linkage. It is she who turns to Beatrice while Dante at random wanders around on earth. As proto-agents of divine grace, saints can perform their acts in different ways. Their appearance can be mysterious. For example, in Purgatory, St. Lucy comes to Dante, while he sleeps, in the form of an eagle, and carries him up to the Gate of Purgatory (*Purg.* 9: 55-63). But saints can send another agent who then acts as a messenger and mediator of divine grace. Such an agent is often one who stands close or is dear to the person in distress. In Dante's case, Beatrice is such an agent. On her request, Vergil guides Dante through Hell and assists him in the climb of Mount of Purgatory.

Virtue of Courage

Dante sees another soul in the Venus light next to Folco and wishes to know its identity. Without being asked, Folco tells him who it is that "scintillates like sunbeams on crystal water" (*Par.* 9: 113-14). It is Rahab of Jericho, now at peace with herself. Folco says that she has impressed her seal upon the order of Venus "at the highest rank"—*nel sommo grado* (*Par.* 9: 117). Her soul is the most luminous in the Venus heaven; it sparkles over the whole group of souls. In her the virtue of the Venus heaven is most intense. With her appearance the Venus discourse finally reveals the representational function of the sphere.

Folco says that the soul of Rahab was the first to be redeemed and rise to heaven when Christ harrowed Hell before his return to the Father. The reason is that she made possible Joshua's first glory in the Holy Land, whereby the Coming of Christ was prefigured (*Par.* 9: 118-20):

> *"Da questo cielo, in cui l'ombra s'appunta*
> *che'l vostro mondo face, pria ch' altr' alma*
> *de triunfo di Christo fu assunta."*
>
> "To this sphere where the shadow of your earth
> comes to an end, she was the first to rise
> among the souls redeemed in Christ's great triumph."
> (Trans. Mark Musa)

Thus Folco mentions the shadow of the earth that falls on the Moon, Mercury, and Venus. But Folco says nothing about their power and function. On the contrary, he continues his speech by emphasizing that it matters little to the pope what happens in the Holy Land. What the pope cares about is Dante's native city of Florence, founded by Satan, whose envious revolt against the creator disturbed the world. In that city a damned flower is produced and circulated (the coin of the Florin), which diverts the sheep and lambs of the Christian flock and makes shepherds into wolves (*Par.* 9: 130-32). Finally, Folco—once a man of the church—ends *Paradiso* 9 with a devastating criticism of the conduct of the church that once again strikes the theme of evil rule (*Par.* 9: 133-42).

Folco speaks of what has caused the social disorder both in Dante's homeland and in the Christian world as a whole. Thus he continues both Carlo's and Marco's speeches and, as we shall see in the next chapter, also Brunetto Latini's speech in the seventh circle of Hell. For that reason, it is rather peculiar that Dante scholars insist on taking his reference to the earth's shadow to mean that the first three spheres display some deficiency; they make the same mistake in coding the meaning of Folco's reference as in the case of Cunizza's reference to the refulgence of her soul. Cunizza and Folco speak of social disorder, but Dante scholars focus on one sentence in the two speeches, which they use in support of their notion of deficiency. The two references contain different meanings and create different interpretive problems. Cunizza's sentence can be taken to refer to the providential influence that enabled her to develop the virtuousness necessary for overcoming her violent past. Folco's sentence, however, seems to imply no decisive meaning apart from the delineation of the three spheres' cosmological or astrological status. Since Folco's speech does not elucidate the meaning of the reference, it may not be significant at all, and if it does contain some meaning, it may not be the one Dante scholars maintain. However, in order to propose another meaning on the basis of Seung's theory, it would require an extended interpretation of the relation between the Venus heaven and the heaven of the Sun, which Seung associates with the active and the passive virtue of the irascible power of the tripartite soul. My reading of the Venus cantos is therefore not exhaustive, because it deals only with a certain part or segment of the whole.

Many Dante scholars insist on drawing a line of demarcation between the heaven of the Sun and the three heavens below, because they claim to detect a change of tone at the beginning of canto 10 of *Paradiso*. For example, Attilio Momigliano says that with the fourth heaven, that part of *Paradiso* starts that comprises only the perfect souls who no longer have any earthly attachment. For that reason, he says, the beginning of the canto constitutes a "solemn prelude" (*solenne preludio*) to that part of *Paradiso* that thematizes heavenly perfection.[32] Likewise, commenting on Dante's direct address to his reader at the beginning of the canto (*Par.* 10: 7), Singleton says:

> This invitation to the reader, which extends through vs. 27, is to a "feast of contemplation" of this total order. The first twenty-seven verses of this canto which bears the perfect number ten have quite correctly been viewed by commentators as marking, thematically, a fresh beginning, so that the first nine cantos, which deal with the first three of the heavenly spheres, are an initial subdivision of the *Paradiso*.[33]

But this argument is untenable if we take account of the fact that at the beginning of canto 17 of *Purgatorio*, Dante also addresses himself directly to his reader. Hence canto 17 of *Purgatorio* and canto 10 of *Para-*

diso make use of the same rhetorical figure. This is just one of several thematic similarities between the two cantos. For example, in the former Dante speaks of the power of imagination (*Purg*. 13-24). In the latter he calls upon the reader's capacity to reflect upon his words and contemplate the vision he describes (*Par*. 10: 7-9 and 22-24). He says that he has put the food out, but the reader has to feed himself (*Par*. 10: 25). The reader has to combine the different elements of the description in order to make the vision of God's universal order emerge before his inner eyes. That requires the power of imagination.

In *Paradiso* 10 Dante arrives at the heaven of the Sun. In *Purgatorio* 17, as he moves out of the heavy smoke that encloses the penitents of wrath, he speaks of "how the sun's pale disc feebly begins to penetrate the mist" (*Purg*. 17: 5-6). He figuratively emphasizes the sun's power for curing the blindness that characterizes the outlook of the wrathful and leads them astray. In *Paradiso* 10 he is overwhelmed by the sun's brilliance; it is indescribable (*Par*. 10: 46-48). Dante does not notice his ascent from the third to the fourth heaven (*Par*. 10: 34-36). While still on the third terrace, he does not understand why his powers start to fail (*Purg*. 17: 52-54). After hearing the words "*Beati pacifici*, who feel no sinful wrath," he asks Vergil why his strength is fading away (*Purg*. 17: 73). Vergil explains that it is because they have arrived at the terrace where "the oar once sluggish now is plied with zeal" (*Purg*. 17: 87). In *Purgatorio* 17 Dante is already unknowingly under the influence of sloth before arriving at the fourth terrace. *Paradiso* 10 thematizes a similar change since Dante arrives at the heaven of the Sun unknowingly. But there is a difference between the transition from the third to the fourth terrace and the transition from the Venus heaven to the heaven of the Sun. The difference does not undermine the thematic correspondence between the two cantos. It underlines the fact that Purgatory is the realm of transition, while Paradise is the realm of virtuousness.

Purgatorio describes a transition from a state of imperfection to a state of perfection. The end is the redemption of the soul. To achieve that end, all seven capital sins have to be purged. Since the transition occurs through a chain of events, the different stages of the purgatorial process can easily overlap each other. For that reason, Dante feels his strength fading away before his arrival at the terrace of sloth. He is only an observer of the purgatorial process, but he is affected by it. In *Paradiso*, however, there is no process. Whereas the penitents of Purgatory have yet to achieve the ultimate end, the souls of Paradise have already achieved it. The ascent from one heaven to another involves a move from one type of perfection to another type of perfection. In contrast, the mounting of the seven terraces describes the acquisition of the virtues the heavens display as a whole. This does not mean, however, that the souls Dante encounters, for example, in the Venus heaven only have the virtue of meekness. On the contrary, all souls of the heavens have acquired all virtues. This is the end of the purgatorial process. When Folco, for example, appears before Dante, it is because the relation between his earthly existence and otherworldly appearance exemplifies the virtue of meekness.

Due to the thematic affinity between canto 17 of *Purgatorio* and canto 10 of *Paradiso*, the idea that the initial part of the latter constitutes a solemn prelude or marks a fresh beginning is tenable only if our interpretive perspective is that of segmental reading. Momigliano and Singleton do not compare the segment of canto 10 of *Paradiso* with similar segments in the other two parts of the poem, because their perspective reflects the principle of serial reading. The segmental approach should be rejected because it often leads to serious misconceptions. For example, when Foster defines the unique character of *Paradiso* by saying that it is basically a discourse about God, the result is a serious misconception of Dante's discourse about God. As Raimundi Panikkar points out, Hell makes sense only if it is seen as the work of divine wisdom and love.[34] *Inferno* is a discourse about God, although its narrative content is the world of sin. The same goes for *Purgatorio*, since it deals with how to enter God's kingdom. The discourses about God in *Inferno* and *Purgatorio* are not as directly concerned with the essence of God's nature as *Paradiso* is. But to speak indirectly of God is also to speak of God.

To further emphasize why the traditional coding of Folco's reference to the earth's shadow is insubstantial, let us compare it with another aspect of the Venus heaven that connects it to the Sun and not to the Moon and Mercury. The first thing we learn about the motion of the souls in the Venus heaven is that they move in circular motions with one rhythm and one desire; that is, their celestial dance forms one ring (*Par.* 8: 34-36). In the heaven of the Sun we see a similar setting. There the souls also move in circular motions, but their celestial dance forms two rings (*Par.* 10-64; *Par.* 12: 6-27). The number of rings in the Sun is normally enumerated as three, since at the end of the discourse on the Sun Dante sees a third ring. But it is significant that no person of this ring is mentioned. As Seung explains in *The Fragile Leaves of the Sibyl*, the last ring represents the Holy Spirit:

> The two circles of the theologians represent the two types of theology, the Franciscan and the Dominican, the theology of love and the theol-

> ogy of the intellect. Their union is represented by the third circle which appears and encircles the two circles of the theologians just before Dante leaves the Sun. Dante hails the third circle in a single line: "Oh true sparkling of the Holy Breath (*santo spiro*)" (*Par.* xiv. 76) (*FLS* 234 and *MC* 201).

Seung explains how the Holy Spirit and its love are essentially related to the Sun. Furthermore, although the number of rings differs in Venus and the Sun, the circular motion is a unique feature of these two spheres among the seven planetary heavens. This is a much stronger textual evidence for correlating the third and the fourth heaven than Folco's reference to the earth's shadow made in passing.

Let me mention one more formal element that supports Seung's theory. The circular motion described in Venus and the Sun is repeated later on in the ninth heaven in Beatrice's description of the circular motions of the spheres of the created world and the circular motions of the angelic orders in the Empyrean realm. In *Paradiso* 27 (106-14) Beatrice explains that in the divine mind the love burns, which moves that sphere and thereby the other spheres below. By this motion the power of the divine mind is transmitted to all the spheres below. In *Paradiso* 28 Beatrice further reveals the correspondence between the spheres of geocentric realm and the angelic rings of the theocentric realm.

However, in many studies of the *Commedia*, it is only the cosmological aspects of Beatrice's explanation that are explained; that is, how the ultimate motionless sphere, where the *mente divina* is situated, contains all the others, of which the ninth heaven is the one that sets all the rest below in motion. But in order to understand the description it should be emphasized that the divine mind does not simply signify God as a singular divine figure, which translations and commentaries on the passage often state. The divine mind implies the attributes of the three persons of the Trinity. According to the traditional medieval view, which the *Convivio* reproduces, these attributes are the wisdom of the Son, the love of the Holy Spirit, and the power of the Father. In the heaven of the Prime Mover, the theme is love and power. It is the love of the divine mind that governs the motions of the angelic orders; that is, they are under the governance of the Holy Spirit. Due to the circular motions caused by the effect of this love, the power of the divine mind (the attribute of the Father) is transmitted below. When Dante in Venus and the Sun uses the circular motion, it is most likely that he is thematically correlating the two spheres to the love of the Holy Spirit, under whose governance the nine celestial heavens are set in motion.

This suggests that the Holy Spirit is formally present in the nine spheres of the created world in two ways. First, as the third person of the Trinity, the Holy Spirit governs the motions of the universe through the power of the Father. Seung says:

> It is the spiral motion of the Holy Spirit that our Angelic Poet sees on the ninth rung of the angelic ladder of divine love. The spiral motion is the Love of the Spirit revolving in the Light of the Father and governing with his Power. The grace which flows out through His spiral motion nurtures and sanctifies the seeds of the faithful sown by the sower of the Divine Word. The Spirit is the Motion of all motion; He is the center of the *Primum Mobile* (*FLS* 372).

Second, the love of the Spirit is manifest in Venus and the Sun through the circular motion by which their souls move around. The reason why this thematic correspondence needs to be taken into consideration is that in the third and the fourth heaven, it is the circular motion that formally presents the individual souls as one unit. What these two units stand for, however, is revealed only through the discourses made on the two heavens. When we consider the Venus heaven, neither its celestial setting nor its discourse should be overshadowed by a few textual and extratextual aspects that indicate an association with lust. The results are two superficial assertions. First, Dante's use of the circular motion is taken to be only a poetic vision without any significant thematic meaning. Second, a few sentences are emphasized at the expense of the thematic content of the entire discourse.

Since Dante scholars maintain that Venus displays some deficiency, they do not take account of the content of Folco's speech when he points out Rahab in the Venus heaven. Instead, they focus on the fact that she was a harlot. This has long been taken as an evidence for associating Venus with lust. But the basis for the association is extratextual. Dante never mentions her status as a prostitute. It can be argued that he does not mention it because most Christians of his time were well aware of it. Moreover, they knew how disgraceful prostitution was. To emphasize the disgracefulness, let us point out the difference between the medieval and the modern attitude towards prostitution. As Ruth Mazo Karras argues:

> In modern society, prostitution is generally considered as a matter of behavior. In law, it is no longer a status offense; a woman is arrested for soliciting money for sex, not for "being in a common prostitute." Definitions of prostitution are based on action, not inclination—serious scholars no longer believe, for example, that a prostitute might choose

> this career because of nymphomania—and prostitutes are an occupational category.

On the other hand, as Karras continues, in the medieval period,

> a woman was a prostitute (*meretrix*) because she was a lustful woman, not because of the specific behavior of accepting money. Her sinfulness made her behave badly, her behavior did not classify her as a sinner. The state of being a whore was not innate—a whore could repent and abandon her sin. But the sin encompassed more than just the commission of certain acts; it was what medieval people considered a state of the soul—what we today call an identity.[35]

In medieval legal terms, prostitution was a crime committed by one who had the disposition for lustful acts. Prostitutes were social outcasts and classified among the other stereotypes of the common enemy in medieval Europe, such as Jews, heretics, lepers, and male homosexuals.[36] It meant little that women most commonly became prostitutes for economic reasons—in order to survive or support a family. The fact that their state of being was not innate but due to the corruption of the innate form of their souls proved that their uncontrolled sexual behavior was due to the misuse of their divinely given free will. Since they did not repent their sins but continued their disgraceful behavior, they deserved their lives as social outcasts in this world and as eternally damned in the other world.

However, nothing of all this is of any importance when we consider Rahab's presence in the Venus heaven. When considered in a medieval theological context, it makes perfectly sense that Dante does not mention her sinful past but emphasizes her virtuous deed. The reason is that a sinner is no longer a sinner once he or she has repented his or her sins and is forgiven. For example, Mary Magdalen was also a prostitute and perhaps the most popular saint in the medieval period after the Virgin Mary, but her sins were forgiven even without confession.[37] She was healed of evil spirits and infirmities by Christ and seven demons left her. She was saved because she had loved much and had faith. Because of her faith she was the first to see Christ after his death and before the resurrection (Luke 7: 48-49, Luke 8: 2, Mark 16: 9, John 20: 1-18). To be sure, aspects of Cunizza's earthly past elucidate how she overcame the violence she experienced. But her past makes no part of her spiritual afterlife, because she has been forgiven. This is also the case with Folco and every other soul in *Paradiso*, whose mortal life might have been sinful. It goes directly against the teachings of the church to assume that any soul in Paradise can be marked by the transgressions of its mortal life.

Therefore, when Dante scholars emphasize Rahab's sinful past and assert that it is still somehow imprinted in her spiritual afterlife, they make a serious error. Forgiveness is always total, never partial. If Rahab's sins as a harlot have been forgiven, her soul is no longer corrupted by the sins; they have been erased. This does not mean that when a sinful soul is forgiven, it becomes a blank tablet. The former sins are replaced by the virtues the act of repentance generates. In Rahab's case, it was not strictly speaking an act of repentance that transformed her. But by helping Joshua, whom medieval Christians saw as a figure of Christ, Rahab prepared the way for Christ's passion, because Joshua's conquest of Jericho prefigured Christ's triumphant entry into Jerusalem. To apply the medieval exegetical method of reading, Joshua's conquest was considered to be a historical fact with a specific moral meaning. When the walls of Jericho came down at the sound of the trumpets, the world of sin was conquered by a man of faith. This event was then transferred to Christ's passion by way of analogy. Christ's entry in Jerusalem was analogous to Joshua's conquest, and through this analogy the ultimate meaning was established: at universal judgment, the walls of the sinful world shall come down, when the trumpets of divine justice shall sound.[38] Since Rahab was saved because she helped Joshua, her act was not accidental. Although she was a prostitute, her soul was not totally corrupted, but virtuously disposed.

On this ground, it might seem reasonable to suggest, as Kay does, that Rahab is "a *figura* of faith."[39] But this identification of her virtuousness is inadequate for two reasons. First, it does not establish the essential quality of her virtuous act. Second, the emphasis on faith as her figural meaning is misleading when considered in a Christian teleological perspective. Let us consider the first problem. For medieval Christians, an act of faith was a virtuous act. But to identify such an act as virtuous does not reveal the virtuous disposition that inspires the act. In order to understand this problem, let us once again apply Seung's notion of orientation and powers of operation. To risk one's life in helping people whose lives are in danger undeservedly is a virtuous act. A person who takes such a risk shows courage in helping others; his or her acts display the virtue of courage. Such a virtue is not an orientational virtue but an operational virtue, and the identification of the specific virtue underlines how a person handles a dangerous situation, but it does not reveal what orients him or her to act courageously. If a courageous act arises from a disposition, it is due to a conviction that people undeservedly in danger should be helped. This conviction is comparable to faith in a Christian context and is an orientational virtue—that is, the acts of a courageous person are due to a fundamental commitment.

The commitment generates dispositions in his or her character that can result in courageous acts. Although the commitment is the ultimate cause of every act a courageous person makes, it is not the same as the virtuous disposition that inspires the acts. In a medieval Christian context, faith is a virtue that orients the person to act righteously. But when it comes to specific acts of virtue, their inspirational ground is identified with other virtues that underline the intimate relation between act and disposition. These virtues are the results of what the commitment has generated in the person's character. To say that Rahab is a figure of faith is inadequate, because the association with faith only indicates what oriented her in helping Joshua; it does not reveal the true quality of her virtuous act. If courage was the virtue that inspired her act, as Seung argues, the essential quality of the act is properly defined in terms of virtuous operation. Rahab was the sole person in Jericho who dared to help the enemy. Since Joshua was a man of faith and his conquest was divinely justified, her act was ultimately courageous.

As for the second problem, it is misleading to identify Rahab as a figure of faith, because the Christian faith was established only with the visible mission of the Son. For that reason, Rahab's representational function should rather be associated with the orientational virtue of hope that is sustained by the invisible mission of the Holy Spirit through preservation and providence. In a teleological perspective, Joshua's conquest displays the hope of Christ's Coming. But with Christ's Coming and the establishment of the Christian faith, Joshua's conquest comes to display the hope that sustains the faith revealed in Christ. Rahab's courageous act was in accordance with the faith established by Christ. But it was the providential power of the Holy Spirit that oriented her to the development of the disposition that inspired her act. For that reason, Rahab's salvation is not just an example of divine inscrutability, which some Dante scholars assert. On the contrary, she was saved because she participated in the implementation of the divine plan that led to the Coming of Christ. The ways of the Lord are inscrutable, but only as long as man has not understood the signs of the divine plan.

Notes

1. Lino Pertile, "Paradiso: A Drama of Desire," in *Word and Drama in Dante: Essays on the Divina Commedia*, ed. J. C. Barnes and J. Petrie (Dublin: Irish Academic Press, 1993), 143.

2. Dante scholars might object to my use of the word "lust" in characterizing the theme of the Venus heaven, because they prefer to speak of "terrestrial love," as, for instance, Cogan does, and characterize the souls of the Venus heaven as *spiriti amanti*. But I find such expressions misleading. If the souls of the third heaven took pleasure in sexual behavior while still on earth, their acts were acts of lust.

3. C. H. Grandgent, *Companion to The Divine Comedy*, ed. C. S. Singleton (Cambridge, Mass.: Harvard University Press, 1975), 212-15. John A. Scott's *Dante's Political Purgatory* is a more recent example of the reasoning of this interpretive tradition. John A. Scott, *Dante's Political Purgatory* (Philadelphia: University of Pennsylvania Press, 1996), 128.

4. Rachel Jacoff, "'Shadowy Prefaces': An Introduction to *Paradiso*," in *The Cambridge Companion to Dante*, ed. Rachel Jacoff (Cambridge: Cambridge University Press, 1993), 211.

5. Robert Hollander, *Dante: A Life in Works* (New Haven, Conn.: Yale University Press, 2001), 109, and Frank Ordiway, "In the Earth's Shadow: The Theological Virtues Marred," in *Dante Studies* 100 (1982), 77-92. Richard Kay is more sensitive to the ambiguity in determining what Venus stands for, but he ends up reproducing the traditional view. Richard Kay, *Dante's Christian Astrology* (Philadelphia: University of Pennsylvania Press, 1994), 66-97.

6. Dante Alighieri, *Dante's Il Convivio (The Banquet)*, trans. Richard H. Lansing (New York: Garland Publishing, 1990), 53.

7. Frank Ordiway, "In the Earth's Shadow," 85.

8. Dante Alighieri, *Dante's Il Convivio*, 46.

9. Dante Alighieri, *Dante's Il Convivio*, 53-54.

10. Dante Alighieri, *Dante's Il Convivio*, 70.

11. Kenelm Foster, *The Two Dantes and Other Studies* (Berkeley: University of California Press, 1977), 48.

12. Kenelm Foster, *The Two Dantes*, 49.

13. C. H. Grandgent, *Companion to The Divine Comedy*, 233.

14. Richard Kay, *Dante's Swift and Strong: Essays on Inferno XV* (Lawrence: University of Kansas Press, 1978), 85-87. Kay suggests that the grammarian Priscian might have an "antitype" in Aelius Donatus, who is placed in the heaven of the Sun (Richard Kay, *Dante's Swift and Strong*, 27). This seems to undermine Seung's connectionist reading, since Donatus is not placed in the Venus heaven. But if we take account of Seung's theory that Venus and the Sun are the two heavens that display the active and the passive virtue of the irascible power of the tripartite soul, the two grammarians are still thematically connected.

15. John A. Scott, *Dante's Political Purgatory*, 151.
16. John A. Scott, *Dante's Political Purgatory*, 250-51.
17. Frank Ordiway, "In the Earth's Shadow," 85.
18. *DDP* Singleton on *Par.* 9: 34; *DDP* Bosco-Reggio on *Par.* 9: 32.
19. *DDP* Singleton on *Par.* 9: 46-48.
20. *DDP* Singleton on *Purg.* 16: 124 and 125.
21. Dante Alighieri, *Dante's Il Convivio*, 191-92: "Suppose that Gherardo da Cammino had been the grandson of the basest peasant who ever drank from the waters of the Sile or the Cagnano, and lack of remembrance of his grandfather had not yet occurred. Who would dare to say that Gherardo was a base man? Who would not agree with me and say that he was noble? No one, surely, as presumptuous as he might be, for he was noble, and so will his memory be forever."
22. The letter was written around the time when the cardinals were assembled at Carpentras in 1314 in order to elect the successive pope after the death of Clemente V. For further information on the letter and for a critical edition of the text, see Raffaello Morghen, *Dante profeta: tra la storia e l'etterno* (Milano: Jaca Book Ed, 1983), 109-38. For more on the characteristics of the letter, see Raffaello Morghen, *Dante profeta*, 152.
23. *DDP* Singleton on *Par.* 9: 52-54.
24. The doctrine is found in Gregory's *Homiliae in Evangelia*, XXXIV, 10, and it is cited in *Summa Theologiae* pt. 1, q. 108, a. 6.
25. *DDP* Singleton on *Par.* 9: 63.
26. See, for example, Mercury's warning in Vergil's *Aeneidos* (IV. 563-65): "illa [Dido] dolos dirumque nefas in pectore uersat/ certa mori, uatiosque irarum concitat aestus." Vergil, *Opera*, ed. R. A. B. Mynors (Oxford: Oxford University Press, 1972), 193. For the translation, see Vergil, *The Aeneid*, trans. W. F. Jackson Knight (London: Penguin, 1958), 114: "She plans in her thought a fearful and treacherous wrong. In her a violent rage surges and surges again, and she is resolved to die."
27. *DDP* Singleton on *Par.* 9: 94.
28. Ovid, *Heroides*, trans. Harold Isbell (London: Penguin, 1990), and Ovid, *Heroides*, ed. Peter E. Knox (Cambridge: Cambridge University Press, 1995).
29. Ralph J. Hexter, *Ovid and Medieval Schooling Studies in Medieval Commentaries on Ovid's Ars Amatoria, Epustalee ex Ponto, and Epistulae Heroidum* (Munich: Arbeo-Gesellschaft, 1986), 7 and 211.
30. Brunetto Latini gives Lucretia the following characterization in his *Li Livres dou Tresor* (I. 36. 3): "She was one of the best and most chaste women in the world." Brunetto Latini, *The Book of the Treasure*, trans. Paul Barrette and Spurgeon Baldwin (New York: Garland, 1993), 25. In *De civitate Dei*, Augustine treats both Lucretia's and Cato's suicides. As for the former case, Augustine admits the dilemma of judging her self-violence. She killed herself because she was subjected to an outrage in which she had no guilt, and because she was overwhelmed by the burden of shame (I.19). As for the latter, the prob-

lem is more complicated because Cato was a learned and excellent man (I.23) whose virtuousness, however, did not fully reflect the true value of virtuousness according to the Christian conception of virtue (V.12). Although his suicide was unacceptable, Augustine finds it necessary to ask whether it was weakness or fortitude that prompted Cato to kill himself. Cato was too weak to endure Caesar's victory and his fortitude so thoroughly overcome that he abandoned his life on earth (XIX.4). But now in the *Commedia*, due to the help of divine grace, he is given a chance to purge his weakness.

31. For more on this issue, see Jesper Hede, "Unity and Difference in Dante's Universal Vision," in *Classica et Mediaevalia* no. 57 (2006), 239-82.

32. *DDP* Momigliano on *Par.* 10: 1-34.

33. *DDP* Singleton on *Par.* 10: 7.

34. Raimundo Panikkar, *Cultural Disarmament: The Way to Peace*, trans. Robert R. Barr (Louisville, Ky.: Westminster John Knox Press, 1995), 65.

35. Ruth Mazo Karras, "Prostitution and the Question of Sexual Identity in Medieval Europe," in *Journal of Women's History* 11: 2 (1999),160-61.

36. Robert Ian Moore, *The Formation of a Persecuting Society: Power and Deviance in Western Europe, 950-1250* (Cambridge, Mass.: Harvard University Press, 1990), 94-98.

37. For more on the popularity of Mary Magdalen in the medieval period, see Ruth Mazo Karras, "Holy Harlots: Prostitute Saints in Medieval Legend," in *Journal of the History of Sexuality* 1: 1 (1990), 17.

38. Jeffrey Burton Russell, *A History of Medieval Christianity: Prophecy and Order* (New York: T.Y. Crowell, 1968), 48.

39. Richard Kay, *Dante's Christian Astrology* (Philadelphia: University of Pennsylvania Press, 1994), 96.

Chapter Six

Circle of Violence

The thematic reading of the Venus heaven proposed in chapter five outlines what can be accomplished if a segmental reading takes account of Seung's theory of what constitutes the unity of the *Commedia*. In this chapter I will exemplify what can be attained if an episodic reading is placed within the context of a segmental reading based on Seung's theory. The focal point is the problem of Brunetto Latini's presence in the seventh circle of Hell. In many studies of Dante's poem, this circle is identified as the circle of violence and Brunetto is most commonly regarded as a sinner of sodomy. However, according to Seung's theory, the seventh circle is the section of Hell that thematizes the capital sin of wrath, and, as I will further argue, there are no sinners of sodomy in this section. The sin of wrath is the subject of discourse on the third terrace of Purgatory, where wrath is transformed into the virtue of meekness or courage by way of repentance, and the Venus heaven is the sphere of Paradise, where meekness (or courage) is displayed and exemplified. However, in order to fully understand the virtue of meekness, it is necessary to come to terms with its opposite, the sin of wrath.

Friendship and Anger

In his *Preception and Passion in Dante's Comedy*, Patrick Boyde argues that by the presence of Carlo in the Venus heaven, we are perhaps meant to infer "that the rays of Venus may dispose a 'gentle heart' to disinterested friendship, as well as to *luxuria*." Boyde's suggestion is an example of how the association of Venus with lust can lead to the distortion of a theological doctrine. His argument is that "*Similtudo est causa amoris.*

The young poet, we are told, had 'greatly loved' the even-younger prince, and had been loved in return."[1]

The Latin citation is taken from *Summa Theologiae*, where Aquinas discusses whether similarity is a cause of love and distinguishes between two types—it is either actual or potential (pt. 1-2, q. 27, a. 3). In the one case, similarity arises when two things have the same quality actually. In the other, similarity arises when one thing has a quality potentially that the other has actually.[2] Actual similarity causes the love of friendship in which two persons wish to do good to each other as well as to themselves because they are alike. Potential similarity causes a love of concupiscence or friendship for personal profit or pleasure because what is potential has the desire for being actual and takes pleasure in its realization. This type of friendship has formally the character of friendship, since one person wishes another person some good. But when friendship is connected to love of concupiscence, it is no longer a true friendship, since the one person's wish for the other person's good involves a wish that the good be profitable or pleasant to himself (pt. 1-2, q. 26, a. 4). Boyde takes this distinction to mean that the friendship between Carlo and Dante may exemplify the notion of actual similarity because their friendship was "disinterested." This is a plausible suggestion, since friendship is an essential theme of the Venus discourse. But the conclusion Boyde draws from Carlo's presence in Venus in contrast to the other souls, whereby he creates a thematic relation between friendship and lust, is problematic. The idea that potential similarity should give rise to lustful behavior involves both a simplification of the concept of concupiscence and a disregard for Aquinas's distinctive exemplification in the passage in question.

According to Aquinas, concupiscence is a strong desire that graves for what is pleasant (pt. 1-2, q. 30, aa. 1-4). It is caused by love, and it is either natural and irrational or unnatural and rational. When concupiscence is natural, the rational part of the soul is not involved in the act, and when it is not natural, the rational part is involved. When a man in accordance with nature fulfills his hunger or thirst by eating or drinking, he satisfies a desire that is a natural appetite, and its fulfillment does not require rationality for being accomplished. Hence man is irrational when he fulfills this desire naturally. When man fulfills his hunger or thirst in a manner that is beyond what nature requires, his desire is unnatural and involves a sentiment of pleasure in its realization, and this sentiment requires rationality in the pursuit of fulfilling the desire. Man is rational when he strives for fulfilling an unnatural desire. The natural desire is finite and fixed, while the unnatural desire is infinite. For example, if a man drinks or eats what nature requires, he does not desire infinite meat or drink. Conversely, if he drinks or eats beyond what nature requires, he desires infinite meat or drink. The latter results in the sin of gluttony (pt. 2-2, q. 146, aa. 1-2) or drunkenness (pt. 2-2, q. 149, aa. 1-4), while the former is represented by the virtue of abstinence (pt. 2-2, q. 148, aa. 1-6) or sobriety (pt. 2-2, q. 150, aa. 1-4). The opposition between finite and infinite ends is applicable to other kinds of desire. For example, if a man takes pleasure in becoming as rich as possible, his end is infinite riches, which is the sin of avarice (pt. 2-2, q. 118, aa. 1-8), opposed to the virtue of liberality (pt. 2-2, q. 117, aa. 1-6).

The interesting thing about Aquinas's explanation of concupiscence and similarity in friendship is his choice of exemplification. In the passage Boyde draws upon, Aquinas says (pt. 1-2, q. 27, a. 3):

> In the love of concupiscence, the lover, properly speaking, loves himself, in willing the good that he desires. But a man loves himself more than another, because he is one with himself substantially, whereas with another he is one only in the likeness of some form. Consequently, if this other's likeness to him arising from the participation of a form, hinders him from gaining the good that he loves, he becomes hateful to him, not for being like him, but for hindering him from gaining his own good. This is why "potters quarrel among themselves," because they hinder one another's gain, and why "there are contentions among the proud," because they hinder one another in attaining the position they covet.[3]

In dealing with the two types of friendship, Aquinas does not propose the association of friendship with lust. Boyde's use of Aquinas in analyzing the Venus cantos must be due to the preconceived idea of Venus as associated with lust. Lust can have something in common with the problems involved in profitable or pleasant friendship (*ST* pt. 2-2, q. 153, a. 5), but in the passage on friendship, Aquinas is concerned with more serious matters than lust. As originally stated by Gregory the Great (*Moralia in Job* XXXIII. xii) and repeated by Aquinas on several occasions, sins of the flesh such as lust and gluttony are less grievous than spiritual sins such as envy and pride. When Boyde argues for a thematic connection between actual friendship and lust, he simplifies Aquinas's doctrines by disregarding both the Gregorian distinction and the central issue in the discourse on friendship.

If we follow Aquinas's line of thought, it is particularly important that he focuses on "quarrelling" as the significant distinction between similarity by love of friendship and similarity by love of concupiscence.

There are two ways of interpreting the consequences of quarrelling as explained in the *Summa*. On one hand, Aquinas says that quarrel and strife arise from anger (pt. 2-2, q. 158, a. 7 and pt. 2-2, q. 41, a. 2). Anger belongs to the irascible faculty of the soul (pt. 1-2, q. 46, a. 3), and its objective is to hurt another by means of revenge (pt. 2-2, q. 158, a. 5). On the other hand, the fact that profitable and pleasant friendship can give rise to hatred puts quarrelling into a graver perspective, since hatred is worse than anger (pt. 1-2, q. 46, a. 6). Hatred is caused by love, and its object is evil (pt. 1-2, q. 29, aa. 1-2). Hatred comes out of envy (pt. 2-2, q. 34, a. 6), which is in the intellectual faculty of the soul (pt. 1-2, q. 29, a. 6). When love of concupiscence is involved in friendship, anger and envy are the most serious vices that can arise from potential similarity in friendship.

Boyde does not use Aquinas's notion of similarity as evidence of an intertextual relationship between the *Commedia* and the *Summa*. He uses it only in order to elucidate an aspect of Dante's conceptual outlook. Since the basis is a conceptual comparison, it would also be reasonable to consider Dante's encounter with Carlo in relation to Aquinas's emphasis on anger and envy. If we compare Boyde's suggestion with this other interpretive possibility, the latter provides a more consistent characterization of Carlo's and Dante's friendship than the idea that similarity can give rise to actual friendship as well as to lust. On the one hand, if we interpret their friendship thematically in relation to anger, the "disinterestedness" refers to the opposite of quarrelling, which arises from anger. As a result, it suggests an association with the virtue of meekness according to Aquinas's method of oppositional thinking (pt. 2-2, q. 158, aa. 1-8).[4] If so, their friendship can be said to represent actual similarity. This proposal is reasonable. For, on the other hand, if we interpreted their friendship in relation to envy, their friendship would represent the opposite of envy. Envy is sorrow for another's good, while sorrow for another's evil involves pity (pt. 1-2, q. 35, a. 8), which expresses the virtue of mercy (pt. 2-2, q. 30, aa. 1-4). But no such feeling is involved in Carlo's and Dante's friendship. If we try to establish, in Thomistic terms, what characterizes their friendship, it is most likely thematically related, by way of opposition, to the vice of anger, whose opposite is the virtue of meekness. According to Aquinas, meekness restrains the onslaught of sinful anger. It is an obstacle for man's free judgment of truths. Meekness mitigates and moderates anger according to right reason. It disposes man to the knowledge of God by removing the obstacle of anger. A meek person does not contradict the words of truth, while a person who contradicts the words of truth is disturbed by anger.

The significance of this thematic opposition becomes evident if we apply Seung's method of thematic parallelism. In the seventh circle of Hell we find an example of friendship, which according to the Thomistic distinctions stands for the kind of similarity opposite of that between Carlo and Dante. In the third rung of that circle, which is normally said to contain clerics and respected men of letters, Dante encounters his former teacher Brunetto Latini. One of the striking things about Dante's presentation of their friendship is that it stands out as one characterized by dissimilarity both on earth and now in Hell. Throughout their conversation Dante addresses himself to Brunetto with the respectful *Voi* and Brunetto responds with the paternal *tu* and calls Dante twice his son (*Inf.* 15: 31 and 37). There is nothing unusual in the difference of addresses. It reflects a common practice; Brunetto was an elderly and honorable man when Dante met him, and Dante was still in a formative stage of his life when Brunetto died.

However, when we examine the question of friendship, it should be noticed that at the very outset of their conversation, the difference of addressees stresses the formal character of their friendship—it was unequal. This dissimilarity is emphasized at least in two ways. First of all, Dante says that he bent his head in reverence during their conversation (*Inf.* 15: 44-45), and assured his teacher that he would speak of his debt and gratitude to him for the rest of his life (*Inf.* 15: 86-87). He also characterizes Brunetto as kind, loving, and paternal. He says that Brunetto taught him "how man makes himself eternal" (*Inf.* 15: 82-85). Brunetto, on the other hand, says that he wished to have lived longer to comfort and support Dante in all his work, whether it be in poetry or political matters (*Inf.* 15: 58-60). But if Dante follows his star, Brunetto says, he will not fail to reach his goal (*Inf.* 15: 55-56). Hence Dante shows his respect and admiration for his teacher, while Brunetto expresses his concern for his pupil. This dissimilarity can even be seen as an echo of the educational structure of Brunetto's encyclopedia *Li Livres dou Trèsor*. There the Master (*Mestre Brunet Latin*) speaks to his pupil-friend (*amis*). However, the physical setting of their meeting, now in Hell, reflects the reverse order of their friendship—Dante walks on a dike and has to look down during their conversation, while Brunetto walks on the plain below and has to look up. Both the formal character of their conversation and the physical setting emphasize the dissimilarity of their relationship.

Besides the thematic contrast between Dante's and Carlo's friendship of similarity and Dante's and Brunetto's friendship of dissimilarity, there are textual instances in Brunetto's speech that support the method of thematic parallelism. For example, the fact that the relationship between

Brunetto and Dante is textually presented as one between a father and his son can be seen as an anticipation of Carlo's notion of how two persons of the same family can have two diverging characters. Brunetto and Dante did not belong to the same family, but they had communal roots—they were Florentines. The importance of their communal roots is manifest in Brunetto's words about the foundation of Florence. He says that it was the result of the mixture of good Romans and wild beasts of old Fiesole (*Inf.* 15: 73). He regards the mixture as tragic, and the state of his soul in Hell reflects the tragedy. Brunetto was an educated man, but in Hell he resembles a wild beast rather than a good Roman. In considering the tragic mixture, Brunetto becomes full of rage. In his view, the Florentines are an ungrateful and malignant race. Because of their descent, they are brusque like the rock and mountain on which Fiesole was founded. They are avaricious, envious, and proud and Dante's enemy. Among the bitter berries of Florence, there is no place for such a sweet fig as Dante. The political factions of the city will try to devour him. Their members are like goats that try to eat up all the grass, but there is no grass where the goat is. They will try to eat up each other and leave untouched the plant in which the holy seed of the Romans is carried on (*Inf.* 15: 61-78). The picture Brunetto paints of Florence resembles that of Jericho and Sodom in the Old Testament. In both biblical cities there were only few righteous people. When Jericho was conquered, only Rahab and the members of her house were saved. In Sodom, only Lot and his two daughters escaped the destruction of the city (Genesis 18 and 19).

Brunetto conceives the order of the world as if everything were a matter of nature and fortune. He expresses the blind belief in the influence of the stars Marco Lombardi rejects on the third terrace. In the *Livres* Brunetto gives the following account of the foundation of Florence, which might be the inspirational source for Brunetto's assault on Florence in the *Commedia* (I.37.2):

> The Roman besieged the city of Fiesole, and they conquered it and subjugated it. Then they built in the middle of the plain, which is at the foot of the other hills where this city stood another city, which is now called Florence . . . the piece of land where Florence now is was formerly called the Head of Mars, that is, the House of Battles, for Mars, which is one of the seven planets, is called the God of Battles . . . For this reason it is not surprising if the Florentines are always at war and in discord, for the planet rules over them. Master Brunetto Latini should certainly know the truth about this, for he was born in that city, and he was exiled when he compiled this book, because of the wars among the Florentines.[5]

Brunetto's reference to Mars is incompatible with the basic concepts in Marco's and Carlo's speeches. In the *Livres* there is nothing that resembles the notion of providential influence as explained by Carlo. Brunetto provides no coherent explanation of the relation between man's natural and providential dispositions and the function of his free will. In fact, he is caught up in a conflict between materialistic and pantheistic views of the universe (III.52.3):

> It is very difficult to describe the essence of nature, for some say that nature is the beginning of all things; others say that it is not, for if it were, God would have had his beginning through nature. But Plato says that nature is God's will, and for this reason it appears that God and nature are the same thing. But nature is double, one which causes things to be born and another which comes from what is born. Of the things which are born, some are divine, others are worldly, and of the worldly things, some pertain to men and others to beasts.[6]

And yet he fully accepts the notion of an external cause for the creation of the universe (I.8.1): "God ordained the nature of all things individually, and gave them a way in which they should be born and die, and the strength and characteristics and nature of each one . . . He who made everything can adjust and change the course of its nature by divine miracle."[7]

Brunetto's assault on Florence puts into perspective the limitations of the perception of the world he and his fellow sinners maintain. The differences between Dante's and Brunetto's worldview are the thematic material out of which Dante makes the portrait of his former teacher as one in whom a violent anger rages against nature, exemplified by his characterization of the Florentines as hybrid products of the good Romans and the beast of Fiesole (*FLS* 198). However, many Dante scholars do not consider the limitations of Brunetto's worldview when they interpret his appearance in the seventh circle. In Dante studies the so-called sodomites, to which Brunetto belongs, have most frequently been interpreted as homosexual sinners. But some scholars have opposed this interpretation and prefer to see him as a blasphemer.[8] For example, Brunetto defiled his Tuscan mother tongue by choosing to write his *Livres* in French, he had "bad intentions against God" and stands for a perverter of the mind, or the structural difference between prone, seated, and standing sinners in the seventh circle indicates that Brunetto belongs to the category of blasphemers.[9]

The problem with these suggestions is that they are all contextually inconsistent. None of them finds support in historical sources. In the first case, as pointed out by Bianca Ceva, Dante is the only source to the verdict on Brunetto as a sodomite.[10] Only two verses in Brunetto's *Tesoretto* (2559-60) and a passage in Villani's *Chronicles*, written after the *Commedia*, support the verdict, however, only vaguely. Moreover, in the *Livres* Brunetto explicitly says that with regard to the type of pleasure that involves lust, the precondition for a chaste practice is the union of man and woman (II.77.1).[11] It is true that if we follow the practice of interpreting Brunetto's condemnation as a sinner against nature, the examined dissimilarity of friendship between Dante and his former teacher becomes more evident. It suggests that in general Brunetto regarded friendship between men as involving the kind of similarity whose cause Aquinas would define as love of concupiscence. It therefore seems reasonable to assert that the friendship between Dante and Brunetto could never be a true friendship, because the latter's interest in his own sex comprised the possibility that his wish for the pupil's good would implicate the fulfillment of a desire in himself.

The seriousness of this sin is made clear by Aquinas. In the *Summa* Aquinas says that all types of lust are characterized by the transgression of what is determined by right reason. But he emphasizes that sodomy implies something more serious than the transgression of reason. It is worse than incest, adultery, seduction, rape, or sacrilege. It is not as grievous as bestiality, which violates nature by not observing the use of due species. But like bestiality, it involves the violation of what is determined by nature. If we rely on Aquinas, by sinning against nature Brunetto should be interpreted as a sinner against God because what is contrary to nature is contrary to God (pt. 2-2, q. 154, a. 12). In that case, Brunetto would exemplify how lust is a sin that can be overridden by a more aggravating sin that justifies a more severe punishment. This might seem to be a plausible explanation of Brunetto's presence in Dante's infernal Sodom. But it disregards the content of his speech. We neglect the fact that Brunetto's speech is concerned with the influence of the stars and the misfortune of Florence and Dante.

The same misfitting coding of the content of Brunetto's speech also characterizes the other suggestion that Dante should have regarded his choice of the French as an act of blasphemy. It involves a serious misunderstanding of the doctrines concerning blasphemy.[12] In the *Convivio* Dante accuses some respected men of praising the vernacular of others and disregarding their own. But he does not mention Brunetto, nor does he relate blasphemy to the detestable causes from which, as he says, the impulse of these men arise: blindness of discernment, disingenuous excusing, desire for glory, reasoning prompted by envy, and baseness of mind or pusillanimity (I.11).[13] In the *Livres* Brunetto gives two reasons for writing in French: "One, that we are in France; the other, that French is more pleasant and has more in common with all other languages."[14] It might be that Dante would regard such a statement as expressing ignorance, incapacity, ambition, criticism, or inferiority. But the fact that the *Commedia* identifies blasphemy as a violent act against God makes it impossible to interpret Brunetto's choice of the French as blasphemy on the basis of the *Convivio*. Blasphemy aims at dishonoring God, whose power descends to the natural world from the supernatural world. The choice of language in the distribution of human thoughts concerns only the natural world. To commit a violent sin against nature involves something graver than a certain choice of means of expression.

For Dante the question of the relation between nature and providence and the question of the function of the human free will are essential issues for his theory about the divine implementation of the empire in the temporal world. That Brunetto makes only a matter-of-fact treatment of the foundation of the empire (I.27.2 and I.36.2) and the church (I.86.4) might be due to the fact that the conflict between the two institutions was less severe when Brunetto wrote his *Livres* than when Dante wrote his *Commedia*. But since Dante looks at the two institutions from a teleological perspective, the contrast between his and Brunetto's view is evident. Brunetto takes it for granted that the church is divinely instituted, but since he does not consider the legitimacy of the empire, Dante might have regarded his view as dangerous, because it does not resolve the conflict between secular and spiritual power and the problem of the spiritual dimension of secular rule. As a result, the empire is reduced to a mere historical phenomenon in the *Livres*.

Like Carlo, Brunetto wishes to have lived longer. But there is a major difference between their wishes. Whereas the object of the former is for the benefit of mankind, the object of the latter is for the benefit of an individual. One concerns the righteous rule of the empire, which ought to govern the whole world. The other concerns only Dante's fortune. Here again the problem of similar and dissimilar friendship is made manifest. Since Dante makes Carlo the spokesman of his own wish and stresses their friendship of similarity, it stands clear that the friendship between Dante and Brunetto was never actual, only potential. That Brunetto's wish is not just an innocent wish for the future life of a former friend is manifest in the fact that Jacopo Rusticucci, who was once a rich Florentine merchant and often engaged in political and diplomatic affairs, makes a similar statement. Jacopo wishes that Dante's light of fame may shine after he has gone (*Inf.* 16: 64-66). The concern for fortune, fame, and personal profit is a special characteristic of the sinners of the third rung of the seventh circle, which includes the usurers. It indicates that the sinful disposition these sinners now enact in Hell involves selfishness. The selfishness is not as grievous as the disposition that motivates acts of envy and pride. Envy and pride are vices of the intellect that result in two different kinds of selfish act. The selfishness of the envious is hidden in his secret calculation and execution of evils. The selfishness of the proud is openly manifest in his arrogant behavior in order to attain singular excellence. However, since wrath is a vice of the irascible or sensitive part of the soul, which human beings share with animals, the wrathful acts selfishly because he has fallen for his bestial passions. As we learn from Marco Lombardi, whenever human acts are governed by bestial passions, the reason can always be traced back to a free choice of the human will, but as soon as a person acts out of bestial passions, his free will starts to deteriorate and his acts come to resemble those of animals. This is not the case with acts of envy and pride. The envious and the proud act out of their will, but their acts are forceful perversions of God's gift of the free will to human beings. As a result, their acts are more grievous than those of the wrathful.

Rhetoric of Violence

If we take account of these aspects when we examine the difference between the political positions of Dante and Brunetto, a thematic connection emerges between the latter's political ideas and the former's condemnation of the latter as a sinner of wrath. By considering this connection in detail, it becomes possible prepare the consistent basis for interpreting Brunetto's appearance in Hell. To do that, Plato's theory of government is of particular importance, because it brings forth the Platonic current in Dante. Aristotle is the principal source for the political positions of Brunetto and Dante, but in essential ways, Dante's theory of government resembles that of Plato more than that of Aristotle. This has to do with the fact that Dante's concern is the implementation of the perfect state on the global scale. When he considers the governmental practices of actual local states, the purpose is always to point out their deficiency and injustice and to underline the necessity of implementing the perfect state—that is, the rule of world monarchy.

In Brunetto, however, we detect a stronger inclination toward the Aristotelian inquiry into actual states. In this respect, Brunetto can be seen as a forerunner to Marsilius of Padua. It has been said that with the evocation of the *legislator* in Marsilius's *Defensor pacis* (1324), we hear "the first word of the secular state"[15] or see "something like the idea of the modern state."[16] But the secularized political conceptions that emerge in *Defensor pacis* should not be seen as the evocation of the future model for power organization in Western Europe. As Eric Voegelin remarks, the human legislator "is simply the stratified medieval society in any political unit,"[17] and the elements that can be discerned in Marsilius's conception of the human legislator are descriptions of actual medieval town institutions.[18] There is nothing unusual in such an existential and cultural context-boundness. Dante's identification of the local disorder of Florence with the global disorder of the temporal world is also context-bound. On the basis of an existential experience of local disorder, Dante develops a theory about how to secure order in local contexts with the implementation of a global institution. But in Brunetto and Marsilius we detect a change from the global and ideal perspective, characteristic of Dante and other medieval political theorists, to the local and practical perspective. This change reflects a preoccupation with the Aristotelian concern for actual states. To be sure, Brunetto and Marsilius speak in the language of the perfect state, but by idealizing existing forms of government, they undermine the ideal of the perfect institution for global government.

The essential topic of discourse in Brunetto's *Livres* is rhetoric, especially Aristotelian rhetoric. Brunetto's reliance on Aristotle's *Rhetoric* is clear from the general outline of his work. The first book deals with the creation, history, geography, and the physical world. The second book deals with ethics, and the third with rhetoric and politics. The order of topics treated in the *Livres* is by no means arbitrary. Since rhetoric is about consistent argumentation, it is necessary to be well-educated to produce consistent arguments, and it is necessary to possess some basic knowledge of the world and its history and to have appropriated basic ethical standards. However, the end of education is not knowledge in itself, but righteous government. According to Brunetto, government of cities is "the highest science and the most noble office there is on earth" (III.73.1).[19] Rhetoric is what ties the educational basis to the political end. For that reason, rhetoric becomes the essential topic of discourse in the *Livres*. Without consistent argumentation, knowledge and ethical standards are poorly distributed. Without consistent argumentation, the end cannot be achieved.

Brunetto's concern for rhetoric elucidates Dante's motivation for placing him in the seventh circle of Hell, but it does not provide a full explanation of his condemnation. The problem of rhetoric is that just as it can serve a righteous purpose, it can serve the opposite. The end of rhetoric is persuasion; it is not a particular type of persuasion. Whether it serves a righteous purpose or not is an ethical matter, not a rhetorical matter. As a result, the attitudes toward rhetoric were mixed both in antiquity and in the medieval period. For example, as Paul Oskar Kristeller says, the ancient philosophers moved between two poles—they either rejected rhetoric altogether, as did the early Plato and Epicurus, or they treated it as a subordinate part of philosophy, as did Aristotle and the Stoics.[20] It is the latter view Brunetto presents in the *Livres*. According to Brunetto: "Philosophy is the root from which grows all of the knowledge man can have . . . Philosophy is the true inquiry into things, divine and human, insofar as man is capable of understanding" (I.1.5-I.2.1.).[21] Hence rhetoric is a discipline only within the practical branch of philosophy.

By placing Brunetto in Hell together with Priscian and Francesco d'Accorso, Dante seems to take the Platonic stand toward rhetoric; he seems to identify it as fake knowledge that produces opinions and not knowledge.[22] The three sinners were all practitioners of rhetoric, either in politics, in law, or in education. Brunetto wrote his *Livres* and made translations of Cicero's works on rhetoric, and he was directly involved in politics. In short, he was a teacher of rhetoric and a practitioner of political rhetoric. Francesco was a celebrated lawyer and a professor of law in Bologna and a teacher and practitioner of legal rhetoric. As for Priscian, Dante scholars have mostly been concerned with trying to explain why this famous grammatician of late antiquity is apparently condemned for sodomy.[23] However, Priscian was not only a grammatician but also a rhetorician. This is seldom noticed in Dante studies because his renowned work is the *Institutiones grammaticae*. This work was a standard text in grammar from the sixth to the fourteenth century, together with the *Ars minor* of Donatus, whom Dante has placed in the heaven of the Sun (*Par.* 12: 137-38).

But Priscian also wrote a rhetorical tract on Hermogenes' *Progymnasmata* (second century). The tract is formally a translation, but it diverges considerably from the original.[24] Priscian's text mainly deals with how to build up different types of arguments. As such, it is a harmless text. But as soon as we read it as a source for rhetorical training in schools, whose principles would later be practiced in legal matters and political affairs, it becomes clear that Dante could easily have regarded it as a cynical text concerned with manipulation and opinion, not knowledge and truth. This is not a fair reading of Priscian's tract or a fair judgment of his conception of rhetoric, whether in education, law, or politics. The same objection can be made against Dante's judgment of Brunetto's political position. But our concern in understanding the appearances of Priscian and Brunetto in Hell is not the historical Priscian and the historical Brunetto but Dante's attitude toward them. The fact that Brunetto, Francesco, and Priscian were preoccupied with rhetoric, both in theory and in practice, provides a better answer to the question of why they are grouped together than the traditional suggestion that it is because they were sodomites, for which there is no textual evidence whatsoever.

But Dante's attitude toward rhetoric does not provide a full explanation of why he apparently condemns these three rhetoricians. This has to do with the nature of rhetoric itself. If rhetoric is accepted as a necessary means in the service of justice, it can be justified. Consequently, if it does not serve justice, it should be condemned. But since rhetoric is a matter of persuasion, which can turn into manipulation, even when its purpose is just, its function is not necessarily the distribution of truth. By thematizing this ambivalent nature of rhetoric, Dante seems to correct yet another of his assertions about the Venus heaven in the *Convivio*. In the treatise, he associates Venus with the discipline of rhetoric, especially because of its sweetness (II.13). If we follow Seung's method of thematic connectionism and regard the circle of violence as thematically related to the Venus heaven, the condemnation of the three rhetoricians can be seen as an implicit correction of his former assertion about Venus and the sweetness of rhetoric. When rhetoric is manipulative, its sweetness is deceptive.

To paraphrase the opening lines of canto 8 of the *Paradiso*, the ancients once believed that rhetorical sweetness was a virtue and developed and worshiped its means of seduction and manipulation. But this belief was dangerous and erroneous, because instead of worshiping the sweetness of truth, they worshiped the sweetness of rhetorical seduction and deception. Folco's concluding lines in canto 9 of the *Paradiso* about how the study of canon law has replaced the study of the Holy Scriptures and the Church Fathers emphasize the same problem in Dante's historical context. The pope and the cardinals are more concerned with rhetorical manipulation in the world of political affairs than with the distribution of revealed truth. The placement of Andrea de' Mozzi together with the three rhetoricians underlines the same problem. Richard Kay is right in suggesting that Andrea, who was the bishop of Florence in Dante's youth, should be seen as an "antitype" or "antithesis" to Folco. The early commentators describe him as vicious and dishonest and not a very intelligent person who was under the influence of Pope Boniface VIII, and Boccaccio says that he was detested by the citizens.[25] Andrea exemplifies how deep the church falls when it is more concerned with political scheming than with spiritual truth. Andrea was a shepherd who turned into a ravening wolf and let the lambs run wild (*Par.* 9: 130-32). The fact that he is described as one whose nerves were badly protected (*Inf.* 16: 114) spells out his incapacity to control anger in human affairs.

What purpose did Brunetto's rhetorical practice serve, or what was the content of his rhetorical speeches? On reading the episode of canto 16 of the *Inferno*, it is not possible to answer that question. Since he is placed in the circle of violence, his rhetorical practice must have served a violent purpose. His verbal assault on old Fiesole and the Florentines makes him stand out as a violent rhetorician. There is no trace of meekness in his character. Only toward his former pupil does his speech display some sweetness of discourse and gentle concern. The fact that the episode in itself does not reveal the reason for Brunetto's condemnation emphasizes the limits of episodic reading. In order to understand the episode, it is necessary to expand the perspective. As a result, episodic reading becomes subsidiary to segmental reading, which in turn is subsidiary to systematic parallel reading. Segmental reading is capable of collecting the acts of these sinners under the heading of violent sins. But it is incapable of placing these three types of sins within the context of Dante's description of God's universal order.

Seung's reading provides the principles for determining that the circle contains violent sinners opposed to the penitents of wrath and the souls of meekness. But Seung's view of the third ring of the seventh circle has one deficiency. In *The Fragile Leaves of the Sibyl* Seung argues that the sins on each terrace of Purgatory reflect the design of the corresponding circle in Hell, except in one case. This case is the sin of sodomy in the seventh circle, which is not displayed in the process of purgation on the third terrace but on the seventh terrace (*FLS* 311). How can this anomaly be resolved? My argument is that it is not Dante who is inconsistent in his exposition of the universal order. By placing the so-called sodomites in the seventh circle, he does not make an exception from the rule. The problem is that only on this minor issue, Seung relies too much on the standard view of traditional Dante studies. By this I mean that he takes it for granted that the sinners of the third ring are sinners of sodomy. It should be noticed, however, that in his treatment of these sinners he stresses their wrathful character, not the potential relation between sodomy and the capital sin of wrath. The problem of the so-called sodomites does not disturb his overall theory of their nature as sinners of wrath.

My solution to the problem is radical. My thesis is that there are no sinners of sodomy in the seventh circle if sodomy is identified with unnatural sexual behavior or homosexual lust. In order to substantiate this thesis, we have to move from the episodic level to the segmental level, while still maintaining the global view established by Seung's systematic parallel reading. On the global level, we can say that all sinners of the seventh circle are sinners of the capital sin of wrath. We can also say that they have corrupted the irascible power of their souls. On the segmental level, we can say that they are violent sinners. We can also say that they are divided into three types of violent sinners—the first ring contains sinners against one's neighbor and his property, the second ring contains sinners against oneself and one's property, and the third ring contains sinners against God, nature, and art. These three demarcations should be sufficient for understanding Dante's description of violent sins of the irascible power arising from the capital sin of wrath. But since many Dante scholars interpret the three divisions without the psychological and ethical understanding Seung's reading provides, they try to determine which particular sinful act has determined the destination of each sinner in one of the three sections of violent sins. In explaining the particular sin in question, they make use of theological—namely, Thomistic—distinctions. For example, the reference to Sodom in *Inferno* 11 is taken to demarcate the sin of the second group of sinners in the third ring. Their acts of violence are said to have been directed against nature. Since Aquinas says that sodomy is a sin against nature, many Dante scholars conclude that the sinful act of these violent sinners is that of sodomy. On this ground, Brunetto becomes as a sodomite, although Dante scholars agree that the historical Brunetto was not a sodomite. It matters more what Aquinas says about sodomy than what our historical sources reveal about the lives of Brunetto and his fellow sinners. For that reason, the use of Thomistic distinctions often leads to problematic interpretations of the three divisions.

In suggesting my solution to the problem of sodomy, I maintain that the meaning of Dante's infernal Sodom cannot be found if we focus mainly on medieval theological discourse. We have to take account of medieval political discourse. Of course, since Dante's view of the universe is integral and aims at embracing it as a whole, political discourse eventually becomes theological discourse. For example, the problem of friendship is, first of all, an ethical matter. But as soon as it is viewed in an integral manner, it can take two courses—the political and the theological. In books 8-10 of the *Ethics*, Aristotle shows that friendship is essential in politics. However, since friendship is an ethical matter concerned with virtues and vices and the human psyche, it will eventually become a theological matter, because the human psyche is an image of the Trinity, and virtues and vices concern the human will to comply with the divine will. The reason for approaching the seventh circle from the perspective of medieval political discourse is that it naturally follows from Dante's discourse on government on the third terrace and the third heaven. The terrace of wrath and the heaven of meekness deal with the problems of implementing a righteous form of government in the temporal world. Since the circle of violence belongs to the realm of sinful perversions, it is reasonable to expect that it thematizes what haunts the world of politics as long as the authority of the divinely instituted empire is undermined and its power is weakened.

Symbol of Sodom

The three divisions of the seventh circle display violent perversions of the three cornerstones of man's existence—his relation to his fellow beings, his self-perception, and his relation to the divine. As for the latter, the relation includes his relation to nature, because nature is a divine creation. In short, natural law is the manifestation of eternal law in the natural order. When Dante speaks of violence against God, he intends blasphemy, the act of despising God. But all souls of the third ring can be seen as sinners who despise God and his creation. To further elucidate the three types of sin in the seventh circle, we can also say that they represent three ways of violating the sacredness of life. Since every human being is a divine creation and therefore imprinted with sacredness of life, to act against one's neighbor is to violate the sacredness of life in fellow beings. Such an act is ultimately an act against God. The same goes for the act against oneself; it violates the sacredness of life.

That the seventh circle thematizes the capital sin of wrath is manifest in a number of descriptions in the three rings of violent sins. Let us point out some essential indicators in the first two rings before settling the problem of sodomy in the third ring. In the first ring Dante encounters the Minotaur, who goes "crazy with the fever of his rage" and bites his flesh when he sees Dante and Vergil (*Inf.* 12: 14-15). He meets the centaurs Chiron, Pholus, and Nessus. Chiron "reared and taught Achilles,"

Pholus "was known for his drunken wrath," and Nessus "died from loving lovely Deianira and made of himself, of his blood, his own revenge" (*Inf.* 12: 67-72). The latter points out four tyrants of heartless crimes in the river of boiling blood. Two of them belong to the ancient past: the fierce Dionysius of Syracuse and a tyrant called Alexander, who is either Alexander of Pherae or Alexander the Great. The other two are brutal Italian tyrants of the thirteenth century—Ezzelino da Romano (Cunizza's brother) and Obizzo d'Esti (*Inf.* 12: 104-12).

The theme of boiling blood is essential for identifying the capital sin of the seventh circle. As Seung points out, Aristotle's material definition of anger in *De anima* (I.1, 403a32) provides the basis for Dante's description of the bloody river of the seventh circle: "Anger is the boiling of the blood around the heart, the animal's central organ" (*FLS* 193). This material definition was a standard in ancient and medieval psychology and ethics. For example, Seneca says in *De ira* (II.19.2-3), which Dante might have known:

> A natural endowment of *heat* in the mind makes men irascible, fire being active and stubborn, while a mixture of *cold*—sometime inert and congealed—makes them timid. (Some of our [Stoic] school, accordingly, maintain that anger is roused when the blood boils around the heart, their reason for locating anger in this particular area being simply that the breast is the warmest part of the whole body).[26]

Seneca states a firm relation between anger and the irascible. For Dante, who believes in the seven capital sins, this implies a firm relation between the capital sin of wrath and the irascible power of the soul. The sinners of the seventh circle have corrupted the sensitive part of their souls. With the river of boiling blood, Dante presents an image with at least two essential connotations—it describes the internal manifestation of wrath, according to medieval psychology, and it alludes to the waters colored with blood following the scourge of war and strife.

Then follows a revengeful murderer, Guy de Montfort, an emissary of Charles of Anjou, who along with Boniface VIII brought Corso Donati back to power in Florence, whereby Dante was forced into exile (*Inf.* 12: 118-20).[27] Nessus mentions three atrocious warriors against whom "Heaven's justice strikes its blow" (*Inf.* 12: 133-35): Attila or "the scourge of earth," Achilles' son Pyrrhus or Neoptolemus, who was an enraged warrior in the Trojan War (Vergil, *Aeneide* II.526-58), and Pompey's son Sextus, who, after the murder of Caesar, became a ferocious pirate (Lucan, *Pharsalia* VI. 113-15 and 420-22). Finally, Nessus points out two highway robbers who were also murderers: Rinieri da Corneto and Rinieri de' Pazzi, the latter a Ghibelline leader who was excommunicated (*Inf.* 12: 135-38). These sinners acted only to their own advantage, whether their goal was sovereign power, ferocious revenge, or hard cash. Since they were not concerned with their fellow beings and only pursued their own interest, their sins can rightly be defined as sins against one's neighbor, whom they ought to love.

In the second ring Dante encounters two suicides, Pier della Vigna and an unknown Florentine (*Inf.* 13: 143-50). The latter has been associated either with a Florentine judge who hanged himself after having delivered an unjust sentence, or with a very rich Florentine who hanged himself in despair at finding himself bankrupt.[28] Then Dante meets the spendthrift Lano da Siena, who was a gentleman of court who squandered all his property in riotous living (*Inf.* 13: 115-21). Giacomo da Sant'Andrea, who is said to have been put to death by order of Ezzelino, committed the same sin. He was extremely rich but wasted an enormous treasure of wealth. While expecting some guests, he set all the cottages of his estate on fire to celebrate their arrival. As the early commentator Benvenuto da Imola says: "In this, surely, he was more violent and more foolish than Nero; for Nero had the houses of the city burned, but his own."[29] That these sinners are sinners of wrath is manifest, for example, in Pier's remark that he fell victim of calumny, initiated by a courtesan, "who inflamed the hearts of everyone against me and these, inflamed, inflamed in turn Augustus" (*Inf.* 13: 67-68). To put it in Aristotelian terms, with her envious slander, the courtesan made the blood boil around the hearts of everyone, including Emperor Frederick. In the end, Pier's heart was also inflamed just like Folco's heart. However, the fire within himself made him blind to reason, whereas the virtue of meekness in Folco made him act with reason. Now in Hell, Pier is still marked by the blindness; he puts all the blame on his enemies and does not admit his fault. He cannot admit it because as a sinner of Hell he is absorbed in his sin of wrath. Through Pier's description of his suicide, Dante gives an example the external manifestation of wrath. The same is case with Giacomo's burning down his property. At the same time there is a clear thematic relation between the fire of the burning cottages and the material definition of anger as the boiling of blood around the heart.

When we turn to the third ring, the theme of wrath is even more manifest. In this ring flames are falling on all three groups of sinners. These flames refer to the brimstone and fire by which God destroyed Sodom, Gomorrah, Adama, and Seboin. In the medieval period the names of these cities were synonymous with impertinent sin and their destruction was regarded as an almost proverbial manifestation of God's wrath, or *indigneris Domine* (Genesis 18: 30).[30] Genesis 13 calls the people of Sodom "wicked" (*pessimi*) and "sinners" (*peccatores*). Lust is only one aspect of the sin associated with the people of Sodom. The general term used for their condemnable sin is most often "wickedness." In Genesis 18 we read that if some "just" (*iustos*) people could be found in the city, they would be spared, but all except for Lot were "wicked" (*impius*). Hence the question of the wickedness of the people of Sodom is, first of all, a matter of justice and injustice, not lust or chastity. It is under the heading of the cardinal virtue of justice that Aquinas examines the majority of sins portrayed in the seventh circle, such as murder and usury, whereas lust, including sodomy, is treated under the heading of the cardinal virtue of temperance.

In Genesis 19 the people of Sodom are described as being full of rage and violence. This is particularly the case with the siege of the house in which Lot is protecting his angelic guests, whom the people outside regard as strangers. They are intent on raping the two men under Lot's care. The problem they are posing is not sodomy but rape. Since Lot offers his daughters as substitutes for the two men, the Sodomites cannot be restricted to the pleasure of sodomy. If the sin of Sodom is seen as the sin of rage and violence, it is thematically connected to the discourse on government by Marco and Carlo. According to the latter two, good government is a matter of practical reason; it requires the subordination and cooperation of the irascible part of the soul. But when the irascible element overpowers the rational element, the governing process becomes a regime of violent rampage. The government of violence and fury leads to the government by factions as in the case of the Guelphs and the Ghibellines.

The sin of impiety is obvious in the behavior of the people of Sodom; they lack reverence. Since the impious have no reverence for God and other human beings, they are usually outright arrogant and contemptuous of all others and have no fear. There is a long tradition of associating Sodom with unnatural sexual desire. For example, Gregor of Nyssa makes the association in his treatise *On Virginity*, Augustine in his *Confessions*, John Chrysotom in his *Homilies on the Gospel of Matthew*, Tertullian in his treatise *On Monogamy*, and Gregory the Great in his *Moralia in Job*. Moreover, Jude 1 describes the people of Sodom and Gomorrah as immoral and indulged in unnatural lust. For that reason, they should serve as examples by undergoing eternal punishment by fire. There seems to be good reason in interpreting the third ring as associated with homosexual lust. But to see Sodom as representing only sodomitic lust is a misunderstanding. The general setting of the third ring with the rain of fire makes it clear that Dante's infernal Sodom comprises more than homosexual lust.

In Luke 17 (26-33) it is made clear that the sin of Sodom was sometimes given a different interpretation than the one on which Dante scholars normally rely:

> As it was in the days of Noah, so will it be in the days of the Son of man. They ate, they drank, they married, they were given in marriage, until the day when Noah entered the ark, and the flood came and destroyed them all. Likewise as it was in the days of Lot—they ate, they drank, they bought, they sold, they planted, they built, but on the day when Lot went out from Sodom fire and sulphur rained from heaven and destroyed them all—so will it be on the day when the Son of man is revealed. On that day, let him who is on the housetop, with his goods in the house, not come down to take them away; and likewise let him who is in the field not turn back. Remember Lot's wife. Whoever seeks to gain his life will lose it, but whoever loses his life will preserve it (*RSV*).

On reading this passage, it is clear that the people of Sodom did not commit only the sin of sodomy but a complex of different sins. Dante relates these sins to the capital sin of wrath. By disregarding reason in their social behavior, economic affairs, and governmental practices, they followed their violent impulses and raged against God, nature, and art.

In addition, Mark D. Jordan has argued that in the medieval period, there was no consistent concept of sodomy and that Aquinas's version in the *Summa Theologiae*, on which Dante scholars most often rely, is one of the least convincing ones.[31] The concept of sodomy was constantly renegotiated, redefined, and recategorized. When Dante scholars argue that the so-called sodomites in the seventh circle are homosexual sinners, they need to substantiate the reason why Dante's view is apparently unequivocal compared with other views of the medieval period. Whenever homosexuals were condemned in the medieval period, the term "sodomite" was often used, but the lack of a consistent concept and the absence of any direct reference to sexual misbehavior in the seventh circle suggest that Dante regarded Sodom as the name of the city whose violation of God's law had several symbolic connotations, of which impiousness is one of the most important ones.

Let us substantiate the reason for rejecting the traditional interpretation of the group of sodomites by considering in detail those aspects of the third ring that I have not examined. "There I saw God's justice in its dreadful operation," says Dante after entering the third ring of the seventh circle (*Inf.* 14: 5-6); he sees God's wrath fully manifest in the last ring of the seventh circle. In that ring there are formally three types of sinners—first the blasphemers, who are lying on the ground, then the sodomites, who wander aimlessly around, and finally the usurers, who are crouching. Besides the encounters with these three groups, two other important events take place in this ring—Vergil recounts the story of the Old Man of Crete, and Dante sees the Geryon, which will bring him and Vergil down to the eighth circle. Since Dante meets the usurers only after having seen the Geryon, Seung argues that "the category of the violent against Art is borderline-case between the Seventh and Eighth Circle; their animal anger has become quasi-guile" (*FLS* 205). But the presence of the usurers in the seventh circle sheds light on Dante's attitude toward the political disorder of his time.

The representative of the blasphemers is Capaneus. Given the emphasis on impiousness of the people of Sodom, Capaneus represents the lack of reverence. He was one of the seven legendary kings who besieged Thebes. According to Statius in his *Thebaid* (X), since Capaneus defied Jupiter, while he was scaling the walls of the city, he was struck dead with a thunderbolt. Since the pagan myth emphasizes the power of the supreme deity in punishing those who do wrong to him, Capaneus's appearance alludes to the stories of the destruction of Sodom and the conquest of Jericho. As in the case of the ancient myth of Venus, Dante might regard the story of Capaneus's death as yet another example of the pagan way of groping for the ultimate truth without revelation. The thunderbolt corresponds to the brimstone and fire that destroyed Sodom and to the sound of the trumpet that made the walls of Jericho crumble. Just as Sodom was destroyed because of God's wrath, Capaneus was struck dead because of Jupiter's wrath. The pagans had no knowledge of the true God, but they knew that the supreme deity sometimes destroys cities and men out of anger.

Then follows Vergil's story of the Old Man of Crete, whose tears are the sources of the rivers in Hell (Acheron, Styx, and Phlegethon), which ultimately form the lake of Cocytus at the bottom of the infernal pit (*Inf.* 14: 94-120). Dante's primary source is the Book of Daniel (2: 37-45) and Christian sources that examine Nebuchadnezzar's dream, perhaps supported by a reading of Ovid's *Metamorphoses* (I.89-150). But when we consider the function of the myth in the seventh circle, it resembles Plato's myth of metals in the *Republic*, whose inspiration is Hesiod's *Works and Days* (II), which was known in the medieval period.[32] Of course, Dante had no direct knowledge of Plato's myth of metals and his theory of government. Whatever he knew of Plato, he got from other sources. If some of his ideas resemble those of Plato, it is due to his way of combining these sources and reflecting upon their content. However, by considering Plato's myth of metals together with the myth of ages in the Book of Daniel and Hesiod's *Work and Days*, it becomes clear how strong the political implications of Vergil's story of the Old Man of Crete are. My objective is not to point out the proximate sources for the story but to underline the essential aspects of its thematic content.

Let us first consider Dante's version of the myth. Vergil says about the statue (*Inf.* 14: 106-11):

> *"La sua testa è di fino oro formata,*
> *e puro argento son le braccia e il petto,*
> *poi è di rame infono all forcata;*
> *da indi in giuso è tutto ferror eletto*
> *salvo che'l destro piede è terraccotta."*
>
> "His head is fashioned of the finest gold;
> pure silver are his arms and hand and chest;
> from there to where his legs spread, he is brass;
> the rest of him is all of chosen iron,
> except his right foot which is terracotta."
> (Trans. Mark Musa)

Dante makes use of the same myth as the Monk of Saint Gall of the ninth century.[33] But Dante's version is a sad one (*Inf.* 14: 112-14), whereas the Monk of Saint Gall celebrates Charlemagne:

> *"Ciascuna parte, fuor che l'oro, è rotta*
> *d'una fissura che lagrime goccia,*
> *le quali, accolte, foran quella grotta."*
>
> "Every part of him, except the gold, is broken
> by a fissure dripping tears down to his feet,
> where they collect to erode the cavern's rock."
> (Trans. Mark Musa)

In Dante studies the Old Man of Crete has most commonly been interpreted as a symbol of the moral decline of mankind throughout the times. No doubt, there is good reason for maintaining the assertion. Different sources speak in favor of it. For example, according to Richard of Saint-Victor in his *De mystica somnia statuae Nabucodonosor* (I), the biblical statue represents mankind as it has grown old because of sin since Adam and Eve. This view reflects the Augustinian division of history into six ages. These ages correspond to the human periods of infancy, childhood, adolescence, youth, mature age, and old age. For Augustine, his present age of the world was the *saeculum senescens*—the age of growing old.[34] Richard maintains the same view.

According to Richard, the different parts of the statue and their materials represent the wounded parts of mankind: silver stands for reason, copper for the will to do good, iron for the sensitive affections, and the terracotta for the concupiscence. Only gold is still intact, according to Richard, and stands for the free will. Richard's interpretation of the statue is characteristic of a thinker who focuses mainly on the theological aspects of the redemption. But for Dante, who believes that the empire has been installed by divine providence, the statue facing Rome "as its mirror" (*Inf.* 14: 105) also indicates the progressive degeneration of mankind's ability to govern the temporal world for its common good. This view, however, is rejected by John A. Scott, who claims that "there is no evidence to support the idea that Dante saw the history of the empire as one of constant degeneration." He admits that the statue's orientation combines religious and political elements, but he restricts its political dimension to the two feet of iron and terracotta, identifying them with the empire and the papacy.[35]

In books 2-4 of the *Republic*, Plato delineates the composition of the state. It consists of three classes: the guardians or rulers, the auxiliaries or administrative assistants, and the productive or artisan class. The guardians will be the highest grade of citizens; they are the philosopher-kings and have the intellectual virtue of wisdom. The auxiliaries are the next highest; they are the warriors. They are not intelligent enough to be the rulers. The artisans are the lowest grade; they produce the necessities of life for the state. In the myth of metals (415a-c), those destined to be the rulers are compared to gold, the next class to silver, and the lowest to iron and bronze. The myth of metals ends with reference to an oracle saying that the state will be ruined if it is ruled by an iron or bronze guardian. This idea is expanded in Plato's theory of the rise and fall of a state in books 8 and 9.

When gold (philosopher-king) rules, the state fulfills its ideal condition. It is Plato's *Kallipolis* (the beautiful city). The deterioration of the state begins when the gold class is overthrown by the lower classes. It degenerates into a timocracy, when the silver class replaces the gold class as the ruler. It further deteriorates into oligarchy, democracy, and tyranny when the silver class is replaced by the iron and bronze class as the ruler. The progressive deterioration brings about the transformation of the state from a community of unity and harmony into civil war and strife. When the gold class rules, the government aims only at the well-being of the whole state rather than of any of its part or the individuals. The basic principle of government is replaced by the principle of self-interest and private gains when the gold class is overthrown by the lower classes, and the rulers do their best to seek their own advantages, thereby producing a war of factions. Such a civil war becomes most pronounced in a democracy, which lacks a strong centralized power to control the warring factions. This chaotic condition is eventually resolved by the emergence of the tyrant. Hence tyranny is the culmination of this long process of deterioration.

In Plato's theory there are two governing classes, the rulers and the auxiliaries, whose roles are different. The gold class formulates the principles and policies of government, and the silver class dutifully implements or executes them. The first is the role of legislation; the second is the role of execution. In the medieval world, the binary division of power coincided with the division of power between the church and the empire, or between kingdoms and ecclesiastical institutions. When Dante talks about government, he is chiefly concerned with the role of the executive—the empire. He takes it for granted that the goals of government (its principles and policies) are set by the teaching of the church. In Plato's theory, the executive or the auxiliary class corresponds to the second element of the soul, the irascible or the animal spirit, which can be manifested in two forms. One form is aggression, fury, and violence; the other is sloth, timidity, and passivity. These two phases of animal spirit, which Seung identifies as the active and the passive dimensions of the irascible part of the soul, are portrayed on the third and the fourth rung of Dante's ladder of divine love.

The active element of the animal spirit is the basic force for the executive role of government. Since this phase of animal spirit is located on the third rung on the ladder of divine love, his theory of government is given in the seventh circle, on the third terrace, and in the third heaven. The primary task for the executive class is to be obedient to the rulers, and to execute their orders faithfully. When they revolt and assert their own power, they will become violent and destructive. In the *Republic* Plato says that the role of the warrior class is delicate. On the one hand, the warriors should be fierce fighters against enemies to protect their fellow citizens. On the other, they should be gentle with their own citizens. If they cannot maintain this delicate balance between gentleness and fierceness, they will not wait around for other enemies to destroy the city but will do it themselves (375c). In short, the role of government is to institute a social order and harmony for the citizens whose natural inclinations for private gains inevitably lead to a war of all against all. This is the ultimate function of government, especially for the executive class.

Let us try to use this theory of government for resolving some of the particular questions in relation to the circle of violence. The Minotaur and the centaurs represent the condition of the soul, in which the animal spirit overpowers the intellect. In the case of the Old Man of Crete, I mentioned two interpretive possibilities. The statue can be taken as a symbol of the moral decline of mankind, or it can be taken as a symbol of the progressive degeneration of government. However, on reading Plato and Aristotle, it is clear that these two interpretive suggestions are just two sides of the same phenomenon. Nowadays, we usually assume that a bad government can be hoisted upon a good people by misfortune. But according to Plato and Aristotle, the moral decline of government is the reflection of the moral decline of the people. The moral improvement of government can be achieved only by the moral improvement of the people. Plato and Aristotle believed that the quality of government was determined by the quality of its leaders. This is why they advocated for the government by virtue. Dante subscribes to the same doctrine. Since the human race has been corrupted morally, it has produced the progressive deterioration of government. This is the story of the Old Man of Crete, whose political dimension has never been fully recognized by the commentators on the passage.

The Old Man of Crete resembles the object of the king's dream, which Daniel interprets as a succession of ever inferior governments or a progressive deterioration as described in Plato's theory of deterioration. The process of deterioration can be taken in two temporal modes. It can be taken as a future projection, as in the case of Daniel, or it can be taken as a current ongoing process (whose end is either near or still distant), as in the account of Richard of Saint-Victor. The latter perspective is Dante's. The deterioration of the empire has already taken place. According to Plato, the deterioration takes place when the lower classes (silver, iron, and bronze) usurp the political power and abuse it for their private gains. This leads to the war of factions, and the fissures in the Old Man of Crete stand for the divisions of the body politic produced by internal strife and conflict. The blood flowing down from the Old Man is the blood of internecine war, as manifested, for example, in the brutal fights between the Guelphs and the Ghibellines.

The savagery of internecine war is vividly presented in Hesiod's account. According to Hesiod, the first human race was gold, the second human race was silver, the third was bronze, the fourth was the heroes, and the fifth was iron. The race of gold was perfect; they lived in peace and happiness. The race of silver was much inferior to the race of gold. The former did not have the intelligence of the latter and perished. The race of bronze was even worse. They were monstrous and heavy (like the Minotaur and the centaurs). All they cared about was fighting and war, and killed each other off (like the Guelphs and the Ghibellines). All of them went down to Hades. The worst race was that of iron; they were godless rascals. They started taking justice into their own hands, sacking each other's cities.

These five races do not exactly correspond to Plato's theory of three grades of human beings, but their morals elucidate the political implications of the story of Old Man of Crete. On a couple of points, Dante's story diverges from the version in the Book of Daniel. First, the Old Man stands on the island of Crete, and second, he looks toward Rome. These are Dante's inventions. Because of these two elements, many commentators have associated the Old Man with the Latin sources of Ovid and Vergil. According to these sources, Crete was the cradle for the Golden Age and its king was Saturn. Dante may have fused the biblical and the pagan sources in making up the story of the Old Man. But the ultimate source for Ovid and Vergil and perhaps also for the author of the Book of Daniel may have been Hesiod. In Dante's version, Crete and Rome are two important sign posts. Crete stands for the Golden Age that is gone. It was not only the seat for Saturn's kingdom of justice; its constitution was long regarded as the best in ancient Greece. For that reason, Plato uses the Cretan constitution along with that of Sparta as the model for the construction of the ideal constitution in the *Laws*. Although the symbolism of Crete is clear, that of Rome is ambiguous. It may stand for the corrupt government of Rome or for the hope of the new Roman Empire; it may stand for both.

Government by Factions

Brunetto's political position is a significant extratextual pointer of the thematic content of the seventh circle. In considering the political map of Europe in the *Livres*, Brunetto says that there are two types by which a city is governed (III.73.5-6):

> One exists in France and in other countries, who are subjects to the lordships of kings and other perpetual princes who sell the office of

> magistrates and give it to those who seek it (they are little concerned with their goodness or the advantage to the citydwellers). The other is in Italy, for the citizens and the citydwellers and the communities of cities elect as magistrates and lords those they consider to be better and more profitable to the common good of the city and all its subjects.[36]

In choosing between these two types of government, Brunetto prefers the lordship of communes. To further substantiate his argument, he makes a distinction between three principal forms of government. The distinction seems based on book 8 of the *Ethics*, where Aristotle gives his two triads of good and evil forms of government (1160a-61a). Brunetto distinguishes between the lordships of kings (*de roi*), the lordships of men (*de bons*), and the lordships of communes (*de communes*) (II.44.1). He says that each form of government has its opposite. The opposite of kingship is tyranny. The conflict between kingship and tyranny is Brunetto's major concern (II.44.2-3):

> When good men and great men cease doing what is good, with the intent of not letting the lordship leave their family, and do not consider their honor, merit or dignity, then their lordship changes into the lordship of the commune. The lordship of the commune is corrupted when good customs and good and praiseworthy law are abandoned.[37]

Brunetto does not use the Aristotelian political terminology about the different forms of government. But since he stresses the practice of electing magistrates and lords by qualification, his ideal resembles that of timocracy, whose opposite is democracy according to Aristotle. However, in order to determine whether Brunetto maintained that view and whether Dante believed that he did, let us consider the question of timocracy in some detail.

In book 8 of the *Republic*, Plato enumerates the various forms of government from the best to the worst: aristocracy, timocracy, oligarchy, democracy, and tyranny. The hierarchy is made in accordance with the three parts of the soul: the intellect, the spirit, and the appetites. Aristocracy is the government by the best, which is the intellect or the philospher-king; timocracy is the government by the spirit, the warrior class; and the other three forms are the governments by the appetites, the artisan class. Timocracy is the second best form of government, because it is the second element of the soul, the faculty of feeling and emotion, which is the source of violence and courage. In *The Fragile Leaves of the Sibyl* Seung calls this part of the soul the irascible. If Brunetto regarded timocracy as the best form of government, it is reasonable that he appears in the circle of violence, which is associated with the irascible or the spirit, in Platonic terms. According to Plato, timocracy is a form of government intermediate between aristocracy and oligarchy, between the rule of the intellect and the rule of the appetites (the concupiscible). Since it is the rule of the spirit (the irascible), it maintains certain standards of the rule of the intellect and is yet inclined to the rule of the appetites (*Republic* 547c-48b). To emphasize the thematic resemblances between Plato and Dante, it should be remembered that the same reasoning pervades Aristotle's ranking of the different forms of government. He accepts the essentials of Plato's theory of government as given in the *Republic* when he proposes his version of true and perverted forms of government.

There are differences between Plato and Aristotle on the different forms of government. For example, Plato derives "timocracy" from the Greek word *time*, which refers to "honor," whereas Aristotle derives it from the Greek *timema*, which refers to property qualification. For Aristotle timocracy is a special form of democracy, in which the citizens participate only if they can meet the property qualification. Nevertheless, Plato and Aristotle both maintain that timocracy is not a fully perverted form of government; it is a form of government that occurs before the state deteriorates into perverted forms of government or forms governed by the appetites, according to Plato. In book 3 of the *Politics*, Aristotle maintains that the first form of government was monarchical (1286b). But when the stability of the monarchical society produced many people of equal merit, they established a constitutional government. Under this pressure, the ruling classes deteriorated and confined themselves to the pursuit of their own interests. As a result, they decayed into oligarchies, which in the end became democracies. In short, according to Aristotle, democracies tend to arise through a natural cycle of decay. Dante does not hold the notion of a natural cycle of decay, since his teleological view of the course of the world has the touch of the Joachitic evocation of the Third Age. However, he fully agrees with the theory of progressive decay.[38]

Moreover, Aristotle accepts Plato's tripartite theory of the soul in *De anima*, which is explicated in Aquinas's commentary on *De anima*. Aristotle does not explicitly connect the different forms of government to the three parts of the soul. But he uses the tripartite theory of the soul as the basis for his doctrines of virtues and vices as Plato does. The three parts of the soul are the sources of its power, whose perfection becomes virtues and whose corruption becomes vices. These virtues and vices take effect, not only in the private domain of ethics, but also in the public domain of politics. For example, if the animal power of aggressive disposition goes out of control, it will become the vice of anger and violence. When a person of this vice gains political power, he will produce a government of violence and aggression. As Cicero puts it in *De officiis* (I.89.), "anger is in every circumstance to be eradicated; and it is to be desired that they who administer the government should be like the laws, which are led to inflict punishment not by wrath but by justice."[39] However, as Aquinas explains the relation between wrath and meekness in the *Summa* (pt. 2-2, q. 157, aa. 1-2), with special reference to Aristotle's *Ethics* (1125b25-1126a10), the same disposition will become the virtue of meekness, if it is well-trained. When a person of this virtue manages public affairs, he will institute a government of peace and reconciliation instead of violence and aggression.

The examples of violence and meekness are given on the third terrace. For example, Peisistratus, whose reign in Athens, according to Aristotle, was a golden age because his sons were much harsher in their government than the father, is portrayed as a person who knows how to control anger.[40] The source is Valerius Maximus who recounts how Peisistratus reacted when a young man in love with one of his daughters kissed his beloved in the street. Peisistratus's wife urged that the young man be put to death because of his act.[41] But Peisistratus replied (*Inf.* 15: 104-5):

> *"Che farem noi a chi mal ne disira,*
> *se quei che ci ama è per noi condannato?"*
>
> "What shall we do to those who wish us harm
> if we condemn the ones who show us love?"
> (Trans. Mark Musa)

The exchange between Peisistratus and his wife comes to the question of which is going to win, the momentary anger or the sensible anger. With his soft reply, Peisistratus rebukes his wife's momentary anger and makes it subdue to reason. In the seventh circle the same problem underlies Jacopo Rusticucci's remark that he was driven to violent acts by his fierce wife. We do not know which acts Dante has in mind, but if we follow Seung's method of parallel reading, the remark can be thematically related to the Peisistratus story. As a result, there is no need to know which acts Jacopo committed. The parallel reading makes it probable that they were acts similar to the one Peisistratus's wife tried to provoke with her momentary anger.

The fact that Peisistratus was a king does not mean that he should be linked to Dante's theory of government. His behavior can be taken as a political act because he was a king, or as a private act because it only involved his private affair. The same virtue and vice can be manifested in both the private and the public domains. The influence by Jacopo's wife on her husband formally belongs to the private domain. But if her fierceness influenced his decisions in the public domain, there is no longer any clear demarcation between the private and the public domain. With the episode of St. Stephen (Acts 7: 54-60), which is the third example of meekness of the third terrace, Dante thematizes how anger overpowers reason in the public domain. The mob shouting "Kill him, kill" stones the poor Stephen. However, even in his final agony, Stephen asks God to forgive his persecutors (*Purg.* 15: 106-14). His wish of forgiveness underlines meekness as a private affair. The mob that stones St. Stephen resembles the mob that comes to Lot's house in order to violate his angelic guests (Genesis 19: 5). Lot's faith in the two angels also underlines meekness as a private affair. The two mobs, however, exemplify how anger manifests itself in the public domain when it overpowers reason. When the mob tries to enter Lot's house, the two angels strike all men blind. Brunetto says that the Florentines are blind. Marco corrects this assertion by saying that the world is blind. As a result, Brunetto's statement about the Florentines comes to represent the blindness Marco identifies as the state of the world. Hence blindness is an essential characteristic of those people whose acts are governed by the irascible power of their souls, which suppresses the intellectual power. Brunetto's blindness is manifest in his contemptuous assault on his fellow citizens. The assault displays his impiousness, arrogance, and fearlessness.

However, here we need to take into account a certain ambivalence in considering Brunetto's political ideal. Brunetto does not say that timocracy is the best form of government. Instead, he speaks of the lordship of communes, which resembles the timocractic rule of the warrior class according to Plato. But the lordship of communes also resembles the democratic rule of the artisan class. If so, it might be objected that in my Platonic exposition of the thematic content of Dante's infernal Sodom, I need to explain why he is not assigned to a section of Hell that thematizes the perversions of the appetites or the concupiscible, since his political ideal displays a democractic inclination. However, my motive for turning to Plato, whose work was virtually unknown in Dante's time, but whose influence is detectable almost everywhere due to the transmission of Platonic ideas through other writers (ancient, Christian, Jewish, or Muslim), is not to impose Platonic ideas on Dante's poem but to bring forth its political themes. It is Brunetto's appearance in the *Commedia* that indicates his affinity with the executive class of warriors according to Plato. For example, Brunetto shows concern for his former pupil, whom he regards as a son. But when he speaks of what he regards as their enemies, he becomes full of rage. The assault on Florence and the theme of friendship in the Brunetto episode comes to display the perversion of the delicate role of the warrior class; the warriors should be fierce fighters against enemies in the protection of fellow citizens, but they should be gentle with their own citizens. Brunetto does not master this delicate role. He rages against his and Dante's enemies, but the enemies are their fellow citizens.

The fact that Brunetto's political ideal has the touch of the democratic ideal only emphasizes its complete dissimilarity from Dante's political ideal. The ancient and medieval attitude toward democracy was radically different from ours. Whereas we assume that democracy is the only just form of government, the ancient and medieval people believed that it was one of the basest forms of government, which leads to government by factions. When considered most negatively, democracy was seen as a form of government in which all citizens seek only their own respective advantages. Their conception of people (*demos* or *populus*) was different from ours. When we say that democracy is the government by the people, of the people, and for the people, we exalt the people to the sacred level of unity and harmony. The ancients and the medievals did not have such an exalted notion of people. For them the *demos* or *populus* was a bunch of ill-educated and ill-tempered rabbles, each of whom was concerned only with his self-interest and had no concern for the well-being of the state as a whole. Given this nature of the people, there is no guarantee that the people of a state will have any unity or harmony. The degeneration of a people into a state of warring factions is most likely if they are overpowered by rage and fear. As a result, a democratic government will become a government by vengeance as exemplified by the factional strife between the Guelphs and the Ghibellines.

Though neither a democracy nor a timocracy, the lordship of communes Brunetto prefers implies a government by factions. As such, the difference between democracy and timocracy is not essential for understanding Dante's rejection of Brunetto's ideal. The point of the matter is that Dante regards the government by factions as incapable of providing peace and order to cities and kingdoms. In the *Politics* Aristotle says that democracy is the worst form of government, but the best when all are bad (1289b). The difference between oligarchy and democracy is the choice between the rich or the poor looking after themselves. Had Brunetto known Aristotle's *Politics* when he wrote his *Livres*, he might have been more cautious in his argumentation in favor of the lordship of communes.

He was well-acquainted with the *Ethics*, but his preference for the lordship of the communes is significantly influenced by his reading of the *Rhetoric*. In book 1 of the *Rhetoric*, Aristotle does not present the two triads of true and perverted forms of government, but gives a fourfold distinction of democracy, oligarchy, aristocracy, and monarchy (1365b-1366a).

Aristotle says that monarchy is the supreme rule of one man alone; aristocracy is the rule of those who possess an educational qualification laid down by the law; and oligarchy is the rule of those who possess a certain property-qualification. Brunetto's preference for the Italian communes does not fully correspond to any of these forms of government. In Florence citizens entered its governmental institutions, not because they possessed property, but because they were members of guilds. Aristotle's definition of democracy is the only form of government that resembles the lordship of communes. Aristotle defines democracy as a form of government under which the citizens distribute the offices of the state by lot and whose end is freedom. For Brunetto, it appears, the end of freedom stands in contrast to the practice of power by the French king, and the distribution of offices among the citizens by lot stands in contrast to the trading of offices in the French kingdom.

In the *Livres* Brunetto relies heavily on Aristotle, but in the end he uses him to promote an argument for city-republicanism. For Dante, who was well-acquainted with Aristotle's *Politics* and *Ethics*, Brunetto must have been a dangerous violator of Aristotle's ethical and political ideas. But the central issue is not Brunetto's misreading or misuse of Aristotle, but the fact that Brunetto's political ideal is the opposite of Dante's. According to the latter, as explained in *De monarchia* (I.xiii), mankind is in its ideal state when it is ruled by one person. For Dante, the government by factions is a violent form of government because each faction tries to attain the power over all other factions in order to maintain its freedom and to obtain more wealth. In *De monarchy* (1.xii) he explicitly says that democracies along with oligarchies and tyrannies "force mankind into slavery."[42] In book 6 of the *Politics*, Aristotle says that "where absolute freedom is allowed there is nothing to restrain the evil which is inherent in every man" (1318b).[43] In book 8 of the *Ethics*, Aristotle says that "democracy is found chiefly in masterless dwellings (for here every one is on an equality), and in those in which the ruler is weak and every one has license to do as he pleases" (1161a).[44] These statements spell out, as Dante most likely saw it, the danger of Brunetto's preference for city-republicanism. In a city-state there is no secure principle of unity as in the case of a monarchy. The principle of order will constantly change as it suits the rulers. The result is disorder, according to Dante. The ideal of absolute freedom is firmly rejected by Marco on the third terrace with his remark that mankind needs the restraint of laws. In the Venus heaven Cunizza exemplifies what happens in masterless dwellings when there are no laws or the laws are not respected. Carlo elucidates the failure of secular rulers in implementing the necessary laws. Marco and Folco emphasize the role of the church in undermining the implementation of laws by secular authorities.

Dante holds that the relation between emperor and mankind is equivalent to the natural bond between a father and a son. Government by factions breaks this bond. Each faction seeks only its own interest. The son need not respect his father, although he is the head of the family. Since the natural bond is broken, the son is free to pursue his fortune. For that reason, since Brunetto favors the government by factions, he is condemned as a sinner against nature. But he can also be seen as a sinner against God, who is the ultimate source for the imperial institution, which the government by factions undermines. Finally, he can be associated with the sin against art because in a community governed by factions, the increase of wealth is not for the benefit of the community as a whole; it is only for the benefit of the faction that possesses the power or the individual who expands his wealth by the accumulation of interest payment. By considering Brunetto's condemnation, it becomes clear that the third ring should not necessarily been as describing three types of violent sins; it can be taken as one type of sin with three essential implications.

The second group of sinners against nature Dante encounters in the third ring further elucidates the problem of government by factions. These sinners are usually lumped together as the three Florentines: Guido Guerra, Tegghiaio Aldobrandini, and Jacopo Rusticucci. But according to Susan Noakes, it is more adequate to describe them as the "three Guelphs" or "three heroes of the Golden Age of the Guelph party."[45] The latter description could have been true if they had not been placed in Hell. Since their souls are depraved, there is nothing heroic about them. The age they represent can only be the age that has led to deterioration. To the Guelphs it might be the golden age, but since Dante opposes the government by factions, in which the Guelph party is in constant conflict with the Ghibelline party, the three Guelphs are monstrous warriors who share the same tendency to prefer war for peace. One of them is even referred to by his nickname *Guerra*, meaning war. Dante the traveler shows empathy for many of the depraved souls in Hell, but for Dante the writer, each condemnation is unconditional. Since the three Guelphs were influential Florentine citizens, they could have prevented the deterioration of the city. But they chose the government by factions and encouraged the deterioration.

Jacopo says to Dante that the recently deceased Guglielmo Borsiere has told him and his fellow Guelphs about the wicked state of their hometown (*Inf.* 16: 70-72). But they want to hear more about it. Then Dante makes a short eloquent answer that puts further into perspective the process of deterioration, for which the three Guelphs are responsible (*Inf.* 16: 73-75):

> *"La gente nova e' subiti guadagni*
> *orgoglio e dismisura han generata,*
> *Fiorenza, in te, sì che tu già ten piagni."*
>
> "A new breed of people with their sudden wealth
> have stimulated pride and unrestraint
> in you, O Florence, made to weep so soon."
> (Trans. Mark Musa)

The three Guelphs are impressed by Dante's "gift of ready, open speech" (*Inf.* 16: 81). His answer is as sharp and precise as a doctor's scalpel. Florence has deteriorated, and all the citizens seek their own self-interests. This is the truth as Dante sees it. Since it is the truth, it even impresses the sinful souls that encouraged the deterioration.

But who are this new breed of people? The three Guelphs do not belong to them. But with their practice of government by factions, they have prepared the way for them. The central issue is the gain of wealth. In book 1 of the *Politics*, Aristotle says that there are two ways of getting wealthy (1258a-58b):

> One is a part of household management, the other is retail trade: the former is necessary and honourable, while that which consists in exchange is justly censured; for it is unnatural, and a mode by which men gain from one another. The most hated sort, and with the greatest reason, is usury, which makes a gain out of money itself, and not from the natural object of it. For money was intended to be used in exchange, but not increase at interest. And this term interest, which means the birth of money from money, is applied to the breeding of money because the offspring resembles the parent. That is why of all modes of getting wealth this is the most unnatural.[46]

The usurers in the seventh circle, says Dante, try to protect themselves from the flames "like a dog in summertime busy, now with his paw, now with his snout, tormented by the fleas and flies that bite him" (*Inf.* 17: 49-51). In short, they act like bestial creatures. By placing the usurers in the third ring, Dante emphasizes that the ruling principle in his hometown is the gain of wealth, of which usury is the most distasteful.

As we have seen, Dante's discourse on government on the rung of meekness and wrath is specifically concerned with the question of opposite characters within the same family. Carlo explains the influence of nature and providence in the formation of the individual character. On the basis of Marco's speech on the free will, he underlines the necessity of using the free will in accordance with the natural and providential dispositions. Usury is the complete perversion of the truth Carlo reveals. The principle of money breeding money resembles the principle of nature and providence in the generation of human beings. For the usurer money is a natural condition in human relations and its increase at interest is the result of good fortune. But this view is condemned by Marco. The belief in fortune implies a perverted view of the influence of providence. The workings of providence are not like rates of interest. Providence cannot be predicted, nor can it be negotiated. Like the other sinners of the seventh circle, the usurers suffer from the blindness that characterizes the wrathful. Their unnatural pursuit of wealth is a bestial passion. It makes them blind to the truth about the natural and providential dispositions in the generation of human beings. But, as Seung points out, the usurers are a borderline case. The calculation of interest entails the intellectual power of the soul. Since their object is deliberate deceit, their sin has a certain affinity with the souls of the eighth circle, the envious who love secrecy and never reveal their malicious will.

New Breed of People

In *Intuition and Construction*, Seung argues that "loss of confidence in natural intuition leads to normative subjectivism and skepticism":

> Such a loss can take place on an individual or a collective level and at any time in history. It has produced massive cultural upheavals on two occasions in the West: in Renaissance Europe and Sophistic Athens. On both occasions, distrust of natural or positive intuition created a normative crisis for the whole culture. Under those circumstances, there are two ways to overcome normative chaos. One of them is the positivistic

> appeal to the power that can sustain a social order. The other is the idealistic appeal to transcendental norms, which requires transcendental intuition. In ancient Athens, Socrates and Plato proposed transcendental intuitionism against the positivism of Thrasymachus and Callicles. In Renaissance Europe, the positivism of Machiavelli and his heirs was countered by rational intuitionism. Both versions of intuitionism presuppose transcendental norms or ideals (*IC* xii).

In *Cultural Thematics* and *Plato Rediscovered*, Seung examines the motives for the cultural upheavals of Renaissance Europe and sophistic Athens. In the latter he elucidates Plato's response to the normative crisis of his time. He argues that his whole work reflects an ongoing dialectical treatment of the same basic issues. These issues are essentially related to the problem of power politics (*PR* ix-x). Historically, Seung identifies Plato's dialectical project as a persistent criticism of the Athenian imperialism that emerged from the Persian Wars (*PR* xv). This criticism is categorically stated in the early dialogue of the *Gorgias*, where Socrates accuses the Athenians of having become "idle, works-shy, garrulous and mercenary" under the reign of Pericles (515e).[47]

To elucidate Plato's criticism, Seung makes a distinction between "theonomy" and "anthroponomy": "This distinction concerns the origin of *nomos* (normative standards or rules), that is, the question of whether they are given by the gods or made by human beings" (*PR* 8). To exemplify the theonomic culture, Seung refers to Lucurgus, who, according to Herodotus in his *History* (I), was believed to have received the entire system of laws, observed by the Spartans, from Apollo of Delphi. But this view was no longer the prevalent one in Plato's time. According to Seung, the Protagorian doctrine of man as the measure of all things marks the advent of the anthroponomic culture. With reference to the Socratic notion of appetites, Seung says that the cultural transition involved a conflict between "the culture of restrained (by the fear of God) appetites and the culture of released (from the fear of God) appetites"′(*PR* 11). He points out that especially the sophists were instrumental in the radical transformation of normative standards.

The transition led to agnosticism and even atheism and created serious problems about the legitimacy of laws. If the gods were no longer the origins of order, new normative standards had to be invented or discovered in order to maintain and legitimize, not only the existent, but every conceivable order. References to conventions were one way to uphold normative standards. Another way is the one represented by Callicles in the *Gorgias*. This way implies a law of natural selection, in which personal ambition and power possession are the regulating forces (*PR* 267). However, for Plato the constitution of normative standards became a matter of the relation between the world of phenomena and the world of forms. He tried to settle this relation in different ways, but ultimately he came to realize that it could not be settled if the two worlds were recognized as separate entities. Instead, they were to be fused and combined. Due to this realization, Seung argues, Plato gave up the idea, as displayed in the *Republic*, that the understanding of the relation can establish "a complete system of normative rules and standards." Instead, in the *Laws*, Plato argues that such an understanding can only provide "the basic normative ideals" (*PR* xi-xii and 240-45, and *IC* xii-xiii).

Although the difference between these two conceptions of the foundation of normative standards is significant, they underline the decisiveness of Plato's dialectical project. This is manifest in the fact that he wrote two major dialogues (the *Republic* and the *Laws*), which in Seung's words "stand out like two huge landmasses in a vast ocean of many smaller islands" and present two different versions of the ideal society (*PR* xv). In Dante we detect a similar close connection between argumentative insistence and historical circumstances. His theory of dual ends and authorities is also motivated by cultural problems concerning the foundation of normative standards or ideals by transcendental intuition. These problems, however, did not bring about the massive cultural upheaval of the Renaissance, but they can be seen as pointing towards it. For example, although the Parisian bishop Etienne Tempier's reaction against materialist conceptions concerned the tendency to give prevalence to philosophical knowledge at the expense of theological truths, it elucidates the increasing problems of giving political evocations a tenable transcendent foundation. As soon as the principles of inquiry into natural causes, which the natural philosopher employs, are transferred to the political sphere, it is no longer possible to maintain, as Dante does, that the foundation of the empire is transcendent. Since the natural philosopher cannot consider the creation, as, for example, Boethius of Dacia held, the natural politician needs not to consider whether his power has a transcendent foundation. If his power is kingly, he can justify it by appealing to heritage, which is a normative standard based on conventions. But the disregard for transcendental intuition in justifying political institutions can lead to the Calliclean doctrine of natural selection; those who hold power are those who are best at gaining and maintaining that power. The radical Aristotelians of the thirteenth century were not sophists; their approach to knowledge was different and their influence was less decisive than that of the sophists. But by focusing only on natural causes, they held a worldview that undermined the transcendental intuition. As a result, they indirectly contributed to the transformation of normative standards and prepared the way for the anthropocentric culture of the Renaissance.

Another symptom of crisis is the dispute about the hierachical division of secular and spiritual power in the beginning of the fourteenth century. It demarcates the increasing difficulty in maintaining the ideal of a unifying power organization in medieval Europe. Joan M. Ferrante argues that Dante's overall objective with writing the *Commedia* is "to deliver a political message" and "preach the need for political unity."[48] But this view tends to reduce Dante's theory of dual ends and authorities to a pragmatic construct that is more concerned with rhetorical persuasion than with the distribution of a coherent vision of God's universal order. Richard Kay makes a similar argument about *De monarchia*. He argues that the treatise should be seen as an occasional piece designed to persuade more than to instruct. According to Kay, it was most likely written around 1317 in response to the Pope John XXII's bull *Si fratum*, whose aim was to break up the alliance of pro-imperial rulers in Northern Italy. Can Grande della Scala, who was Dante's patron at the time and member of the alliance, might have commissioned the treatise in order to strengthen his position as imperial vicar. As a result, Kay argues, Dante might have been under pressure to produce a scholarly response as quickly as possible. Consequently, he drew on materials at hand and what he had written in the same vein, such as book 4 of the *Convivio* and some of his political letters, and relied on rhetoric to gloss over tenuous arguments.[49]

To be sure, in considering especially the political conflicts during Boniface VIII's papacy, to which Dante often refers in the *Commedia*, the need for a pragmatic solution to the division of secular and spiritual power is evident. The contending parties were irreconcilable. On the one hand, there is the glorious celebration of the Jubilee of 1300, which marks the peak of the pope's power. It was followed up by his bull *Unam sanctam* (1302), in which the pope claims that both the spiritual and the material sword are in the hands of the church; the former is exercised by the church itself and the latter by secular rulers on its command. On the other hand, there is the pope's violent death in 1303 due to starvation and torture during his imprisonment by the French troops. It was the outcome of a hideous conflict between the pope and the French king. In the bull *Clericos laicos* (1296), the pope had forbidden the clergy of France and England to pay taxes. In response, the French king forbade the export of gold and silver from his kingdom and spread rumors about the legitimacy of the pope's election. However, the pope was not intent on making trouble with the French king. As a result, he issued the bull *Etsi de statu* (1297), allowing levies from the clergy in defense of the kingdom without papal authorities.[50]

This controversy was not yet another conflict between papacy and secular rulers. As R. W. Dyson points out, the consequences were far-reaching in a historical perspective:

> Boniface's death marks the end of the medieval papacy's vision of its own world-wide political authority. The struggles of 1296-1303 were, indeed, not so much a personal contest between Boniface VIII and Philip the Fair as a collision of two incompatible principles: on the one hand, the ideal, which had largely animated papal diplomacy since the time of Gregory VII, of a universal papal monarchy transcending territorial boundaries and uniting the Christian world in the peaceful and harmonious community of Christendom; and, on the other, the new conception, so rapidly supplanting older feudal loyalties, of the consolidated nation state, brooking no interference from without and acknowledging no sovereign but its king.[51]

For Dante the conflict between Boniface and Philip was not a conflict between two incompatible principles. Since the *Commedia* announces the future damnation of Boniface and calls Philip the "Plague of France" (*Purg*. 7: 109), he saw it rather as a struggle over control, wealth, and possessions that resulted in tyranny and disorder. With his evocation of a new model for the Gelasian distinction between secular and spiritual power, Dante tries to find the means for resolving such conflicts. By reconstituting the empire, the church might be prevented from deteriorating into a secular institution in constant conflict with other secular institutions. The reinforced imperial authority could control by force and regulate by law the different institutions of secular government.

In *De monarchia* (I.xiv) Dante admits that nations, kingdoms, and cities have their own characteristics that legitimate the use of different laws, since the climate and the length of days and nights differ from one area to another. But mankind should be guided by one ruler "in those matters which are common to all men and of relevance to all, and it is to be guided towards peace by a common law."[52] However, by emphasizing that the Roman people won the race to rule the world against all competition by the aid of divine providence, Dante makes it clear that any appeal to imperial reinforcement is ineffective if its transcendent foundation is unsettled. For that reason, Dante's motivation cannot be explained only with reference to the need for cooperation between states, cities, and kingdoms for a common cause. In *De monarchia* (I.ix) he tries to explicate the transcendent foundation of the empire by way of syllogistic reasoning. In the *Commedia* he further substantiates his arguments, but he moves away from the literal sensibility of syllogistic reasoning and takes a big leap into the spiritual sensibility of allegorical expression.

To emphasize further Dante's reaction against the political disorder of his time, let us turn to Marsilius's *Defensor pacis*, which was burned at the University of Paris the same year of its publication and condemned as heretical by Pope John XXII (1327).[53] In making this connection, it should be remembered that, as Brian Tierney puts it, "although Marsilius was pursuing his own agenda, different from that of contemporary Franciscan controversialists, the whole pattern of his argument was shaped by John XXII's condemnation [in 1322] of the Franciscan doctrine of evangelical poverty."[54] The *Defensor pacis* departs from a historical situation Dante could only have seen coming. But when we try to come to terms with the nature of Dante's criticism, Marsilius's treatise substantiates the sad picture of the Italian peninsula Dante draws up in the *Commedia* and that underlies his appeal to imperial reinforcement in *De monarchia*.

According to Marsilius, priestly power is by nature spiritual. It is entirely concerned with the spiritual order, whose reference is the world beyond, where God will state his judgment on human behavior. Priests can teach men how to act righteously in this world. They can also admonish human conduct. But they have never been given coercive power to intervene in temporal affairs. Thus, in criticizing papal intervention in political affairs, Marsilius presents a reading of the Holy Scriptures that undermines the papal idea of hierarchical power division. He claims that "all bishops are of equal authority immediately through Christ," and it cannot "be proven by divine law that there is any superiority or subjection among them in spiritual or temporal affairs" (III.2.17). Hence the authority of the Roman bishop who holds the papal office is not superior to any other bishop. In short, there is no head of the church, or the head is Christ, whose kingdom is of the other world. In this world the authority lies in the hands of the human legislator who is "the whole body of citizens, or the weightier part thereof" (III.2.6).[55]

The existential reality that animates Marsilius's political thought makes it clear that Dante's identification of the local disorder with the global one is not just an audacious response to a personal defeat in political affairs resulting in exile. Marsilius and Dante pursue different and incompatible political ideals. But their evocations reflect a culture that has lost its bonds of order. To emphasize this further, we might mention, for example, that with the fall of the Hohenstaufens at the battle of Tagliacozzo (1268), the empire was, as Thomas G. Bergin puts it, "dead in Italy from that day forth."[56] To this we can add that with the sack of Acre (1291), the Western crusades in the eastern Mediterranean came to an end and with them also the aspirations for unifying the Christian world through a common cause. None of the ruling powers in Western Europe responded to the definitive loss of the Holy Land; they were all too absorbed in local and regional conflicts.[57] Moreover, with the Babylonian Captivity from 1309 with Pope Clement V's settlement in Avignon, the dissolution of the unity of the church was symbolically marked and made the advancement of regional churches linked to regional power politics inevitable.

In *Cultural Thematics* Seung examines the transformation of the medieval ethos into the modern ethos, which led to the positivism of Machiavelli. Schematically speaking, he identifies Dante's worldview with the medieval ethos of theocentricism and humility. Dante's epic displays a worldview different from that of the Renaissance. However, as soon as we recognize the political content of Dante's discourse on meekness and wrath, it becomes clear that the *Commedia* is a constructive reaction against the surfacing culture of the Renaissance, which Seung identifies with the Faustian culture. Due to Dante's emphasis on their irascibility, the sinners of wrath can be seen as the medieval forerunners to the sovereign or Machiavellian individuals of the Renaissance. According to Seung:

> Machiavellian individuals are a new breed of human beings that emerge by the end of the Middle Ages and reshape European culture during the Renaissance. Obsessed with freedom and power, they are bent on controlling and conquering others by fraud and force. They are bold and brutal, cunning and cruel, resilient and resourceful. The prototype of the Machiavellian individual is portrayed in Boccaccio's *Decameron.* The heroes and heroines, whose exploits are described in one hundred stories over ten days, distinguish themselves by their ingenuity and audacity in coping with their adversaries (*IC* 133-34).

In *Cultural Thematics* Seung defines these characters as sovereign individuals to stress their determination to preserve their liberty and autonomy (*CT* 207-16).

Dante's identification of the irascible element of these sinners resembles the Machiavellian idea of *animo* (soul): "Its meaning is completely dissociated from the Christian idea of the soul. It is the center of force of energy, from which all human actions emanate. It is the source of political ambition and militant spirit." However, Dante's sinners of wrath are different from the Machiavellian individuals in one particular respect. For Machiavelli, *ambizione* (ambition)

> is the drive for glory and power, the power to dominate others and to avoid domination by others. Power alone is not enough to sustain ambition; it should be supplemented by *ragione* (reason). Machiavelli conception of rationality is instrumental rationality par excellence. The combination of reason and power is expressed by the Machiavellian tactics of fraud and force and by the Machiavellian metaphor of the fox and the lion in his description of the ideal prince (*IC* 134).

Whereas Dante's new breed of people are sinners whose reason has been overpowered by bestial passions, the Machiavellian individuals are the new breed of people in whom reason or the intellectual power of the soul has become instrumental in their passionate pursuit of power. In this respect, Dante's sinners of wrath are not sovereign individuals, but his portrayal of the usurers as a borderline case between bestial passion and intellectual fraud indicates that the premises for the Machiavellian tactics of fraud and force had already emerged in the public domain in Dante's time. Although Dante's vision of God's universal order in the *Commedia* belongs to the medieval ethos, the world of depravation, violence, and fraud he describes reflects the emergence of the Renaissance ethos.

In *Cultural Thematics* Seung examines this transformation by focusing on two triads of intellectuals in medieval Europe. The one consists of Bonaventure, Aquinas, and Duns Scotus, and the other consists of Dante, Petrarch, and Boccaccio. In a review of the book, Aloysius P. Martinich says that Seung needs to account for the separation by nearly a half century between the two triads he examines in order to explicate what he defines as the formation of the Faustian ethos.[58] According to Martinich, Seung's appeal to "relative backwardness of Florence in comparison with Paris" seems incomplete (*CT* 248): "It does not explain why Paris never produced a literary triad nor why Florence never produced a philosophical one. Why did Florence and not Paris become one of the lights of the Renaissance? This remains a mystery." There are no easy answers to these questions. But Dante's reaction against the emergence of the Faustian ethos helps to clarify the time lag between the two triads.

In examining the Parisian and the Florentine triads, Seung emphasizes the similarity of the two triads with respect to their forms of expression. Both triads display a movement from the allegorical to the literal form of expression. Since the Parisian triad used the Latin of the church, there was no need to invent a new language. It used the established style of expression that had been developed in philosophy and theology. The Florentine triad used the vernacular and had to invent a new style of exposition. It took some time to do that and to polish the invention. This is one of the reasons for the time lag between the two triads. But the form of expression is not the same as its cultural content. The Parisian triad is situated in a medieval culture, whereas the Florentine triad moves into a secular culture. In this regard, the Florentine culture was more modern and more advanced than the Parisian, if modernization and secularization are taken as the traits of progress and advance.

Dante's new breed of people is the new breed of secular people, who can be identified as Faustians or Machiavellians. The transformation of the medieval Christian into the Faustian or Machiavellian is the transformation of the man of humility to the man of ambition and arrogance. This transformation involves all three parts of the soul—the intellect, the animal passion (the irascible), and the appetite (the concupiscible). The intellect becomes scheming and manipulative. The animal passion becomes aggressive and expansionistic, and the appetite becomes greedy and acquisitive. All these changes were accomplished in the genesis of the usurers during Dante's lifetime. Economically, the institution of usury was the first embodiment of European capitalism and expansionism. The transformation of the humble medieval Christian into the modern Machiavellian can be described in different ways. First, the transformation can be regarded as an inversion of humility into arrogance. Second, it can be regarded as the imitation of the almighty God. Technically speaking, God is the only sovereign individual. Instead of humbling themselves before God, human beings tried to be like God. The first and the second way describe the same phenomenon. Since the humble Christian is the opposite of the almighty God, to invert the former is to imitate the latter. Finally, the transformation can be taken as the secularization of Christian culture, which can also be described as the inversion of the Christian ethos.

The common ground of these descriptions is the human rebellion against God. In this respect, all sinners of Dante's Hell can be seen as sovereign individuals who recognize no master over themselves. Consider the tyrants in the first ring of the seventh circle. All of them stand out as sovereign individuals. The same goes for the suicides. In ancient Rome, suicide was not permitted for the slaves because they did not have control over their bodies. For the same reason, suicide was not permitted for the Christians. They considered their bodies, not as their own, but as gifts from God. As a result, suicide was considered to be an act of defiance for the Christians. As such, it is an act of a sovereign individual.

Sovereignty is supremely expressed by Satan at the bottom of Hell. All the sinners of Dante's Hell participate in his sovereignty one way or another. If we took the sinners out of Hell and removed the labels of terrible sins, we might have the kind of resourceful people that populate Boccaccio's *Decameron*.

Dante's criticism of the new breed of people is his reaction to the Faustian ethos that became acute during his lifetime. But it took him a long time to reach this conservative position of reaction. For example, in the *Convivio* he tried to work through the problem of secularization as a champion of a new culture, but he failed in this endeavor. *De monarchia* displays the same preoccupation with its preference for syllogistic reasoning. But in the *Commedia* Dante has lost faith in the secular ethos. Instead, he makes a full commitment to the medieval ethos. In today's language, he is a born-again Christian, and the *Commedia* is the record of his conversion. There are especially two passages in the *Commedia* that reflect his excursion into the secular ethos and his return to the spiritual ethos of medieval Christianity. One is the opening tercet of the poem with Dante lost in the dark wood (*Inf.* 1: 1-3). The other passage is Dante's confession of infidelity to Beatrice in the Terrestrial Paradise (*Purg.* 31: 34-36):

> *Piangendo dissi: "Le presenti cose*
> *col falso lor piacer volser miei passi,*
> *tosto che'l vostro viso si nascose."*
>
> Weeping, I said: "Those things with their false joys,
> offered me by the world, led me astray
> when I no longer saw your countenance."
> (Trans. Mark Musa)

Notes

1. Patrick Boyde, *Perception and Passion in Dante's Comedy* (Cambridge: Cambridge University Press, 1993), 285.

2. Thomas Aquinas, "De Principiis Naturae," in *Opusula Omnia necnon Opera minora. Tomus Primus: Opuscula Philosophica*, ed. R. P. Johannes Perrier and O. P. Joannes (Paris: Lethielleux 1949), 3-17. For an English translation, see Thomas Aquinas, "On the Principles of Nature," in *An Aquinas Reader*, ed. by M. T. Clark (New York: Image Books, 1972), 163-77.

3. The two statements concerning "potters" and "proud men" are taken from Aristotle's *Ethics* VIII.1 (1155a) and Proverbs 13: 10.

4. Aquinas is aware of the complexity with regard to the relation between anger and quarrelling (*ST* pt. 2-2, q. 116, a. 1, ad. 2): "The direct opposition of virtues to vices depends, not on their causes, since one vice may arise from many causes, but on the species of their acts. And although quarrelling arises at times from anger, it may also arise from other causes, hence it does not follow that it is directly opposed to meekness." What Aquinas stresses is that quarrelling is a vice, while anger is a capital sin. As repeated several times in the *Summa* the difference consists in the fact that "a capital sin is one from which other vices arise most frequently" (*ST* pt. 2-2, q. 34, a. 5). Quarrelling is opposed to the virtue of meekness only if it arises from anger, since it can arise from envy, which is not opposed to meekness.

5. Brunetto Latini, *The Book of the Treasure*, trans. Paul Barrette and Spurgeon Baldwin (New York: Garland, 1993), 26.

6. Brunetto Latini, *The Book of the Treasure*, 321.

7. Brunetto Latini, *The Book of the Treasure*, 7. See also Brunetto Latini, *The Book of the Treasure*, 60: "Nature is to God as a hammer to a blacksmith, who at one time forms a spear, at another a helmet, or a nail, or a needle" (I.99.3).

8. For an overview over recent studies of Brunetto's placement in Hell, see Deborah Contrada, "Brunetto's Sin: Ten Years of Criticism (1977-1897)," in *Dante: Summa Medievalis*, ed. C. Franco and L. Morgan (Stony Brook, N.Y.: Forum Italicum, 1995), 192-207.

9. André Pézard, "Dante sous le pluie de feu—Enfer XV," in *Etudes de philosophie médiévale no. 40* (Paris, 1950), 468; Thomas Vece, "Brunetto Latini's Sin: False Rhetoric," in *NEMLA Italian Studies* 3 (1979), 21-30; Marco Giacomelli, "In Difesa di Ser Brunetto Latini," in *Dante Studies, Vol. 1: Dante in the Twentieth Century* (1982), 99-107.

10. Bianca Ceva, *Brunetto Latini: L'uomo e l'opera* (Milano-Napoli: Riccardo Ricciardi, 1965), 214-15.

11. Brunetto Latini, *The Book of the Treasure*, 222.

12. In the *Summa*, Aquinas gives the following definition of blasphemy (*ST* pt. 2-2, q. 13, a. 1, ad. 1): "He that speaks against God, with the intention of reviling Him, disparages the divine goodness, not only in respect of the falsehood in his intellect, but also by reason of the wickedness of his will, whereby he detests and strives to hinder the honor due to God, and this is perfect blasphemy." Aquinas compares it to murder, but he makes a clear distinction (pt. 2-2, q. 13, a. 3): "If we compare murder and blasphemy as regards the objects of those sins, it is clear that blasphemy, which is a sin committed directly against God, is more grave than murder, which is a sin against one's neighbor. On the other hand, if we compare them in respect of the harm wrought by them, murder is the graver sin, for murder does more harm to one's neighbor than blasphemy does to God. Since, however, the gravity of s sin depends on the intention of the evil will, rather than on the effect of the deed, it follows that, as the blasphemer intends to do harm to God's honor, absolutely speaking, he sins more grievously

than the murder. Nevertheless, murder takes precedence, as to punishment, among sins committed against our neighbor."

13. Dante Alighieri, *Dante's Il Convivio (The Banquet)*, trans. Richard H. Lansing (New York: Garland Publishing, 1990), 25.

14. Brunetto Latini, *The Book of the Treasure*, 2.

15. Eric Voegelin, *History of Political Ideas, Vol. III: The Later Middle Ages*, ed. David Walsh (Columbia: University of Missouri Press, 1998), 86-87.

16. Antony Black, *Political Thought in Europe, 1250-1450* (Cambridge: Cambridge University Press, 1993), 67.

17. Eric Voegelin, *The Later Middle Ages*, 90.

18. Eric Voegelin, *The Later Middle Ages*, 91.

19. Brunetto Latini, *The Book of the Treasure*, 350.

20. Paul Oskar Kristeller, *Renaissance Thought and Its Sources*, ed. Michael Mooney (New York: Columbia University Press, 1979), 219 and 228.

21. Brunetto Latini, *The Book of the Treasure*, 1-2.

22. Paul Oskar Kristeller, *Renaissance Thought and Its Sources*, 218.

23. In his comment on Priscian's appearance in the seventh circle, Charles S. Singleton remarks: "What basis Dante had for imputing to Priscian guilt of sexual nature is not known; there is nothing to justify the accusation in any of the scanty notices of him that have reached us. The early commentators believe he is meant to represent the whole tribe 'pedagogi' and would justify Dante's condemnation of him by the argument, 'pedagogus ergo sodomiticus' ('teacher, therefore sodomite')." Singleton quotes a passage from Giovanni Boccaccio's *Commento* on the *Inferno*, where he says that he has never read or heard that Priscian was guilty of such a sin: "Rather, I judge he [Dante] put him [Priscian] here [in the third rung of the seventh circle], since the majority of them [teachers] are believed to be tainted with that evil. For most of their students are young; and being young, are timorous and obey both the proper and the improper demands of their teachers. And because the students are so accessible, it is believed that the teachers often fall into this sin." *DDP* Singleton on *Inf.* 15: 109.

24. For an excerpt of Priscian's attitude toward rhetoric, see Joseph M. Miller, ed, *Readings in Medieval Rhetoric* (Bloomington: Indiana University Press, 1973), 52-68.

25. *DDP* Singleton on *Inf.* 15: 112; *DDP* Sapegno on *Inf.* 15: 114.

26. Seneca, "On Anger," in *Moral and Political Essays*, trans. John M. Cooper and J. F. Procopé (Cambridge: Cambridge University Press, 1995), 58.

27. *DDP* Singleton on *Inf.* 12: 18: "In revenge for his father's death and for the indignities offered his corpse, Guy murdered his first cousin, Prince Henry of Cornwall, in the church of San Silvestro at Viterbo in March 1271, during the assembly of the cardinals to elect a successor to Pope Clement IV. The crime is popularly supposed to have taken place at the moment of the elevation of the Host, when Henry was on his knee. To compound the atrocity, Guy, upon being reminded that his father's body had been trailed, seized Henry by the hair and dragged his corpse out into the open street."

28. *DDP* Singleton on *Inf.* 13: 143.

29. *DDP* Singleton on *Inf.* 13: 119.

30. In Deuteronomy 29: 23, we read that God overthrew the cities of Sodom, Gomorrah, Adama, and Seboin "in anger and fury" (*in ira et furore*).

31. Mark D. Jordan, *The Invention of Sodomy in Christian Theology* (Chicago: University of Chicago Press, 1997).

32. M. L. West, "The Medieval Manuscripts of the *Works and Days*," in *The Classical Quaterly* 24 (1974), 161-85.

33. A. J. Grant, *Early Lives of Charlemagne by Eginhard and the Monk of Saint Gall* (London: Chatto & Windus, 1926).

34. Eric Voegelin, *History of Political Ideas, Vol. I: Hellenism, Rome, and Early Christianity,* ed. Athanasios Moulakis (Columbia: University of Missouri Press, 1997), 210-13.

35. John A. Scott, "Canto XIV: Capaneus and the Old Man Crete," in *Inferno: A Canto-by-Canto Commentary*, ed. Allen Mandelbaum (Los Angeles: University of California Press, 1998), 192-95.

36. Brunetto Latini, *The Book of the Treasure*, 351-52.

37. Brunetto Latini, *The Book of the Treasure*, 179.

38. To see how the Platonic and Aristotelian theory of governmental decay or deterioration can be combined with the theory of ages, we only need to recall Seneca's *Letter XC*, in which the state of the golden age is described as one of peace and harmony. Seneca, *Letters from a Stoic: Epistulae Morales as Lucilium*, trans. Robin Campbell (Harmondsworth: Penguin, 1969), 161-77.

39. Cicero, *De Officiis*, trans. W. Miller (Cambridge, Mass.: Harvard University Press, 1968), 91.

40. This is most clearly stated in *The Constitution of Athens* (XVI.vii). Aristotle, *The Politics and the Constitution of Athens*, trans. J. Barnes and J. M. Moore (Cambridge: Cambridge University Press, 1996), 119-225. Although Dante did not know this work of Aristotle, there are many ancient and medieval sources that reveal that the reign of Peisistratus was commonly identified as a golden age. The reason for underlining this aspect will be made clear when I turn to Vergil's story about the Old Man of Crete.

41. *DDP* Singleton on *Purg.* 15: 94-105.

42. Dante Alighieri, *Monarchy*, trans. Prue Shaw (Cambridge: Cambridge University Press, 1996), 21.

43. Aristotle, *The Politics*, 157.

44. Aristotle, *Nicomachean Ethics* in *The Complete Works of Aristotle, Vol. II*, ed. Jonathan Barnes (Princeton, N.J.: Princeton University Press, 1984), 1834.

45. Susan Noakes, "Canto XVI: From Other Sodomites to Fraud," in *Inferno: A Canto-by-Canto Commentary*, ed. Allen Mandelbaum (Los Angeles: University of California Press, 1998), 215-16.

46. Aristotle, *The Politics*, 25.

47. Plato, *Gorgias*, trans. Robin Waterfield (Oxford: Oxford University Press, 1994), 118. The classical translation of the passage in the Loeb Edition is "idle, cowardly, talkative, and avaricious."

48. Joan M. Ferrante. "Why Did Dante Write the Comedy?" in *Dante Studies* CXI (1993), 9.

49. Dante Alighieri, *Dante's Monarchia*, trans. Richard Kay (Toronto: Pontifical Institute of Medieval Studies, 1998), ix and xxvii-xxxi.

50. John of Paris, *On Royal and Papal Power*, trans. J. A. Watt (Toronto: The Pontifical Institute of Mediaeval Studies, 1971), 16.

51. James of Viterbo, *On Christian Government*, trans. R. W. Dyson. (Woodbridge, UK: The Boydell Press, 1995), xxvi.

52. Dante Alighieri, *Monarchy*, trans. Prue Shaw (Cambridge: Cambridge University Press, 1996), 25.

53. O. J. Thatcher and E. H. McNeal, eds., *A Source Book for Medieval History* (New York: Scribners, 1905), 324-25.

54. Brian Tierney, "Marsilius on Rights," in *Journal of the History of Ideas* 52: 1 (1991), 7.

55. Marsilius of Padua, *The Defender of Peace*, trans. Alan Gewirth (New York: Columbia University Press, 1956), 427 and 428.

56. Thomas G. Bergin, *Dante* (New York: Orion Press, 1965), 7.

57. Eric Voegelin, *The Later Middle Ages*, 39; Robert Bartlett, *The Making of Europe: Conquest, Colonization, and Cultural Change 950-1350* (London: Penguin, 1993), 308.

58. Aloysius P. Martinich, "Review of T. K. Seung's *Cultural Thematics*," in *Journal of the History of Philosophy* 16 (1978), 352-54.

Bibliography

Anderson, William. *Dante the Maker.* London: Routledge and Kegan Paul, 1980.

Aquinas, Thomas. "De Principiis Naturae," in *Opusula Omnia necnon Opera minora. Tomus Primus: Opuscula Philosophica.* Edited by R. P. Johannes Perrier and O. P. Joannes. Paris: Lethielleux, 1949.

———. "On the Principles of Nature," in *An Aquinas Reader.* Edited, with an introduction, by M. T. Clark. New York: Image Books, 1972.

———. *Aquinas Against the Averroists: On There Being Only One Intellect.* Translated and edited by R. McInery. West Lafayette, Ind.: Purdue University Press, 1993.

———. *Aristotelian Commentary Series. Vol. I: Commentary on Aristotle's Nicomachean Ethics.* Translated by I. C. Litzinger. Notre Dame, Ind.: Dumb Ox Books, 1993.

Aristotle. *Nicomachean Ethics* in *The Complete Works of Aristotle, Vol. II.* Edited by Jonathan Barnes. Princeton, N.J.: Princeton University Press, 1984.

———. *The Politics and the Constitution of Athens.* Translated by J. Barnes and J. M. Moore and edited by S. Everson. Cambridge: Cambridge University Press, 1996.

Asìn Palacios, Miguel. *La Escatologìa Musulmana en la Divina Comedia.* Madrid-Granada: Imprenta de Estanislao Maestre, 1943.

Augustine. *Confessions.* Translated by R. S. Pine-Coffin. London: Penguin, 1976.

Auerbach, Erich. *Mimesis: The Representation of Reality in Western Literature.* Translated by W. R. Trask. Princeton, N.J.: Princeton University Press, 1953.

———. "Dante's Addresses to the Reader," in *Romance Philology* VII (1954), 268-78.

———. "Vico's Contribution to Literary Criticism," in *Studia Philologica et Litteraria in Honorem L. Spitzer.* Edited by A. G. Hatcher and K. L. Selig. Bern, Switzerland: Franeke Verlag, 1958.

———. "Figura," in *Scenes from the Drama of European Literature: Six Essays.* Translated by R. Manheim. New York: Meridian Books, Inc., 1959.

———. *Dante: The Poet of the Secular World.* Translated by R. Manheim. Chicago: University of Chicago Press, 1961.

———. "Philology and *Weltliteratur*," in *Centennial Review* 13: 1 (1969), 1-17.

———. "Epilegomena to *Mimesis*," in *Mimesis: The Representation of Reality in Western Literature.* Princeton, N.J.: Princeton University Press, 2003.

Bakhtin, Mikhail. "Discourse in the Novel," in *The Dialogic Imagination: Four Essays*. Translated by C. Emerson and M. Holquist. Austin: University of Texas Press, 1981.

Barbi, Michele. *Problemi di critica dantesca: Prima serie 1893-1918*. Firenze: Sansoni, 1934.

——. "Nuovi problemi della critica dantesca," in *Studi danteschi* XXIII (1938), 5-77.

Barolini, Teodolinda. *The* Undivine *Comedy: Detheologizing Dante*. Princeton, N.J.: Princeton University Press, 1992.

——. "'Why Did Dante Write the *Commedia*?' or The Vision Thing," in *Dante Studies* CXI (1993), 1-8.

Bartlett, Robert. *The Making of Europe: Conquest, Colonization, and Cultural Change, 950-1350*. London: Penguin, 1993.

Bergin, Thomas G. *Dante*. New York: Orion Press, 1965.

——. *Perspectives on the Divine Comedy*. Piscataway, N.J.: Rutgers University Press, 1967.

Black, Antony. *Political Thought in Europe, 1250-1450*. Cambridge: Cambridge University Press, 1993.

Bloom, Harold. *The Anxiety of Influence: A Theory of Poetry*. Oxford: Oxford University Press, 1973.

——. *Ruin the Sacred Truth: Poetry and Belief from the Bible to the Present*. Cambridge, Mass.: Harvard University Press, 1989.

——. *The Western Canon: The Books and Schools of the Ages*. New York: Harcourt Brace & Company, 1994.

Bloomfield, Morton W. *The Seven Deadly Sins: An Introduction to the History of a Religious Concept with Special Reference to Medieval English Literature*. East Lansing: Michigan State University Press, 1967.

Boccaccio, Giovanni. "Trattatello in laude di Dante," in *Opere in versi*. Edited by P. G. Ricci. Milano: Riccardo Ricciardi, 1965.

Bonaventura. "Itinerarium mentis in Deum," in *Opera Omnia. Tomus V*. Quaracchi, 1891.

——. "The Journey of the Mind to God," in *The Works of Bonaventure. Vol. I: Mystical Opuscula*. Translated by J. de Vinck. Patterson. N.J.: St. Anthong Guild Press, 1960.

Botterill, Stephen. *Dante and the Mystical Tradition: Bernard of Clairvaux in the Commedia*. Cambridge: Cambridge University Press, 1994.

Boyde, Patrick. *Dante: Philomythes and Philosopher: Man in the Cosmos*. Cambridge: Cambridge University Press, 1981.

——. *Perception and Passion in Dante's Comedy*. Cambridge: Cambridge University Press, 1993.

Cantarino, Vicente. "Dante and Islam: History and Analysis of a Controversy," in *A Dante Symposium in Commemoration of the 700 Anniversary of the Poet's Birth*. Edited by William de Sua and Gino Rizzo. Chapel Hill: The University of North Carolina Press, 1965.

Cassata, Lettario. "The Hard Begin," in *Lectura Dantis: Inferno: A Canto-by-Canto Commentary*. Edited by Allen Mandelbaum, Anthony Oldcorn, and Charles Ross. Los Angeles: University of California Press, 1998.

Cerulli, Enrico. *Il "Libro della Scala" e la questione delle fonti arabo-spagnole della Divina Commedia*. Città del Vaticano: Biblioteca Apostolica Vaticana, 1949.

Cervigni, D. S., ed. *Annali d'Italianistica: Dante and Modern American Criticism No. 8*. Chapel Hill: The University of North Carolina Press, 1990.

Ceva, Bianca. *Brunetto Latini: L'uomo e l'opera*. Milano-Napoli: Riccardo Ricciardi, 1965.

Charity, A. C. *Events and their Afterlife: The Dialectics of Christian Typology in the Bible and Dante*. Cambridge: Cambridge University Press, 1987.

Cheny, Marie-Dominique. *Nature, Man, and Society in the Twelfth Century: Essays on New Theological Perspectives in the Latin West*. Translated by J. Taylor and L. K. Little. Chicago: University of Chicago Press, 1968.

Cicero. *De Officiis*. Translated by W. Miller. Cambridge, Mass.: Harvard University Press, 1968.

Coleridge, Samuel Taylor. *The Portable Coleridge*. Edited by I. A. Richards. New York, 1950.

Collins, John J. *Daniel: A Commentary on Book of Daniel*. With an essay, "The Influence of Daniel on the New Testament," by A. Y. Collins. Edited by F. Moore Cross. Minneapolis: Augsburg Fortress Publishers, 1993.

Contrada, Deborah. "Brunetto's Sin: Ten Years of Criticism (1977-1897)," in *Dante: Summa Medievalis*. Edited by C. Franco and L. Morgan. Stony Brook, N.Y.: Forum Italicum, 1995.

Copleston, Frederick. *A History of Philosophy. Vol. II: Medieval Philosophy from Augustine to Duns Scotus*. New York: Image Books, 1993.

Corti, Maria. *Dante a un nuovo crocevia*. Firenze: Sansoni, 1981.

———. "Il binomio intertestualità e fonti: funzioni della storia nel sistema letterario," in *La scrittura e la storia: problemi di storiagrafia letteraria*. Edited by Alberto Asor Rosa. Firenze: La Nuova Italia, 1995.

Cosmo, Umberto. *A Handbook to Dante Studies*. Translated by D. Moore. Oxford: Basil Blackwell, 1973.

Cottino-Jones, Marga. "Literary-critical Developments in Sixteenth- and Seventeenth-Century Italy," in *The Cambridge History of Literary Criticism. Vol. III: The Renaissance*. Edited by G. P. Norton. Cambridge: Cambridge University Press, 1999.

Croce, Benedetto. *La Poesia di Dante*. Bari: Laterza, 1921.

Dales, Richard C. "The Origin of the Doctrine of the Double Truth," in *Viator* 15 (1984), 169-79.

Daniel, Norman. *The Arabs and Medieval Europe*. London: Longmans, 1975.

Daniello, Bernardino. *L'espositione di Bernardino Daniello da Lucca sopra la Comedia di Dante*. Edited by R. Hollander and J. Schnapp with K. Brownlee and N. Vickers. Hanover: University Press of New England, 1989.

Dante Alighieri: *The Divine Comedy*. Translated, with a commentary, by Charles S. Singleton. Six volumes. Princeton, N.J.: Princeton University Press, 1970-1975

——. *La Divina Commedia*. Commentated by Umberto Bosco and Giovanni Reggio. Three volumes. Firenze: Sansoni, 1979.

——. *Dante's Il Convivio (The Banquet)*. Translated by Richard H. Lansing. New York: Garland Publishing, 1990.

——. *La commedia secondo l'antica vulgata*. Edited by Giorgio Petrocchi. Four Volumes. Firenze: Le Lettere, 1994.

——. *The Portable Dante*. Translated and edited by Mark Musa. New York: Penguin, 1995.

——. *Monarchy*. Translated and edited by Prue Shaw. Cambridge: Cambridge University Press, 1996.

——. *Dante's Monarchia*. Translated, with a commentary, by Richard Kay. Toronto: Pontifical Institute of Medieval Studies, 1998.

Di Scipio, G. C., and A. Scaglione, eds. *The Divine Comedy and the Encyclopedia of Arts and Sciences*. Amsterdam, Philadelphia: John Benjamins Publishing Co., 1988.

Eliot, T. S. "Dante" (1922), in *Selected Essays*. London: Faber and Faber Limited, 1972.

Fergusson, Francis. *Dante's Drama of the Mind: A Modern Reading of the Purgatorio*. Princeton, N.J.: Princeton University Press, 1953.

Ferrante, Joan M. "Why Did Dante Write the *Comedy*?" in *Dante Studies* CXI (1993), 9-18.

Figurelli, Fernando. "I Canti di Cacciaguida," in *Dante nella critica d'oggi: risultati e prospettive*. Edited by Umberto Bosco. Firenze: Le Monnier, 1965.

Foster, Kenelm. "A Propos of a New Book on Dante," in *Blackfriars* 43 (1962), 477-83.

——. *The Two Dantes and Other Studies*. Berkeley: University of California Press, 1977.

Freccero, John. "Dante's Pilgrim in a Gyre," in *PMLA* LXXVI (1961), 168-81.

——. "The Proloque Scene," in *Dante Studies* 84 (1966), 1-25.

——. *Dante: The Poetics of Conversion*. Edited by Rachel Jacoff. Cambridge, Mass.: Harvard University Press, 1986.

——. "Dante's Cosmos," in *Bernardo Lectures Series No. 6*. New York: Center for Medieval Studies, 1998.

Giacomelli, Marco. "In Difesa di Ser Brunetto Latini," in *Dante Studies. Vol. 1: Dante in the Twentieth* Century (1982), 99-107.

Gilson, Etienne. *Dante the Philosopher*. Translated by D. Moore. New York: Harper & Row, 1952.

——. *The Philosopher and Theology*. Translated by C. Gilson. New York: Random House, 1962.

Grandgent, C. H. *Companion to The Divine Comedy*. Edited by C. S. Singleton. Cambridge, Mass.: Harvard University Press, 1975.

Grant, A. J. *Early Lives of Charlemagne by Eginhard and the Monk of Saint Gall*. London: Chatto & Windus, 1926.

Grant, Edward. "Cosmology," in *Science in the Middle Ages*. Edited by David C. Lindberg. Chicago: University of Chicago Press, 1978.

——. *Planets, Stars, & Orbs: The Medieval Cosmos, 1200-1687*. Cambridge: Cambridge University Press, 1997.

Halliwell, Stephen. "Aristotle's Poetics," in *The Cambridge History of Literary Criticism. Vol. I: Classical Criticism*. Edited by G. A. Kennedy. Cambridge: Cambridge University Press, 1993.

Hallyn, Fernand. "Cosmography and Poetics," in *The Cambridge History of Literary Criticism. Vol. III: The Renaissance*. Edited by G. P. Norton. Cambridge: Cambridge University Press, 1999.

Harris, Wendell V. *Literary Meaning: Reclaiming the Study of Literature*. London: Routledge, 1996.

Hede, Jesper. "Unity and Difference in Dante's Universal Vision," in *Classica et Mediaevalia* no. 57 (2006), 239-81.

Hexter, Ralph J. *Ovid and Medieval Schooling Studies in Medieval Commentaries on Ovid's Ars Amatoria, Epustalee ex Ponto, and Epistulae Heroidum*. München: Arbeo-Gesellschaft, 1986.

Hollander, Robert. *Allegory in Dante's Commedia*. Princeton, N.J.: Princeton University Press, 1969.

——. "Dante *Theologus-Poeta*," in *Studies in Dante*. Ravenna: Longo, 1980.

——. "Dante and his commentators," in *The Cambridge Companion to Dante*. Edited by Rachel Jacoff. Cambridge: Cambridge University Press, 1993.

——. *Dante's Epistle to Cangrande*. Ann Arbor: University of Michigan Press, 1993.

——. *Dante: A Life in Works*. New Haven, Conn.: Yale University Press, 2001.

Irwin, Terence. *Classical Thought*. Oxford: Oxford University Press, 1989.

Jacoff, Rachel. "'Shadowy Prefaces': An Introduction to *Paradiso*," in *The Cambridge Companion to Dante*. Edited by Rachel Jacoff. Cambridge: Cambridge University Press, 1993.

James of Viterbo. *On Christian Government*. Translated by R. W. Dyson. Woodbridge, UK: The Boydell Press, 1995.

John of Paris. *On Royal and Papal Power*. Translated by J. A. Watt. Toronto: The Pontifical Institute of Mediaeval Studies, 1971.

Jordan, Mark D. *The Invention of Sodomy in Christian Theology*. Chicago: University of Chicago Press, 1997.

Kantorowicz, Ernst H. *The King's Two Bodies: A Study of Medieval Political Thought*. Princeton, N.J.: Princeton University Press, 1957.

Karras, Ruth Mazo. "Holy Harlots: Prostitute Saints in Medieval Legend," in *Journal of the History of Sexuality* 1: 1 (1990), 3-32.

——. "Prostitution and the Question of Sexual Identity in Medieval Europe," in *Journal of Women's History* 11: 2 (1999), 159-77.

Kay, Richard. *Dante's Swift and Strong: Essays on Inferno XV*. Lawrence: University of Kansas Press, 1978.

——. *Dante's Christian Astrology*. Philadelphia: University of Pennsylvania Press, 1994.

Keck, David. *Angels & Angelology in the Middle Ages*. Oxford: University of Oxford Press, 1998.

Kennedy, Philip F. "Muslim Sources of Dante?" in *The Arab Influence in Medieval Europe*. Edited by Dionisius A. Agius and Richard Hitchcock. Reading, Pa.: Ithaca Press, 1994.

Kent, Bonnie. *Virtues of the Will: The Transformation of Ethics in the Late Thirteenth Century*. Washington, D.C.: Catholic University of America Press, 1995.

King, Peter. "Ockham's Ethical Theory," in *The Cambridge Companion to Ockham*. Edited by Paul Vincent Spade. Cambridge: Cambridge University Press, 1999.

Kirkpatrick, Robin. *Dante: The Divine Comedy*. Cambridge: Cambridge University Press, 1996.

Kragh, Helge: *Cosmology and Controversy: The Historical Development of Two Theories of the Universe.* Princeton, N.J.: Princeton University Press, 1996.

Kristeller, Paul Oskar. *Renaissance Thought and Its Sources*. Edited by Michael Mooney. New York: Columbia University Press, 1979.

Kritzeck, James. *Peter the Venerable and Islam*. Princeton, N.J.: Princeton University Press, 1964.

Ladner, Gerhart B. "*Homo Viator*: Medieval Ideas on Alienation and Order," in *Speculum* 42: 2 (1967), 233-59.

Latini, Brunetto. *The Book of the Treasure*. Translated by Paul Barrette and Spurgeon Baldwin. New York: Garland, 1993.

Le Goff, Jacques. *The Birth of Purgatory*. Translated by A. Goldhammer. Chicago: University of Chicago Press, 1984.

Lindberg, David C. *The Beginnings of Western Science: The European Scientific Tradition in Philosophical, Religious, and Institutional Context, 600 BC to AD 1450*. Chicago: University of Chicago Press, 1992.

Logan, J. L. "The Poet's Central Numbers," in *MLN* 86: 1 (1971), 95-98.

Mancini, Franco. "Un' 'auctoritas' di Dante," in *Studi danteschi* 45 (1968), 95-119.

Mandelbaum, Allen, Anthony Oldcorn, and Charles Ross, eds. *Inferno: A Canto-by-Canto Commentary*. Los Angeles: University of California Press, 1998.

Marsilius of Padua. *The Defender of Peace*. Translated by Alan Gewirth. New York: Columbia University Press, 1956.

Martinich, Aloysius P. "Review of T. K. Seung's *Cultural Thematics*," in *Journal of the History of Philosophy* 16 (1978), 352-54.

Mastrobuono, Antonio C. *Dante's Journey of Sanctification*. Washington, D.C.: Regnery Gateway, 1990.

Mattalia, Daniele. "Dante Alighieri," in *I Classici Italiani nella Storia della Critica. Vol. I: Da Dante al Marino*. Edited by Walter Binni. Firenze: La Nuova Italia, 1967.

McGinn, Bernard. *The Presence of God: A History of Western Christian Mysticism. Vol. I: The Foundations of Mysticism*. New York: Crossroad, 1991.

——. *The Presence of God: A History of Western Christian Mysticism. Vol. II: The Growth of Mysticism*. New York: Crossroad, 1994.

McNair, Philip. "The Poetry of the 'Comedy,'" in *The Mind of Dante*. Edited by U. Limentani. Cambridge: Cambridge University Press, 1965.

Miller, Joseph M., Micheal H. Prosser, and Thomas W. Benson, eds. *Readings in Medieval Rhetoric*. Bloomington: Indiana University Press, 1973.

Moevs, Christian. *The Metaphysics of Dante's Comedy*. Oxford: Oxford University Press, 2005.

Moore, Robert Ian. *The Formation of a Persecuting Society: Power and Deviance in Western Europe, 950-1250*. Cambridge, Mass.: Harvard University Press, 1990.

Morghen, Raffaello. "Dante Profeta," in *Dante profeta: tra la storia e l'etterno*. Milano: Jaca Book Ed, 1983.

Nardi, Bruno. *Dal Convivio alla Commedia: sei saggi danteschi*. Roma: Edizioni di Storia e Letteratura, 1960.

Newhauser, Richard. *The Treatise on Vices and Virtues in Latin and the Vernacular*. Turnhout, Belgium: Brepols, 1993.

Newman, Francis X. "St. Augustine's Three Visions and the Structure of the *Commedia*," in *MLN* 82: 1 (1967), 58-78.

Noakes, Susan. "Canto XVI: From Other Sodomites to Fraud," in *Inferno: A Canto-by-Canto Commentary*. Edited by Allen Mandelbaum, Anthony Oldcorn, and Charles Ross. Los Angeles: University of California Press, 1998.

Ordiway, Frank. "In the Earth's Shadow: The Theological Virtues Marred," in *Dante Studies* 100 (1982), 77-92.

Ovid. *Heroides*. Translated with introductions and notes by Harold Isbell. London: Penguin, 1990.

——. *Heroides*. Edited by Peter E. Knox. Cambridge: Cambridge University Press, 1995.

Panikkar, Raimundo. *Cultural Disarmament: The Way to Peace*. Translated by Robert R. Barr. Louisville, Ky.: Westminster John Knox Press, 1995.

Pertile, Lino. "Paradiso: A Drama of Desire," in *Word and Drama in Dante: Essays on the Divina Commedia*. Edited by J. C. Barnes and J. Petrie. Dublin: Irish Academic Press, 1993.

——. "Does the *Stilnovo* Go to Heaven?" in *Dante for the New Millennium*. Edited by Teodolinda Barolini and H. Wayne Storey. New York: Fordham University Press, 2003.

Petrocchi, Giorgio. "Dante and Thirteenth-Century Asceticism," in *From Time to Eternity: Essays on Dante's Divine Comedy*. Edited by Thomas G. Bergin. New Haven, Conn.: Yale University Press, 1967.

——. "Canto XII: The Violent against Themselves," in *Inferno: A Canto-by-Canto Commentary*. Edited by Allen Mandelbaum, Anthony Oldcorn, and Charles Ross. Los Angeles: University of California Press, 1998.

Petronio, Giuseppe. *L'attività letteraria in Italia: storia della letteratura*. Palermo: Palumbo, 1977.

Pézard, André. "Dante sous le pluie de feu—Enfer XV," in *Etudes de philosophie médiévale no. 40*. Paris, 1950, 468.

Plato. *Gorgias*. Translated by Robin Waterfield. Oxford: Oxford University Press, 1994.

——. *The Republic*. Translated by Desmond Lee. London: Penguin, 1987.

Richards, I. A. *Practical Criticism: A Study of Literary Judgment*. London: Routledge and Kegan Paul, 1929.

Russell, Jeffrey Burton. *A History of Medieval Christianity: Prophecy and Order*. New York: T.Y. Crowell, 1968.

——. *Lucifer: The Devil in the Middle Ages*. Ithaca, N.Y.: Cornell University Press, 1984.

Sapegno, Natalino. "Genesis and Structure: Two Approaches to the Poetry of the *Comedy*," in *The Mind of Dante*. Edited by U. Limentani. Cambridge: Cambridge University Press, 1965.

Scott, John A. "Review of T. K. Seung's *Cultural Thematics*," in *Italian Studies* 33 (1978), 113-16.

——. *Dante's Political Purgatory*. Philadelphia: University of Pennsylvania Press, 1996.

——. "Canto XIV: Capaneus and the Old Man Crete," in *Inferno: A Canto-by-Canto Commentary*. Edited by Allen Mandelbaum, Anthony Oldcorn, and Charles Ross. Los Angeles: University of California Press, 1998.

Seneca. *Letters from a Stoic: Epistulae Morales ad Lucilium*. Translated by Robin Campbell. Harmondsworth: Penguin, 1969.

——. "On Anger," in *Moral and Political Essays*. Edited and translated by John M. Cooper and J. F. Procopé. Cambridge: Cambridge University Press, 1995.

Siegel, Lee. "Out of the Dark Wood: Dante and the Subversive Ego," in *Harper's Magazine*, May (2002), 79-83.

Sigmund, Paul E. "Law and Politics," in *The Cambridge Companion to Aquinas*. Edited by Norman Kretzmann and Eleonore Stump. Cambridge: Cambridge University Press, 1993.

Singleton, Charles S. *Dante Studies I: Elements of Structure*. Cambridge, Mass.: Harvard University Press, 1954.

——. "The Irreducible Dove," in *Comparative Studies* IX (1957), 129-35.

——. *Dante Studies II: Journey to Beatrice*. Cambridge, Mass.: Harvard University Press, 1958.

——. "The Poet's Number at the Center," in *MLN* 80: 1 (1965), 1-10.

——. "The Vistas in Retrospect," in *MLN* 81: 1 (1966), 55-80.

Skinner, Quentin. *The Foundations of Modern Political Thought. Vol. II: The Age of Reformation*. Cambridge: Cambridge University Press, 1978.

Southern, Richard W. "Dante and Islam," in *Relations between East and West in the Middle Ages*. Edited by Derel Baker. Edinburgh, Scotland: Edinburgh University Press, 1973.

Thatcher, O. J., and E. H. McNeal, eds. *A Source Book for Medieval History*. New York: Scribners, 1905.

Tierney, Brian. "Marsilius on Rights," in *Journal of the History of Ideas* 52: 1 (1991), 3-17.

Vece, Thomas. "Brunetto Latini's Sin: False Rhetoric," in *NEMLA Italian Studies* 3 (1979), 21-30.

Vergil. *The Aeneid*. Translated by W. F. Jackson Knight. London: Penguin, 1958.

——. *Opera*. Edited by R. A. B. Mynors. Oxford: Oxford University Press, 1972.

Voegelin, Eric. *History of Political Ideas. Vol. I: Hellenism, Rome, and Early Christianity*. Edited by Athanasios Moulakis. Columbia: University of Missouri Press, 1997.

——. *History of Political Ideas. Vol. III: The Later Middle Ages*. Edited by David Walsh. Columbia: University of Missouri Press, 1998.

Weisheipl, J. A. "Classification of the Sciences in Medieval Thought," in *Medieval Studies* 27 (1965), 54-90.

West, M. L. "The Medieval Manuscripts of the *Works and Days*," in *The Classical Quaterly* 24 (1974), 161-85.

Witke, Edward Charles. "Review of T. K. Seung's *The Fragile Leaves of the Sibyl*," in *Speculum* 38: 4 (1963), 666-67.

Witte, Karl. "The Ethical Systems of the Inferno and the Purgatorio" (1879), in *Essays on Dante*. London: Lawrence and Philip H. Wicksteed, 1910.

Index

About the Author

Jesper Hede is a postdoctoral scholar of comparative literature and rhetoric at the University of Aarhus in Denmark, specializing in medieval literature and philosophy and the history of rhetoric. He studied Italian language and culture and medieval history at the University of Copenhagen and the University of Rome "La Sapienza," and attained his PhD degree in European Studies at the University of Aarhus. In 2004 he was awarded with Aarhus University Research Foundation's doctoral prize for his dissertation on Dante's *Divina Commedia*. He has written articles on Dante and European literature, and taught Italian language and history at the University of Copenhagen and comparative literature and rhetoric at the University of Aarhus. He is currently writing a book on the hermeneutics of rhetoric funded by the Carlsberg Foundation.